Rose Terry Cooke

The Sphinx's Children and other People's

Rose Terry Cooke

The Sphinx's Children and other People's

ISBN/EAN: 9783337214425

Printed in Europe, USA, Canada, Australia, Japan

Cover: Foto ©Thomas Meinert / pixelio.de

More available books at **www.hansebooks.com**

THE

SPHINX'S CHILDREN

AND

OTHER PEOPLE'S

BY

ROSE TERRY COOKE

Author of " Somebody's Neighbors," etc.

BOSTON
TICKNOR AND COMPANY
1886

PRESS OF
ROCKWELL AND CHURCHILL
BOSTON

NOTE.

The pieces contained in this volume are reprinted chiefly from the "Atlantic Monthly," "Harper's Magazine," and the "Galaxy," although a portion of them have appeared in other periodicals.

CONTENTS.

	PAGE
The Sphinx's Children	11
The Deacon's Week	25
A Black Silk	37
Jericho Jim	59
Lost on a Railway	79
Doctor Parker's Patty	108
Doom and Dan	136
Some Account of Thomas Tucker . .	167
The Forger's Bride	204
Too Late	229
My Thanksgiving	257
How She Found Out	290
Ann Potter's Lesson	317
Aceldama Sparks; or, Old and New .	341
Sallathiel Bump's Stocking . . .	393
Sally Parsons's Duty	410
A Hard Lesson	432
'Liab's First Christmas	459

THE SPHINX'S CHILDREN

THE SPHINX'S CHILDREN.

"Que la volonté soit le destin!"

Long had she sat, crouched upon her breast, — crouched, but not for slumber or for spring. No slumber gloomed darkly in those broad, sad eyes; no dream indefinably softened the lips, whose patient outline breathed only wakefulness and expectation, — a long-deferred, yet constant expectation, — a hope that would have been despair, save that it was just within hope's limits, — a monotonous, reiterate, indestructible chord in the creature's mystic existence, that, once struck by some mighty, shrouded Hand of Power, still reverberated, and trailed its still renewing echoes through every fibre of its secret habitation. Nor yet for spring; — a couchant leopard has posed itself with horrid intent; murder glitters in its fixed golden eye, quivers in the tense loins, creeps in the tawny glitter of the skin, clutches the keen claws, that recoil, and grasp, and recoil again from the velvet ball of that heavy foot; murder grins in the withdrawn lip, the white, red-set teeth, the slavering crunch of the jaw: but nothing of all these fired the quiet and the silence of the crouching Sphinx; nerve and muscle in tranquil strength lay relaxed, though not unconscious. Year after year the yellow Desert robed itself in burning mists, splendid and deadly; year after year the hot simoom licked up its sands, and, whirling them madly over the dead plain, dashed them against the silent Sphinx, and grain by grain heaped her slow-growing grave; the Nile spread its waters across the green valley, and lapped its brink with a watery thirst for land, and then receded to its channel, and poured its ancient flood still downward to the sea; worshipped, or desecrated; threaded by black Nubian boatmen, who mocked its sacred name with such savage mirth as satyrs might have spirted from their hairy lips; navigated by keen-eyed Arabs, lithe and dark and treacherous as the river beneath them; Coptic shepherds, lingering on the brink, drank the sweet waters, and led their flocks to drink at the shallows, when the shepherd's star cleft that deepest sky with its crest, and warned the simple people of their hour; — yet forever stood the Sphinx, passionately patient, looking for sunrise, over desert, vale, and river, — beyond man, — to her hour. — And the hour came.

Once to all things comes their hour. The black column of basalt quivers to its heart with one keen lightning thrill that vindicates its kin to the electric flash without; the granite cliff loses one atom from its bald front, and every other atom quails before the dumb shiver of gravitation and shifts its place; the breathing, breathless marble, which a sculptor has rescued from its primeval sleep, and, repeating after God, though with stammering and insufficient lips, the great drama of Paradise, makes a man out of dust, — once, once, in the deadness of its beauty, that marble thrills with magnetic life, drinks its maker's soul, repeats the Paradisiac amen, and owns that it is good. Yea, greater miracle of transcendental truth, — once, —

perhaps twice, — the sodden, valueless heart of that old man, whose gold has sucked out all that made him a man, beats with a pulse of generous honor; even in the dust of stocks and the ashes of speculation, amid the howling curses of the poor and the bitter weeping of his own flesh, once he hears the Voice of God, and all eternity cleaves the earth at his feet with a glare of truth. Once in her loathsome life, that woman, brazen with sin and shame, flaunting on the pavement, the scorn and jest of decency and indecency, the fearful index of corrupt society, — even she has her hour of softness, when the tiny grass that creeps out from the stones greenly into a spring sunshine, and as with a divine whisper recalls to her the time before she fell, the unburdened heart, the pure childish pleasures, the kind look of her dead mother's eye, the clasp of that sister's arm who passed her but yesterday pallid with disgust and ashamed to own their sacred birth-tie: then the tide rolls back; the hour is come! She, too, called a woman, who leads society, and triumphs over caste and custom with metallic ring and force, — she who forgets the decencies of age in her shameless attire, and supplies its defects with subterfuges, falser in heart even than in aspect, — she, about whom cluster men old and young, applauding with brays of laughter and coarser jeers the rancor of her wit, as it drops its laughing venom or its sneering sophisms of worldly wisdom, — even she, when the lights are fled, when the music has ceased from its own desecration, when the frenzy of wine and laughter mock her in their dead dregs, when the men who flattered and the women who envied are all gone, — she recalls one calm eye in the crowd, that stung her with its pure, contemptuous pity, a look not to be shut out with draperies as the stars are; and even through her soul, harder than the soul of that unowned sister walking the midnight street beneath the window, since it has ceased to know the stab of sin or the choking agony of shame, — even through that world-trodden heart flashes one conscious pang, one glimpse of a possible heaven and an inevitable hell, one naked and open vision of herself.

Long had the Sphinx waited. Year after year the flocking pigeons flitted and wheeled through the sweet skies of spring, built their nests and reared their young; tiny lizards, the new birth of the season, coiled and glittered on the hot sands like wandering jewels; every creature, dying out of conscious life, left its perpetuated self behind it, and repeated its own youth in its young, according to its kind: but the Sphinx lived alone. Nor all-unconscious of her solitude: for he who formed that massive shape, chiselled those calm, expectant lips, and wide eyes pensive as setting moons, he had not failed to do what all true artists do in virtue of their truth, — he had shared his own life with his own creation, and it was his lonely yearning that stirred her pulseless heart. Little did he think, toiling at that stupendous figure, ages gone by, that he transfused into the stone at which he labored, like a patient ant at some stupendous burden, no little share of that creative yearning that inspired him to his task; as little as you think, dear poet, whether poet, painter, or sculptor, — for all are one, and one is all, — that in those dreams which you write, as unconscious of your power as the transcribing stylus of its office, your own heart pulsates for a listening world, and the very linking of words that so respire their own music makes those words self-sentient of their breaking, thrilling melody, and wrings or exalts them, idea-garments as they are, with the restless heaving of the thought that wears them.

Or you, whose sun-steeped brush brings to life on canvas the golden trances of August noons, the high, still splendor of its mountain-tops, which the sun caresses with fiery languor, the unrippled slumber of its warm streams, the broad glory of its woods and meadows fused with light and heat into the resplendent haze that earth exhales in her day of prime, till he who sees the picture hears the cricket's chirping in its moveless grasses and scents the rich, aromatic breath of its summer passion and its rapturous noon, — do you dream, when at last the perfect work repeats your thought, and you rest in the tropic atmosphere you have created, that in very truth the picture itself is full of inward heat and breathless languor? For you have poured out the colors that light makes out of heat, and in them the still inevitable light shall ever stir the recreating heat that clothes itself in color, and bring your thought, no more a dead abstraction, but a living power, into the very substance whereby you have expressed it. And even so far as you were creative, so shall your work be informed by you, and not mere dead pigment and dried oil and dull canvas be your autograph, but the vivid and inspiring blazon of an inspired idea shall glow life-like on some friendly wall, and in its turn inspire some other soul, whose light within needs but the breath from without to burst upward in clear flame.

Or you, who unveil from its marble tomb that figure of a chained and stainless woman, whose atmosphere is as a nun's veil, whose sad divinity is a crown, — do you dare imagine that the holy despair you have imaged, the pause of a saint's resignation and a martyr's courage, is but the outline and the faultless contour of a stone? Come back, Pygmalion, from your mythic sleep! return, Art's divinest mystery, germ of all its power, from the deep dust of ages! and teach these modern men that his story, whose passion fired a statue's breast, was but an immortal fable, a similitude of the truth you feel, but do not see, — that even as our Creator shared his life with his creatures, so do you pour, in far less measure, but obedient to that precedent which is law, your own life and the magnetic instincts of that life, into what you create!

Keep your hearts pure and your hands clean, therefore; for these things that you sell for dead shall one day livingly confront you, and tell their own story of your life and your nature with terrible honesty to men and angels.

But whoever, in those mystic ages that have ceased to be historic and have become mythic, whoever made the Sphinx, — whether it were some Titaness sequestered from all her kind by genie-spells, forced to live amid these desert solitudes fed from the abundant hands of Nature, and taught by dreams inspired and twilight visions, —

> "A daughter of the gods, divinely tall —
> And most divinely fair,"

her only image of human beauty the reflex of her white, symmetric limbs, her wide, dark eyes, her full lips and soft Egyptian features, wherewith the river greeted her from its blue placidity; her only sense of love the unspoken yearning within, when the soft, tumultuous stress of the west wind kissed her, who should have been clasped in tender arms and caressed by loving lips; whose dumb, creative instincts, becoming genius instead of maternity, struggled outward from their home in heart and brain to culminate in this world's wonder, and so build a monument namelessly splendid to the grand nature that found its bread of life was a stone and perished; or whether this creature were the fashioning of some demigod, — " for there were giants in those days," — who, in the fulness of his strength, despairing of a mortal mate, wandered away from men and wrought his patience and his longing into the rock, — as lesser men have carved their memorials on hard Fate, — and then died between its paws, sated with labor and glad to sleep; or whether, indeed, the captive spirits, sealed in Caucasus with the seal of Solomon, did penance for their rebellion in mortal work on mere dull matter, and with anguished essence toiled for ages to mimic in her own clay the dumb pathos of waiting Earth; — whichever of these dreams be nearest truth, one thing is true, — that the maker of the Sphinx infused into his work, in as much greater measure as his nature was greater than that of other men, that yearning of pathetic solitude that most wrings a woman's heart; and the outward semblance, working in, wrought upon the heavy stone with incessant and accumulative power, till through that sluggish sandstone crept a confused thrill of consciousness, and the great creature felt the loneliness that she looked. Far away below her the Nile valley teemed with life; the antelopes coursed beside their young to feed on the green pasture fresh from its long overflow; red foxes sported with their cubs on the tawny sand; the birds taught their infant offspring their own sweet arts of flight and song on every bough; and even the ostrich, lonely Desert-runner, heaped her treasure of white eggs in the sand, or guided her callow young far from the sight and fear of man; — but the Sphinx sat alone.

Mightier and mightier grew the yearning within her, as the full moon floated upward from the east and cast her dewy dreams over land and sea. The hour was come; the whole impulse and persistence of her nature went out in vivid life, and, filling the very stones which the winds had gathered and piled against her breast, cleft them with its sentient spell, clothed them with lean flesh and wiry sinews, shaped them after the fashion of the Desert men, and sent them out alive with intellect and will, but with hearts of flint, into the wide world, — the Sphinx's children!

With a sigh that shook the shores of Egypt and smote the Sicilian midnight with sickening vibrations of earthquake, the Sphinx beheld this culmination of her great desire; in the very hour of fruition hope fled; and as this grim certainty sped away from before her, taking with it all her borrowed life, she dropped that majestic head lower upon her bosom, uplifted it again for one last look at her offspring, and so stiffened, — once more a stone.

Age after age rolled by; storm and tempest hurled their thunders at her head; wave after wave of bright, insidious sand curled about her feet and heaped its sliding grains against her side; men came and went in fleeting generations, and seasons fled like hours through the whirling wheel of Time; but the Sphinx longed and suffered no more. Her hour had come and gone; her dull instinct had burnt out, her comely outline began to disintegrate, her face grew blank and stony, her features crumbled away, altars and inscriptions defaced her breast and hieroglyphed her ponderous sides, men worshipped and wondered there, and travellers from lands beyond the sun pitched their tents before her face and defiled her feet with barbaric orgies; but she knew it no more,—her children were gone out into the world. And the world had need of them. Its rank and miasmatic civilization, — its hot-beds of sin and misery — its civil corruptions and its social lies, — its reeling, rotten principalities, — its sickly atmosphere of effeminate luxury, wherein neither justice nor judgment lived, and the solitary virtues left mere effete shadows of philanthropy and cowardly impulses called love and mercy, — needed a new race, stony and strong, unshrinking in conquest and reformation, full of zeal, and incapable of pity, to rend away the fogs that smothered truth and decency, to disperse the low-lying clouds of weak passion and maudlin luxury, to blow a reveille clear and keen as the trumpet of the north-west wind, when it sweeps down from its mountain-tops in stern exultation, and shouts its Puritanic battle-psalm across the reeking, steaming meadows of sultry August, fever-smitten and pestilent.

Such were the Sphinx's children: had they but died out with their need! Here and there a monk, fresh from his Desert-Laura, hurtles through the eclipse-light of history like the stone from a catapult, — rules a church with iron rods, organizes, denounces, intrigues, executes, keeps an unarmed soldiery to do his behests, and hurls ecclesiastic thunders at kings and emperors with the grand audacity of a commission presumedly divine, while Greeks cringe, and Jews blaspheme, and heathen flee into, or away from, conversion; and the church itself canonizes this spiritual father, this Sphinx-son of an instinct and a stone!

Or an Emperor exalted himself above the legions and the populace of Rome, banqueted his enemies and beheaded them at table, drank in the sight of blood and the sound of human shrieks as if they were his natural light and air, tormented God's creatures and cursed his kind, kindled a fire among the miserable myriads of his own city, and, exulting in a safe height, mixed the leaping, frantic discords of his own music with the horrid sounds of the hell's tragedy below him; seething in crime, steeped in murder, black with blasphemy, the horror and the hate of men, death gaped for his coming, and he went! Men revile him through all posterior ages; women shudder at the legend of his deeds; but the Sphinx stands unconscious in the Desert, — she knew not her child!

Or a Reformer springs up. High above his birth-place the snowy Alps paint themselves against the sky, an aërial dream of beauty, softened by the tender hues of dawn and sunset, serenely fair through the rift of the tempest; even their white death takes a nameless grace from distance and atmosphere, clothing itself in beauty as a spirit in clay, and tempting wanderers to their graves: but no such beauty clothes the man whose daily vision beholds them; hard, clamorous, disputatious, with one hand he rends the rotten splendors of Rome from its tottering image, and with the other plunges baby-souls to inevitable damnation; strong and fiercely rigid, full of burning and slaughter for the idolatries and harlotries of Popery, fired with lurid zeal, and bestriding one stringent idea, he rides on over dead and living, preaches predestination and hell as if the Gospel dwelt only upon destiny and despair, casts no tender look at the loving piety that underlay shrines and woman-worship and bead-counting wherever a true heart sought its God through the sole formulas it knew, but spurs forward to the end, a mighty power to destroy, to do away with old corruptions and break down idols on their altars, — saint and iconoclast! Did the heart of stone within him know its ancestry, — track its hard, loveless descent from the Sphinx's children?

Then a Queen; — a solitary woman, proud of her solitude, isolated in her regnant splendor, a dead planet like the moon, sung and pictured and adored, but keeping on her majestic path in awful beauty, deaf to human entreaty, cold to human love; a great statesman in a queen's robes; a keen, subtle politician, coifed and farthingaled; a revengeful sovereign; a deadly enemy; a woman who forgave nothing to a woman, and retaliated everything upon a man; she who brought unshrinkingly to death a sister queen discrowned and captive, a sister whose grace and loveliness and kindly aspect might have moved the lions of the arena to fawn upon her, but nowise disarmed the tigress who lapped her blood; she who banished and slew the man she would not stoop to love, because he dared to love another; and when death stared her in the face, and open-eyed judgment shook her soul, rose from that death-pallet to grapple and abuse a false woman, penitent for and confessing her falseness; a virgin monarch, pitiless, relentless, cruel as jealousy; an anomalous woman, were she not a stone-born child of the Sphinx!

Or a great General, before whose iron will horse and horseman quailed and fled, like dry stubble before flame; who wielded the sword of Gideon, and cut off the armies of his kindred people and his anointed king as a mower fells the glittering grass on a summer dawn, heedless that he, too, shall be cut down from his flourishing. On his track fire and blood spread their banners, and the raven scented his trophies afar off; age and youth alike were crushed under the tread of his war-horse; honor, and valor, and life's best prime, opposed him as summer opposes the Arctic hail-fury, and lay beaten into mire at his feet. Hated, feared, followed to the death; victorious or vanquished, the same strong, imperturbable, sullen nature; persistent rather than patient in effort, vigorously direct in action; a minister of unconscious good, of half-conscious evil; stern and gloomy to the sacrilegious climax of his well-battled life, even in the regicidal act going as one driven to his deeds by Fate that forgot God; — was he to be wondered at, whose life, in ages far gone, began among the stony Sphinx children?

Nor alone in these great landmarks of their dwelling have the Sphinx's children haunted Earth. Poets have sung them under myriad names; History has chronicled them in groups; Painting and Sculpture have handed down their aspect to a gazing world. From them sprung the Eumenides, pursuers and destroyers of men. They wore the garb of Roman legionaries, when Ramah wept for her children dashed against the walls of the Holy City, and not one stone stood upon another in Zion. They crowded the offices of the Inquisition, and tested the endurance of its victims, with steady finger on the flickering pulse, and calm eye on the death-sweating brow and bitten lip. They put on the Druid's robe and wreath, and held the human sacrifice closer to its altar. In the Asiatic jungle, lurking behind the palm-trunk, they waited, lithe and swarthy Thugs, treacherously to slay whatever victim passed by alone; or in the fair Pacific Islands kept horrid jubilee above their feasts of human flesh, and streaked themselves with kindred blood in their carousals. Holland tells its fearful story of their Spanish rule. Russian serfs record their despotism, cowering at the memory of the knout. France cringes yet at the names of the black few who guided her roaring Revolution as one might guide the ravages of a tiger with curb of adamant and rein of linked steel.

Africa stretches out her hands to testify of their presence. Too well those golden shores recall the wail of women and the yelling curses of men, driven, beast-fashion, to their pen, and floated from home to hell, or — happier fate! — dragged up, in terror of pursuit, and thrown overboard, a brief agony for a long one. They know them, too, whose continual cry of separation, starvation, insult, agony, and death rises from the heart of freedom like the steam of a great pestilence. Pity them, hearts of flesh! pity also the captors, — the Sphinx children, the flint-hearts! pity those who cannot feel, far beyond those who can, — though it be but to suffer!

New England knew them, in band and steeple-hat, hanging and pressing to death helpless women, bewitched with witchcraft. Acadia knew them, when its depopulated shores lay barren before the sun, and its homes sent up no smoke to heaven.

Greece quivers at the phantasm of their Turkish

turbans and gleaming sabres, their skill at massacre and their fiendish tortures; Italy, fair and sad, "woman country," droops shuddering at sight of their Austrian uniforms; and the Brahmin sees them in scarlet, blood-dyed, hurling from the cannon's mouth helpless captives, — killing, not converting.

Wherever, all the wide world over, a nation shrinks from its oppressors, or a slave from its master, — wherever a child flees from the face of a parent who knows neither justice nor mercy, or a wife goes mad under the secret tyranny of her inevitable fate, — wherever pity and mercy and love veil their faces and wring their hands outside the threshold, — there abide the Sphinx's children.

For this she longed and hoped and waited in the desert! for this she envied the red fox and the ostrich! for this her dumb lips parted, in their struggle after speech, to ask of earth and air some solace to her solitude! for this, for these, she poured out her dim life in one strong, wilful aspiration!

Happy Sphinx, to be left even of that dull existence! blessedly unconscious of that granted desire! mouldering away in the curling sand-hills, the prey of hostile elements, the mysterious symbol of a secret yearning and a vain desire! Not for thee the bitterness of success! not for thee the conscious agony of penitence, — the falling temple of the will crushing its idolater! No wild voices in the wind reproach the wilder pulses of a slow-breaking heart; no keen words of taunt sting thee into madness; Memory hurls at thee no flying javelins; broken-winged Hope flutters about thee no more! Thy day is over, thine hour is past!

"*Wherefore I praised the dead which are already dead, more than the living which are yet alive!*"

THE DEACON'S WEEK.

THE communion service of January was just over in the church at Sugar Hollow; and people were waiting for Mr. Parkes to give out the hymn; but he did not give it out, — he laid his book down on the table, and looked about on his church.

He was a man of simplicity and sincerity, fully in earnest to do his Lord's work, and do it with all his might; but he did sometimes feel discouraged. His congregation was a mixture of farmers and mechanics, for Sugar Hollow was cut in two by Sugar Brook, — a brawling, noisy stream that turned the wheel of many a mill and manufactory; yet on the hills around it there was still a scattered population, eating their bread in the full perception of the primeval curse. So he had to contend with the keen brain and sceptical comment of the men who piqued themselves on power to hammer at theological problems as well as hot iron, with the jealousy and repulsion and bitter feeling that has bred the communistic hordes abroad and at home; while perhaps he had a still harder task to awaken the sluggish souls of those who used their days to struggle with barren hill-side and rocky pasture for mere food and clothing, and their nights to sleep the dull sleep of physical fatigue and mental vacuity.

It seemed sometimes to Mr. Parkes that nothing but

the trump of Gabriel could arouse his people from their sins and make them believe on the Lord and follow his footsteps. To-day — no — a long time before to-day — he had mused and prayed till an idea took shape in his thought, and now he was to put it in practice; yet he felt peculiarly responsible and solemnized as he looked about him and foreboded the success of his experiment. Then there flashed across him, as words of Scripture will come back to the habitual Bible-reader, the noble utterance of Gamaliel concerning Peter and his brethren when they stood before the council: "If this counsel or this work be of men, it will come to naught: but if it be of God ye cannot overthrow it." So with a sense of strength the minister spoke.

"My dear friends," he said, " you all know, though I did not give any notice to that effect, that this week is the Week of Prayer. I have a mind to ask you to make it for this once a week of practice instead. I think we may discover some things, some of the things of God, in this manner, that a succession of prayer-meetings would not perhaps so thoroughly reveal to us. Now when I say this I don't mean to have you go home and vaguely endeavor to walk straight in the old way; I want you to take 'topics,' as they are called, for the prayer-meetings. For instance, Monday is prayer for the temperance work. Try all that day to be temperate in speech, in act, in indulgence of any kind that is hurtful to you. The next day is for Sunday-schools; go and visit your scholars, such of you as are teachers, and try to feel that they have living souls to save. Wednesday is a day for fellowship meeting; we are cordially invited to attend a union-meeting of this sort at Bantam. Few of us can go twenty-five miles to be with our brethren there; let us spend that day in cultivating our brethren here; let us go and see those who have been cold to us for some reason, heal up our breaches of friendship, confess our shortcomings one to another, and act as if, in our Master's words, 'all ye are brethren.'

"Thursday is the day to pray for the family relation; let us each try to be to our families on that day in our measure what the Lord is to his family, the church, remembering the words, 'Fathers, provoke not your children to anger;' 'Husbands, love your wives, and be not bitter against them.' These are texts rarely commented upon, I have noticed, in our conference meetings; we are more apt to speak of the obedience due from children, and the submission and meekness our wives owe us, forgetting that duties are always reciprocal.

"Friday, the church is to be prayed for. Let us then, each for himself, try to act that day just as we think Christ, our great Exemplar, would have acted in our places. Let us try to prove to ourselves and the world about us that we have not taken upon us his name lightly or in vain. Saturday is prayer-day for the heathen and foreign missions. Brethren, you know and I know that there are heathen at our doors here; let every one of you who will, take that day to preach the gospel to some one who does not hear it anywhere else. Perhaps you will find work that ye knew not of lying in your midst. And let us all, on Saturday evening, meet here again, and choose some one brother to relate his experience of the week. You who are willing to try this method please to rise."

Everybody rose except old Amos Tucker, who never

stirred, though his wife pulled at him and whispered to him imploringly. He only shook his grizzled head and sat immovable.

"Let us sing the doxology," said Mr. Parkes; and it was sung with full fervor. The new idea had roused the church fully; it was something fixed and positive to do; it was the lever-point Archimedes longed for, and each felt ready and strong to move a world.

Saturday night the church assembled again. The cheerful eagerness was gone from their faces; they looked downcast, troubled, weary, — as the pastor expected. When the box for ballots was passed about, each one tore a bit of paper from the sheet placed in the hymn-books for that purpose, and wrote on it a name. The pastor said, after he had counted them: —

"Deacon Emmons, the lot has fallen on you."

"I'm sorry for't," said the deacon, rising up and taking off his overcoat. "I haint got the best of records, Mr. Parkes, now I tell ye."

"That isn't what we want," said Mr. Parkes. "We want to know the whole experience of some one among us, and we know you will not tell us either more or less than what you did experience."

Deacon Emmons was a short, thick-set man, with a shrewd, kindly face and gray hair, who kept the village store, and had a well-earned reputation for honesty.

"Well, brethren," he said, "I dono why I shouldn't tell it. I am pretty well ashamed of myself, no doubt, but I ought to be, and maybe I shall profit by what I've found out these six days back. I'll tell you just as it come. Monday, I looked about me to begin with. I am amazin' fond of coffee, and it aint good for me — the doctor says it aint; but, dear me, it does set a man up good, cold mornings, to have a cup of hot, sweet, tasty drink, and I haven't had the grit to refuse. I knew it made me what folks call nervous, and I call cross, before night come; and I knew it fetched on spells of low spirits, when our folks couldn't get a word out of me, — not a good one, any way; so I thought I'd try on that to begin with. I tell you it come hard! I hankered after that drink of coffee dreadful! Seemed as though I couldn't eat my breakfast without it. I feel to pity a man that loves liquor more'n I ever did in my life before; but I feel sure they can stop if they try, for I've stopped, and I'm a-goin' to stay stopped.

"Well, come to dinner, there was another fight. I do set by pie the most of anything; I was fetched up on pie, as you may say. Our folks always had it three times a day, and the doctor, he's been talkin' and talkin' to me about eatin' pie. I have the dyspepsy like everything, and it makes me useless by spells, and onreliable as a weathercock. An' Doctor Drake he says there won't nothing help me but to diet. I was readin' the Bible that morning, while I sat waiting for breakfast, for 'twas Monday, and wife was kind of set back with washin' and all, and I come acrost that part where it says that the bodies of Christians are temples of the Holy Ghost. Well, thinks I, we'd ought to take care of 'em if they be, and see that they're kep' clean and pleasant, like the church; and nobody can be clean nor pleasant that has dyspepsy. But, come to pie, I felt as though I couldn't! and, lo ye, I didn't! I eet a piece right against my conscience; facin' what I knew I ought to do, I went and done what I ought not to. I tell ye my conscience made music of me consider'ble, and I said then I wouldn't never sneer at a drinkin' man no more when he slipped up. I'd feel for him and help him, for I see just how it was. So that day's practice giv' out, but it learnt me a good deal more'n I knew before.

"I started out next day to look up my Bible-class. They haven't really tended up to Sunday-school as they ought to, along back; but I was busy, here and there, and there didn't seem to be a real chance to get to it. Well, 'twould take the evenin' to tell it all; but I found one real sick, been abed for three weeks, and was so glad to see me that I felt fair ashamed. Seemed as though I heerd the Lord for the first time sayin', 'Inasmuch as ye did it not to one of the least of these, ye did it not to me.' Then another man's old mother says to me before he come in from the shed, says she, 'He's been a-sayin' that if folks practised what they preached you'd ha' come round to look him up afore now, but he reckoned you kinder looked down on mill-hands. I'm awful glad you come.' Brethring, *so was I!* I tell you that day's work done me good. I got a poor opinion of Josiah Emmons, now I tell ye; but I learned more about the Lord's wisdom than a month o' Sundays ever showed me."

A smile he could not repress passed over Mr. Parkes's earnest face. The deacon had forgotten all external issues in coming so close to the heart of things; but the smile passed as he said:—

"Brother Emmons, do you remember what the Master said,—'If any man will do His will, he shall know of the doctrine, whether it be of God, or whether I speak of myself'?"

"Well, it's *so*," answered the deacon, "it's so right

along. Why, I never thought so much of my Bible-class, nor took no sech int'rest in 'em as I do to-day,— not since I begun to teach. I b'lieve they'll come more reg'lar now, too.

"Now come fellowship-day. I thought that would be all plain sailin'; seemed as though I'd got warmed up till I felt pleasant towardst everybody; so I went around seein' folks that was neighbors, and 'twas easy; but when I come home at noon spell, Philury says, says she, 'Square Tucker's black bull is into th' orchard a-tearin' round, and he's knocked two lengths o' fence down flat!' Well, the old Adam riz up then, you'd better b'lieve. That black bull has been a-breakin' into my lots ever sence we got in th' aftermath, and it's Square Tucker's fence, and he won't make it bull-strong, as he'd oughter, and that orchard was a young one jest comin' to bear, and all the new wood crisp as cracklin's with frost. You'd better b'lieve I didn't have much feller-feelin' with Amos Tucker. I jest put over to his house and spoke up pretty free to him, when he looked up and says, says he, 'Fellowship-meetin' day, aint it, deacon?' I'd ruther he'd ha' slapped my face. I felt as though I should like to slip behind the door. I see pretty distinct what sort of life I'd been livin' all the years I'd been a professor, when I couldn't hold on to my tongue and temper one day!"

"Breth-e-ren," interrupted a slow, harsh voice, somewhat broken with emotion, "*I'll* tell the rest on't. Josiah Emmons come around like a man an' a Christian right there. He asked me for to forgive him, and not to think 'twas the fault of his religion, because 'twas hisn and nothin' else. I think more of him today than

I ever done before. I was one that wouldn't say I'd practise with the rest of ye. I thought 'twas everlastin' nonsense. I'd ruther go to forty-nine prayer-meetin's than work at bein' good a week. I b'lieve my hope has been one of them that perish; it haint worked, and I leave it behind to-day. I mean to begin honest, and it was seein' one honest Christian man fetched me round to't."

Amos Tucker sat down and buried his grizzled head in his rough hands.

"Bless the Lord!" said the quavering tones of a still older man from a far corner of the house, and many a glistening eye gave silent response.

"Go on, Brother Emmons," said the minister.

"Well, when next day come, I got up to make the fire, and my boy Joe had forgot the kindlin's. I'd opened my mouth to give him Jesse, when it come over me suddin that this was the day of prayer for the family relation. I thought I wouldn't say nothin'. I jest fetched in the kindlin's myself, and when the fire burnt up good I called wife.

"'Dear me!' says she. 'I've got such a headache, 'Siah, but I'll come in a minnit.' I didn't mind that, for women are always havin' aches, and I was jest a-goin' to say so, when I remembered the tex' about not bein' bitter against 'em, so I says, 'Philury, you lay abed. I expect Emmy and me can get the vittles to-day.' I declare, she turned over and give me sech a look; why, it struck right in! There was my wife, that had worked for an' waited on me twenty-odd year, 'most scart because I spoke kind of feelin' to her. I went out and fetched in the pail o' water she'd always drawed herself, and then I milked the cow. When I come in Philury was up fryin' the potatoes, and the tears a-shinin' on her white face. She didn't say nothin', she's kinder still; but she hadn't no need to. I felt a leetle meaner'n I did the day before. But 'twant nothin' to my condition when I was goin', towards night, down the sullar stairs for some apples, so's the children could have a roast, and I heered Joe, up in the kitchen, say to Emmy, ' I do b'lieve, Em, pa's goin' to die.' — ' Why, Josiar Emmons, how you talk! —' Well, I do; he's so everlastin' pleasant an' good-natered I can't but think he's struck with death.'

" I tell ye, brethren, I set right down on them sullar stairs and cried. I *did*, reely. Seemed as though the Lord had turned and looked at me jest as he did at Peter. Why, there was my own children never see me act real fatherly and pretty in all their lives. I'd growled and scolded and prayed at 'em, and tried to fetch 'em up,— jest as the twig is bent the tree's inclined, ye know,— but I hadn't never thought that they'd got right and reason to expect I'd do my part as well as they theirn. Seemed as though I was findin' out more about Josiah Emmons's shortcomin's than was real agreeable.

" Come around Friday I got back to the store. I'd kind o' left it to the boys the early part of the week, and things was a little cuterin', but I did have sense not to tear round and use sharp words so much as common. I began to think 'twas gettin' easy to practise after five days, when in come Judge Herrick's wife after some curt'in calico. I had a handsome piece, all done off with roses and things, but there was a fault in the weavin', — every now and then a thin streak. She didn't notice it, but she was pleased with the figures on't, and said she'd take the whole piece.

Well, just as I was wrappin' of it up, what Mr. Parkes here said about tryin' to act jest as the Lord would in our place come acrost me. Why, I turned as red as a beet, I know I did. It made me all of a tremble There was I, a door-keeper in the tents of my God, as David says, really cheatin', and cheatin' a woman. I tell ye, brethren, I was all of a sweat. 'Mis' Herrick,' says I, 'I don't b'lieve you've looked real close at this goods; 'taint thorough wove,' says I. So she didn't take it; but what fetched me was to think how many times I'd done sech mean, onreliable little things to turn a penny, and all the time sayin' and prayin' that I wanted to be like Christ. I kep' a-trippin' of myself up all day jest in the ordinary business, and I was a peg lower down when night come than I was a Thursday. I'd ruther, as far as the hard work is concerned, lay a mile of four-foot stone wall than undertake to do a man's livin' Christian duty for twelve workin' hours; and the heft of that is, it's because I aint used to it, and I ought to be.

"So this mornin' come around, and I felt a mite more cherk. 'Twas missionary mornin', and seemed as if 'twas a sight easier to preach than to practise. I thought I'd begin to old Mis' Vedder's. So I put a Testament in my pocket and knocked to her door. Says I, 'Good-mornin', ma'am', and then I stopped. Words seemed to hang, somehow. I didn't want to pop right out that I'd come over to try'n convert her folks. I hemmed and swallered a little, and fin'lly I said, says I, 'We don't see you to meetin' very frequent, Mis' Vedder.'

"'No, you don't!' ses she, as quick as a wink. 'I stay to home and mind my business.'

"'Well, we should like to hev you come along with us and do ye good,' says I, sort of conciliatin'.

"'Look a here, deacon!' she snapped; 'I've lived alongside of you fifteen year, and you knowed I never went to meetin'; we aint a pious lot, and you knowed it; we're poorer'n death and uglier'n sin. Jim he drinks and swears, and Malviny dono her letters. She knows a heap she hadn't ought to, besides. Now what are you a-comin' here to-day for, I'd like to know, and talkin' so glib about meetin'? Go to meetin'! I'll go or come jest as I darn please, for all you. Now get out o' this!' Why, she come at me with a broomstick. There wasn't no need on't; what she said was enough. I *hadn't* never asked her nor hern to so much as think of goodness before. Then I went to another place jest like that,— I won't call no more names,— and sure enough there was ten children in rags, the hull of 'em, and the man half drunk. He giv' it to me, too; and I don't wonder. I'd never lifted a hand to serve nor save 'em before in all these years. I'd said consider'ble about the heathen in foreign parts, and give some little for to convert 'em, and I had looked right over the heads of them that was next door. Seemed as if I could hear Him say, 'These ought ye to have done, and not have left the other undone.' I couldn't face another soul to-day, brethren. I come home, and here I be. I've been searched through and through and found wantin'. God be merciful to me a sinner!'"

He dropped into his seat, and bowed his head; and many another bent, also. It was plain that the deacon's experience was not the only one among the brethren. Mr. Payson rose, and prayed as he had never prayed before; the week of practice had fired his heart, too. And it began a memorable year for the church in Sugar Hollow; not a year of excitement or enthusiasm, but one when they heard their Lord saying, as to Israel of old, "Go forward;" and they obeyed his voice. The Sunday school flourished, the church services were fully attended, every good thing was helped on its way, and peace reigned in their homes and hearts; imperfect, perhaps, as new growths are, but still an offshoot of the peace past understanding.

And another year they will keep another week of practice, by common consent.

A BLACK SILK.

"Fetch him right in here, pa. Poor little feller! I hope he'll come to!"

The man who had just fished this little pickle of a boy out of the brook obeyed the kind voice, and lugged his dripping burden into the small brown house, laid him on the floor, and hurried away after the doctor, while Aunt Nancy Peck stripped off the wet clothes, rubbed the cold body, and tried all her homely, old-fashioned ways of restoration.

Boys are hard to kill: before the doctor got there Leslie Varick opened his eyes, and laughed in Aunt Nancy's face, and the dear, kindly old face smiled back on the naughty boy. Leslie had been sent to spend the summer in Barrett, while his father and mother were abroad, and being a "human boy," as Mr. Chadband says, he got into every variety of mischief known to that species, his latest exploit being a headlong tumble into the mill-pond, from which Ozias Peck drew him as soon as he rose to the surface, and disposed of him as recorded. But when Master Leslie began to stir in the warm nest of blankets, he also began to howl. If he had only been half drowned, my story would have had the fate of Franklin's instructive rhyme that begins, —

"For want of a nail the shoe was lost."

But the nail was not wanting; in going down he struck sharply on a rock, and broke his leg, so that Aunt Nancy's blankets and his tired little body had long acquaintance. However, at last he got well, and in the late autumn went home, and told his mother how good Aunt Nancy had been to him: to be sure, his board had been duly paid for the six weeks he spent with the good woman; but Mrs. Varick felt as mothers do feel, even about the naughtiest boys, that she still owed her a debt of gratitude, and Leslie had a scrap of heart under all his mischief, — enough to grow a good-sized organ by and by, when he should find out that animals have nerves, and other boys tastes and feelings not unlike his own. He had hardly done capering around the open trunks that held so many pretty foreign things, — so many for him, — when suddenly he threw himself on the floor, and, putting his curly head on his mother's lap, began: —

"Mammy, haven't you got something in all this truck I can give old Aunty Peck? She was tremendously good to me when I cracked my shin-bone down there in Barrett."

Mrs. Varick laughed. "O Lello! what a slangy boy! But no matter; if you want to give Mrs. Peck something, choose for yourself. I meant to send her a nice gift at Christmas, but it would be better for you to do it."

"Oh, I've got it! Send her those red things you got to wear on your neck and ears. Oh, jolly! wouldn't she just take the shine out of Barrett folks on Sunday!"

"My pink corals? Well done, Lello! How do you think those exquisitely cut cameos would look on a black alpaca gown? Why, child, they are set in pearls, and cut by the best artist in Italy; the set cost five hundred dollars. Try again, sir."

"O mammy, what do you s'pose a man knows about women's finery?"

"A man! I like that," laughed his mother. "But try once more, dear, and if you choose wrong this time I will choose for you."

Leslie put his head on one side like a bird eying a beetle, thrust his hands in his pockets, and whistled "Captain Jinks" like a cheerful robin, as he peered into the trunks. At last he dived into the bottom of the largest.

"Here's the very thing!—this dull old shawl. It does look rather dirty, but she could wash it, and it's sort of soft and warm."

Mrs. Varick fell back in her chair, and lifted up her hands and eyes. "Leslie, my camel's-hair shawl that your father *would* buy me, though I protested! The handsomest shawl in Paris, and the dearest!"

"It looks dirty, anyway," stoutly protested Leslie. "I don't care if it cost fifty thousand dollars, mammy, it isn't clean."

"You goosey boy, that's the way they all are."

"Well, I know Aunty Peck wouldn't wear it, anyway, till 'twas washed: she can't abide dirt. I guess you'll have to pick out her present. I seem to miss it every time."

"Don't you think, Lello, a nice black silk dress would be a good thing?"

"Like enough," muttered Leslie, disgusted at such a sombre, commonplace thing for a Christmas present. A crimson satin would have met with his own approbation; but he dared not suggest it after his two failures.

So Mrs. Varick bought twenty-five yards of excellent silk, heavy fringe to trim it, a set of expensive buttons, and all needful linings and thread, having never in her life seen Aunt Nancy or her surroundings, but from Lello's enthusiasm about the house, the barn, the savory and abundant food, and the large garden, supposing Ozias was a well-to-do farmer, instead of a poor blacksmith, whose daily fare was made dainty to Leslie by the keen air of Barrett and the uncompromising appetite of a boy. Mrs. Varick herself would have starved on the rye bread, baked beans, Indian pudding, fried pork, and succotash that were so delicious to her son, and been utterly incredulous of possible comfort in that small brown house, with its stuffy best bedroom opening out of the kitchen, just as the small parlor did; for they lived in the kitchen, and slept in the half-story above it in summer, or in the tiny bedroom at one end in winter.

However, the dress was bought, and packed, and sent at Christmas, with a scrubby little letter from Leslie, expressing his gratitude, and wishing Aunty Peck a merry Christmas; and this was the end of it to the Varicks. But it was only the beginning of things to Aunt Nancy.

When the package arrived she was as pleased as a woman can be. "Why, 'Zias Peck!" she exclaimed, as the glistening length of silk unrolled before her, and the rich fringe and bright buttons inside the dress lay open to her delighted gaze, "this beats all natur'. I never did! What *upon* airth shall I do with it? It's heaps too good for an old creatur' like me."

"'Taint nuther," sturdily retorted Ozias. "I've allers lotted on buyin' of ye a silk gownd some day, Nancy, but somehow things have went ag'inst me mortally. There aint no woman in Barrett deserves it no more'n you do; 'nd I'm thankful to Providence for doin' of it, so be's I couldn't myself."

Aunt Nancy's brown eyes shone with tears. It was not often Ozias allowed himself the luxury of praising his wife; few men do; but it is a precious cordial to the female mind, if they only knew it.

"Well, well, pa, I don't say but what I'm glad on't, though I hed ruther 'twould ha' ben a suit of Sabba'-day clothes for you. My alpacky is good 'nough."

"Sho, mother, you go 'long and sew your gownd, an' put it on, 'nd go to meetin' in't. Sabba'-day clothes do wimmin-folks a heap more good 'n men-folks."

Aunt Nancy laughed; the amiable satire amused her. So she folded up her dress, and the next week took it to Miss Salter to cut and baste, intending to sew it herself. But as the lengths of silk lay across Miss Salter's table, in sailed Mrs. Gross, whose husband kept the Barrett "store."

"Whose dress is that?" she asked, curtly.

"Why, it's Aunt Nancy Peck's; aint it a most an elegant silk?" purred Miss Salter.

"I want to know! What's happened to them Pecks? I thought he was shif'less as a Canady thistle. How come she by that dress? It's cur'us how sech folks is always owin' and always havin'."

"Why, she says 'twas sent to her in a present by that youngster 't 'Zias fished out o' the pond last summer."

"My sakes! I don't believe it. Boys aint so skerce that folks pay that way for haulin' of 'em out o' water. I don't believe but what she's laid by quite a spell to buy it herself."

Mrs. Gross flounced out of the room, and took a straight course for the store.

"Well, Hiram Gross," she began, sitting down on a big cheese-box in the back room, where she found her husband, — a meek, slow man, with a rather delayed utterance, — "here I have been a-slavin' and a-savin' for you this seventeen year, and I haven't never had but one silk gownd to my back, 'nd here's 'Zias Peck's wife has got a satin-finished black silk a-cuttin' to Sabry Salter's, fit for the Judge's wife, trimmin's to match. Don't he owe ye a bill right along?"

"Well," said the easy man, looking gently over his spectacles, "I don't know but what he d—oos, a leetle. 'Z—ias means well — he means real well; b—ut he aint forehanded, 'nd I don' know 's I feel to blame him. He was b—orn tired, I expect — he! he! he!"

"Now I want to see them books o' yourn, Hi Gross. Ef he owes ye thirty dollars, jest you set a lawyer onto him, an' git the money, an' buy me a silk gownd; she'd oughter hev paid ye the money b'fore she buyed sech finery as that, and me goin' everywhere in nothing but a cashmere."

"No, Sary, 'twouldn't be no use for ye to see them books n—ow; they aint footed up." Here the easy man closed his lips with a set firmness that Mrs. Gross knew well; it was his one mode of resistance to her marital authority. He could not scold or domineer, but he could shut his mouth; and he, too, thought silence was golden.

But she would not be baffled. The clerks of the store boarded with Mr. Gross, and the youngest, a tall, growing boy, always hungry, she had made her obedient servant by the simple method of feeding him well when he made himself useful to her, and withholding rations whenever he recalcitrated; she worked upon this principle now, and discovered through him that Ozias was in debt thirty-six dollars to her husband.

So, taking the matter into her own hands, she stepped into the little shanty one bitter cold morning, when Ozias sat crouched over the fire waiting for a job, and told the poor man, in very short and sharp terms, that Mr. Gross wanted him to pay up his bill; he couldn't afford to be out of the money so long.

Ozias was a simple creature, and the proprieties of business were quite unknown to him; he did not know why Mrs. Gross had not as good a right to dun him as her husband, and his face fell.

"I'm dre'dful sorry, Mrs. Gross," he said, plaintively. "I don't see no way to raise the money dyrect. I thought 'twas kind of 'greed on to take a share on't out in shoein' the horse, 'nd there's a little on my side to the good. I do mean to pay Mister Gross as quick as ever I get the means; but times is hard and business is dreadful slack. And"—

"Folks that can buy their wives black-silk gowns had ought to pay their store-bills," snapped the woman, fixing her cold gray eyes on him.

Ozias was struck dumb. The silk dress, that he took such pride in, was, so to speak, crumpled up and thrown in his face; and Mrs. Gross left him staring at her, his mouth open, and his jaw dropped.

"O Lordy!" he ejaculated as she disappeared, dropping down on the nail-keg that was his wonted seat. "What upon airth! She doos beat all! Well, I won't say nothin' to mother. They can't 'tach her gownd noway, if they do the furnitoor, and I'm glad on't."

Just here a pair of horses appeared at the door, and with a heavy sigh Ozias went to his work.

While this happened Aunt Nancy was sitting by the window, stitching away at her new gown, and in sailed Miss Beers, collector for the church contributions. Now, Aunt Nancy had always given of her poverty to various causes presented in the routine, as a matter of duty. But this year her winter bonnet was a hopeless case; she could not press it or retrim it any longer; the felt was broken and rusty, the ribbon frayed, the binding all worn out, and to be decently comparable with her silk dress a new one had to be a little finer; so all her store of money, painfully gathered from the sale of berries, home-knit socks, eggs, and chickens, had been exhausted by the new felt bonnet with satin ribbons, and the warm gloves, that were a real necessity.

"I'm awful sorry," she said, in a half-frightened way, as Miss Semantha Beers showed her forbidding countenance, and took the proffered chair. "I did expect to have somethin' as usual to contriboot, but I haint. Things is so this year that I can't do jest what I hev done."

"H'm!" sniffed Miss Beers, setting her pale lips more closely, and staring at the silk dress. "Them that cares for the poor, perishin' frame to sech an extent as that they can't give no help to the lost souls a-cryin' out for sucker in the ends of the airth will find themselves a-cryin' in vain mabbe when these mortal gods" (she meant gauds) "and vanities is clean vanished away into emptiness and"—

"I'm real sorry," interrupted Aunt Nancy, a little scared by this commination, "but so it is; and ef I haint got it I can't give it."

"I should think if you had sold your goods and gi'n the money to them that needs salvation a sight more'n you need a silk gownd, 'twould be a lot better for your immortal soul," Miss Semantha answered, pursing up her mouth and rolling up her eyes.

"Why, mercy sakes! Miss S'manthy, the dress was gi'n to me. I couldn't give 't away, nor sell it, ye know. That boy o' Varick's that come so near gittin' drownded was here quite a spell with a broke leg, and I nussed him up, for his folks was to Eurup; so when it come Christmas-time, why, he went and sent me this in a present, trimmin's and all. I was real beat when I got it. Course ye know I couldn't never hev afforded no sech gownd; but I don't deny but what I feel consider'ble set up."

"Yes, I dessay ye do," sighed Miss Beers, whose green eyes looked longingly at the heavy silk. "Seems as though 'twould ha' ben more accordin' to your necessities, though, ef they'd hev paid his board right out and out."

"Why, land, they did,— five dollars a week. The gownd Leslie sent me for a present. He's kind of free-hearted, and he and me got to thinkin' a sight of each other whilst he laid here on the comp'ny bed."

"Well, I must say it's sing'lar. I should ha' thought they'd ha' thought five dollars a week was enough. Sence you say so, of course it's so, but seems as though 'twas scatterin' their means to do sech things."

Mrs. Peck felt this remark to be unanswerable, and Miss Semantha got up to go away, convinced in her own mind that the money for Leslie's board had been laid out on the dress, and Aunt Nancy's conscience twisted to make it appear the boy's present. She made much capital of the whole affair at the next sewing society; and, by some of the inscrutable means that spread gossip like spores of disease, her tale got to the ears of Stephen Spencer, the richest man in Barrett, and the holder of a mortgage on Ozias Peck's little homestead.

Five years ago Chester Peck, Ozias's only child, had been seized with a wild desire to go to California. Barrett was a dull place, its only life the great cotton-mill that Mr. Spencer owned, and Chester had no liking for mill work, nor could he buy a farm, or even rent one. He was a bright, energetic young fellow, and Ozias had sense enough, slow as he was, to see that his son ought to go somewhere else to find success, or even occupation; so he mortgaged his house for three hundred dollars, and sent his boy off on his travels. He had gone at once to San Francisco, and after a while got a place as clerk in a hotel; but after two years' absence his letters suddenly ceased, and his father and mother had gradually come to believe him dead. But the mortgage did not die, and year after year it taxed Ozias to the utmost to pay its interest; but for this the bill at the store never would have run on so long, and this year the mortgage would have been foreclosed but for the lucky accident that laid up Leslie Varick in their house six weeks, and brought them in thirty dollars. Now, Stephen Spencer was a man who had made money by the most grinding economy and all kinds of petty shifts and stratagems; he held as an article of faith that no poor man ought to spend any money at all except for the bare necessities of life: pork, and potatoes, and cabbage were nourishing food, and calico and osnaburg cheap; finery was a sin, and palatable food a crime, in his eyes; money was the sole good of life. Yet he took none of the ordinary pleasure people take in the results of wealth; his own dress was shabby, his method of life squalid, his workmen were pinched of their wages and crowded in their work. "Steve" Spencer was a by-word in all the country round for meanness and greed.

Such a man was not likely to lose any money for want of watching his investments. When he heard that Ozias Peck's wife had a new black silk dress, and when he saw it on a bright March Sunday, shining and rustling up the meeting-house aisle on her well-rounded person, — for she laid aside her shabby shawl in the porch, and gave it to Ozias to carry in for her, — he jumped at once to the conclusion that this unlucky couple had been beset by that sudden craze which sometimes attacks poor people, and impels them to launch out into some expenditure, extravagant and quite unwarranted, but indulged in from an impulse of despair, such as makes a slave strike his master, or a prisoner kill his jailer; for what slavery or what imprisonment is worse than the heavy shackles of poverty, the despair of debt, the grind of a life that is endless labor, the pleasureless existence, "the haunting, indefinable dread, of a moneyless man?"

A fear of this sort smote the sense of Stephen

Spencer as he looked at Aunt Nancy shining up the aisle to her seat by the pulpit; for Ozias was deaf, and had to be near the minister to enjoy his sermon. It seemed to him that he was about to lose the interest on his mortgage; but the word carried its own remedy. He could — he would — foreclose at once; such extravagance was no longer to be condoned; his own daughter, a meek and much-oppressed girl, never had a silk dress in her life; there she sat now, in a cheap alpaca and an old straw hat trimmed with worn velvet, looking for all the world like a lily-of-the-valley under dry leaves, so pure and pale was her delicate countenance, so slight her shape, so shrinking her girlish attitudes. That the dress could have been a present to Aunt Nancy never entered his head; in all his long, poor life he had never given anybody so much as a common pin, and to give away a silk dress would have stamped the giver in his eyes as a dangerous lunatic; he comforted himself with reflecting that he could threaten Ozias at least, for he did not pay very punctually the ten per cent. interest, and the last instalment was due this two weeks: he would foreclose as soon as the law allowed, surely. And secure in that resolve he went to sleep in the corner of his slip, and made a day of rest out of the Sunday that was never anything else but rest to him. Ozias sat with his head sunk on his breast: a dreadful shadow of debt hung over him; the sanctuary was not a place of refuge from such troubles; he could not help seeing Mrs. Gross's cold, clear eyes fixed on Aunt Nancy as she rustled up the aisle in her innocent complacency, and he thought her husband eyed him askance, as who should say, "To-day thee, to-morrow me;" and in his mental distress he heaved sighs so deep, though unconscious, that dear Aunt Nancy, devoutly drinking in Parson Fry's sermon, could not but hope her husband was under conviction, and felt more than ever ashamed that her contributions to the missionary-box had fallen short. If only Ozias could be converted, she thought, she would deny herself everything in future to make proper thank-offerings; and as she sat musing on this great mercy the silk gown went out of her simple, pious mind, and did her as little good as the old alpaca that had been her ordinary Sunday garb so long.

But every woman belonging to the sewing-circle had an eye to that transgression in silk, and many a head was shaken over Aunty Peck's fall from grace in the line of apparel, while Miss Beers passed her by on the other side, as the congregation at last emerged from the building, with a look of scornful pity that made Aunt Nancy feel like a sinner of the deepest dye, though her own conscience withheld its blame; but we are so apt to think more of other people's opinion of us than our own.

Monday was a black day to Ozias. He had hardly got to work before Stephen Spencer appeared at the shop door and demanded his due.

"You had ought to have been on time, 'Zias Peck. Every six months punctooal is the way. Th' int'rest money was due Friday last, and I haint seen hide nor hair on't."

"O Lordy!" squeaked Ozias, with the pitiful tone of a mouse in a trap. "Don't ye, now don't ye, Square Spencer. Times is so everlastin' bad, and business hez fell off. I'd ha' did it ef I'd ha' had it to hev done; but it does seem as though folks let their hosses go on the huff ruther'n hev 'em shod, and they'll rig a rail betwixt the exes afore they'll come here an' get me to tinker of 'em up. It's *so*, now I tell ye, Square."

"That's talk," said the Squire, fixing his hard, bold eyes on Ozias with the look of a born tyrant. "Bizness is bizness; folks thet borrer must pay. Ef you can buy your wife a silk gownd to go to meetin' in, you can pay me fifteen dollars, sure as shootin', and you've got to."

"Darn that gownd!" burst from Ozias's despairing lips. "No, don't nuther. The gownd's hern, and she sets by it like everything, I tell ye. 'Twas a present. I didn't buy it no more'n you did. I wisht I could, but I couldn't."

"Don't tell me no sech yarn as that, 'Zias Peck. Folks don't send silk gownds to old women round the country, no more'n they rain out o' the sky. I tell ye ag'in I've got to hev that int'rest money before Sat'day night, or I'll foreclose that moggidge as sure as I stan' here, — you jest depend on't;" and with these words the usurer walked off, confident and self-satisfied, and poor Ozias sank on to his nail-keg, and dropped his face in his hands.

What could he do? There was nothing for it but to sell the heifer, a creature of their own raising, whose mother was already fatting for the butcher. This must be done, and then he could pay Squire Spencer and part of the store-bill; but it was like selling a child. The pretty heifer was Aunt Nancy's pet, and whenever Ozias came to drive her home from pasture she came up to him and pushed her fine muzzle into his hand, hoping for an apple, a crust of bread, a lump of salt. or a crisp turnip, and if she failed to find such a tidbit, turned her soft purple eyes on him with a bland reproach that went to his heart.

And to sell Betty meant to be stinted in milk, pinched in butter, deprived of snowy Dutch cheese in hot summer days, and ripe home-made cheeses the year round; it meant to take away two-thirds of what simple luxuries they had; but it was better, after all, than to lose the house. The poor man had not the courage to tell his wife at once. He went over to the tavern where Selah Hills lived, to see what he could get for his heifer; and finding that worthy ready to pay him thirty dollars in cash, agreed to receive the price, and deliver the animal the next week. He put off the evil day of telling Aunt Nancy as long as he could, though he had to tell Squire Spencer that by the next Thursday he would pay up his debt, — information not altogether pleasant to Stephen, who wanted to end the matter, and secure himself from final loss as soon as possible. Of his bill at the store he heard nothing more. Mrs. Gross went out of town suddenly to see her sick mother, and nothing was farther from her husband's thought than to harass an honest, hard-working man like Ozias Peck; but, as the days went on, Ozias bethought himself that the bill might come in any moment, and his wife be disturbed by it; so he wrote a note to Mr. Gross, assuring him that part of it would be paid the next week, on Thursday; but as the good man had gone to fetch his wife home the labored epistle, so pathetic in its thumbed, misspelled condition and plaintive humility, had to wait for his return.

In the meanwhile Ozias went about his work under

a heavy cloud; he was silent at meals, groaned and sighed in his sleep, seemed to take no interest in the weekly paper, and mightily strengthened his wife's hope that he was struggling with a sense of his sinful condition, and on the high-road to a new life of faith and duty. She watched him in respectful silence, hoping for some word of confidence or emotion, till human nature could endure it no longer, and she burst out one night as he sat by the fire, with his head in his hands : —

"Say, 'Zias, be ye under conviction?"

"Lordy!" exclaimed the astonished man, looking up at her. "Under conviction! If I be, I guess it's conviction of other folks's sins. I'm pestered with them a heap more'n I be with my own, now I tell ye."

"Oh, dear!" said Aunt Nancy, piteously, wiping her spectacles on her checked apron; "I was in hopes you'd seed your errors, and ben a-repentin' of 'em. Ye know, 'Zias, you've set under the droppin's of the sanctooary a consider'ble long time, and I'm dreadful afeard you're getting hardened."

"I wish to gracious I was; I wish I was a stun wall; but I aint!" exclaimed the poor man, getting up hastily and going out of the door. He could not bear another word, for, though he had put the greatest restraint on himself to keep the impending trouble from his wife, it irritated him extremely not to have her sympathize with what she did not know anything about. Such is man!

Aunt Nancy sighed; she, too, had her troubles. Parson Fry had been to see her the day before, and though he did not say anything definitely about that root of evil, the silk gown, he delivered such a homily on the virtues of self-denial, economy, cheerful giving, and humility, together with a discourse on the duties we owe to the heathen in particular, that the poor woman knew that he had heard all about her shortcomings, and observed the sable splendor of her attire in meeting. What she did not suspect, however, was that Mrs. Fry, a little, meek, excellent woman, being exasperated by the minister's insistence that she should accompany him to the next meeting of the Association in Hartford, had, after putting forth sundry small reasons, to have them demolished each in turn by her husband's logic, turned upon him as the worm will turn, and snapped: —

"I haven't got a decent dress to wear, Mr. Fry. If I was 'Zias Peck's wife, I suppose I should have a good black silk; he don't have to buy every book that's printed;" and so, having freed her mind, Mrs. Fry burst into tears, and went out, slamming the door behind her.

Semantha Beers had already urged the parson to admonish Aunt Nancy for not doing her duty; but, being a man much absorbed in study, he had forgotten all about the matter till his wife's sudden and surprising outburst recalled it. He saw his duty in a much stronger light then, and performed it with singular unction; and Mrs. Peck, awed by his dignity of person and position, received his exhortation without a word, and even went down on her knees, and was prayed at full fifteen minutes without any other remonstrance than a few slow tears. She had kept her troubles to herself as silently as her husband kept his up to this hour, and with the same tender motive. "Bear ye one another's burdens." Perhaps this command is as stringent as that to contribute to missions; I cannot at this moment place the latter to compare them.

At last it was Tuesday, and 'Zias went early to the barn to drive his heifer to pasture for the last time; to-day he must tell his wife, and his heart ached as he thought of it. But as he drew near the barn an ominous cough smote on his ear; he hurried in, and there stood Betty, her hair rough and staring, her eyes dull but wild, her breath like the labored puff of rusted bellows, her mouth dripping, and her legs trembling; he could not but see that the dreaded "cattle-ail" had attacked her, and he remembered now how slowly she had dragged herself from the lot the night before, though he had laid it then to the sultry heat of the April weather, coming, as now and then a day of April will come, with all the blaze of July, when the drifts are scarce gone from the hills.

Nothing need be said now about selling the poor creature; remedies must be found and applied; and all day both Ozias and Nancy worked over the suffering animal, sat up with her all night, and were found beside her in the morning, when Selah came over with his money,— Aunt Nancy, with the deer-like head in her lap, crying like a child, as the beautiful purple eyes, fast glazing in death, rolled up at her imploringly, and Ozias, leaning against the manger, sniffing fiercely.

"Well, I declare!" exclaimed Selah, sticking his old white hat in at the door; "good as dead, aint she? What'll ye take for hide an' horns, 'Zias?"

Aunt Nancy looked up, enraged; but a hand was laid on Selah's shoulder, and a kindly countenance peeped over it, while a slow voice said, "Well! well! poor c—ritter! Got the p—pleury—newmoaney, haint she? Why, 'Zias, I am r—eal sorry."

"So be I," said Ozias, firmly, setting his battered hat straight on his head, winking both eyes hard, and uttering a loud "H-m!" to clear his throat; for he saw Stephen Spencer behind the other men, peering in with bold, hard eyes, as if he, too, had scented the prey afar off, and pounced down lest it should escape him, though 'Zias had specially appointed to-morrow for his payment. "But sorry won't help none: the caow's a-dyin'. I'd calc'lated to sell her to Sely here, and pay up that int'rest on the moggidge, and a piece o' that bill o' yourn, Gross; but 'twant so to be. I haint got the money, and I can't git it, and you can't hev it; that's the hull on't."

"But, 'Z—ias," put in the shopkeeper's kindly, stumbling voice, "I've been to P—lymouth, 'nd I haint but jest g—ot your letter you writ. Why, I hadn't n—o idee of pressin' of ye to settle. Th' aint a mite o' hurry. I d—on' know what p—ossessed ye, 'Zias. I haint never dunned ye for't, now, hev I?"

"Your wife come an' said you'd got to hev it right off, and she knowed jest how 'twas, and I expected you'd sent her, and I meant to ha' paid ye some on't ef"—

'Zias's voice stopped here; a stifled sob choked him; he could only hold out his rough, trembling hand toward the dying cow with a gesture of rude dignity and eloquence.

"Well," put in Stephen Spencer, "I come to dun ye, and I'm stayin' to dun ye. Either I'll foreclose that 'ere moggidge, or I'll put a 'tachment on to your goods 'nd chattels. I guess that 'ere silk gownd 'll sell for my claim ef it won't for Gross's."

Aunt Nancy threw her apron over her head in sheer despair; the heifer gave a low groan, shivered all over, and was still, but Nancy did not see nor Ozias hear. Trouble maddened him; he held out his clenched fist at the usurer.

"Do it if ye dare! That there gownd is my wife's own. She came by it in a way you won't never come by a half cent, — by bein' kind an' good to a feller-creatur, in trouble. I'll chuck ye inter the mill-pond, and never look for ye no more, ef you touch a button on't, or so much as take it off'n the peg. Four-close your old moggidge, five-close it ef you want to; we can go to the taown-house to-morrer without howlin', an I shan't care a darn, ef Nancy's along; but you shan't lay a finger on her nor hern."

"No more he shall, father," said a strong young voice behind the group of men.

Aunt Nancy dropped the heifer's head, and sprang up with a loud cry, to be hugged by her boy, come home from California in the nick of time.

It all sounds very like a novel; but, after all, where do people who write novels get their situations but out of real life? Sam had been prospecting in the interior of California since he left San Francisco, where the climate did not agree with him, and had met with wonderful success, not in mining, but by hard, steady work on a ranch. Now he had a stock-farm of his own, and was raising fruit besides. He had made some money, and had a fair prospect of future wealth; but getting no answer to his letters home, and being desirous to pay his debt to his father, having also a stronger reason —

which was a secret between him and one other person — for returning to Barrett, he had come in the very nick of time. In twenty-four hours the mortgage was cancelled, the store-bill paid, and five hundred dollars lodged in a Hartford savings-bank to his father's credit. Aunt Nancy wiped away the few tears she had to shed over poor Betty, with a glow at her heart she felt almost ashamed of, seeing her pet lay stark and stiff already under the sod. Ozias returned to his shell, and Selah Hills, who was a carpenter as well as tavern-keeper, the latter occupation being almost nominal, had already raised the frame of a new barn on 'Zias's lot to accommodate a beautiful full-blood Alderney cow which Sam Peck had bought in Hartford, and thought worthy of a better lodging than the tumble-down structure which had scarce sheltered Betty, when Barrett was electrified by the announcement that Nelly Spencer, the sweet, pale, gentle girl, over whom her father tyrannized always, was married to Sam Peck, and on her way to California.

It was quite true: Sam and Nelly had been little lovers at school, and never grown out of loving. Part of her pallor and meekness was owing to Sam's missing letters; she, too, thought him dead, for they had exchanged stringent promises, and she knew that nothing less than death could so silence him. She forgot that the mail service in those far-away regions might be quite as effectual to that end.

She and Sam both knew it was of no use to ask her father's consent, so she put on her old shawl and worn-out bonnet one morning and walked over to Parson Fry's study. Ozias was there in his Sunday clothes, and Aunt Nancy in the fateful black silk; and when the brief ceremony was over, and the happy pair packed into the stage to meet a New York train at the nearest station, Aunt Nancy stopped on her way home at Semantha Beers's house, and gave her five dollars for foreign missions. After that she wore her black silk gown in peace till it wore out.

JERICHO JIM.

"Say now, marm! Lemme in. I aint half so smart's I look to be. I kin do more'n four things to help ye, and I'm kinder onlucky jess now. Mother's dead, ye see, 'nd "—

Here the simple creature blubbered honestly, and drew his ragged sleeve across his eyes. Mrs. Ellery relented. "Well, who be ye, anyhow? Where d'ye come from?"

"'Ho, Jemimy! Where d'ye come from?
Flat fish 'n flounders! where d'ye come from?'

I'm Jericho Jim; come from Jericho straight, a Tuesday mornin'. No place for Jim there. Dad broke his neck last winter; drunk as David, 'nd slipped up, 'nd the sled fixed him out a-goin' over him; mother she cried some, but he was dead, anyhow;" and, with a sort of furtive grin on his thin, sallow face, and a spark in the hitherto vacant gray eye, Jericho Jim sent his stick spinning in air and caught it again dexterously.

"Where be ye a-goin' to?" inquired the old lady again, resting on her broom-handle, and looking over her spectacles at the queer creature before her.

"I'm goin' here, marm. They said suthin' 'bout the poor-house, down to Jericho; so I quit. Poor-houses aint clean;" and he gave a sidelong glance into the kitchen, neat as a lady's parlor, not passing over the clean calico gown and stainless cap of good Mrs. Ellery.

"That's *so;* they're dirty holes. Well, you come in and set down. I'll give ye some vittles, and ye can stay till husband comes home; he'll see to ye."

So Jericho Jim was set down to an abundant supper of beans, biscuit, pie, and gingerbread, and plenty of hot tea, and proved beyond a doubt that he was hungry.

When Deacon Ellery came home he growled a little at the new inmate of his family, more because it was his way to growl than because he meant it; for his keen eye for business discerned in Jim an inexpensive helper, whom his increasing years and rheumatism made welcome if not needful. Somebody was once overheard by this worthy man to ask: "Why does Deacon Ellery allers go grumblin' round like an old gobbler?" and the deacon saw fit to answer for himself, to the great confusion of the inquirer, who had not seen him coming: "Why, ye see, I have ter; so's to everage things. Wife's orful smoothly; comf'table as a punkin in a corn lot; allers a-smilin' and chirpin'; 'nd it stands to reason all m'lasses aint good for this world; 's got to be some grind, so I do the grindin'." With which exposition of his unconscious heathenism the deacon gave a grunt and walked away. He was better than his words, however, for his heart was warm and his head clear; and poor Jericho Jim soon found that his new home was a haven of rest for his weary body, and did his very best to reward the sheltering goodness that fed and clothed him, and beamed on him like sunshine in kind looks and words.

"I declare for't," grumbled Deacon Ellery, "it beats all to see that are feller work; I dono whether he's a fool or not. See him a-pitchin' into the woodpile, mother? Well, ye'd say there warnt no better feller to pile wood betwixt here'n Danbury; but yesterday, when he was a-sawin', all of a sudden he stopped short 'nd jumped the fence 'nd lay down in the sunshine 'nd kicked his heels. 'Jim,' says I, 'what be ye stoppin' for?' 'So's to grow,' ses he, cooler'n a cucumber. 'Grow?' says I. 'Yes,' ses he. 'It's a reel growin' day; the' aint a heap sech days; sun a-shinin', birds a-singin', wind a-blowin' real soft: mostly we're friz to death in this world; kinder stunted, deacon; I want to grow whilst I can; there's more'n forty days in the wilderness to work, ye know.' Well, if I didn't let him be! 'Taint no use a-talkin' to him when he gets a curus notion like that holt on him."

"There's somethin' to most o' his notions, that's a fact," replied the old lady. "I kinder wonder whether or no he aint got the right on't, Mr. Ellery. Mebbe ef we'd took more sunshine into us along back, you an' me wouldn't ha' been so dreadful rheumaticky."

"He's a queer genius, anyhow," muttered the deacon, walking off; but it was to be observed after this that the old man sat in the south door-way more than he ever had done; and that his wife let in all the sunshine into her bedroom and kitchen that the small, green-paned windows allowed. If they were too old to be cured of rheumatism, at least the rooms grew cheery and the air sweet, and spectacles did them more good than usual.

They would neither have read or remembered a hygienic treatise on the benefits of sun and air, but they had sense enough to accept the homely wisdom of Jericho Jim, and brains enough not to let carpets stand between them and comfort.

Before many months Jim became a sort of neighborhood courier; he peddled milk for the deacon, and dispensed with his quarts and pints all the news of the village. Many a good woman waited eagerly for his coming, and ran out with her apron over her head, not merely for the pitcher of fresh, sweet, rich fluid, but to hear about "Mis'" Allen's sick baby, or Jones's grandmother who broke her leg last week, or Sary Penny's company from York; and it was strange enough to see how quaintly and deftly Jim fitted his story to the hearer. With the curious instinct that sometimes dwells in the souls of those we conceitedly call half-witted, he seemed to comprehend the characters he met, to understand their wants and their ways; and many was the word in season carelessly dropped from his lips that did a blessed errand, all the more because it was uttered by "the foolishness of man."

"Did ye stop to Harris's to-day?" inquired the deacon, as Jim rode up to the gate one frosty morning, with clattering empty cans.

"Well, I expect I did."

"Lef' the quart, I s'pose, 'nd didn't git nothin' for't?"

"No, *sir!* I give 'em somethin' to boot. Ole Harris came to the door for't; she's done up. Doctor's gig was a-stannin' there, an' he was clus up to the winder a-mixin' a mess, 'nd ole Harris sez: 'Be you Ellery's fool?' — 'Yes, I be, you bet,' sez I, pooty cherk. Then he larfed rough as bark. 'Give us a quart,' sez he; 'I haint got no change to-day.' — 'Well,' sez I, 'it aint no matter 's long 's ye're to hum; deacon 's willin' to trust folks t' stay to hum.' He looked orful beat 'nd mad, 'nd I see the doctor larfin'; but he took the milk, 'nd I whipped up, I tell ye."

Jericho Jim never knew that Tim Harris stayed at home through his wife's long illness, simply to be sure, since he had no money to buy it with, that the delicate baby, sole survivor of six, should have its regular food; for, drunkard and idler as he was, he had a passionate, reasonless fondness for his children; and when one after another they died he sought fresh consolation at the whiskey-shop. But this one lived, thanks to its sudden weaning from its heart-broken, worn-out mother, whose bitter troubles and meagre food had poisoned even the draught of life for her babies, and sent them to untimely graves. While she lay helpless and raving with fever for nine long weeks, Tim stayed at home, nursed her as well as he could, tended and fed the baby, who learned to cry for him, instead of crying at the sight of him as all the others had, and getting fat and rosy on the yellow milk that Jim brought daily in a little pail from the deacon's Alderney, wound itself round the father's heart, kept him with bands stronger than iron from his evil haunts, taught him to live without his stimulant, at least for so long, and established a hold on him never lost. It was little Rosy Harris who in after years coaxed her father into good habits, and made her mother's last days bright and calm; but it was Jericho Jim who began the good work with his unauthorized statement of the deacon's willingness to trust a man who " stayed to hum."

Curious enough, too, were Jim's peace-making propensities. These clouded or straying minds sometimes take a certain elfish delight in mischief, but his desire and delight was peace. Miss Nancy Vance was a thin and somewhat bitter old maid, yet gifted with a good deal of sense, and tolerably reasonable; about half a mile from her little brown house, where she lived with a bedridden mother, and did tailoring, lived the Widow Pyne, a noisy, good-natured, high-tempered woman; quick to resent or to fancy an injury, but equally quick to forgive. Between her and Miss Nancy raged a feud of such strength and bitterness as is only to be found in a little country village between people whose minds are narrowed by their limited horizon and slight experience. They were both church-members, but they would neither look at each other across the meeting-house, nor recognize each other in the porch. Miss Nancy always called Mrs. Pyne "that pesky widow," and was styled in return, with more vigor than reticence, "that darned old maid."

Jericho Jim was aware of this, and many a time shrunk as if from a pin-prick or a blow when one began to vituperate the other, and openly evaded the subject.

"I s'pose old Nance Vance takes half a pint o' milk on ye, don't she?" inquired Mrs. Pyne, with a sniff.

"Land o' glory! what splendid red apples them be!" ejaculated Jim, his ears shut to the question, but his eyes very wide open to an Astrachan apple-tree in the corner of the yard.

Now this apple-tree was Widow Pyne's glory; nobody in Sawyer had such a tree; and she petted it like a baby, dug about it with her own hands, manured it every fall, and gave it copious libations of dish-water all through the summer. No tent worms ever found lodgment in its thrifty branches; and in May it was always pink with blossoms, for a tree so coddled had no "off year," but bloomed and bore in every returning season.

It was "a sight to behold," as its gratified owner remarked, and Jim's admiration was so fervent Mrs. Pyne could not do less than reward him with a pocket full of the glowing fruit. Jim was duly gratified, and jogged on his way revolving a scheme in his simple mind which fructified, literally, as he found himself at Miss Vance's door. Miss Nancy came out for her pint of milk looking unusually benign; some of the small items that make up lonely women's lives had been gracious that morning: perhaps her bread had risen just right, or her hens had done their duty in the matter of eggs; but, however that might be, she had a kindly word for Jim, and he poured her full pint with a beaming grin. "Stop a minnit, won't ye?" he called after her. "Won't ye jest set down that are milk, 'nd hold up your apern; here's some o' Miss Pyne's amazin' apples."

"Widder Pyne's apples!" ejaculated the amazed spinster, as she received the crimson spheres into her check apron.

"Yes, them's the fellers; she sent 'em along o' me. Good-day!" With which ambiguous statement Jim whipped up the old horse and went along before Miss Nancy had time to think.

"Well, here's nigh onto a merracle!" she exclaimed to herself. "Widder Pyne's apples! I've heerd she sot by 'em dreadfully, 'nd now she's been 'nd sent 'em to me. Well! well! well! I'd oughter be ashamed o' myself, that's a fact; 'tis shameful for church-members to keep up a querrel the way we've did; but she's got the start o' me, that's a fact. I must kinder show my feelin's now, surely."

So the next day Jim was invited to stop on the way back, and carry Widow Pyne a basket of fresh eggs, for eggs were Miss Nancy's specialty. Imagine Jim's secret joy and Mrs. Pyne's noisy surprise.

"Sent me them eggs? Land o' Goshen! she aint weak in her mind, is she, Jim? Must be a leetle touched; or else I be: I guess she's a good cretur, after all. I dono what on airth hes ailed us two to be allers a-fightin', and now she's begun it I guess I kin be as neighborly as other folks. Don't ye go by here to-morrow without gettin' a pocketful o' apples for Nancy Vance, Jim. Let's see. I'll put 'em in the basket." But the second supply of apples never reached Miss Nancy. Jim had a queer sense of justice, and a squirrel's love for nuts and fruit. He had done a good work with the other apples, and lost them, as far as his own delectation was concerned; these others he would keep for his own eating; and his very simpleness made up for wisdom, for a second supply of fruit would certainly have led to awkward explanations; while, as it was, when the two ladies met on the church steps next Sunday, smiling and beaming to make their mutual acknowledgments, there were no questions to ask or answer, and they parted in friendliest fashion, to remain firm allies thereafter.

Not far from the Ellery farm there lived a bad-tempered, cross-grained old fellow, John Dekin by name, who had driven his boys away from home long ago by dint of being everything a father ought not to be; and whose wife stayed with him simply because she was his wife: a fact which is of some virtue to a good woman. Now this man was a great stickler for his rights: he had a right to do as he liked in his own house, no doubt; and the neighbors agreed that they had an equal right to keep away from it! All but good Mrs. Ellery, whose great, kind heart could not see a woman suffer as she knew Mrs Dekin must, and not try to alleviate her sufferings. She would go there persistently, though she trembled before the big dog, and quivered at the sound of his master's voice; for it was one of John Dekin's "rights" to keep the fiercest dog and the crossest bull anywhere about Sawyer. Jericho Jim volunteered to go with Mrs. Ellery when she paid her visits to the Dekin farm, and as there never was a dog who could withstand Jim's way with the brute creation, he and Tige soon became the best of friends.

"Hullo!" said the farmer one day, as he came suddenly round the corner of the house, and found Jim, who had just escorted Mrs. Ellery to the door, sitting on the step and fondling the great bull-dog, who, with watery eyes and slobbering jaws, rested his muzzle on Jim's knee, and looked up into the thin, kind face above him. "Hullo, you feller! look out for that critter; he'll be into ye 'nd chaw ye up 'fore ye can wink."

"I guess not," said Jim, with one of his half silly, gentle smiles. "He knows real well I don't want to hurt him none; so he don' keer to hurt me; no more he will, will ye, Tige?"

The dog's stump of a tail wagged affectionate answers.

"Well, mebbe it'll do with dogs; you seem to kinder get round that one; but it aint folkses ways," growled the farmer.

"Aint it?" said Jim, looking up innocently. "Why, I thought folks knew more'n dogs!"

There was no answer to this. John Dekin walked away; and there ran through his mind, oddly enough, a scrap of a text he had heard somewhere; perhaps his mother read it to him; may be he had heard it at meeting, though he generally went to sleep there, — "Is thy servant a dog, that he should do this thing?" It clung to him with that curious persistence peculiar to texts, which defies philosophical explanation, and more than once thereafter modified some currish act, or silenced some growl, before he fully recognized the invisible restraint upon him. Not long after, that violent bull of Mr. Dekin's broke into Deacon Ellery's lot of winter wheat, just about two inches high, and made a general mess of the whole field, already soaked by a wet autumn. Jim discovered the creature in full tide of devastation, browsing on the tallest spires, and trampling down the rest into undistinguishable mud. He sat down a moment and considered; then filled his pockets with potatoes, left in the next lot after digging, as too small to save, and carefully tossed one over the fence just before the old bull's nose; the bait was too tempting, the creature nipped it up at once, another fell about a foot in front of him, then another still further off, and following the fence, which tended toward the barn-yard, Master Taurus, before he really understood the snare, was beguiled into his own quarters, and the gate shut fast behind him. Then Jim hunted up the farmer.

"Say, Mr. Dekin; hed you jest as lives keep that are splendid ole bull o' yourn in the barn a spell, till I git our folkses fence sot up?"

"Why, what harm's he ben a-doin'? Haint I a right to keep a bull in my own lot, I want to know?"

"Sartinly, sartinly! but ye see the poor cretur wanted a fresh bite, an' he kinder pushed down the fence like, an' got into some winter wheat; so I guessed I'd git him out on't fust"—

"How in thunder did ye get him out? That's the pint."

"Well, I coaxed him a leetle; sorter tolled him along with a mess o' raw potatoes t'other side the stun wall. I see he hankered after fresh victuals, so to speak; 'nd I dono's I blame him."

John Dekin could not help a laugh; but Jim went on quietly:—

"So ef you'd jest as lives keep him in a spell, I'll hurry up an' fix the fence, 'nd then he can go out to pastur' ag'in, leastways while there *is* pastur'; 'twont last no great now, that's a fact."

Now the fence between the lots was Dekin's, as he very well knew, and he could have been made to pay well for the damage his beast had done; but he also knew Deacon Ellery was laid up with an attack of rheumatism, and Jim had all the work to do; if the fence was once up it would be hard work to make the bull's owner pay for it, so he grimly assented.

"Yes, I'll keep him tethered; but you hurry up with your old fence."

Jim went to work directly; hauled the rails, dug the post-holes, and hired a few hours' help to set them; before the next night that winter wheat was safely railed in, and Deacon Ellery, feeling a little better, had his factotum into the bedroom to hear an account of the day's proceedings, which Jim composedly gave him.

"Why, you darned fool!" exclaimed the old man, cross with pain, and testy naturally, "you've been a building John Dekin's fence to keep his own bull out o' my lot! What upon the globe did ye do that for?"

"Well, ye see, mister," said Jim, assuming a comfortable sort of attitude, as who should say, "Come now, let us reason together," "I did kinder mistrust from the looks o' things twas his'n; but thinks me, he aint the kind to up and do right off; he don't care much ef his bull does eat up your wheat; I expect he's one o' them that didn't hev a good mother. My! ef he'd ha' had my mother he'd known better, ef he had ha' been a fool. But, you see, folks is folksy; they aint as they had ought ter be, and you can't fix 'em no way, reely. I calc'lated that if you waited for him the grain 'd be clean lost; ef ye took the law on him, why, that would be time an' money spent, and the wheat had oughter be a-growin'; 'twouldn't never grow without fencin', for that bull's dreadful obstropolous; and we hed them old rails handy. Anyway it's fixed now; 'nd ef ye want to jaw him, or set Squire Jinks outer him, why, there's time enough while the wheat's a-growin' ag'in to satisfy ye that way."

"You go 'long," growled the deacon, falling back on his pillow; "it's a pretty piece o' business to come to my time o' life to learn how to handle thistles. I don't deny but what I've learned suthin', but I guess you'd better go to bed now; you're all-fired tired."

"Well I be, some," and, stretching and yawning, Jim obeyed.

"That aint nobody's fool," ejaculated the deacon, looking after him; "'r if he is, 't's a plaguy sight better folly than most folkses wisdom."

There was no lawyer sent to John Dekin; the fence stood firm against wintry storms, but Jim noticed that the bull was not turned into that lot again; and when spring returned the grain shot up in full luxuriance, thick and heavy-headed; none the worse for its accidental pruning, perhaps all the better. And, besides, there was certainly a softening in John Dekin's aspect toward his neighbor; perhaps not unmingled with contempt for the deacon's "softness;" but still a grain of leaven had been planted in this unpromising lump; time — perhaps eternity only — could show how it worked. So Jim went his way in and about Sawyer: a being of no account in the eyes of most people; of less than none in his own; but planting here and there by the wayside little seeds of kindness and humanity that blossomed to some soul's delight and benefit. "She hath done what she could," was the Lord's own commendation, and this was the lowly measure of Jim's desert; but can any of us do more? How many of us do as much? How many of the great and rich leave behind them a grateful record in even as many hearts as always remembered with tender affection poor Jericho Jim?

But it was reserved for him to do the great service of his life for his good old friends, the Ellerys. It has not been declared to you, dear reader, any more than it was to Jim, that Deacon Ellery had a son living in a distant city, who for some years had never been seen in Sawyer, nor spoken of in his father's house. Sam Ellery had been the very core of his father's heart, to use the pathetic Irish phrase, and yet he never found it out; for, with the painful shyness and reticence of his race and nature, Deacon Ellery hid this affection deep in silence and coldness. He was a rigid Calvinist, and had striven to bring up Samuel in the straitest sect of that sort. Dogmas and doctrines are husky food for a bright, brave, joyful soul like this boy's; he never took to them kindly; his mother's love made her religion just tolerable to him, for professedly she held her husband's faith. Sam could believe in the goodness and tenderness of God when he saw and heard his mother; but his father's stern and unflinching hand closed the gates which he was most desirous of opening. He went away from home to a position in a bank in Boston, where he began as "boy," and had now arrived at the office of cashier. At first he had returned once or twice a year to the old home, to mother, and also to keep up a certain youthful sweethearting with Annie Palmer, the minister's pretty daughter; but as he grew to be a man, and remembered bitterly his father's stern belief, he made use of his freedom to examine into religious faiths, and naturally enough rebounded into Unitarianism. That his son should become a member of that sect in particular was the very gall and bitterness of iniquity to the old deacon, who could better have borne a defection in almost any other direction; and in what he called righteous wrath he wrote a dreadful letter to Samuel, and forbade him ever to enter his doors again till he had repented of this great sin, and humbled himself in dust and ashes for betraying his Master, as the deacon was pleased to style it. Although a loving and entreating letter from his mother went after this fulmination, and somewhat calmed Sam's first contemptuous anger, and though that letter was answered, and a fitful correspondence carried on between mother and son through Annie Palmer, Sam accepted his father's alternative, and stayed away from his home as persistently as the deacon ignored him; for he was, indeed, " a chip of the old block."

His name was never named in the family, nor uttered in the daily prayer, and if his father's heart ever cried after him, it cried in silence.

Now Jericho Jim adored the minister's daughter with the dumb passion of a faithful dog. It was the great joy of his life to have her come to the door with the milk-pitcher for him to fill, as she sometimes did; and one pleasant word or lovely smile made Jim happy all day. After the fashion of wiser folks he paid tribute to this goddess continually. He brought her every wild flower in its season, and the rarest of all; he knew where the rhodora grew, and gathered its early blooms for Annie; delicate orchids unveiled their shy haunts for him, and the slight sweet flowers of spring all lay at Annie's feet from her faithful worshipper. Cardinal flowers and spotless pond-lilies came in their season; for her he stored the biggest nuts, and begged the sweetest fruits that grew in any garden, nor ever begged in vain, for Jim was petted and privileged in Sawyer. Annie was mightily joked about her fervent admirer, but nobody ever laughed at Jim; his pathetic simplicity shielded him like a young girl's innocence. But Annie knew very well that this poor boy liked her, though not how deeply; and knowing, too, his curious power of setting people to rights, it occurred to her that he might perhaps pave the way for her lover's reconciliation with his father; for the careless admiration of the deacon's son had long ago deepened into love, and Sam Ellery had been many times to Sawyer to see Annie Palmer since he finally left his father's door; and now they were soon to be married, and Annie longed with all her heart to have peace between father and son.

One July evening, just at twilight, Jericho Jim arrived at the door of Parson Palmer's house with the milk for Sunday, which was always carried round Saturday night, and also with a pail of fresh lilies from Warren pond.

Annie came out to take them, fresh and cool as their spotless blooms herself; her dark hair waved above a sweet, colorless face, and her clear, sad, hazel eyes looked at Jim both gratefully and wistfully.

"O Jim! thank you! these are so lovely. Jim, there is one thing I wish you could help me about."

"I'll do anything I can in the natur' of things to help ye, ma'am, as sure's you're born," he answered to the half question.

"I do want so much to have Deacon Ellery make friends with his son."

"Why, he haint got any!" said Jim, with simple confidence.

"Yes, he has, Jim; he has indeed; but they haven't spoken for years."

"Sho now! that are can't be; guess you dreamed it, Miss Annie. Why, Deacon Ellery's a good man; a Christian cretur as ever was; can't be; somebody's ben a " —

"Annie!" called Mrs. Palmer, evidently in haste; and Jim drove off, feeling in an uncertain sort of way as if he hadn't heard, or ought not to have heard, such things about his best friend, even from the adorable Annie. But the thing worked in his feeble head, and as "Fools rush in where angels fear to tread," and sometimes do good service by their folly, so Jim plunged into the middle of things the very next morning as he was brushing the shoes for church-going, while the deacon read over his Sunday-school lesson by the window.

"Say! you haint got any son, have ye, deacon?"

The old man looked at Jim with an air of terror as well as wonder, and turned pale as ashes.

"Yes, I've got a son," he answered mechanically.

"Why, I haint never seen him," exclaimed Jim, as if still he scarcely believed.

"He has not been at home for five long years, Jim; he is a prodigal who filleth himself with husks," solemnly replied the deacon, who had somewhat recovered his poise.

"Well, why don't ye fetch him home 'nd give him suthin' better to eat?"

The deacon stared at Jim, but could not answer.

"What's he ben 'nd done anyway?" went on the simple torturer. "Killed anybody? Stole anythin'?"

"No! no! no!" ejaculated the deacon, raging inwardly between the persistency of his questioner and the impossibility of explaining to him the reason of Sam's banishment. Perhaps, too, the reason why this was so difficult to explain began to wrestle with his conscience.

"Well, I'm dretful sorry," said Jim, musingly. "My daddy, now, was a poor cretur, drunk, mostly;

but he was real good to me. I'm glad he wa'n't no better; mebbe I shouldn't ha' ben good enough for him to speak to, too."

The deacon could have struck Jim, who went on brushing the shoes as seriously as if they were an algebraic problem.

"Well, Jim, the fact is, he didn't believe in the Bible — Sam didn't."

"Poor cretur! poor cretur!" said Jim, warming into sympathy at once. "Well, deacon; ye know what you was a-readin' about to me last Sabba'-day; a tryin' to drive in ter my head, ye know? — takes a lot o' time to drive anythin' into a fool's head; but I can't disremember that, 'twas so kinder marciful like, 'bout how the good Lord forgiv' them fellers that killed him, 'cause he said they didn't know what they was a-doin'. Mebbe your Sam don't; what ef ye was to take him to Sabba'-school, an' larn him better? You tell me where he stays, 'nd I'll go fetch him."

Jim was in eager earnest; his eyes were lit with unusual rays, and one hand held awkwardly out toward the deacon; but the old man could not answer; he stumbled away to the bedroom and fell on his knees by the bedside. What he said to God is not for us to know; what he did was to write a letter that very night to Samuel, and beg him to come home to his old father and his loving mother.

As for Jim, the matter passed clear out of his oddly made-up mind; he had satisfied himself the deacon had a son; the immediate curiosity was at rest. He did not see Annie Palmer the next day; in fact so inconsequent were his mental processes when under the external excitement he did not once think of what she said to him; but only missed her as he would miss sunshine, or fire, or food; for Annie had become a necessity to the largest share of his nature — his heart.

A week after Mrs. Ellery came out into the garden where Jim was weeding.

"O Jim!" said she, "my dear son, my Sam, is comin' home to-morrer; and goin' to be married."

"Well, I'm glad on't," cheerfully answered Jim.

"Yes, he's a-comin' home to-morrer. I haint sot eyes on him this five year an' more; and a Thursday he's a-goin' to be married to Annie Palmer."

"O Lord!" said Jim, with a gasp; but the good woman did not hear him: heart and head were full of Sam, and she turned and went into the house.

Jim did not come in after milking that night; the deacon found him curled down in a corner of the barn.

"I guess I'm sick," was all he said; but somehow he reminded the deacon of an old dog he once had, that was mortally wounded by accident, and stole into that very corner to die. There was the same hurt, protesting look in both pairs of eyes.

They took Jim into his own room, and in a day or two he was better, but never well again; he lived a few months, feeble, patient, smiling, and doing all he could. The only queer thing about him was that he never asked to see Annie Palmer, or even spoke her name again. Sam went upstairs to see him, but Jim was asleep, he said, and he wouldn't waken him. Perhaps Deacon Ellery, being a reticent man, never told his son how much he owed to the poor fool. Annie forgot him too, probably; but what can you expect of a happy young bride? When winter came, Jim went.

Dr. Green said the cold was too great for such a low state of vitality; perhaps it was. However that might be, one starry and splendid night a quick flash sprung into the languid eyes. "Mother!" he said, with an accent of rapture, and Jericho Jim was gone to the Jerusalem which is above.

LOST ON A RAILWAY.

"Moosop Station!" roared the conductor on the H. P. & F. R.R., as advertisements economically style that line of road that cuts Connecticut in two, — as far as it goes, — probably on the principle that it might go farther and fare worse, or rather get no fares.

The train stopped, the axles screeched, the whistle shrieked, and the engine sent out side-puffs of spiteful steam, and on the platform stood a little old lady with a big new bandbox, in that state of mingled confusion and excitement common to old ladies from the country in prospect of a journey, particularly a journey after that incarnation of Young America, — a locomotive.

"Good-by, mother!" said a mild-looking, dark-eyed woman, giving the old lady a kiss.

"Good-by, gran'ma," shouted a thick-set boy from his station beside the engine, which he was surveying, much as if he had taken an order to build one, and meant to improve on this pattern.

"Oh, dear me! where's my bundle? — no, my bandbox! I declare if I haint got it in my hand, after all! — Good-by, Sary! Good-by, Sammy! Where's John? Oh, here he is! John, where's my umberell?"

"Here it is, mother; now get in," answered an elderly man, who stood at her elbow.

"But where's my piece of string? — and the apples? — and you haint lost that fennel, have ye, Sary?"

"All aboard!" again roared the conductor, and the old lady made for the car, with John after her, holding in his hand the basket of apples, with a piece of string knotted to the handle, a bundle of dry fennel, and a blue cotton umbrella. John could get no farther than the door, for the cars began to move. He piled the things upon the old lady's bandbox, and swung himself off, just in time to get upon the end of the platform, leaving his mother-in-law a picture of confusion.

However, the old lady righted herself pretty quickly; she tied her fennel to one end of the string, took the umbrella in one hand and the bandbox in the other, hung the basket on the umbrella handle, which she held horizontally, and proceeded to find a seat. There were none empty, but several occupied by only one woman; and, guided by the instinct of dress that almost all women possess, she stopped beside one of those whose occupant's peculiar array stamped her as a country woman, and gave her a familiar aspect to our heroine.

"Can I set here?" said the old lady, giving a little poke to the woman's elbow, who looked round with the forbidding expression common to single or solitary females when assaulted by that question in the cars. But as soon as she caught sight of her questioner's face within the frill of her black bonnet, she smiled a benignant smile of welcome, and said, in a loud, cheerful voice: —

"Why, 'taint you, Miss Dodd, is it?"

"Well, I declare," said the old lady, who recognized a neighbor from the town next her own, "I *am* beat now! When did you leave home, Miss Packard?"

"Why, I come away this morning. But set down, set down. I'm real glad it's you; I never do fellowship strange folks settin' in the same seat with me on the railroad; seems so intimate like, and they 'most always crowd."

"I'm goin' to hang my basket up before I set down," remarked Mrs. Dodd. "John, he put a string on't so as to be handy."

She stretched up her arm across Mrs. Packard's head to hang up her apples, but at that unlucky moment a sharp jar shook the car, and the apples rolling out of the basket fell on the head below, and Mrs. Packard sprung up in a fury, her straw bonnet, liberally adorned with red flowers, thoroughly smashed, and her head well bruised.

"Good gracious!" said she, darting a sharp look at Mrs. Dodd, who was holding on to the seat, pretty well frightened. "Good gracious! them apples have a'most broke my skull! and they've smashed my bunnet all up! I don't see what folks do want to carry sech things for!"

"Dear me!" said the old lady, "it is too bad, I do say! But what on airth jounced all these cars so? I do believe we've run away!"

"Well," was Mrs. Packard's indignant reply, "I guess if we had, you wouldn't be a-talkin' about it!"

"Don't you want some rum onto your head?" said Mrs. Dodd, anxious to repair the injuries her apples had committed.

"I guess I had better have some," was the mollified reply, evidently expecting the old lady to hand over the lotion from her bandbox or her pocket. But she innocently answered: —

"I wonder if the conductor haint got any. I should think he'd keep some in case of bruises and cuts."

An indignant sniff was the sole remark Mrs. Packard hazarded; and the old lady, after picking up her apples, which had rolled hither and yon through the car, quietly established herself in the seat beside her friend, who was occupied in pinching up and pulling out the crushed bonnet and its decorations. Just as bandbox, umbrella, apples, and fennel were all finally arranged, the conductor came by.

"Ticket, ma'am!"

Mrs. Dodd was a long time getting it. Out of her deep pocket came all its contents before the missing card was found: three keys on a blue string, one red silk handkerchief and one white cambric one, two pieces of flag-root, an old silk purse with change in it, half a nutmeg, a silver thimble, a tape-needle, a little almanac, a box of Dally's Pain Extractor, and one of corn salve, a pin-ball, and a pair of scissors, a lemon, and two peppermints, a small ball of blue yarn, a bit of Turkey rhubarb, three peanuts, and a pair of black silk gloves, in whose folds was the ticket. But while this investigation was going on Mrs. Dodd improved her time in questioning the conductor.

"What did make these cars jump so a little while back, sir?"

"Cow on the track," laconically growled the man.

"Dew tell!" said the old lady, in an accent of horror, — "was't a red caow?"

"Pretty red when I see her," grimly remarked he.

"I shouldn't wonder now if 'twas Miss Jacob Smith's old Red," went on she. "I heerd her tell how her caow would run acrost the track comin' home from pastur'. Why, here's my yarn, and Sammy's peanuts 't I took away from him last night when he was goin' to eat 'em in bed; poor little fellow, he'll think gran'ma is dreadful! I declare I did mean 't he should have 'em again. You didn't hear whose caow it was, did you, sir?"

"No!" emphasized the conductor, who wanted the ticket, — and at last got it!

By this time Mrs. Packard's bonnet was bent out to its pristine shape and splendor, and Mrs. Dodd, recalled from her ticket-hunt, remembered the bruises and called the conductor back in so loud and earnest a voice that he could not affect not to hear her, and unwillingly turned.

"Say, Mr. Conductor, you haven't got any old rum, have you? I want to wet her head with 't."

The conductor, I regret to say, became profane.

"Why, he swears!" ejaculated the old lady, with an accent of horror and surprise.

Mrs. Packard laughed; a touch of superiority restored her temper; she could afford to be amiable to a woman who knew so little of the ways of the world as Mrs. Dodd. So she resumed the conversation.

"You haven't told me yet where you're goin', Miss Dodd."

"Me? Why, I'm goin' to Albany, to see my son Jehiel, he that studied for the ministry, and was settled a spell in Westbury, and then down to Fall River, and now he's ben in Albany quite a spell, — five years I guess, — and I haven't ben to see him never.

You see Sary she's hed young childern, and I hevn't felt as though I could leave her to worry it through alone. But now they're pretty well grown; Sammy he's the smallest, and Jehiel wouldn't hear to my stayin' away no longer; I was bound to go and stay there a year. So John he sent my trunk somehow, by express, I expect, so 't I shouldn't hev no trouble, and I'm a-goin' in to Hartford and down to York, and John's brother he's goin' to meet me there, and find somebody that's goin' that way, who'll take me along. It's quite a voyage out to Indianny, and I don't hanker much to go."

"Out to Indianny!" exclaimed Mrs. Packard. "Why, Albany's in York State; 'taint out there."

"Why, yes it is," stoutly answered Mrs. Dodd.

"Why, Miss Dodd, it aint! I guess I know where Albany is; *his* sister's son, Joe Weed, lives to Albany; and when he had a liver complaint, and had to go to Saratogue a spell (he's got a nephew 't keeps a bakery to Saratogue, so it didn't cost no great), he slep to Albany, to Joe Weed's house, and he said 'twas queer why they had it for the capital to York State when York City was so much the biggest. I *know* 'taint in Indianny!"

(Dear reader, let me tell you, *par parenthèse*, that "he," to a Connecticut woman, always means "my husband." Grammar fails before conjugal devotion; there is but one man to our Mrs. Packards, and the personal pronoun is sacred to that one.)

"Well," rather irresolutely replied Mrs. Dodd, "I know Jehiel said 'twas Indianny, and so did John; and, come to think on't,' Jehiel's letters always have New Albany on 'em, but I never heerd John call it *New*."

"I don't say but what there may be an Albany or even a *New* Albany out to Indianny," retorted Mrs. Packard, with dignity; "but I *do* say I haint never heerd of no Albany except the one in York State; and if there was one out in Indianny I don't see why John should send you to York to go there; it appears more likely you should go to the York State Albany from there."

"Well, I don't know," feebly answered the old lady; "I expect John's brother 'll know. I feel rather uncertain about changin' cars to Hartford. After that, I expect I'll go straight."

"There aint no difficulty to Hartford," condescended Mrs. Packard. "You've jest got to step acrost the depott, and there 'll come along a train by-'n-by, and you jest ask ef that's the Albany train — I would say the York train — and they'll tell you, somebody will. I wish 't I was a-goin' as fur as that myself, but I aint. I'm goin' to stop to Manchester to see my sister Lucy-Ann; she's got a bad complaint of her vitals, and I ruther expect she won't survive. Anyway, I'm goin' to nuss her for a spell."

"I declare I do wish you was goin' along," said the old lady, in a wistful voice. "I'm kind o' hampered with these bundles and things. But my trunk was packed, and I thought maybe I'd have to stop quite a while in York, and this pongee I'm ridin' in isn't very much to look at, so I put up my best black silk gown, and two frilled caps, and some handkerchers, so't I needn't appear otherwise than conformable to city folks's ways; and then I knew James Greene (that's John's brother, leastways his step-brother) was extreme fond of Roxbury russets; so I concluded to take along a few; they have kept over so well — why, it's June the tenth to-day; and I couldn't go without my umberell no way, if it should come on to rain; and then I had the fennel so 't if I should be sick to my stomach a-ridin' in the cars, it's very warmin'" —

"Manchester!" interposed the conductor, and Mrs. Packard bundled out of the cars with a rapid farewell to her travelling companion, and left the old lady alone. Before long the train rolled into the Hartford station, and Mrs. Dodd, somewhat confused by the rush of people out of the cars, and the vociferations of the hackmen, gathered up her "things" and stepped off the train, coming down the long step quite unawares, with a bounce that made her drop her bandbox and exclaim: —

"Oh, goodness! I believe I have bumped my bunnet off!"

But the approach of a predatory hackman made her grasp the precious box again, and let go of the bonnet.

"Allyn House, ma'am?"

"Hay?" replied the bewildered old lady, as another man behind her screamed, "United States Hotel! — where's yer checks?"

"Why, I left 'em to home," was the naïve reply, "a-hangin' behind the milk-room door."

"City Hotel! — give *me* your box, ma'am. Any more baggage?"

"Why, what *do* you want of my box? I haint got no trunk, it's gone to Albany."

Just then a train screeched into the station and completed Mrs. Dodd's confusion, while it drowned the drivers' voices; and, seeing there was nothing to be done with the old lady, they left her staring at the locomotive, as thoroughly confused as ever any old lady was. "Dear me!" soliloquized she; "seems as though my head would bust." Just then her eye caught a placard, "Beware of pickpockets!" A look of alarm and horror crossed her face; she shifted the apples and the "umberell" all to one hand, and grasped her pocket firmly with the other, thereby drawing up her gray pongee dress, and displaying to all beholders a pair of thick-set ankles cased in blue cotton stockings, and the goodly feet to which they belonged clothed with prunella shoes, whose shape betrayed the swollen joints and crooked shapes that were the reward of hard work and cheap shoe-leather. Certainly Mrs. Dodd did not look one whit less funny to the loungers and employés in that station-house because she was one of the kindest and best old ladies in the world! If love and truth and unselfishness want to be appreciated, they must wear hoops and sacques and coats with big sleeves; not pongee-skirts and black bombazine bonnets, or even blue yarn stockings! As she stood there glaring through her silver-rimmed spectacles, and trying to recall Mrs. Packard's advice, the station-master came by, and she appealed to him, for she despaired of finding out for herself.

"Sir," said she, tremulously, quite forgetting in her confusion where she was going, "are them the Albany cars?"

"That's the New Haven, Hartford, and Springfield train, ma'am; you can go to Albany by it, or you can go to New York or to Boston."

"Oh, well! it's York I'm going to; thankee, sir."

Somebody called the station-master, and he walked rapidly away, while the old lady picked her way across the tracks, and with some difficulty clambered into the cars on the wrong side, nothing doubting but that she was all right, when in fact she had taken the up train.

She sat down behind two ladies, young and fashionably dressed, and presently the train moved off. Poor Mrs. Dodd, tired with the worry and bustle of the morning, fell asleep, and the conductor, having an old mother himself, compassionately forbore to wake her on his first round. But next time he tried to rouse her, as they neared a station, and possibly she might wish to get off; the old lady slept, however, so soundly that shakings and callings seemed all in vain, much to the amusement of the two women before her. But one behind, more considerate, offered her bottle of salts to the conductor, who applied it with such effect that Mrs. Dodd jumped up, spilled her basket of apples out of her lap, and looked about her with a dismayed and alarmed expression, irresistible to behold. Even the conductor laughed.

"Do you want to get off here, ma'am?" said he.

"Where is't? where is't? We haven't got to York, have we? Oh, my apples! I declare for 't, they've all rolled away!"

"Thompsonville!" shouted the brakeman, as the conductor did not fulfil that particular part of his duty, being occupied with Mrs. Dodd. "Are you going off here, ma'am?" repeated this latter functionary.

"No, I'm goin' further. I'm goin' to York."

The conductor did not wait to hear the latter part of her answer, he was obliged to see to other affairs. So long as the old lady didn't mean to get off, he could wait for her ticket till their brief stop at the station was over. And she, by this time wide awake, began to collect her scattered apples, — a task of no small difficulty, between the mischievousness of two schoolboys who had already possessed themselves of three or four, and the spread of sundry hoops that concealed others. At length she had gathered the better part of her fruit, feeling rather puzzled by the earnest declaration of the boys that they hadn't seen such a thing, when she had found three rolled beyond them; and just as she stooped to pick up one more the train started and pitched her forward. Luckily the bombazine bonnet took the brunt of her fall, the front crushed in and saved her face, but the bonnet was deplorable; and the poor old lady's discomfiture was completed by the malicious tittering of the "ladies" before her.

As soon as she was seated the conductor came back; his face twitched a little at Mrs. Dodd's aspect: the pongee was streaked with dust from the car-floor; the bonnet bent in angles that were none of them right angles, and her attempts at straightening it had only multiplied them; her face was flushed with heat and mortification, and she had put down her basket of apples on the floor between her feet, which steadied it as resolutely as if they were glued to either side.

"Where's your ticket, ma'am?" said he.

"Why, I haint got none," she answered, meekly.

"I thought you kep' 'em."

"Didn't you get one at the office?"

"Well, I declare, I forgot John told me to, I was in sech a hurry. You see I come in on the Providence train, and I see this train come in right off, and I didn't recollect nothing about a ticket."

"Where do you want to go?" said he.

"Why, I want to go to York. You see I'm goin' to Albany, but I'm goin' to York fust."

"You're in the wrong train, ma'am. This train goes to Boston."

"Oh, dear!" exclaimed she, in a tone of heart-felt confusion and distress. "What be I goin' to do?"

"Why, we stop at Springfield in a few minutes, and you can get on the down train there, and go right on to New York."

"Well, can you give me a ticket, sir? I've got the money all right. I held on to't down to Hartford depott so't there shouldn't no pick-pockets git it."

"I guess I sha'n't ask you to pay for this ride," said he, smiling. "You can get a ticket for New York at the Springfield office, and the down train starts in five minutes, right alongside t'other side of the waiting-room; you won't have any stop to make there. Is this all your baggage?"

"I expect it is, sir. John, he sent my trunk by express, and these is all besides, if I don't tip over them apples ag'in."

Pretty soon the train did stop, and the old lady bundled out, and after much questioning and explanation discovered a ticket-office, and in her fresh confusion asked for and bought a ticket to Albany, and deposited herself in the train for Boston.

It was some time before the cars began to move, and Mrs. Dodd thought her friendly conductor must have mistaken the time, so she left her box and walked forward to an elderly man, who sat reading a paper just before her, and said: —

"I thought these here cars wa'n't goin' to wait very long."

"Time changed," gruffly replied he.

So Mrs. Dodd sat down again, and in a few minutes the same two women who had been before her on the Springfield train came in, and took the same seat. Mrs. Dodd was hardly pleased by this encounter, and it puzzled her somewhat that these two ladies who had just come up should be going down again; but she said nothing, and in ten minutes the train was off. It was an express train, and stopped at but few places, so that she was well on her journey before the conductor claimed her ticket, which was safe at the bottom of her pocket.

"I'll get it in a minute," said she, deprecatingly, as the conductor began to look impatiently at the heterogeneous articles that one by one were being fished up out of her pocket.

"Hurry up, ma'am!" said he, at length, crossly. "I can't wait all day!"

So urged, the poor old lady thrust her hand energetically down, deeper yet, and ran a sharp pin from the pin-ball into her thumb: her hand was withdrawn with as much force as it went in, and her elbow hit the basket of apples, which, for the third time that day, went rolling along the floor. This last catastrophe was too much for poor Mrs. Dodd. She was tired, and puzzled, and hungry withal; she had had no dinner, and had brought nothing to eat with her; and tears of fatigue as well as vexation dimmed her spectacles as she tried to inspect the wounded thumb.

"I'll get your ticket when I come back," said the conductor, tired of waiting.

But the old lady scarcely heard him; she could not see the place that was hurt on her thumb, which she was most anxious to do, and in her simplicity she quite forgot that the ladies in front of her had been rude in the morning; so, quite regardless of her apples, she lifted herself half-way off the seat, and leaning forward thrust her hand between the two ladies, and asked, in perfect good faith : —

"Say, ma'am! can you see the hole?"

The lady on the right turned round and looked at Mrs. Dodd with a pair of eyes that expression made more insolent even than nature had made them, and said, in the sweetest voice of ice and snow, tingling with a fine suggestion of astonishment : —

"What?"

Mrs. Dodd never winced, she was so absorbed in her hurt. "Why, you see I sticked a pin into my thumb, and pins are p'isonous, they say. Hester Smith's daughter, she 't worked to a pin-factory, she got pricked and didn't take no pains to heal up the wownd, and she swelled up awfully, got mortified and re'lly died; so I always carry Dally in my pocket to put on first jump; but I can't see real well in the cars so as to apply it right. Do you see the hole?"

The green eyes and amber hair confronted her again, and the same discriminating voice remarked, "I see a very dirty thumb."

Now Mrs. Dodd's thumb did not look clean ; she had taken off her clinging silk gloves to straighten out her bonnet and pick up her apples, and the dust had left unmistakable traces on that puckered and pierced member. But Mrs. Dodd's hobby was cleanliness; she was scrupulously, religiously neat; however old, and faded, and stained her dress might be, it was always faultlessly clean as soap and water could make it; and to have a strange woman in a public conveyance tell her that her thumb was "dirty" was not to be endured. She bent her head slightly to facilitate the manœuvre, and directed a look over her spectacles at the offender,— a look of that transfixing kind peculiar to indignant old ladies, in which they assume something of the severely virtuous aspect common to those dragon-flies that have four eyes, though they do not wear spectacles. But the green eyes and amber hair were turned away, and poor Mrs. Dodd's Medusean artillery was wasted. She gave no further license to her tongue than to remark quite audibly : —

"I wish you better manners!"

No notice was taken of this little remark by the green eyes. An icicle could not have been more insensitive, and Mrs. Dodd had spent all her ammunition; so after anointing her whole thumb with her favorite remedy, and tying it up in a rag extracted from that voluminous pocket — which certainly was clean — she betook herself to gathering up the scattered apples, — a work of time and patience, for they had rolled further than ever. Just as she was fairly settled again the conductor came back for her ticket, which she had discovered, and taken the precaution to pin to her shawl. She handed it up to him with a look of serene satisfaction.

"Wrong ticket!" said he.

"Why, sir! isn't this the York train?"

"No; this is the Boston express, and your ticket is for Albany."

"Goodness gracious! I haint got lost again, have I? Oh, dear! what shall I do?"

"Get out at the next station," said he.

"Where is't?"

"Worcester, — fare, a dollar sixty-two."

"Aint my ticket good for nothing?" said Mrs. Dodd, with a dismayed accent.

"Don't you see," answered he, running his finger along the card, "'Good for this day and train only'?"

"Well, can't I get back to anywhere afore it's dark?" said she.

The conductor did not hear her; the cars were stopping without leave. He hurried through to find the trouble, leaving the poor old woman more perplexed than ever. Opposite to her sat a lady much less elaborately dressed than those before her. Something quiet and well-bred marked her whole aspect, though her dress was of a gray, unnoticeable fabric, and her thin cloak and hat of a delicate transparent material, dull in tint, but without crease or spot. She looked across at Mrs. Dodd, and said in a low, pleasant voice: —

"Can I help you, ma'am?"

"Oh, dear! I don't know," said she. "You don't know nothin' about the trains, do you, nor what time we get to Worcester?"

"We ought to get to Worcester by half-past three," said the lady.

"Where be we a-stoppin' now?"

"I don't know. I think something is wrong; there is no station here."

Just as she spoke one of the gentlemen who had got out — as gentlemen always do on such occasions, to see for themselves — came back and took his seat behind Mrs. Dodd. The lady addressed him in her sweet and delicate tones. "What is the matter, sir?" said she. It was the same man who had given so laconic an answer to the old lady when she spoke to him on coming into the cars at Springfield; but he was neither gruff nor brief to his present querist.

"The locomotive has burst a flue, ma'am, I believe. If so, we shall be detained some time on the track."

Mrs. Dodd looked aghast. "Oh, dear me!" said she; "what shall I do?"

"I think you will have to spend the night at Worcester, and go back in the morning," said the lady.

"Well, if I go to York now, I don't know where to go, for James he won't expect me," was the piteous reply.

So the lady — a woman who deserved the name — addressed herself kindly to quiet the poor old woman's apprehensions; and, having gradually extracted the history of Mrs. Dodd's wanderings, advised her to ask somebody in the station at Worcester to show her a hotel, and then to proceed in the first morning train to Albany — the kind adviser not suspecting that *New* Albany was her proper destination.

"I thank you kindly," said Mrs. Dodd. "'Taint everybody that's willin' to take so much pains and trouble for an old cretur like me."

"You are very welcome," said the lady. "I shall be old myself sometime and want help."

"Well, I'll be bound you'll get it," was the earnest response of Mrs. Dodd, as the lady returned, smiling, to her seat and her book, while the pair of women on the seat in front stared at her with undisguised wonder, one of them having recognized her, on entering, as a Boston lady, to attain whose position and reputation she would have given all her luxuriant amber hair and one of her green eyes.

After long delay the train moved on, and at Worcester our old lady left the cars, not without a hearty shake of the hand from her unknown friend, to whom she offered her basket of apples, begging her to take them all, — an offer graciously declined, though she did take one, by way of showing her appreciation of the kindness intended.

When Mrs. Dodd found herself once more left to her own devices in a strange place she made a resolute effort to keep her wits about her, not to get lost again. She asked one hackman after another "where the tavern was." And as fast as they discovered she was no fare for them they turned away; and soon both men and women had left the station empty, except for the ticket-seller, who waited for another train and had shut his window, so that not even the strenuous inquisitiveness of spectacles could discover him. In this strait was poor Mrs. Dodd left: tired, dusty, thirsty, hungry, and perplexed, when, just as her withered lip began to quiver and her eyes to fill, a stout, rosy Irish girl, in the most wonderful figured cotton dress, and a red shawl over her head, came in at one door of the station, and the old lady, determined to intercept her, planted herself right before her, brandishing the umbrella feebly, and accosted Bridget with : —

"Say! do you know where the tavern is?"

"Shure there's more 'n one to this big place, mem," said she; "whichever is it ye'll be afther?"

"Well, I don't care much, only I've got kinder lost on the railroad, 'n I've got to stay here overnight, so's to go back in the mornin' to Albany, and I want a place to sleep, and get some vittles, pretty near by."

"Well, an' if it aint a big hott-el ye've set your mind on, here's Mrs. Donovan's close by, an' she keeps a fust-rate boordin'-house, and it's meself waits, an' cooks, and does up the chamber-work; and Miss Flynn, she left the place last week, and there aint a sowl in her room, and I think ye'd better be afther comin' along wid me, where ye'll get boord an' lodgin' av the best, an' it's right forninst the dapott."

Mrs. Dodd yielded: she knew nothing else to do, and after a supper at Mrs. Donovan's "boordin'-house" — which made her recall the clean and savory food she was used to at her daughter's table with regretful astonishment — she was shown into a dark, close room, upstairs, where the fluffy bed and very objectionable linen — or rather cotton — thereof, shocked Mrs. Dodd quite as much as it would have the green-eyed lady who insulted her thumb. But the extremity of her fatigue made her less fastidious practically; she went to bed, and forgot everything in so sound a sleep that she did not wake till half-past seven of the brightest possible June morning, when a sound shake from Bridget effected that desirable event.

"Shure, mem, the accomydashin's goin' by in a half an hour, an' ye've overslep' yerself, an' the brekfist is ready."

Mrs. Dodd yawned, and rubbed her eyes, and yawned again, but at length awoke to what the newspapers call "a sense of her situation," and dressed herself as hastily as the methodical ways of an old lady would permit; for such brushings and shakings as gown, shawl, cap, handkerchief, and bonnet had to go through were a work of time, and the breakfast-bell rung impatiently twice before the dust of three railways was expelled from every gather and plait, and when at length she appeared downstairs, much the better for the aforesaid processes, she was greeted by Bridget standing at the foot of the stairs with arms akimbo: "An' there's the accomydashin' train a whustlin' this blessed minit, an' you haven't ate yer brekfist, as shure's I'm Bridget Flanigin!"

"Oh, dear!" said Mrs. Dodd, "if I aint the unluckiest woman! Can't I get over to 't, Bridget?"

"Shure ye can't aven put on yer bonnet quick enough, for it's afther goin' out as quick as iver it comes in!"

"Oh, what shall I do!" exclaimed the old lady, who felt as one does when, after waking out of one nightmare, breathless and oppressed, is felt the creeping, curdling horror of another, and, conscious of its presence, cannot stir to escape.

"Shure, whativer else ye'll do, ye'd betther ate yer brekfist. Hev'n't I been an' br'iled a beautful salt fish meself for that same, wid chopped petatys, an' fine hot caffee?"

Mrs. Dodd followed her to the dining-room, which was deserted even by Mrs. Donovan; and if cold or tepid salt mackerel, greasy potatoes, coffee that never grew on any Javan or Arabian soil,— being unblushingly burned beans,— and stale baker's bread could have tempted her appetite, our old lady would have scarcely eaten with less apparent notice of her food than now. She did not know what to do till at last a bright thought visited her, and she turned to Bridget, who sat at ease in a chair behind her, heaving Irish sighs, and wiping her hot face with an apron that was far from clean, saying:—

"Aint there no more trains besides this, Bridget?"

"Shure an' there is. 'Taint a twopenny railroad that runs twice't an' then gives over. It's sivin or tin trains a day they do be havin', I don't remimber which."

"Well, then, I can go in the next one, can't I? When does it go?"

"There's the express comes by at tin o'clock, mem; but I undtherstood ye to say ye wanted the first train, and that's the accomydashin that's agoin' out beyant now."

"Then I'll go by express. I'll put on my bunnit right away, and take my things, and go and set in the depott till it comes along, so 't I'll be sure next time."

"And I'll come afther I get the dishes done, about tin o'clock, an' see ye safe in," said Bridget, muttering as she retreated, " she's a rale plisant ould lady, and as like to me Aunt Honour Maguire — the heavens be her bed this day! — as one pay is like to another in the pod; and it's more nor likely she'll make me the complimint of a quarther for bein' attintive!"

Mrs. Dodd paid for her board at the rate of a great hotel, and gladly left Mrs. Donovan smiling from under her be-ribboned cap at the meek inexperience of the old lady. After a few inquiries she found her way to the station, and seated herself in the gentlemen's waiting-room, as if the spirit of all blunders possessed her! She was somewhat chagrined at not finding a rocking-chair, but compromised affairs by sitting in one common one, with her feet on the rungs of another, that held her box, basket, and umbrella. Thus perched she waited quietly till the hour for the train should come. As the time drew near, and only men began to come in, one after another, she wondered mightily what was the reason that no women were going, and why all the men looked at her so. Presently two coarse-looking youths entered, tolerably well-dressed except in the article of vests, which were of the showiest character, — brilliant pink and blue checked Marseilles, overhung with the gaudiest and most elaborate chains, — while Mosaic studs, rings big enough for the finger of Gog or Magog, and blue neck-ties stamped them as undoubted "swells."

"Hullo!" said the reddest of them, as his eye caught Mrs. Dodd's quaint figure. "Jim! I say, look there!"

Jim turned round, struck an attitude, and whistled; while Joe quoted audibly, "Big box, little box, band-box, bundle."

Mrs. Dodd couldn't hear them, or she might perhaps have taken herself out of the way of the next manœuvre, which was, after buying their tickets, to seat themselves one on each side of her, and begin a conversation.

"Good-morning, ma'am!" said Joe, which was reciprocated by Mrs. Dodd. "Got your ticket, ma'am?"

"Well, no, I hevn't. I calculate to get it in the cars, so's I can't make no mistakes no more. Can I get it way through to Albany, sir?"

"Lord, yes!" answered Jim. "They ticket through to the Rocky Mountains, and overland to China, on this track."

"Dew tell!" said the old lady. "I thought Chiney was acrost the water."

"Well, they've bridged it over on the telegraph cable," said Joe, gravely.

Mrs. Dodd looked at him over her spectacles, not indignantly, but inquiringly.

"Dew tell!" said she. "I didn't know as they could!"

"Why," said Jim, "that feller next you, ma'am, he ticketed through to Japan, and shot buffaloes flying for seven hundred and forty miles of the way — lightning speed."

"Why, buffaloes don't fly!" said Mrs. Dodd, indignantly.

"Oh, no!" said Joe; "but I did, after the engine: it's the same principle. I used to aim a mile ahead, and hit every time."

"Dear me!" said the old lady, quite reassured by Joe's grave air. "Be they quite large critters?"

"Oh, immense!" said Jim; "they use their horns for church-steeples out in Kansas, and make a bell-rope of the tail."

Mrs. Dodd began to look dubious, and just then Joe's eye lit on a number of an agricultural paper lying on the floor, that some one had dropped, where were depicted certain diagrams illustrating the shape that a well-fed ox should be, inclosing him in a parallelogram except his head and legs; he availed himself of the accident directly.

"Well, that does sound rather largish," said he; "but we shall get a look at 'em in this part of the country before long. They're goin' to be imported."

"I should like to see a man drive a herd of 'em into New York!" said Jim, affecting a great scorn for the idea.

"Oh, they're going to be boxed up!" returned Joe. "Look here, ma'am: here's a description of the way, in the last 'Syracuse Harrow.' You see how it's to be done!"

"What!" said the pitiful old lady, eying the diagram, that presented a view of the ox's back,—"a-settin' up on end! Why, it must hurt their tails dreadfully. Poor creturs! I should think they'd beller all the way."

This was too much for Jim and Joe; they disappeared in a roar of laughter, leaving the mortified and astonished Mrs. Dodd to her own reflections. Presently the train came up, and the old lady betook herself to the cars, being seized on the way by Bridget, who put her into a seat, and bade her an affectionate good-by, lingering in hope of some more tangible souvenir, but lingering in vain. Mrs. Dodd was "of prudent mind," and she thought the two dollars she had paid Mrs. Donovan quite enough, to say the least, for her scanty accommodations; so she only said, "Good-by, Bridget; I wish you well." Just then the bell rung.

"Ye stingy ould nagur!" sputtered the indignant serving-maid; "the divil's own luck go wid ye!"

"All aboard!" sung out the conductor, and Bridget beat a hasty retreat without her "complimint," whereon Mrs. Dodd uttered but one reflection, in soliloquy, which we preserve for its point and pith:—

"She's real Irish,—sweet one minute and sassy the next."

The cars had passed Springfield, and were well on their way toward Albany. Mrs. Dodd had procured the right ticket this time, and sat peacefully nibbling a great piece of cake she had bought of a boy; for nothing could have induced her to leave her seat a moment till she arrived at Albany,—hardly the necessity of the ferry,—when suddenly it occurred to her she could get away from the troublesome sunshine in her face by taking the other end of the seat. To do so, bandbox, umbrella, and apple-basket must change places, and of course she knocked down the apples, and was obliged to grope for them here and there as they had rolled. Just before her sat a young man, with a deep weed on his hat, which had given rise to various sympathetic conjectures in the old lady's mind. He had taken that seat at Westfield, and remained apparently absorbed in his papers ever since. He was not handsome, but there was something serious and sweet about his dark face, and his dress was quiet and serviceable. Just as Mrs. Dodd stooped by his seat to look for one of the unfortunate russets, he perceived her errand, and offered to help her so kindly that the weary old lady looked up at him with a glow of satisfaction.

"Well, I wish you would," said she. "Them apples do pester me dreadfully; they've kep' a-tumblin' down ever since I come away from home."

"Let me tie a paper over the basket," said he, "and then you will have no more trouble;" and he proceeded to tie a bit of his newspaper over the re-collected russets.

"I declare for't," said she, "it's a great thing to have one's faculties handy! I don't see why I never thought of that myself."

The gentleman smiled, and, arranging the old lady's possessions, offered her a pictorial paper, and for the next hour she was happy; but the paper being finished she began to think with apprehension of her search through Albany after Jehiel. She returned the paper with thanks, and proceeded — encouraged by the smile with which it was acknowledged — to inquire of him as follows: —

"You haven't never been to Albany, have you, sir?"

He smiled again, at the intensely Yankee idiom.

"Oh, yes, ma'am; a great many times."

"Well, do you know the Reverend Jehiel Dodd there?"

"No; there is no settled clergyman of that name in Albany."

"Why, yes, there is, sure. He's my son; he's settled in the Pilgrim Church, I b'lieve 'tis they call it."

"But there is no such church in Albany."

Several new wrinkles gathered on the wistful, troubled face that looked into his, and the wonted exclamation came to her lips: —

"Dear me! what *shall* I do? Well, do you know one thing, — is Albany in Indianny or York?"

"The Albany we are going to is in New York State. There is a *New* Albany in Indiana."

"Well, that is it, I expect; but everybody told me it was in York. And here I am a-goin' all wrong! Oh, dear me, sus!"

This was the extreme of Mrs. Dodd's ejaculations; language reached its limits with her in that climax of phraseology; and the hot, slow tears began to creep out of her poor old eyes. Something about her look touched her listener's heart to the quick. The weed on his hat was not the token of a lost love, or wife, or child; it signified to him a loss never to be amended, — a dead mother, who also had been gray-haired, wrinkled, faded out of her young bloom, but lovely with the undying beauty of a lovely soul that transfigured her forever, and left its fair ghost behind in the hearts and the memories of all who knew her. Her son, remembering her, soothed poor old Mrs. Dodd into quiet, drew from her all her story, and, after thinking it over, decided that it was not best for her to go to New York, but to keep right on to Cleveland, and from there, by various railways, to Indianapolis and New Albany.

"But I don't believe I've got money enough," said she. "It must take quite a spell o' travellin' to get out there; and John Greene, that's my son-in-law down to Moosop"—

"John Greene! Why, I know him quite well. I've bought wool of him many a time," said the young man, speaking with visible pleasure, as everybody who knew John Greene did speak of him.

"Why, dew tell! I want to know if you know our John! Well, now, I feel kind o' familiar, I declare! Well, I was goin' on to say, he said't James, his brother, when I was goin' down to York, would hand over the money for my passage to whoever should take me along, so't I shouldn't have no trouble; and I brought along ten dollars for little things, and for to pay my passage from Hartford to York, and I haint got more'n three of it left, I've been a-wanderin' round so." Here the old lady's lip began to quiver.

"Well, you're all right now!" said he, soothingly. "I'm going on out West, and I've got money enough for both of us. I shall go as far as Indianapolis, and there I'll put you in a train straight for New Albany."

"Oh, I don't know how to be thankful enough!" said she. "I'm greatly obleeged; and you'll be sure to get your money — though that's the least part on't."

"Oh, yes; I'll get that out of Mr. Greene on our

next wool bargain. He'll trust Frank Scarborough's word for the debt, I'll be bound."

"I guess he'd trust a look out o' them eyes o' yourn as quick," said the old lady, thinking aloud.

Mr. Scarborough turned her thoughts by saying, "We'll telegraph from Albany to Moosop Station that you're all safe with me."

"Oh, yes, sir; and you needn't never go to John for wool after this without makin' it your home while you stay. They'll always befriend anybody that befriends mother."

They arrived at Albany very soon after this agreement; and, deciding to take a night train on, Mr. Scarborough arranged his shawl carefully for the old lady's rest, and cared for her as if he had indeed been her son, — better, perhaps; for Mr. Scarborough was that rarest of modern curiosities — a gentleman!

Mrs. Dodd's troubles were all ended now, and she ceases to be interesting. Suffice it to say, that she had a weary yet a very pleasant journey to Indianapolis, entertaining her friend all the way with her family histories, and praises of a little girl, named Lizzy, belonging to Jehiel, — "The prettiest little cretur you ever see!"

They parted with a promise on Frank Scarborough's part to surely visit New Albany on his return home in a month or two; and August was just fading away when he rung the bell of the Rev. Jehiel Dodd's door, in the quietest street of New Albany, — a door which was opened to him by Lizzy herself, — a young lady, instead of the pretty little girl her grandmother had painted. Pretty she was, nevertheless, with a true Saxon complexion of milk and roses; sweet, honest blue eyes, still innocent and childish; waves on waves of braided golden hair, and the kind, sweet beauty of a heart as true and gentle as her grandmother's.

More than once on his Western tours did Mr. Frank Scarborough find his way to New Albany; once, just in time to say good-by to his travelling companion, now bound on a longer journey, yet fearing not to be lost, though she went alone. The old lady drew that grave, yet tender, face down to hers, and kissed him for good-by, even as his mother had.

"The Lord bless you!" whispered she. "He will. He is faithful!"

Frank Scarborough never saw her again; but a year after he came back to New Albany, and, with much unwillingness on the Rev. Jehiel Dodd's part, that venerable man nevertheless performed a certain ceremony that gave his Lizzy over into the young man's hands for life; and I am credibly informed that old Mrs. Dodd's opinion of Mr. Scarborough is fully indorsed by Lizzy, who had heard many and many a time that he was "the best of all the Lord's creturs, ef he was a man!"

DOCTOR PARKER'S PATTY.

"Patty! Patty!" called the doctor's cheery voice from the little ell he used as an office, "tell Eph to harness up old Whitey."

"Into the 'chay' or the sulky, father?" answered a clear note from the kitchen.

"The 'chay.' I've got to go down to Dog's Misery. Friend Abraham Best has broken his leg."

Patty did her errand, and then tripping to the open window of the ell, which stood at right angles with the kitchen, put her pretty head in, and asked:—

"Can I go with you, father?"

The doctor nodded assent; he was very busy sorting splints, and one long one athwart his big mouth prevented his speaking. Doctor Billious Parker, though he bore so ominous and medical a name, was a kind, friendly, jolly soul, carrying a big heart in a big body. His coarse, humorous face, his always cheerful smile, hearty laugh, and warm, strong hand-grip, did his patients quite as much good as medicine; and he had plenty of patients.

Ths profession generally did not fraternize with him. He did not walk just as the Medical Association would have him. He had cast a certain doubt on the free use of calomel, and was known to distrust opium; and in those days the sheet-anchors of the profession were those of Scott's farrier friend, —"joost twa simples: laudamy and calamy;" and if they did not, as in his case, "mak' up for Flodden," they certainly slew their thousands, and to the accompaniment of the jawbones of more than one ass.

Doctor Parker, you see, was somewhat in advance of his age, and no profession likes a member to step out of its ranks. But he did not care about that; he was a man of independence in weighty matters, having worldly wisdom enough to conform in little things, or keep his opinions to himself about them, that he might the more freely use his liberty when it was truly needful.

If the medical tribes in and about Tenterden had been aware of the bread pills, burnt sugar and water draughts, and baths medicated with a powder composed of rye flour and common salt, which this man administered under long Latin names, they would have put him in the pillory, which still stood on Tenterden green, or ducked him in the frog-pond. They wanted to now, he had cured so many patients; but there was no legal chance to do so, therefore he still went on his way rejoicing.

Another thing was against him: he was not orthodox, people suspected. To be sure, a doctor could not go to church regularly; the exigencies of the profession forbid this, particularly with so popular a physician; but then when he did go he almost always fell asleep before Father Marsh got to " tenthly, beloved;" and once, — I shudder to reveal it, — once he gave forth a horrid snore, and when it woke him with its long reverberations he was seen to smile, and Patty tittered audibly. Moreover, had he not forbidden Hannah

Marsh to attend meeting all one winter? If she did have a weak spine and a cough, and the straight pew-backs and unwarmed edifice were bad for her, was it not still worse for her soul to absent herself from the courts of the tabernacle?

When Deacon Green solemnly remonstrated with the doctor on this ground he was horrified to hear him swear. If he had been a member Mr. Green would have dealt with him summarily; but the good man never had joined any church, and escaped censure from the meeting on that account. No wonder Tenterden people thought he was not orthodox! But, for all that, they continued to employ him. Mrs. Parker was pious enough for both. I say pious, advisedly; for I do not consider that she was religious. Of the two I should say the doctor had more religion.

"Sabriny" Gunn had been a patient of his when he first came to Tenterden; and after a year of visiting and prescribing, everybody was surprised at their sudden marriage; perhaps nobody more so than the bridegroom. Miss Gunn was not pretty, or healthy, or even graceful; she had thick, dull, light hair; gray eyes that really were green, but passed for gray, and had a queer way of looking steel-blue in certain lights, — eyes as cold and hard as bits of mountain crystal, but capable of flashing with fierce passion. A pale skin, strong jaw, plausible mouth, and cruel white teeth, completed this feline type. She was "smart as a steel-trap," besides. Some people loved — no, not loved her — were under her dominion, soul and body; others hated her. She was of that German proverb's class: "*Strass-engel Haus-teufel.*" Professedly a saint of the highest style, she made religion so distasteful in her daily life that neither her husband nor her children believed in her, and all were repelled from the real paths of pleasantness because her pretence and arrogance made them seem so unpleasant. Of this she also made outside capital, openly praying in meetings for her " unconverted husband," to his deep disgust; and when Patty, under the wonderful preaching of George Whitefield, was converted, and joined the church at the early age of sixteen, it only gave her mother a new lever of torture.

Thenceforward Patty was watched, mouse-fashion, by an untiring cat. All the innocent diversions of youth were denied her, as being worldly snares. Books were forbidden, few as they were. " Boston's Fourfold State," " Taylor's Holy Living," " Pilgrim's Progress," — these were allowed; but " Clarissa," " Pamela," " Sir Charles Grandison," a torn copy of " Amadis of Gaul," and sundry remnants of still older and more high-flown stories were burned up in the kitchen fire with summary judgment. It was just as well for Patty; for if Mrs. Parker had stolen a march upon the doctor as regarded matrimony, she was thereafter thoroughly understood by him, and made to understand that he was master whenever he saw fit to assert it, and always master of his own especial domain, the office. So there Patty read at will the works of William Shakespeare, the elaborate allegories of Spenser, and a full edition of English Classics, — as certain British publishers chose to call a set of those old papers, the " Spectator," the " Tattler," the " Rambler, and sundry lesser sparks from the era of Addison, Steele, and Sterne.

Odd reading enough for a young girl; but in those

days the modern novel was unknown, and Patty at least read pure and lucid English, — which is more than can be said of girls to-day.

By the time the "chay" came round Patty was ready, and a very pretty Patty she was, in a skirt of pink calimanco, a white dimity short-gown, a flat of straw she had braided and sewn herself, from the bright fine stems of Leghorn grass, tied down over her abundant and riotous curls, a black silk tippet upon her shapely shoulders, and black mitts on her little brown hands. But, though dress adorned her, as it does any woman, she more than returned the compliment; for even in her homespun gown tucked up over a stuff petticoat she was still beautiful. She inherited her sturdy constitution and splendid coloring from her father's family, as well as the regular, delicate features which her rich brunette complexion and laughing dark eyes illuminated. Not slight nor slender, but well filled out, dimpled at wrist and elbow as well as in cheek and chin, as graceful as unconscious nature and a total absence of stays and whalebone (for which she had the doctor to thank) could make her, Patty Parker was about as charming a bit of flesh and blood as one could see on a summer's day; and it was generally summer where she was, for she had a sweet, sunny temper, with enough will to strengthen the cheeriness, and as much energy and common-sense as steadied her for the conflicts that we all share, sooner or later.

When I say her temper was sweet I do not mean that she never lost it; for there were times when Miss Patty could thunder and lighten like any other summer squall; but she always cleared off thoroughly and smiling, as brief tempests are apt to. Dr. Parker said the explosion did her good, aerated her moral nature, and restored the disturbed equilibrium. He was of good old Fuller's opinion: "Anger is one of the sinews of the soul. He that wants it hath a maimed mind."

How Patty would endure real grief and thwarting remained to be seen. Her mother was steadily preparing her for trouble by the daily fret that took out much sweetness from the girl's life, and the rigid observances that tried hard to misinterpret both heaven and earth for this young soul that knew neither. But here the doctor's counteractive force came in. He took his daughter with him on his daily rounds whenever the "housewife-skep" could spare her, and sometimes when it could not. He opened her eyes to all the healing and delighting forces of nature. There was not a flower in Wyannis County unknown to Patty, a bird whose song she could not recognize before she saw its plumage, or a tree she could not name from its bark, though it were already cut and chopped and laid up in the wood-pile. All the simples of the neighborhood and their properties were familiar to her. She could tell you what black cohosh, and blue cohosh, and meadow rue, and mullein, and elecampane, and prince's piney, hardhack, and hemlock, were good for. Had not she gathered them all, and fairly tapestried the great garret with their odorous and inodorous sheaves? For the doctor was much given to use these things when he used any medicine; and it was considered a feather in his cap that he never used any "mineral doses." How the doctor laughed when Patty told him of this boast, made by one of his patients!

"I like that, Patty," he said. "That's *vox populi* with a vengeance. 'Mineral doses,' quotha! A few boluses of mandrake root, a little drink of nightshade tea, or a pinch of dried stink-weed, or St. Ignatius's bean, would change their tune, I reckon! I'd engage to kill more men to-day, twice over, with messes out of the swamp down at Dog's Misery, than anything in all the minerals in the county!"

And with this the doctor gave a smart lash to Old Whitey that was really meant for the ignorance of his admiring patients.

But to-day the doctor was bent on a purely surgical errand; and he jogged quietly along with Patty by his side, as congruous companions to behold as a damask rose and a lobster, but a pair of dear friends for all that; and in due time drew up at Abraham Best's farm-house in the district, called "Dog's Misery," — a name given it in old times when all the intervale had been a swamp of tangled thicket and boggy ground, into which the dogs of the first settlers were always straying after wild animals, and between the mire and the beasts rarely coming back. The land had long been drained and reclaimed, except a few acres that lay too low, and were too full of springs to repay so much expense and trouble as their drainage would have cost; and the Best farm stood just at the head of the little valley where the hills converged.

Abraham Best was the descendant of a persecuted remnant of Quakers, driven into the wilderness years ago for their faith's sake, and clinging for that very reason still closer to the creed that had exiled them from their earlier homes.

There were twenty or thirty families scattered in

and about Tenterden, who had a little meeting-house at one end of the village, and adhered in their walk and conversation to the most rigid tenets of the sect. Abraham Best was grim as Giant Despair in his outer aspect. He was a preacher, and in early life had married a beautiful English girl converted under his own exhortations, and who had herself become a preacher too. Long ago Elizabeth Best's beauty had gone from her thin face and spare form; the rich golden hair, whose waves had been tucked away under a Quaker cap, was gray and sparse now; the milk and roses of her complexion had faded to true American sallowness, and the scarlet lips grown pallid and set; but her dark blue eyes were still beautiful and tender, and a certain divine patience and sweet serenity seemed to glorify those wan tints and sharpened outlines with a beauty that was truly not of this world.

The house where they lived was bare of all external charm, though thrift, neatness, and order made it thoroughly respectable. If no roses or lilies lit up its brown walls, or clambering honeysuckles floriated its angles, there were no scattered chips, broken wagons, or neglected implements in sight; and the inside of the house was as exquisitely neat as it was formal and unlovely.

Abraham Best lay on the bed, quite silent, though he had bitten his lips till they bled, in stern determination to suffer without a murmur. His wife was in the kitchen preparing dinner, but a young man stood by his father's side, who was not known to the doctor, but carried his name in his face, and advertised himself thereby as Friend Best's only son.

Why a Quaker, and a rigid Quaker, should have

thought of calling a boy "Liverius" is a problem I cannot solve; but that was the youth's name. Perhaps there was a spell in it, for he was the sole survivor of five; and while Friend Best regarded carnal affection as a snare, and had trained Liverius in the way he wished him to go, with unflinching sternness and apparent success, Friend Elizabeth "clave unto the lad," in the lovely phrase of Scripture, with all the passion of a mother's heart who had been bereaved of her children, and refused to be comforted because they were not, till the Lord sent her this son of consolation. The doctor looked at Liverius with approbation; he had never happened to see him before, because the Bests had little to do with the medical profession; whether it was the effect of that habitual self-control that calms the nervous system, and so equalizes the circulation, and speaks peace to that perpetual duel between mind and body which affects most people; or the ease which abundant possessions give, since their possessor never knows the rack of debt, the terror of poverty, or " that nameless fear which haunts the steps of the moneyless man ;" or whether the simple life and out-door labor of the family fortified them against disease, this, at any rate, was the first time Dr. Parker had been called to their aid, and the splendid beauty of the young Quaker struck him with delight: for Liverius had his mother's gift of outline and coloring, and added to that a noble masculine figure and a rarely intelligent expression. It is all very well for people to prate about mental charms and the loveliness of the soul; that

"Beauty is unripe childhood's cheat,"—

the stamp of God on flesh and blood has and must have a charm for every healthy and honest nature. It gave the doctor keen pleasure, as he proceeded to set and bandage Friend Best's badly broken leg, to look up now and then at this Quaker Apollo, who handed him splints and bandages with quick apprehension of his wants, and seemed as deft and gentle as he was handsome.

At last the old man was put in order, the bed carefully smoothed, and a cup of hot sassafras tea brought for his refreshment, and, promising to come next day, the doctor nodded good-morning. But Liverius followed him to the fence to ask such questions as people unused to sickness always crave to ask the doctor, feeling dimly that in his hands are the issues of life and death, though they really know better.

"How long will it be, doctor?" said the young man, eagerly.

"Well, I can't tell," said Dr. Parker, with a smile. "It depends on the turn things take. It's a bad breakage,— what we doctors call a compound fracture." And, picking a couple of slender twigs from the apple-tree-shoot beside him, the doctor proceeded to illustrate; but suddenly Liverius ceased to attend. The doctor, a little touched, followed his eyes, and soon saw the cause of the diversion, — no less than his own Patty, who had made herself more radiant than even calimanco and dimity allowed, by straying off to a wild apple-tree by the road-side, and returning to the "chay" laden with blushing, budding apple-blossoms. The exercise of breaking those thorny and tough boughs had heightened her glowing color and half knocked off her flat hat, thereby pulling over her little ear and against her peachy cheek a thick and glittering tress of dark curls, and her lips were redder than alder-berries as she laughed and nodded to her father.

"Adam and Eve," said the doctor to himself, but quite to himself; adding to Liverius: "Good-day, sir! good-day! I shall be back to-morrow;" and again, *sotto voce*, "but I shan't bring Patty!"

"What do you think about that young fellow?" said the doctor to Patty, as he whipped up the old horse over Milking-Yard Hill. "Handsome, aint he?"

> "As tall and straight as a poplar tree,
> His cheeks as red as a rose;
> He looks like a squire of high degree
> When dressed in his Sunday clothes,"

sang Patty, mockingly. Her father laughed with an air of relief; the girl certainly was not taken with that fellow's aspect.

Poor doctor! that which is common to man had befallen him. His girl had grown up safe in the fold, the delight of his eyes and the joy of his heart, and here now was a young springald ready to walk off with her for the term of her natural life, and deprive the father, who had reared and adored her, of his most cherished possession. All this misery his foreboding soul had conjured out of that one bewildered stare Liverius had bestowed on Patty. But jealousy is prophetic, and well he knew that if Friend Best's son were to die to-morrow, there were still enough youths in Tenterden to woo Patty; for half a dozen were already casting sheep's eyes at her of a Sunday, and appearing now and then of a Sunday night, as awkward as their own flocks and herds, to sit on the settle by the fire an hour or so, red and speechless, chewing "meetin'-seed," and apparently afflicted with stiff neck, every one of them; then at the nine-o'clock bell departing in shame-faced haste, with dreadful squeaks of best boots and mumbling of adieux. Further than this mystic demonstration none of them had gotten, so far; for Mrs. Parker kept her glittering eye on them like an Ancient Marineress, and

"The boldest held his breath, for a time!"

She had her own ideas for Patty, and no one yet had met her requisitions. I suppose this woman loved her daughter; but there is love, and love. I have known a love, so called, that could bear no other affection to serve or please its objects; that demanded as the dreadful price of peace that the few it clung to should receive or recognize no other affection, social or natural; a love that was a daily prison and thumb-screw to its beloved; that became life and breath by its own strenuous force to one or two, and when it died and went — somewhere! — took that breath and life with it: a sort of post-mortem homicide. This was Mrs. Parker's way of loving. And I have known another love that set all doors of sunshine open to its loves; that brought adorers from all quarters to its precious shrine; that heaped every good gift upon its idols, whatever hand proffered them, and forgot itself and its own passion in a fervor of anxiety for the happiness of its objects, however that might be best secured, even at the cost of its own mortal agony. But this diviner air was not for Patty's breathing; it is the atmosphere of heaven, and too good for this poor world.

The doctor went again to Friend Best's, and again; indeed, he went many times, for Abraham was not young, and his bones knit slowly; beside, his strong repression of the nervous irritation that will beset even Quaker flesh and blood, under some circumstances, made him feverish.

"I wish to the Lord he would swear!" said the doctor, shaking his head, as he jogged home one day by himself. "It would do him so much good. There's enough electric force stopped up there to turn a mill; his blood's all afire, and there must be an explosion, or leeches; and I don't like leeches, he's too old."

But leeches it had to be. The world might have stopped on its axis sooner than Friend Best swear. All this time Doctor Parker kept an eye on Liverius; noted how he peered into the "chay" to see if Patty nestled in its dusty corner; and, though his face always fell not to find her, still kept his daily watch, while the cruel parent chuckled inwardly to see it. Not that he had any objection to Friend Best's son personally, but he did not want Patty to marry anybody yet. He desired to put off the evil day as far as possible, to keep his treasure as long as he could. Common sense and common observation warned him that Patty, like all other girls, must sometime leave the nest and fly for herself, but he did not want to think about it. He would accept the inevitable, but he would evade it as long as he could.

But the eternal forces were too much for him, as they are for all of us. Liverius Best was young, and a man, if he was a Quaker. Hitherto shut out from women's society, — for the few girls who were of his own faith lived far from his home, and in their Seventh-Day gear of poke bonnets and gray duffle cloaks were not a delight to behold, being for the most part fat and stolid or sallow and skinny, — Patty Parker fairly dazzled him. Color, grace, freedom, — these were unknown female splendors to this formal youth. His ears rung with her sweet, gay voice, his eyes were blinded with her brilliant beauty, which shone on him in dreams and haunted his daytime; her laugh echoed with bewitching mockery from every bubbling brook that crossed the fields; the orioles seemed to sing about her, and the bobolinks to shout her name. In short, Liverius Best was madly in love, and what more is to be said? For it is not to be supposed that Dr. Parker, or any other doctor or father in the land, succeeded in keeping Liverius and Patty apart! Not at all. What did a wise old poet say?

> "Where there is no space
> For the glow-worm to lie;
> Where there is no place
> For receipt of a fly;
> Where the midge dare not venture
> Lest herself fast she lay;
> If Love come he will enter
> And find out the way."

And Liverius was neither midge nor fly, that the three miles between Dog's Misery and Tenterden village should daunt him. He thought nothing of the walk when some advice was needed of the doctor, when the saline draughts gave out, or the last Dover's powder had been used; and he thought still less of forgetting to mention these little items when the doctor made his visits, though he might have saved himself much shoe-leather as well as weariness to the flesh; but what are these poor earthly things to a blissful sight of the beloved object? Liverius would have walked right over Meriden Mountain and into the griffins that tradition peopled the Peak of Lamentation withal, if they lay between him and Patty. What to him were three miles and back of highway? Nor is it to be denied that before many days Patty perceived that this handsome young fellow grovelled, so to speak, at her feet. Curiously enough he never found the doctor in, and Patty always dispensed the medicines in such cases. Perhaps it was fortuitous; perhaps owing to the fact that young Best always stopped to flip the dust from his shoes, and shake his coat, in a certain clump of firs on the hill above Tenterden, at the foot of which lay Dr. Parker's mansion, plainly discernible from the aforesaid firs; but, however it was, the doctor never could be found in the office when Liverius called, and Patty had to wait on him.

The consequence was inevitable. In all her little life Patty had never before met such a youth; Romeo was not a circumstance to him: Romeo, the prince of lovers! To be sure Liverius could not talk blank verse, but to be thee'd and thou'd was almost poetry, and he was so awfully handsome! Before father or mother opened their careless eyes; while Friend Elizabeth's tender old heart glowed afresh over her boy's filial devotion, and Friend Abraham began to feel some meltings and soundings of the inner man in view of Liverius's unexpected care and painstaking; yes, while the cat looked the other way, these young mice began their *grande ronde*, regardless of their doom, like thousands before them. Do not let us protract the prelude or describe at length the growth of Patty's love or the headlong leap of her lover's passion; the blossoms on the apple-trees had long fallen, decked in which Patty made her *entrée* into Liverius's heart; the fruit had set, swelled, become streaked and painted in autumnal suns, before Tenterden and Dog's Misery awoke to the fact that Liverius Best and Patty Parker were keeping company. The earthquake at Lisbon was nothing to it! Quakers and Presbyterians had been in full cry against a small remnant of Prelatists, commonly called Episcopalians, who had dared to build a little log chapel at Tenterden North End, and nail a cross to the gable; thereby flapping a rag of Papacy into the very face and eyes of Puritanism and John Fox. Indeed, this chapel had been a rendezvous more than once for Liverius and Patty, who chose it as a place of perfect security from either of their own sects, and had learned to love the beautiful liturgy, partly from association, partly for itself.

But this was only a new drop in their cup; it added fresh force to the fury of their respective brethren to learn that they had been seen coming together from Priest Punderson's chapel on Pard Hill more than once. Though Episcopacy was permitted by government, it was still an offence and a hissing to both Presbyterians and Quakers; like the cat and dog they could run after a rat together, but here was other game. Yes; here on one hand was a bred and born Quaker intent on marrying out of meeting; and on the other a member of good and regular standing in the Presbyterian body, not only desirous to marry a Quaker, but actually found out in attendance upon the Prelatical services of Priest Punderson!

By this time Friend Best had gotten to his feet, and was able to work a little and to supervise a great deal. This defection of his only child moved him mightily; he uplifted his voice in a way that might have consoled Doctor Parker for his assumed inability to swear, since the spirit, if not the letter, of profanity took possession of him. Stern, rigid, white-hot with passion, he made life a torture to his wife and son after the most orthodox fashion. Friend Elizabeth felt a sacred rage, it is true, when she heard of Liverius's defalcation; but it was the sinless wrath that Scripture itself commends, and melted into pity like a cloud into rain when her sweet, motherly heart fully comprehended how her boy's life was absorbed and centred in Patty Parker. But Friend Abraham was deaf to any softer emotion, and both blamed and despised his wife for giving way to "carnal weakness;" and in this he was backed up by the brethren. One and all of this small conclave felt a call to visit Liverius, and wrestle with him in spirit. No matter where he was, — in field or barn, — these long-coated gentry found him out, and dealt with him more or less gently according to their own nature, but the burden of all their song was: —

"Thee will be read out of meeting, surely, Liverius, if thee takes to wife one of the world's people;" and to be "read out of meeting" is to a Quaker what an interdict or a Papal anathema is to the Romanist. Consider, you who smile that such a threat should have terrors for our hero, that it meant separation from all he had been born and taught to believe most sacred, most necessary to salvation; and that at the period of which we write political freedom had not yet inspired religious liberty in the individual soul. Whether the intoxicating draught of absolute freedom is best for soul or body is not to be discussed here; however that may be, it was a draught unknown to Liverius Best, and he was in a bondage of spirit hard for any of us to recognize to-day. He shuddered and trembled and turned pale under the pressure brought to bear upon him; conscious through all of one inevitable fact, that he loved Patty Parker; but mortally in dread of the threatened consequences, though he could not and would not abjure his love to prevent them.

Nor did Patty come off scathless; her mother's tongue was let loose upon her with devouring fury; it is true the office was always her refuge, and no storm allowed to pass its door, but the doctor himself was dull and unhappy, evidently, — kind to Patty, but with a visible effort. He was disappointed, cut to the heart. Here, in spite of all his foresight, right under his nose, as it were, this young sprig had made love to his girl, turned her heart and her head, and set the whole town talking angrily and coarsely about her. The doctor had old-fashioned ideas about women folks; he believed their place was

"That still, safe corner by the household fire,"

which some women never find, and some never wish for, but which is, after all, the true woman's place; and it vexed him thoroughly that Patty should suffer from the strife of tongues. He was a candid man, and he allowed to himself that there was no personal objection to Liverius. He even made a poor joke to Patty, when he was striving to keep up her spirits one day about their being an eternal fitness of things in Liver-ius being connected with Billious! Patty felt as if he had joked about the Bible, and burst into tears.

Poor old doctor! If Pickwick had been born then, how heartily would he have agreed with the immortal Weller, that "women are rum creeturs"! To think his mild, professional joke should have made Patty cry! He turned sadly away, and went to work at his books. He saw trouble before his darling; he knew what her life would be if she entered a divided family, though love should have triumphed so far as to allow her entrance. He knew the poison and fury of his wife's tongue and temper, and he knew something worse than either: that his own tenure of life was uncertain, and that it behooved him to do what he could for Patty while he had opportunity and time. He was seen more than once to enter Squire Morton's office; but then the Squire had hereditary gout, so nobody made any remark, and nobody knew, till months after, what patient was provided for in that little shanty.

But Patty suffered in spite of her father's sad kindness quite as much as was necessary. Her mother reviled, reproached, and entreated her, till her very soul was sick and sore within. The elders of the church visited her and remonstrated with her. Parson Hyde summoned her into his study, and prayed with her by the hour, and Parson Hyde, as old Moll Pitcher said, could "pray like a house-a-fire." Patty herself was shocked — a little — to find how interested she became in the struggles of a fly to escape from a spider who had netted it in his web, while the parson was praying; but her knees did ache so; and it was so dreadful to be put down and prayed for as if you were dead! Poor Patty!

But worse than all were the visitations of the mothers

in Israel, who must needs have a finger in the pie, being competent to deal with a woman because they were women! Patty did not agree with them there; she had borne with the elders in a sort of sullen patience because she had been brought up in an orthodox fashion to consider, theoretically, that the man was the head of the woman, collectively as well as individually. But when Madam Hall, and Aunt Peters, and Goody Pogue, one after another, took her to do, wagged their wide-ruffled caps at her, and nodded their gray heads in awful prophecy, nagging and baiting her as only women can nag and bait each other, Patty's patience gave way, and, by a sort of poetic justice, which I take to be real, not legal, justice, the forces of gossip came to her aid. She had not been to quiltings, and huskings, and apple-parings in vain; she had eaten of the tree of knowledge like her grandam in Eden, and now she used that knowledge to effect, — politely recalling to Madam Hall how her own eldest daughter had skipped out of window to elope with Aminadab Edwards, the gayest rake in all Connecticut, but now a brilliant and hard-working lawyer, of whom the Halls were proud enough. Then she laid before Goody Pogue the reckless fact that *she* for her part intended to *marry* the man she loved: an announcement which silenced that old lady, and set her face homeward. For Goody was well known to be a late repentant sinner, and to have had high words with the late Jeremiah concerning some passages of her youth. And on Aunt Peters she turned with the fury of long-borne exasperation : —

"And I should like to know, Mis' Peters, what earthly business 'tis of yours what my father's daughter does? He can take care of me, I guess! 'nd you aint my aunt save and except out of civility" (Mrs. Peters being the doctor's step-sister), "and I wouldn't bear it if you was. So there!"

With which Patty fled upstairs, slamming the door behind her, feminine fashion, and leaving Aunt Peters with upraised hands, pouring out vials of wrath not to be exceeded by Mrs. Parker herself.

It was a hard time for Patty and Liverius both. It is all very well to read about these things; to be deeply interested in the struggles and sufferings of the poor lovers who are annually and by thousands —

"Butchered to make a" reader's "holiday."

But when one comes to go through the agonies so pleasant to hear, that is quite another matter. It is far easier to grind than to be ground; and no wonder Patty's cheek lost its splendid glow, her eyes their light, her voice its sweet ring; or that Liverius also became pale, stooping, dull of aspect, and weary always.

When a storm has lasted long and drenched all nature with dark, chill floods day after day, filled heaven with sobbing winds and earth with turbid streams, there comes sometimes a gust of thunder and lightning and whirlwind, and "the old order changes, giving place to new." It is true men are smitten sometimes, houses levelled, forests mowed as by a reaper; but the long, cold storm is swept away, and the blue sky lifts its benign arch again over a sweet, untroubled world.

Such a thunderstroke burst on Patty, when, one bitter December day, old Whitey jogged up to the door with Liverius Best driving, and a strange, prone burden lying at length on the floor of the box sleigh. The doctor had been down beyond Milking-Yard Hill to see a patient, had done his office, and set out for home. What further chanced no man could know. Liverius had seen the sleigh standing still on the turnpike just at the edge of the Dog's Misery intervale, and, foreboding evil, gone on to investigate, and found, still breathing, but utterly unconscious, poor Dr. Parker.

It is hard to die: hard to the natural man, even when friends gather, and loving tendance aids, and there are kind and conscious words passing between the living and the dying. But to die alone and speechless; to go out of life unshriven, unreconciled, without one parting word, one tender look, one smallest token of love and peace, what must this be to the departed? Alas! what is it not to those who are left? For such loss there is no compensation; for such wounds no healing. They will throb, and ache, and burn, while time endures; the soul will be haunted and the heart wrung even in its deepest and most utter submission to the will of God, and the only utterance, even out of the Divine Book, that is left to such survivor, is the despairing outcry of Uz: —

"Though he slay me, yet will I trust in Him."

In all Patty's after life, happy as it was, she never forgot or ceased to mourn her father, for he "died and gave no sign."

Not that he died at once, for day, and night, and still another day, went by, and there he lay, dead to every appeal of love or pity, — dead to every sense; dead to thought and feeling, but alive in gasping breath; a terror to those who stood about him, perhaps an agony to himself; but of that who shall tell? Patty was stunned by the shock. The voluble grief of her mother fell idly on her ear. The talk of the neighbors, the intruding sympathy of relatives, the exhortations of Parson Hyde, assailed on her heedless sense like the babble of children. She could not feel; she could not weep; she could do what was to be done, with her ordinary aspect and usual deftness of touch and executive talent; but her heart slept while her brain woke. A man in her place would have given way, perhaps; made his audible moan, stirred up the ready sympathies of friends, and been set down forever as a tender and profound mourner; but Patty passed as unfeeling. She was called hard-hearted, even, by the old women she had routed when they came to exhort her, and supposed (audibly) to cherish resentment against her dead father for interfering with her love affair; when in fact she was simply stunned by a blow she had not foreseen.

When the funeral was over, and that cheery life-long presence gone forever, Patty gave way, and a slow fever beset her, — a fever so slow that it made no haste to leave her, and for nine long weeks she lay somewhere near death's door, and not much aided or comforted by the draughts and leeches of old Dr. Potter from Meriden, who was called to her help as soon as might be. But youth and a good constitution are sometimes too much even for a doctor. Spring drew near, and Patty began to mend. Liverius had been like one beside himself all these weeks. He grew thin, hectic, irritable; sleep did not rest him or food nourish him. Patty was or might be dying, and he could not even see her! His only comfort was to waylay the doctor, and torment him with inquiries. But, when Patty began at last to mend, Liverius took heart again. The "meeting" had let him alone of late, though his father was still severe and contemptuous, and his mother sad to dreariness. He had at least time to possess his soul in patience, and he had thought much and deeply in that solitude. There was a firm set to his lips and a steady light in his eye unknown before, and a certain determinate energy moved his axe and saw that might have told their story to the acute observer.

When Patty was well again and able to be downstairs, though still weak and languid, Squire Morton came to see her, to tell her about her father's will, which she had neither known nor thought of all this time. Poor Patty could have spared the information, considerate as it was; for to learn how carefully and tenderly her father had provided for her future, even while she was paining the very depths of his great, kind heart, was like losing him over again, and set free all the bitter floods that illness and stunned apprehension had held so long in their fountains. Squire Morton had not expected his tidings to be received with passionate and profuse tears; but he was an old man and a lawyer, and had seen women before, so he only took an extra pinch of snuff, and proceeded to impress on Patty the fact that her mother was left a life-use of the homestead and farm attached; after that life-use, to revert to Patty; and that to the girl herself was left another and larger farm in the neighboring township, with good house and barns thereon, and also a certain store of money, amounting to some five hundred pounds sterling, now in the hands of Squire Morton, awaiting her orders.

Patty took heart wonderfully in the next few weeks, although her mother raved and raged worse than ever, seeing that the heiress of such a portion was clean out of her power and able to do what she would, — a fact the heiress began quickly to appreciate.

But of all this Liverius knew nothing. Out of sheer love to Patty and conscious inability to endure his life without her, he had resolved on sudden and stringent measures; and by some of those sly means known to desperate lovers he conveyed to her a missive, begging, nay, insisting, on a meeting. And after much suspense and delay — for Patty was spied upon and hindered in a way he knew not of — he received a tiny note to tell him she should be in the graveyard an hour before sunset on Wednesday.

Forlorn tryst! but its selection showed Patty's feminine acuteness. Wednesday afternoon a quilting was to be held at Mrs. Hall's, and nothing could have kept the Widow Parker back from that decorous gathering, permitted, as so few social joys were, even to recent widowhood. She did not dream that Patty would or could leave the house, for as yet she had made no such effort; but she engaged old Moll Thunder, the half-breed vagabond, who filled all gaps of service in Tenterden (provided she could be found) to stay in the house lest Patty should need something.

It was easy to calm Moll's vigilance and fix her by the kitchen fire, if once her cider-pitcher and her tobacco-pouch were full, and Patty replenished both before she slipped on her levantine hood and sacque and stole out of the door to meet Liverius.

The graveyard lay, according to Yankee fashion, on a hill-side; but it was not on any high road, and clumps of self-sown young white pines, fragrant and shadowy, afforded shelter to such visitors as would avoid sun, wind, rain, or, as in this case, detection. As soon as Patty's trembling steps closed the rude gate behind her Liverius appeared from one of these rustling, sighing, odorous arbors, and, drawing her into the shade, gave sweet, if silent, greeting to the scarlet lips and tender eyes he had not seen for so long.

"O Patty!" he said at last, with a long sigh, "I never, never will lose sight of thee again! We must marry in spite of everything!"

"But, dear," half sobbed Patty, "we can't! we can't!" for Patty's resolution failed her, and all her old terrors returned as this dictatorial youth laid down the law.

"I don't know why we can't," the man answered, manfully.

"O Liverius, it will be so wicked! I can't possibly turn Friend, and you won't come to our meeting?"

This was half a question, and it was quickly answered.

"Come to thy meeting? Fellowship those who have hunted thee like a partridge upon the mountains? Never! I will never sit down with them who have made thee and me wretched, because we loved one another, even as the Book commandeth. Patty, is thee afraid to be poor — with me?"

Liverius's handsome face glowed with resolute passion and pride, as he asked the question. But wicked Patty answered it with a little giggle; for well she knew there was no poverty in question, and it tickled her secret soul to think Liverius did not know it. But she saw his face darken at her ill-timed mirth;

he was in as deadly earnest as ever Luther, going into the councils of his foes. So she constrained herself to whisper: —

"No, *I* aint afraid."

"Then my mind is resolved, and thee will come with me. We will break away from this godless slavery that holds us in unreasonable bonds. I will give up my religion, and thee shall give up thine. We will marry, and go into the Church of England, and go to the devil together!"

"Oh!" shrieked Patty.

But the veracious chronicler who recorded the above story adds: —

"And they fulfilled their resolution, *soe farre* as goeing intoe the churche, and marrieing, and abyding there for lyfe."

And if the testimony of descendants, who followed the footsteps of Liverius Best, and Patty his wife, down into these present years, still possessing the farm where this happy pair settled after Priest Punderson married them, is of any worth beyond mere legendary lore, then Liverius and Patty went no further; for they are still told of as blessings to their neighbors, — kindly, hospitable, charitable, — as the most devoted parents and faithful friends.

Mrs. Parker never forgave Patty, and Goody Pogue spoke evil of her always. But Friend Elizabeth, after her husband's sudden death, came to live with them, and her last days were gilded with serenest sunshine. Several of their children returned to the Presbyterian fold, with their parents' full consent, having been led thither by strong affection for some youth or maiden of that flock. Patty, the second, seceded to Quakerism, beguiled by a second cousin, who had taken the Dog's Misery Farm.

"Are you glad, granny?" she said to Friend Elizabeth, — now an old angel of fourscore, just ready for her homeward flight, — when she told her of her intention.

"I am glad thee is happy, my child," said the sweet, old, tremulous voice. "I am too near to the General Assembly and Church of the First-Born to care by which road my beloved hasten thither. My spirit was once sore unto death over thy father and mother leading into Episcopal meeting; but the Lord hath taught me better, Patty. I know now that all nations, and people, and kindred, and tongues shall come into one habitation, but that Christ is all, and is in all! For I am persuaded that no sect or form of worship of man's contriving, — 'neither death, nor life, nor angels, nor principalities, nor powers, nor things present, nor things to come, nor height, nor depth, nor any other creature, — shall be able to separate us from the love of God, which is in Christ Jesus our Lord!'"

"Amen!" solemnly answered Liverius, who had waited at the open door till his mother's testimony finished.

DOOM AND DAN.

Moses Dyer was a Quaker; one of the straitest sort. In him strong natural passion, keen enthusiasm, deep feeling, had all been repressed and compressed by creed and training; under his calm and rigid exterior lay sleeping fires ready to desolate his life, but, being yet young and strong when he comes into our vision, these fires within, like steam at high pressure, only served to impel him in all the activities of life, and make of him a hard-working, thrifty, quietly energetic young man, whose deep, dark eyes now and then flashed but never flamed, whose crisp, dark hair defied in its abundant rings even the shears of the village barber, and whose stalwart form displayed strength, vigor, and symmetry that would have served Praxiteles as a model. The few old men of his sect in the near neighborhood of Dorset, where he was born, shook their gray heads over his probable life.

"There is a hard wrastle for Moses, I expect," said old Jacob Morris; "thee will see, Friend Harding, the youth will have much to strive with before he can enter into quietness; the flesh and the devil will be pecooliar hard on him, appears to me."

"It may be so, Jacob; thee knows Moses better than I do. I should say that he will make a man of mark among the brethren. I trust he will be guided in the choice of a partner in life. I am free to believe that will be a turning-point with the youth."

A faint glimmer of chastened humor played over Jacob's face.

"I think thee may be right, Friend Harding; I feel to be grateful that Divine Providence did not place the guiding of the youth in my hands."

"I think thee has much to be thankful for," dryly replied Friend Harding; for, being an older man than Jacob, and once a power in "meeting," before Quakerism had dwindled to the mere handful now left in Dorset, he had been through a wider experience of human nature than this placid old man, whose home high on White Mountain had been a sort of hermit's cell all his life, and saved him from that knowledge of good and evil which destroys as often as it educates.

Moses Dyer was indeed left to no direction but that of the Divine leading now, for his father and mother, both rigid devotees of their faith, died within six months of each other, soon after he was twenty-one, and even the small brown house in Dorset street, which he remembered all his life as an ideal of a Friend's dwelling, so spotless was its purity, so stern its order, so fixed its routine, had been burned to the ground the next year, and ever since, Moses had boarded with Friend Morris up on White Mountain, and come down every day to his grist-mill on Black river, his dinner-pail on his arm. With all their peculiarities of doctrine and living the Friends are a thrifty tribe, and old Solomon Dyer had done the milling for a circle of twenty miles' diameter a great many years, laid up store of money in Rutland bank, and held mortgages on many a goodly farm in Dorset; all of these worldly possessions coming into his son's hands, since he was an only child; but Moses still kept to "plain" customs. Friend Harding's good wishes for Moses did not seem near of fulfilment, for there were few maidens of the faith about that part of the country now, and none of these were comely and pleasant enough to attract Moses Dyer. It was out of his own experience that John Harding had spoken; he knew in his heart that his own anchor to peace and patience was his wife Susannah, whose face was still as smooth, as placid, and almost as fair, beneath the gleaming silver of her parted hair, as when they two stood up in meeting together, — two pallid statues, timidity and emotion sending her soft color and his ruddy blood into banishment, and filling her tender eyes with shyness and tears.

But for her, he very well knew what his life would have been, for this man's nature, too, was stormy; but this gentle voice, this soft touch, guided him past all quicksands, and kept him in the Friends' fellowship till he attained to being a minister among them; the agitations of his youth were laid to rest forever, and his home became a foretaste of the world that now lay so close before him.

For Moses no such angel waited, at least in Dorset; so he plodded on his daily way, grinding and bolting, taking toll, filling barrels and emptying bags, taking his pleasure only in a keen delight in nature, a delight that was his secret treasure; for he knew that Dorset people considered that a man who would climb a hill to see the sun set was a fool or a lunatic, and would pass the same judgment on him if he dared to hint at the beauty of a field strewn white with ox-eyed daisies, swayed by every gentle wind, following the sun with fair faces from east to west, drooping their light stems with graceful spring and rebound under each swift drop of summer rain, when they were only weeds, and "pesky weeds" at that.

It almost seemed to him that he had found one of these, incarnate, when, one May morning, as he opened the mill door, he looked across the little river and saw on a gray rock, that jutted out into the stream just below, a slight girl's figure, with a fishing-rod in hand, balancing it above the water with unpractised fingers. "A slip of a girl" an Irishman would have said, yet Moses stared at her as if she were a heavenly vision; her wide hat had fallen off, and hanging at the back of her head made an oval black background for the tender face flushed with the keen freshness of the hour; her light brown hair had fallen, too; and the sun-rays touched it with golden lights. Her clear, gray eyes and dark lashes gave a peculiar interest to the almost childish features and delicate, languid lips half parted above her white teeth. Dress did not enhance this loveliness. Nelly Wood was clothed upon with nothing more elegant than a clean, cheap calico; only a little blue silk handkerchief tied about her throat gave the one touch of color to the picture; but Moses never forgot that picture to his dying day.

He looked and looked, with his soul in his eyes, standing as if palsied on the threshold of his mill till a sharp old voice called, "Nelly! Nelly!" and the vision turned, dropped the rod, and sprang down the rock.

He knew that voice very well. Orlando Wood kept the Dorset tavern and dispensed in its dirty, noisy barroom half the misery in the township under the names of cider, brandy and rum. He was a drunken, disreputable old miscreant himself, and despised by Moses in that hearty way that consciously moral and upright people do despise disreputable sinners.

But, for all that, the daisy face and swaying figure haunted the miller all day; he saw it when he inspected the dark and dripping wheel, appearing and disappearing between the buckets; it seemed to hover over the hopper and hide behind the great, upright beams of the mill, and as he jogged up White Mountain the soft gray beech trunks, brocaded with velvety black moss, the tall pine boles reddened by the sinking sun, — all seemed to him possible haunt and shelter for the slight shape that had eluded his gaze so soon when Orlando Wood's sharp voice called her.

"Ay, that's the rub," was the thought of his heart, but he thrust it aside; for once his self-control did evil service to him; when he should have thought he would not think. He gave rather free rein to passion hitherto kept so firmly in hand, and, refusing inwardly to perceive the unfitness of yielding to a moment's fancy, gave himself up to the wild reign of a dream; human nature can master even a Quaker.

Yet whom does it not master?

"Breathes there a man with soul so dead"

that the delirium of primeval love never possessed and overwhelmed, and illuminated him? that he never tasted the divine, uplifting, transforming rapture that in its fresh beginning is the one exponent of heaven to the most earthly soul? Perhaps there is, but that man was not Moses Dyer; all the more for his monotonous past, his denied and restrained life, his full and powerful manhood with all its sternly repressed emotions and longings, did he come under the sway of this sceptre which rules now and forever in " the court, the camp, the grove." Like a mountain torrent which the strong, sweet sun sets free from its winter prison, he swept on toward his goal with a swiftness and power that startled all the neighborhood.

In spite of warning and remonstrance, of advice and entreaty, knowing that he lost caste with all the town in seeking out and adoring the niece of a man like Orlando Wood, and that he would be turned out of meeting in Rutland for marrying one of the world's people, he not only made Nelly Wood's acquaintance, but in one short month thereafter asked her to marry him.

Poor little Nelly! — she was a gentle, silly, loving creature, with small education. An orphan, and almost friendless, she earned her scant living by tending at the counter of a milliner's shop in Boston till her health failed entirely, and in despair she wrote a pitiful letter to her uncle, whom she knew to be a reprobate, but who was, after all, her only kin, asking him to let her come to Dorset and rest. He had let her come, for he was kindly enough when he was sober, and his lazy wife hoped to get a little help about the house, or save the wages of a table-girl. But Nelly found here more than she dreamed of; as wan and frail as any daisy, she found her sun, and both light and life in him. As long as those great gray eyes lifted their dark fringes and looked into his with utter love, as long as the full, languid lips trembled under his kisses, and those clinging arms hung about his bended neck, Moses Dyer did not care the wing of a midge for all the tongues of men or penalties of the church; the earth might have yawned under his feet and the floods poured about him from an angry heaven, if he could clasp that slight shape close to his heart and know that it was his own in life or death.

Yet, to other eyes, to all outward appearance he was even more rigid than ever; there was no observer in Dorset keen enough to interpret the dark, steady flush on his cheek, the deep gleam of his eyes, or the controlled depths of his voice, held in tight leash, lest it should tremble with the passion that possessed him, and betray the sweet madness rioting in his veins. Friend Harding alone refrained from word or sign of remonstrance, though he alone understood even partially the state of things.

"I wouldn't, if I was thee, William, say much to Moses," Susannah had incidentally remarked, when William told her of Moses's infatuation, and what the Meeting in Rutland thought about it, they having asked him to deal with Moses with a view to his restoration.

"Thee knows Moses is strong in spirit, and cleaves to the girl mightily; it is not clear to me that thee can mend the matter. Men-folks are not to be moved like saplings; and the dealings of Providence are, I sometimes think, like the ark of the Lord, which may not be touched by man, even to help."

"I had not designed to speak with him, Susannah; I had no leading to do this business for the Meeting. Thee knows I do not mean to be guided by man; and it is possible that I have a deeper sense of the youth's nature than some have. I surely do not think it is the part of wisdom to hold speech with him on this occasion."

And he looked at his fair old wife with eyes that told, could she have read their language, how ill it would have fared with Meeting or man who had dared to intermeddle with his love for her!

So Moses Dyer, in spite of all the town and all his brethren in the faith, went on triumphantly in his course of true love; and a mortgage falling in about this time on one of the finest farms in Dorset, whose owner had borrowed the money on it to go to California, and died there, making no provision to redeem the property, Moses resolved to build a house on that portion of the land nearest the mill; so before the end of July, when he and Nelly were married, the frame of a stately mansion, for those days and that place, was raised, and the barn in its rear completed in season to house the hay crop.

To say that Moses was happy is a weak phrase; it did not concern him at all that he had to be married by a " hireling ministry," or that the Quaker brethren eyed him with disfavor and the sisters with disgust. He was beyond these things forever; the whole force of his nature, free for the first time, flowed on with abounding exultation through a land goodly as Eden. The very weaknesses and wants of his wife opened strange springs of tenderness within him, a pain of pity and love, a very passion of devotion, that lapped her in a care and indulgence so great and so infinite in detail that she thrived as a rose does, long prisoned in a cellar, when the spring sunshine and the fervent air at last bathe and caress it, and draw forth verdant leaves, abundant buds, and fragrant opening blossoms. Nothing that his hands could do or his money buy failed to be lavished on Nelly; a long kiss, a love-look from those lovely eyes, a happy sigh, more than repaid him; and when in the early winter his house was finished and furnished, by Nelly's experience in observation and his own native taste, with all the soft, bright stuffs and luxurious furniture his purse could command, though, in obedience to his early training, no pictures adorned the tinted walls, and no musical instruments tempted Nelly's little fingers, there was not so pleasant a house in the country as Moses Dyer's.

Pictures, indeed, were needless; the house stood on a slight rise of ground, in the midst of a green field itself high above the road through Dorset, and every window showed a landscape beyond the genius of man to reproduce. White Mountain rose fair and mighty to the east, clothed with foliage to the foot of the great limestone rock on its summit; to the north the picturesque old mill and flashing river met the eye; southward lay the lovely Dorset valley, with Equinox Mountain on the right; and westward the Ledge, an abrupt precipice fringed with cedars, hung over the placid waters of Bright Lake. What more could one ask for the delight of the eye than all this changing loveliness?

So the winter went on for these lovers in a fulness of bliss such as love only knows, a surfeit of happiness that of its own fulness grows precarious in its hold, and Moses began to fear the tender promise of the future, which dropped Nelly's white lids and added a soft pallor to her hitherto blooming face, might be only a blow of fate in store for him. It is the irony of life that our purest bliss frightens us, so weak are we in joy, so distrustful of God, while sorrow arms us with sharp weapons and drives us into the lists.

The first hot days of May came in about its second

week, and ended in a furious thunder-storm; hail rushed down from the lurid cloud that hung over Dorset, though the Mill farm only received the edge of the tempest and escaped the broken windows of the village; but while the rain was at its fiercest a bolt sped from the blackness above, and in one moment Moses Dyer's barn burst into quivering flame. Nelly had hidden her head on his shoulder and his arms were clasped about her when the clap came, and with a stifled shriek she fainted and slipped from his hold to the floor. Little did he care for the howling storm or blazing barn. He laid her gently on the sofa, called Amanda, the hired girl, a stout and faithful Yankee, from the kitchen, and, catching his horse, fortunately for him at pasture in the home lot, he rode right out, through hail and rain, after the Dorset doctor.

"Let it blaze!" he said to hurrying neighbors who met him, on their way to save the barn or see it burn; "my wife's dying!"

Astounded neighbors! Not a man of them all but would have left wife or child at the last gasp to save their own barns. They stared and laughed, and stood about with their hands in their pockets till the last rafter tumbled in. But Nelly was not dying; she had fainted, and the shock had somewhat hastened impending events. Before morning a stout, hearty baby lay in her bosom, and she smiled faintly as Moses bent over her, not at all to see the child, who was an atom in the balance compared with Nelly, but to assure himself that his wife lived and loved still.

Things went on smoothly again, now. Nelly and the baby grew and strengthened daily; soon she was about again, crooning sleep songs to her dark-eyed daughter, the very image of Moses, if, indeed, one could imagine him in long white frock and pink ribbons; making dainty garments for her live doll; waiting for Moses at the window with baby in her arms, or drawing the child about the garden after the dews were dried.

So summer passed; the new barn was filled with hay, two good horses put in the ample stables, and Tulip, the black cow, was munching a forkful of hay, one September day just at twilight, when another storm came hurrying up, and another bolt fell and lit up the new barn with destroying blaze.

This time the loss was heavier far; but Moses could bear it, his worldly goods had increased; and he only thanked God that the house had not been struck, built his new barn on the other side of the rise where it first stood, a good deal lower down, and took up his life where it was before, a daily round of accustomed happiness and prosperity. Summer came again, and in July another child entered this twice-blessed family, this time a boy. Little Love, the dark-eyed baby, had been sent to Dr. Strong's for a while, till Nelly could bear the burden of two babies in the house a little better, and one morning the nurse rose early to make some posset for the child who had cried too much through the night. As she went out from the downstairs bedroom into the hall a low growl of thunder met her ear, and, looking from the window of the kitchen, she saw a low and lurid cloud hanging above the Ledge, — a cloud so peculiar in its greenish darkness that she always remembered it; but Dorset people are used to thunder in summer, and Aunt Nancy went on to make her mess at the kitchen stove where she had kindled a fire, not at all observant of the rapidly rising gloom.

"Is there going to be a storm?" said Nelly, as the nurse came back.

"Looks mighty like it!" said the woman. "I shouldn't wonder if we ketched a smart rain-spell; you know the sayin',—

"'Thunder in the mornin',
Sailors take warnin'!'"

"Oh, dear! just hear that!" said the poor little mother, clasping her baby to her bosom, as a low, deep growl smote the air, heavy and threatening as a menace of battle among the Powers of air.

"Please, Aunt Nancy, go and fetch Moses, I'm so scared with thunder. I guess he's gone to the barn to turn out the stock. I heard him come down before you went into the kitchen."

"Why, you blessed creetur! you aint afeared, be you? I never did! Shan't I set on the bed besides of ye? He'll be in in a miunit!"

"Oh, no! no! *Do* call Moses!" said the trembling, terrified Nelly; "he always comes when I'm scared;" and the good-natured old woman flung a shawl over her head and trotted out to the barn, where Moses had just unfastened the stanchions and driven out the last of his cows; the horses were already flying across the pasture, wild with sudden freedom and the roaring storm.

Moses scarce stayed to shut the door, but hastened toward the house, with the woman at his heels, when a flash of supernal light blazed in their faces, and a simultaneous roar, as if heaven and earth were rent asunder, stunned their ears. Alas! it had severed heaven from earth for Moses Dyer. When, blinded and reeling, he staggered through the house, now full of smoke and hissing with fire, he beheld the blackened corpses of wife and child stretched on their flaming bed, and fell senseless. If the nurse had not followed closely, and been a gaunt and powerful woman, he would have perished with them; but, in the strength of desperation, she pulled him out of a near door into the yard, and the man at the mill came hurrying and breathless in time to help her place him out of reach of the falling timbers. When Moses Dyer awoke from that long unconsciousness, wife, child, house, were all in ashes. For weeks and months he was incapable of business; his heart was broken as far as a strong man's heart can be. That full and rapturous life that had satisfied his soul was suddenly ended; he stood like a man who sees the verdurous and waving mountain-side open at his feet and thunder into the valley, leaving him alone on the edge of a precipice whose front is ruin, whose outlook despair.

It was a long year before he could do anything at the mill; happily for him he had a trustworthy man there, who could supervise the business and, with a little help, carry it on. Moses, from sheer force of habit, fed his "creatures," slept in his barn on the old hay, took his rare meals at the village tavern, and never went near his child, who seemed to be forgotten. Dr. Strong's wife, however, was glad to shelter the little creature, knowing well that time would awaken her father's affection at last, knowing, also, that he was incapable now of caring for such a mere baby.

But time went on, and all that seemed to interest

Moses Dyer was his daily pacing about the ruins of his home; so complete had been the consuming power of the flames that not a trace of the mother or child had remained; a heap of ashes only lay in that crumbling cellar, and these he had gathered reverently and with his own hands into a coffin, and buried beside the green mounds where his parents lay. Gloomy, dark, speechless, he went his way, and the first thing that aroused him was a whisper in the village, he overheard accidentally, to the effect that his house was doomed. This curled his lip with a sneer. Moses Dyer did not believe in fate; in all his woful trouble he still believed that God sent it, but he was furiously angry with him for the infliction.

He had been somewhat roused by the scorn the village belief awakened in him, when the Meeting in Rutland thought fit to send one of the brethren to deal with him, to restore him if possible, but at any rate to strive with him for his good.

Barzillai Guest accordingly sought him out one wintry morning in the second November after Nelly's death, and, being a simple, conceited, moderate sort of man, delivered to the silent Moses quite a little address on his sin in marrying out of Meeting, and the evident judgment of God for such sin displayed in the repeated strokes he had experienced; ending with what Barzillai thought an affecting appeal to him to repent and return into the arms of Meeting again.

Moses Dyer's face blackened ominously.

"Stop right there! Friend Guest," he said. "Thee has said a plenty. Shall I repent that I married my wife? Not if the heavens fall upon me now and here! If, as thee says, it is a judgment upon me that fire came down and consumed my life, it is well: does thee think I put faith in any God who so judged me for loving my wife? If it is the voice of the Meeting that I have been a sinner above all other sinners, then I hold no longer with Meeting. Thee says I am judged; the fools in the village say my house was doomed. Does thee know I have got a living child — money in the bank — and a goodly farm? Thee can go back to Meeting, and say I do not repent of my life. I did well to love my wife. I do well to be angry with that Power which blasted my life. And while life lasts, such as it is, I will never hold with men that suffer such talk. I had rather be of this world, since thee believes the next is so hard upon me. I will build my house over again, and fetch my child back, and till my ground till it be time to die."

Friend Guest reported Moses Dyer to be a hardened and irreclaimable brother, and the Meeting meddled with him no more. He was as good as his word, and before another year was over a new house, as like the first in every detail as his memory could reproduce it, rose in place of the other; but long before it could be furnished, even while the plaster was wet on the walls, another bolt pierced the roof and floors; but, owing to the heavy rain and the open condition of the building, that admitted it freely as it drove through unglazed windows and gaping door-frames, the boards were only shattered and scorched, and with grim resolution Moses had them replaced and went on to complete the structure.

In vain the carpenters remonstrated.

"Do you think the lightnin' strikes three times in one spot? Go on with your work, the risk is mine. I take it!" he answered, words long remembered in Dorset.

However the house was safely finished, and when it was ready for habitation Moses chose for his own occupation the lower bedroom, and recalled his child, a rosy, grave, intelligent little maid of four. It was difficult to get a house-keeper, for everybody in Dorset knew the Dyer place was doomed, and no woman from the village would think of living there; but at last Moses found a widow in Rutland, who came the more willingly because she was poor, and not strong enough for factory work or sewing.

For two or three years there was peace in the new house, if not happiness. Time had its healing effect on Moses Dyer, as it has on all of us; he even took a sort of grievous pleasure when he shut the bedroom door on himself at night in recalling the gentle creature who dwelt in that room before. He longed with the awful hunger of loss for one touch of her lips, one look from her tender eyes; and, so far from being terrified at the idea of her returning spirit, he would have given his life to have even her phantom semblance hovering about his pillow. The only sign of weakness he showed was his extreme nervous excitement in thunder-storms, a thing not to be wondered at after his past experience; for other people still felt an unwillingness to take shelter in the Dyer house during such storms, however drenched they might become before reaching the village. It was only after three years had elapsed with no accident of the sort that Lemuel Hough, who was the mill man, consented to board at Moses Dyer's, though Moses himself urged it, not only as a matter of economy, but with an unconfessed feeling of anxiety lest something should again happen and he be helpless as before.

Love was eight years old, and had grown to be the only dear thing on earth to her father, and Lem had lived in the house about a year, when, one October night, after a day sultry as in August, a violent storm came up suddenly while all the inmates of the Dyer house were sound asleep. Love was upstairs in a room next to Hannah Smith's; Lem in the back-chamber, whose window opened out on a shed roof, and Moses, as usual, downstairs. A simultaneous crack and blaze aroused them, and smoke rapidly filled the house. Lemuel, who was a cool-headed Yankee, hurried the woman and child through his room on to the shed-roof, from which they easily slipped to the ground, and, driven by terror, made their way to the mill-shed.

Once having disposed of them Lemuel went round outside to the bedroom door, and knocked it inward with a heavy beetle fetched from the wood-house. A ghastly vision met his eyes there: Moses Dyer sat upright in his bed, staring straight before him; the partition opposite burst into licking tongues of flame as the fallen door admitted air, and the suffocating smoke rolled outward. Lemuel seized the stricken man by the shoulders and dragged him from the bed, helpless as a child of days, right out into the pouring rain; it was not till his suspended senses returned that it was discovered he was a helpless cripple, both legs paralyzed by the bolt that had fired the house. The red light of the fire called out all Dorset to help, but help was in vain; as the angry tempest rolled away its black hosts to the southward, and the tranquil hunter's moon rose fair and still above the crest of White Mountain, her light shone on a heap of smoking ruins, a helpless, hopeless man, and a frightened child clinging, sobbing, to his neck.

The villagers looked at one another with wise eyes and nodding heads.

"I told you so!" mumbled old Aunt Nancy. "I wouldn't ha' gone there to live for half Dorset. My sakes! he wanted me to, the wust kind; but money wouldn't count for that puppus. It's a doomed house if ever there was one, and I guess he'll have to own up to't now, whether or no!"

But it was a long time before Dorset people arrived at Moses Dyer's thought on this matter. He was now in a condition that reversed all his former life and experience; in one instant from the full strength of unusually vigorous manhood he had become helpless as a feeble old man. The shock to his whole system had been severe, and for weeks he lay on his bed unable to lift his hands or his head. Gradually strength came back so far that he could sit up and be moved into a chair; but the best medical advice in the country, called to his aid by Dr. Strong, who was determined to spare nothing in his behalf, pronounced the paralysis of his lower limbs hopeless; he might live for years, but he would never walk again.

Think what a doom this was to a man in the prime of his life, accustomed to be in the open air constantly, striding abroad over his possessions, or riding up and down the wild mountain roads enjoying every aspect of nature, every draught of the keen, pure air that filled him with fresh life! Now he was to pass his lingering existence under a roof between four walls; his proud and independent spirit bent in bitter humiliation, his purposes broken off, the only staff left to him the love of a child.

At this juncture Friend Harding, who had hitherto kept silence toward Moses, though his heart ached with compassionate pity over all his trials, stepped forward to help. He possessed one of those great, old-fashioned houses once common in New England, with four rooms on a floor, a wide hall running between them both above and below stairs, and making so complete a separation that often two families inhabit now where one alone formerly lived. It was Susannah who planned, and William who proposed, that Moses Dyer should hire half their house, which would accommodate him well with Love and Hannah.

Moses considered the proposal with dim eyes; he had been carried to the tavern when he was first pulled from his bed, and the low, dirty rooms, the noise, the vulgar guests who alone came to the old place, made it unpleasant for him and unfit for Love. At last, as William Harding sat waiting for an answer, a grim smile flickered across Moses Dyer's face.

"Isn't thee afraid the lightning will follow me, Friend Harding?" he said.

"No," answered William, steadily. "I do not so apprehend the dealings of the Lord. I think he is one who loveth mercy rather than judgment. If thee has sinned, other men also have done the like. 'Suppose ye that these Galileans were sinners above all Galileans, because they suffered such things?' I know not why thy house was so stricken. 'Lo, these are parts of his ways,' only; I can trust him to do right, Moses. I think thee will in time."

Moses lay back on his pillow with a groan. Would it ever seem to him right that he was bereaved and crippled?

He did not, however, dispute the matter with Friend Harding; the man's calm trust gave even Moses Dyer a sort of awe; but he did accept the kindly offer of house-room, and was glad to divert Love from her sad contemplation of his helplessness by sending her to Rutland with Susannah Harding to make purchases of furniture for the new dwelling; for, though his house was burnt, he was still a rich man, and the mill ground away as merrily as ever under Lemuel's charge. So it came about that the next ten years of Love's life and Moses Dyer's existence were spent under the roof of William Harding, and with Susannah's gentle guidance, added to such education as the village academy afforded, Love Dyer grew up into a beautiful, stately girl, adding to her mother's grace her father's deep coloring and abundant health. Her thick, soft hair crowned a shapely head with rich plaits; her great, dark eyes, grave as her father's, were far sweeter than his had ever been, and could flash from their dusky depths with fun as his had never done; her lips were full and red, and under her clear, olive skin shone a crimson color that told of native vigor and a strong constitution. The young men in Dorset had already found out what a beauty dwelt among them; but Moses Dyer was as jealous of his solitary possession as any father could be, and his post was always at the front window, where he could watch the village street and see if any man dared to attend Love's walks or come to call on her. Ten years had not materially altered his nature; he had grown outwardly more patient, for habit is strong in us, and the things that are inevitable have to be accepted. In his helplessness he had begun to take a sort of morbid pride; he dwelt in thought much on the fact, at last obvious even to him, that he was a sort of moral target for the arrows of the Almighty. It was a kind of balm to his pride to think he had been so singled out from his fellows by a divine hand; a certificate of weight to his own character that it should need such special visitations to be amended. He took to reading the Bible, as we most of us read it,— to find his peculiar case either depicted or provided for,— and in the Old Testament found ample vindications of his theory. He was almost gratified to have strangers in Dorset brought by the house where he now lived, and to see that he was pointed out to them as the hero of a spiritual tragedy. The burnt house on the farm had never been rebuilt; the barn had gone with it; the home-lot was a wilderness of unpruned trees and neglected grass, and the garden a tangle of half-dead roses, clambering briers, tall, rank yellow lilies and straggling peonies. The farm he sold soon after he became unable to manage it, but no one would buy the house-site and the three acres about it; it was known all through Dorset as the Doomed House, and not a man in the township would have taken it for a gift if a palace had been erected there, and the gift been conditioned with its use as a residence.

His life from day to day had only the alleviations of this conscious dignity and the affection which Love showered upon him. She superintended his comfort in every way; read to him, sang to him, waited on him, and sat at his bedside every night till he slept; for his nervous system seemed to have been startled into abnormal vivacity of action by the very shock that paralyzed him physically. Under the sweet influences of Susannah Harding, Love had grown to be lovely as well as beautiful; she was like life and breath to her father; her tender voice, her deft fingers, her loving eyes, were all that fate had left him. He who had so loved every trick and tracery of nature was shut in now to the space of four walls, the outlook of a village street; but it may be that he was in reality more content than ever before; his sense of personal dignity was increased rather than diminished, and a certain regal consciousness attached itself to his isolation and its one ministering spirit.

However, Moses Dyer had not yet learned his lesson. When Love was about eighteen Lemuel Hough took it into his head to emigrate to California, and among the candidates for his place in the mill there appeared a far-away cousin of the Dyer tribe, from Connecticut, Daniel Dyer, a young fellow of the best Yankee type. Cool-headed, energetic, cheerful, with a certain audacity that gave force to his energy, he was one of those people who never expect to fail, and, for that very reason, always succeed. His honest, resolute face, not quite handsome, yet what all Dorset called " good-looking," prepossessed Moses Dyer in his favor; those keen, gray eyes were hawk-like in their outlook, and the crisp, light curls above them gave a sort of character to the square forehead, that might have been too solid but for this ornamentation, which meant quick temper, and implied fire behind the machine.

Moses Dyer was not a physiognomist, consciously, but he could give no better reason for selecting this man to run his mill than that he liked his looks.

Others had as good recommendations; some he knew from childhood; but he "took" to Dan Dyer at once, and when Lemuel Hough went away from Dorset he left behind him a substitute whom men allowed very soon more than filled his place.

Everybody liked the new-comer; he had a kind word, a hearty greeting, a joke for everybody. He was as eager at his work as a boy at play, but equally ready for play in its time. Nobody could husk as much corn or pare as many apples at bees as Dan Dyer, and nobody could tell such funny stories. He sang a fine tenor, and installed himself in the village choir at once, becoming its chorister before the year was out, and drilling that somewhat idle and desultory group of singers into the best choir of the county. He skated as if skates had grown on his feet from his birth, and fished great trout out of brooks in which nobody else had ever discovered a fin of that sort; and, above all, he made some wonderful improvement in the mill machinery that brought him into frequent association with the mill-owner, and crowned all his well-doing with one great folly; for the poor fellow fell over head and ears in love with Love Dyer!

And Love, brought for the first time into contact with a nature at once sunny, fearless, and victorious, — what other result could be expected than that she should strike her colors directly?

Her education had been such as to make her simple in heart and life, with that simplicity Fenelon paints and praises; she had lived under the shadow of a cloud all her days, and here was pure sunshine; why should she not open her heart to it? Dan Dyer came and went day after day, in and out of Moses Dyer's room, talking of cogs and bands and bolt-cloths, of wheels and buckets, beams to be renewed, floors to repair, trap-doors to be put here and a shoot to be built there; but all the time he talked he saw Love's soft, dark eyes and beautiful face instead of her father's grim visage and gray locks, and she sat by in breathless interest. If he had talked of Sanscrit verbs or Hebrew points it would have interested her as much, for his voice had a speech of its own older than the confusion of tongues, and his face a legend open as the stars in heaven. Yet it was a great while before Moses Dyer's eyes were opened to the fact which every woman in Dorset knew long ago; which Love's mother, had she lived, would have known before the lovers knew it; but, to Moses Dyer, Love was still a child, and his wrath was full of contempt when Hannah, with the conscious smirk of a willing gossip, hinted one day, when Love had gone out, "That there Dan Dyer sets a heap by Lovey, don't he?"

"Thee is a fool, Hannah!" sharply answered Moses, his face darkening as he spoke.

"Be I?" she snapped back; "then Dorset's full on 'em; everybody's a-snickerin' 'n' a-gigglin' about it, all over. I should ha' thought your eyes would ha' seen what was right afore 'em. I shouldn't ha' peeped nor muttered about it if I hedn't supposed you was privy to't quite a spell back."

"What does thee mean, woman? Can't thee curb thy silly tongue better than this? Love is a child; does thee think a grown man, with his head full of wheels and such like, has it turned after little girls?" And yet as he spoke he remembered how long he had watched Love's comings and goings from his front window lest some such catastrophe should happen.

"Well, I don't call nineteen year old no child's age!" sniffed Hannah. "Fust you know you'll lose her slap off,' n' then I guess you'll sorter figger up better on folkses age!"

Moses Dyer groaned; he was inwardly furious, and now that his eyes were opened a thousand tiny recollections pressed upon him, driving the unwelcome truth home. Why had Dan come in so unnecessarily often to consult him on the most trivial matters? Why had Love always stayed by and seemed so interested in the mill business? How she lingered of late in her daily walks, and brought home ferns, mosses, and berries, that grew only on the river edges! Well, he would put an end to it at once; that was all. Dan was coming up to-night; there were plain words enough in the English language, and he would not spare them. But to Love when she came in, blooming, yet pensive, her hands full of the pink arbutus blossoms that grew so rosy only on that pine-shaded bank just below the mill, he said nothing, only just before Dan appeared he asked her gently to go in and sit a while with Susannah, for he had private business that evening with a visitor.

Dan came in whistling, his face alight and his heart buoyant; but Moses was like a black bar of thundercloud. Scarcely was the guest seated before his host accused him in no measured terms of coming there on false pretences, to ensnare his daughter's heart and beguile her away.

"You think I come here like a sneak, do you?" retorted Dan, his eyes glowing; "you know better than that, Moses Dyer! You know I've had reg'lar business every time; if you say to the contrary, why, then you say what aint so. As for your girl"—and here his voice fell—"I don't deny but what I think a heap of her; why shouldn't I? She's as han'some as a picture and as good as gold! Why shouldn't I like her? Wa'n't you never young yourself?"

Moses put out his hand to check him, for he could not speak; there rose up before him that rock by the river-side, the fair, young face, the glittering hair, and then the short years of rapture; it almost seemed to him for a moment that those clinging arms were about his neck once more, those fragrant lips pressed to his, those tender eyes looking up to him as a bird from its nest looks to the sky. His face darkened with emotion. Dan saw his opportunity and went on:—

"Yes, I do love her; more'n tongue can tell, I love her. If I aint good enough for her I know it jest as well as you do, but I don't know anybody that is; and I expect I love her enough to make up the goodness that's wanting. I haven't never spoke one word to her about the matter, for I wa'n't ready to, not yet. But I tell you, Squire Dyer, I mean to marry her, whether or no!"

There was something about Dan's very frank speech that touched a kindred chord in the old man; this determination was an echo of his own nature, yet all the more for that it enraged him.

"Thee is a presumptuous fool, Daniel Dyer!" he answered. "Does thee think nothing of taking my girl into poverty,—she that has known no want of this world's goods in all her life?"

"Squire, I aint one of the poor sort! I own up that

I haint got no great of cash in hand now, but I've got my health, and I'm strong, and I aint no fool, if you do say so; but I'm willing to overlook that, for I see you're riled a mite. No, sir! If I live, I'll be the best-off man in Dorset, and if Love is willing to take me she won't ever want for a thing, I say for't!"

Moses Dyer began to feel cowed by this persistent audacity; he fell back on his rights.

"Thee does not know my daughter; she is a dutiful child. Thee could not persuade her to leave her father contrary to his wish."

"I don't know about that, Squire Dyer. Women-folks are kind of queer; they'll mostly foller their inclinations, I've observed." There was an exasperating truth in this statement that crushed Moses.

"What does thee want to come here and take her away for?" he cried, in sudden grief,— "all that is left to me, a man doomed to suffer from the arrows of the Almighty? Does thee think I will spare my ewe-lamb to such as thee?"

"I wouldn't take her away from you for nothing," generously exclaimed Dan. "You *have* had a lot of affliction, and you aint like to be any smarter nor any chircker than you be now; rather the contrary, I expect; and I'd take care of you myself as good as she can. I'd be helpful as though I belonged to you, Squire. You'd get a son and you wouldn't lose your daughter."

Sublime egotism of youth and passion! But it had no sublime effect on Moses Dyer. Trembling with passion he leaned forward in his chair.

"Look here, young man," he said, in a broken voice; "thee drives me to the edge. Love Dyer shall never marry thee till thee can give her a good home and twenty thousand dollars in the bank. Thee has got no feelings I can move. I shall try the facts of filthy lucre; may be thy pocket will comprehend. I will drive the girl out from before my face to starve if she dares to marry thee before I say Amen. Yea, I will curse her as the Lord hath cursed me for my sin!"

Dan looked at the old man steadily. "I'll take you up at that, Squire Dyer. I'll engage, swear to't if you say so, never to ask her till I've got that amount."

Moses Dyer stared. Was this fellow crazy? At any rate, in or out of his senses, the agreement would keep him away from Love; so they struck hands on it, and from that time on Dan's visits ceased at the Harding house, and though Love's fresh color paled, her eyes grew sad, and her voice plaintive rather than gay, with the bitter selfishness of age and his nature Moses Dyer did not relent. He would not spare Love to her lover, for her own pleasure or peace, because he wanted her care, her tendance, her affection, all for himself!

Hannah, in the next room, had overheard all this interview, and her tongue was never tied. Dorset people were soon possessed of the situation, and with one accord pitied the lovers and blamed the cruel father; but pity did not console Love, and Dan's brain seemed to be suddenly turned, for early the next autumn it was declared by the wise ones of the town that he had bought the old ruins of the Dyer house, the home-lot, and all of the farm, about ten acres, lying between the house and the mill.

Nobody believed it at first, for that land had been a drug in the market, owing to its past history as well as to the fact that more than once since the last catastrophe somebody or other had seen lightning strike on that knoll, though nothing stood there capable of injury. But examination of recent records showed the tale to be true; the land had sold for a song, or at least for a note, and that only two hundred dollars; and soon Dan left the mill, hired a man to help him, and began to clear out the cellar of its rubbish. Even Moses Dyer was full of astonishment and a sort of horror; it seemed to him he ought to warn any man who tried to rebuild that house of its doom and its past experience; but he knew Dan must be aware of this, and as days went on and no frame was set up, but certain strange men with little bags and small hammers came to Dorset, visited that cellar, and went away smiling, Dorset people were more and more perplexed. Before winter set in Dan had put up a shanty in the home-lot, and heaps of earth, like the preparations for a railway embankment, lay piled all about the old cellar. The mystery leaked out at last. Under the Dyer house had lain a mine of the best sort of iron; wide and deep, it had attracted the electric fluid with compelling force, and the shrewd sense of one Yankee, who, looking at the events which other people called Fate, had used his reason, had found only a propitious Fact.

Certain capitalists were found ready and willing to help Dan Dyer forward in his work of mining and smelting, for the ore was extremely valuable, and instead of lying in a " pocket," as much of the Vermont ore does, proved to be a solid vein. A great furnace was erected on the river bank, and lit up the water with savage glow by night, sending wreaths of smoke into the keen air by day, and Dan Dyer ruled over the fiery confusion within, exultant and happy; for before him lay a near prospect of the house and money that should qualify him for Moses Dyer's daughter, and Love's shy eyes had long ago given him all the encouragement eyes can give.

But Moses Dyer underwent a strange inward experience. Here was the mystic doom which had set him apart from and above his fellows reduced to a simple matter of mineralogy. He thought it was Providence, and it proved to be iron! The visitation of God had not humbled him when he accepted it as a visitation; but the facts of nature did. The throne of his spiritual pride was abased forever, and he was only a man like other men; rather less than other men, in that he had not seen for himself the open fact that electricity is not the wrath of God, but the law of nature; that lightning does not strike over and over in one place without a reason any more than water flows uphill. He was helpless, useless, bereaved, from his own fault, his defiant pride; and, as he brooded day after day over this new insight into his Maker and himself, he was forced to put his hand on his mouth and his mouth in the dust, recognizing at last the Father, who does not willingly afflict nor grieve us, but in wisdom, as well as mercy, lets us find out for ourselves how good he is, how weak and vain we are.

The heart of Moses Dyer melted within him and became as the heart of a little child. He sent for Dan, and acknowledged his selfishness and his sin.

"If thee loves the child, Daniel," he said, "I will not forbid thee to strive after her affections. I have been a self-seeker, but the Lord hath opened my eyes."

Dan's honest face changed and his keen eyes dropped as he grasped the old man's hand.

"I don't know what to say, Squire!" he answered. "You're everlastin' clever to me. I do expect to make consider'ble more than twenty thousand out of that mine, fust and last; but it'll be quite a while before I fetch it, and I don't think a man's good for shucks without a wife and a home. Besides, there's Love to ask yet; mabbe at the last she won't have me. But I can try; there's never any harm in trying. As for the mine, I kinder suspected there was a wherefore to the why about those thunder-bolts, so I figured on't. I haint any faith in 'doom.' I b'lieve in the Lord, of course; but I don't think he goes about pitchin' into folks with lightnin' to convert 'em. I guess he's converted you quite recent, and without strikin' of you, neither. When it comes to talkin' about doom I'd rather b'lieve in Dan. It works a heap better!"

And Dan's brief creed has certainly vindicated itself, for to-day a fair white house stands on the slope of the hills just out of Dorset, and old Moses Dyer, looking from its sunny windows down on the farm and the furnace with a face peaceful as the autumnal skies above the Ledge, is waited on and caressed by a trio of small Dyers, and guarded from their somewhat rampant affections by a gentle, beautiful woman, who is now and forever Dan Dyer's Love.

SOME ACCOUNT OF THOMAS TUCKER.

"Whom now seekinge, O Diogenes! have I found: ye Sunne's shine Beinge more Discoverable untoe that whiche is Sunne-like, than Thy poore Blinkinge Lanthorne."
— *Marriages of Ye Deade.*

AMASA TUCKER and his wife lived on a lonely farm in Vermont, remote from villages or neighbors. Amasa's work was that hardest of all work, forcing from rocky and reluctant fields enough produce to feed and clothe his family; to do more, with the most strenuous exertion, was impossible, and he did not expect it. To him life was a brief and bitter pilgrimage toward heaven. If it had amenities, they were snares; its pleasures were unknown to him. Rugged, stern, hard as the granite rocks beneath the sward he tilled, he found no consolations in the outer world, on which he walked as they that have eyes and see not, ears and hear not, nor even human interests to cloud their awed and reverent look into the world which is to come. Alone in his arid fields, Amasa Tucker revolved within himself the vast problems of theology, — free-will, election, infant damnation, the origin of evil, and like dogmas; for to such thoughts had he been trained from childhood by the widowed mother who owned and inhabited this solitary mountain farm. Duty was ground into the very bone and sinew of his life. He walked always between a dreadful hell and an awful heaven, set aside from the ordinary temptations of life, and taught to believe that every leaning toward transgression was the whisper of an omnipresent devil, eager to enlist him in his own service; and learning to feel that untruth, disobedience, a thought he could not utter to his mother, or a wish that could not be uplifted to God, were crimes of fatal and total depravity.

He ploughed the brown sod of the sad New England hills under the full force of the primeval curse; uncomplaining, because Adam had sinned for him, and he must bear the doom; and unquestioning, because Job, under a worse pressure of suffering, had taught him that he who challenges the will of God does so in vain.

He saw the sun rise above the purple mountains, and wheel its splendid way through the sky, life-giving and wonderful, with only a sombre thought of that impending day when the sun shall be turned into darkness and the moon into blood, for which it behooved him to be ready and waiting. The melancholy glory of the moon and the keen sparkle of the starry heavens gave him no joy: their story was alone of that creative and judging Lord who should roll them away as a scroll. To him the fear of God was not only the beginning of wisdom, but its course and end; the perfect love that casteth out fear was strange to him as heaven; he knew not its soft steppings about him, nor its clear shining in the beauty that beset his path. He lived only to prepare for death, and to see that his kindred followed in that straight way.

Philura, whom he had married from a sense of the fitness of things, was a meek, spiritless creature, with no sentiment and little feeling; always conscious that she was an unprofitable servant, afraid to love her children lest it should be idolatry, and struck with as keen a pang as her slender nature could know, if her butter was streaky or her cheese crumbled.

She considered her husband lord and head, after the old-fashioned Scriptural order, and listened to his daily prayers with deep reverence for such striking piety, though she knew very well that Amasa was a hard man, gathering where he had not strewed, and reaping where he had not sown, and a tyrant where a man can be tyrannical in safety, — in his own home.

Two children out of ten survived to this pair. Abundant dosing, insufficient food, and a neglected sink-drain had killed all the others who outlived their earliest infancy; but these two evaded the doom that had fallen on their brothers and sisters, by the fate which modern science calls the survival of the fittest, and spindled up among the mullein-stalks of their stone-strewn pastures as gray, lank, dry, and forlorn as the mulleins themselves; with pale eyes, straight white hair, sallow faces, and the shy aspect of creatures who live in the woods, and are startled at a strange footstep.

They were taught to work as soon as they could walk, to consider sin and holiness the only things worth consideration, to attend meeting as a necessity, and take deserved punishment in silence. To obedience and endurance their physical training, or want of training, conduced also; alternate pie and pork are not an enlivening diet to soul or body, and play was an unknown factor in their dreary existence. Keziah grew up a repetition of her mother, — dull, simple, and dutiful; but Thomas, from the moment he entered the little red school-house, two miles away, to complete the education which his father had begun by the evening fire at home, showed a hunger for books and knowledge that amounted to a passion.

Not a particle did he care for the girls who laughed at him, or the boys who tried to torment him. His soul was filled with the joy of the born student, to whom every fresh study is a rapture that never palls, every new book a possession outvaluing gold; to whom the daily needs and pangs of life are as a tale that is told.

It was but a very little while before Thomas knew all his teacher could impart, far better than the teacher herself knew it; but his thirst was scarcely appeased. He longed for ampler opportunity, for better instruction, as earnestly as Amasa longed for the kingdom of heaven, and at last plucked up shamefaced courage enough to beg his father that he might go to the academy at Bantam, ten miles down the valley.

If one of his oxen had made a like request Amasa Tucker could not have been more astounded. What his boy could want with more education than sufficed himself was past his imagining. To farm an upland in Vermont, after the hereditary fashion of those lonely hills, did not seem to him to require any special science. Hard work, perpetual battle with the elements and the soil, primarily doomed to bear thorns and thistles, — surely this could be carried on with no higher education!

Yet, though he neither answered the boy's request nor the entreating look in his eyes, his inmost heart softened with pride in his son. No genuine New Englander ever despises a desire for knowledge, or sneers at learning without an inward feeling of having been profane; and Amasa Tucker was a typical New Englander of the old sort, now so fast passing away.

When Thomas turned back to his work, in that habit of dumb obedience which is stronger than nature, he did not know that he had dropped into his father's mind a seed that would take root and grow as surely as the corn he had just dropped into the furrow, or that the harvest of its planting would be for him; and it was not till that corn had sprouted, grown to rustling, glittering blades, tasselled out, ripened, been husked, and heaped in shining golden ears in the corn-house, till the apples were brought in to their long bins, and purple-streaked turnips and yellow carrots stored in the barn-cellar, that the boy knew how this other grain had at last come to the full ear.

One Saturday night, as they put the last cow into the stanchions after milking was done, his father said grimly: —

"Thomas, ef you want more edication than what you have had, and can pay your way to go to Bantam 'cademy this winter, why, I'll give ye your time."

Thomas was not demonstrative; the dark blood rushed up to his face, and it seemed to him as if the sudden joy seized him by the throat; but he only answered, "I'll try."

So the next week he walked down to Bantam, applied at once to Parson Lathrop for advice, and, arriving at the nick of time, when Semanthy Pratt, the parson's old house-keeper, was threatened with her annual attack of "rheumatiz," he was taken at once into the minister's house to "do chores" for his board. His schooling was free, since he lived in the county of which Bantam was the shire town; for Parsons

Academy was an endowed school, and only pupils from other counties paid for instruction; and there were many such, for the school had a wide reputation.

Perhaps Thomas was not the best chore-boy in the world. Absorbed in pure mathematics, Greek roots, or the proportions and problems of chemistry, he too often forgot the kindlings, or neglected to comb and curry the old white horse. But then he never went out nights; no husking, or apple-bee, or quilting frolic, no sleigh-ride or turkey-shoot, tempted him from his beloved books.

If anybody complained of him it was Semanthy, who declared to her cronies, "Well, he's good enough, for 't I know. He don't find fault with his vittles, nor yet he don't set by 'em no great. He's as big a dreamer as Joseph in the Bible. I don't more'n half believe he knows what he doos eat. But land! he aint no company; you might as well set down along of a rake-tail, an' try to visit with it; he's dumber'n a dumb critter, for they do make a sound. I say, mabbe, 'Come, Thomas, you fetch me in a pail o' water, real spry; and take that air squash off 'n the hooks, and get me a piggin o' soft soap down sullar." Well, he'll lay down his book, and fetch them things slow as molasses,— not a peep nor mutter,— and smack right to ag'in at that book o' hisn, and peg away at it till bed-time. I do mistrust he takes it to bed along with him; he would ef I'd let him have a taller dip! I'd jest as lives have old Bose around, as fur as talkin' goes; p'r'aps ruther, for he does wag his tail real knowin', jest as though he'd speak ef he could; but Thomas, he wouldn't ef he could, now I tell ye!"

Parson Lathrop grew interested in the lad, because

he was such a student, for there was nothing lovable about Thomas. His aspect was more ungainly than ever, since age had added to his height without rounding or filling out his lank and angular figure; and by long study in imperfect light — for Semanthy's " taller dips " served for little more than to show the darkness — he had become very near-sighted, winking and blinking like an owl when he looked away from his book, and wearing the perpetual anxious frown of imperfect vision. In the summer he returned to his work on the farm, more dull than ever to the outer world's beauty and joy. One thing alone possessed his soul, — an eager longing for winter and his return to the precious opportunities of Bantam; regardless entirely of Semanthy's scorn, the laughter of his companions, or any lack or discomfort in his daily existence, if he could resume the study that was his delight and life. Before the second winter was over, Parson Lathrop, observing the boy as he had done from day to day, made up his mind as to Thomas's vocation, and determined to come up to his aid in fulfilling so marked and earnest a call. So one day he had the old white horse put into the high-backed sleigh, bundled himself up in his fox-skin coat, put in a hot brick to set his feet upon, tied his otter cap close about his ears, drew on his double-knit mittens, and, tucking a big buffalo robe closely about him, set off for the Tucker farm.

It is a great strain on a man's benevolence to drive an old horse ten miles of an uphill country road, with the thermometer below zero; but Parson Lathrop was one of the uncanonized saints who used to glorify the waste places of New England, and of whom the world was not worthy. It was enough for him that he was about his Master's work; in that, he did not consider himself or his inconveniences.

It was "borne in upon his mind," as he phrased it, that Thomas Tucker's devotion to study was an open indication of Providence concerning his future career, and therefore he must talk with his father about it. Amasa had met the parson now and then, when business took him to Bantam, so they were not strangers. He laid down the axe with which he was chopping wood when the parson drove into the yard, and went out to meet him. A man of softer nature and less faith might have feared that this visit meant some harm had happened to his boy, but Amasa's soul was firm in a confidence that was half nature and half grace; he was not afraid.

"'Mazin' cold weather, Parson Lathrop," was his greeting; and after hospitably stabling the old horse he followed the minister into the house, where, before the blazing kitchen fire, and over a mighty mug of steaming flip, still hissing from its hot guest the poker, the two "reasoned high" as the recalcitrant spirits of hell, and on the same themes, until the parson, at last, wearied of mystic theological doctrine, and came to the point of his errand. He set down the blue and yellow mug, and opened the subject abruptly: "Well, Brother Tucker, I came up especially to say to you that I believe your son Thomas hath a call to minister in divine things."

"I dono!" said Amasa. Thomas was as yet his boy; he could not look upon him in any other light without further experience.

"I think it is even so," went on the parson. "He is like Samuel of old in that he was early called; I have found him a close walker, strict in attention to ordinances, well grounded in Scripture; not given to foolishness, such as youths are too apt to seek after, but one that studies to be quiet. And such a lover of knowledge, such a hungerer after learning, I have scarce ever met with."

"Well, Parson Lathrop, I should as lieves take your judgment as any man's. I had calc'lated on Thomas's keepin' right along here, and cultivatin' the airth in the sweat of his brow, same as I do, and his grandsir' did afore me. I don't wan't to stand in the way of he's got a call to the ministry, though. I wouldn't hold him back from the Lord's work, no way; but yet I aint clear in my mind, I'm free to confess, how to fetch it. This farm has gi'n me and mine a livin', no more; it's 'sows, an' grows, and goes,' as the sayin' is; but I have striv' always, havin' food and raiment, therewith to be content, but I haint laid up a cent, nor I aint in debt nuther. I didn't rightly know how to spare Thomas to the 'cademy; I couldn't, only that he paid his way; and I don't know how he can get through college. Seems as though there was a lion in the path, don't there?"

"I foresaw this, Brother Tucker," answered the parson, gently. "It has been a trial to me that in that day I cannot say to the Master, 'Lo, here am I, and the children that thou gavest me.' I have a silent house. My beloved wife was under a weary dispensation of bodily ailment all her days, and it pleased the Lord to deny us offspring. It was the last drop in her bitter cup of suffering that she had to leave me, humanly speaking, alone; and I have always purposed to use the small portion of earthly riches she left behind her for the good of those who had the blessing I wanted, and needed the gifts I had. If so be you can spare Thomas, I will help him to his desired education; not so that he shall cease from self-help,— I would not have him weighted with a sense of utter dependence. I propose to have him teach a school when his academic course is over, and remain with me till I can fit him for college myself. He will have laid up something then, and can further teach in vacations. I will see that his funds do not come short. All this if you consent."

Amasa pushed back his chair with a sharp, creaking scrape, his face set, his eyes cold and stern as ever. The most acute observer could not have seen one softening quiver, one tremulous line, to indicate gratitude or assent; yet the heart within him glowed, chill and rayless as it seemed. "I'm obleeged to ye," he said at last, in the dryest fashion, tilting his chair back against the wall and clearing his throat, as if that said all. But Parson Lathrop knew the man and the race; nor was he himself one of those uneasy souls who exact their pound of effusive gratitude for every ounce of good expended on their fellows. His left hand did not know nor inquire what his right hand did, nor even shake that comrade palm in self-congratulation. He had obtained the father's consent to take care of Thomas; now he would go home and do it. So, with a kindly farewell, the good man replaced his wraps, and took his way down the mountain, meditating on heavenly things, an unconscious saint, if indeed saints ever are conscious!

Thomas Tucker's school-teaching, however, did not prove efficient. Wrapped up in his studies, he was so absent-minded that he lacked that modified omniscience which is the *sine qua non* of a country school-teacher. The boys played marbles under his very nose, and he did not see them; they told him the most audacious lies, and he believed them, because he had never told a lie himself; they filched his pens and spilt his ink; they put burrs in the crown of his hat, and smeared his mittens with pitch scraped from the pine-logs in the open fireplace; they ate his dinner, and tied his comforter into knots. But he endured it all with amazement and patience, never thinking his pupils could or would be hard at heart. Then they began to serenade him with the old nursery rhymes of Little Tommy Tucker; to draw pictures of him on the slate, with that vivacious legend attached; and in short to learn so little and misbehave so much that after one term Thomas was "advised to resign," and Parson Lathrop saw that his *protégé* would never earn even the clothes needful to his college course. But the good man had counted the cost when he set out to build this tower of learning, and he sent Thomas at once to the nearest college; becoming answerable for all his expenses, which were somewhat lessened by the fact that a brother clergyman at Deerford gave Thomas his board on condition that he did the "chores" of the family and took care of the horse.

During his first year in this institution the mountain farm where he was born, always, heretofore, considered beyond the reach of fevers such as haunted the lowlands, was suddenly stricken. Amasa Tucker and his wife both fell ill with one of those malignant diseases that were once regarded with a mystical horror as "visitations of God," but are now referred to contaminated wells and neglected drainage. Amasa came in from the woods where he was chopping, one afternoon, livid and ghastly with pain, exclaiming, like the child of the Shunammite woman, "My head! my head!" and fell upon the bed senseless. He lay there unconscious all night, and the next morning Keziah set out at dawn to walk two miles to the nearest neighbor, and send him to Bantam for a doctor. He went at once, but when she got home her father was still senseless, and her mother sat by his side, with both hands clasped about her own head, and her face scarcely less changed than her husband's. Amasa was dead when Dr. Knight arrived, and in twenty-four hours Philura had followed him; both dying speechless, without one parting word or look for their bereft daughter, and before Thomas could come from Deerford. It was a strange, sad funeral at which Parson Lathrop officiated, early on a sweet spring day, the air fragrant with the new buds and fresh scent of the upturned earth, birds twittering among the lofty pine-trees, that set the north winds at defiance on two sides of that quiet graveyard, and the tiny lake below repeating the fair blue heaven above. A divine peace seemed to fill that solitude among the sheltering mountains, and as the good man looked about him he reverently removed his hat, and, before the dead were laid among their kindred dust, he burst involuntarily into the sublime cadences of that psalm so fitted for the time and place: —

"Lord! Thou hast been our dwelling-place in all generations.
Before the mountains were brought forth,
Or ever Thou hadst formed the earth and the world,
Even from everlasting to everlasting,
Thou art God."

But the triumphant submission, the lofty ascription, awoke no thrill in Thomas's heart. He stood by the double grave like one in a dream; no tear dimmed his eye, no quiver moved his set lips. He knew well that these deaths were no real loss to him, and he was too vitally and thoroughly honest to put on any outward aspect of mourning. Neither father nor mother had ever tried to awaken in their children one spark of affection. Duty, grim, hard duty, had been the spring of Amasa Tucker's life toward God and man. He had toiled, and prayed, and striven to fulfil his tale of debt toward One whom he knew only as an exacting Master, and to "set loose by the things of this world," as he expressed it, lest he might not be ready for the summons to another; and from him Keziah had learned to dread the indulgence of natural affection as idolatry and a weakness of the carnal heart, which was always "at enmity with God." Consequently the children had grown up unloving, because they were unloved. There were no tender recollections to wring their souls to-day; no unspeakable longings for the hand that had been ever ready to guide, or the voice always eager to cheer. Even Parson Lathrop was astonished and grieved to see that prim composure of the one and dreamy indifference of the other, and forbore to pray that God would bind up the broken in heart, being too honest to be conventional.

Happily for Keziah, Parson Lathrop's widowed sister had come to Bantam to "make it home with him," as the country phrase is; and, never weary in well-doing, the good man took Keziah home, and sent her to Parsons Academy; and in due time she became a school-teacher, more successful than Thomas, for she only attempted to teach little children, whom her dull, quiet nature enabled her to drill in their earliest education with unwearied patience and smiling endurance.

Thomas himself went on in his college course utterly unmoved by the tricks of sophomores or the contempt of seniors. He was called "Little Tommy Tucker" through the recurring terms in every tone of scorn, amusement, and disgust, without seeming to know that it was not his proper title. Nothing interested him but his books. Society was a meaningless waste of time in his eyes, and he respected holidays only because he could spend them undisturbed in the college library, without need to stir for any purpose save the necessities of food and rest, always at their mimimum with him. He went to the end of the career here with absolute success as far as learning goes, graduated with the highest honors, and passed on into the theological seminary in Hartland, an epitome of learning, but without a single friend.

Here he revelled in Greek and Hebrew; became still more lank, bent, pale, and introverted than ever; and when he was at last through with his divinity course knew more of his studies and less of his fellow-creatures than any other man of his class. He was temporarily placed in charge of the college chapel when he returned to Deerford, its pulpit being vacant for the time; and he preached to the students before him such discourses as might have edified a body of old Puritan divines,— erudite, doctrinal, logical, orthodox, but without one spark of human sympathy or divine love. The eager crowd refused such husks, and expressed their disgust, as a crowd of boys will; but Thomas Tucker took no more notice of their scuffling feet, their laughter, their feigned sleep, or their simultaneous attacks of cold in the head or distressing cough than he took of the wintry winds without that dashed the elm-tree boughs against the lofty chapel windows, or the streaming rain that pattered on its roof. He was there to preach, and preach he did; gladly, however, retiring from the office when the clergyman for whom he had been *locum tenens* arrived. It was evident to those who knew him best in the city that it was not his vocation to preach; and as he was respected among those learned men for his devotion to study and his vast acquisition of knowledge for so young a man, and as the professor of ancient languages was about to resign his position, and his life too, it was brought about that Thomas Tucker should be offered his place. It was true, he was comparatively young; but there was no real youth about him. He went his way with the absorption of a sexagenarian, only that his were the cares of learning and meditation rather than of this world and declining years.

Soon after his acceptance of the professorship he was sent for to say good-by to Parson Lathrop. For this good man, who had been a real father to him in the best fatherly sense, Thomas felt all the affection in his power; and as he stood by his death-bed, the dreamy, deep-set eyes sparkled with unshed tears, and the melancholy lips trembled. He could not speak; he could only grasp the emaciated and burning hand held out to him, and see through a dim haze the faint, sweet smile on the old man's face.

"I am going home, my son," whispered the parson. "I sent for you to say it is best now that you should take Keziah to be with you. Sister Keery has gone before me, having had an abundant entrance into the kingdom." Here he paused, and Keziah gave him a sip of restorative. "My tongue is parched, even as the tongue of Dives, but I am not afraid of his fate. I know in whom I have believed. Thomas, as I said, take Keziah home with you. Well sayeth the Apocrypha, though it be not with inspiration, 'Without women cannot men live.' It is better for you, in this new honor that hath come to you, to have the dignity of a home, and it is best that she should have its comfort. 'He setteth the solitary in families,' and what better earthly thing could he do for them?"

"I will!" said Thomas, as solemnly as if this were a marriage ceremony.

The parson smiled, but the wandering of death was on him. It seemed as if his will had controlled the fluttering of the spirit, eager to break its chrysalis and soar, until he had finished his good work on earth; now he ceased from his labors, but his heart yet beat, and his disordered mind babbled on those clay-cold lips.

"They're all in the yard, Celia," he said; "and the sun isn't down yet; it's above Saltash; and I cocked all the hay on the lower meadow. Tell Semanthy to fetch the milk-pails." Then he muttered something they could not hear. Celia was his wife's name, and that recurred audibly over and over. Suddenly his look changed, his eyes opened, a radiant gleam broke across the pallid face, and, lifting one hand upward, he said, "Why, Celia! Come! rise! let us be going; the Master calleth for thee;" so he went as bidden.

Thomas and Keziah walked behind the coffin, when Parson Lathrop's funeral train wound its way along the shore of the tranquil lake to the same lonely graveyard where their parents lay, feeling in their hearts that here and now they buried a nearer and dearer friend than either father or mother had been; and the silent crowd who followed them were all alike mourners, for the parson had been a power and a presence of goodness in their midst for many a long year. They stayed, too, after they had lain the worn-out body to sleep in the tender shadow of the hills he loved, to hear his funeral sermon, preached by a neighboring brother, who was in such pathetic earnest that his misuse of speech could not stir a smile in the attentive audience, even when he said, in describing the good man's last hours, that "a heavenly smile eradicated his countenance."

Then the brother and sister went back to Deerford, and, hiring a small house, began their life together. Parson Lathrop had left his little property to Keziah, and these few thousands, added to the yearly rental of the old farm and the house in Bantam, kept her independent soul from feeling that she was a burden upon Thomas, and his salary was more than sufficient for their daily needs. So for a year or two they lived in peace, until Satan, or some lesser minion of evil, put it into the head of a student, whose mischief always over-rode his manners, to play a joke upon "Old Tommy."

Professor Tucker, throughout his college life, had never been known to address the least attention, scarcely the least civility, to any woman; he avoided all society but that of his books, refused all invitations, and lived in his room like a hermit in his cell. But when his sister arrived, and he became a householder, the maids and matrons collateral to the faculty of which he was a member at once felt it their duty to call on Keziah, and welcome her to their social enjoyments. But she was as shy as her brother, and proved impracticable to almost every one. Her nearest neighbor alone, a maiden lady of good family and fine, cheerful presence, well-to-do, and having the courageous *aplomb* that all these gifts bestow on a woman, made some headway in the good graces of the quiet rustic spinster. Miss Eleanor Yale would, welcomed or not, invade Keziah's solitude now and then, insist on driving her out to show her the beautiful environs of Hartland, send her flowers from her own elaborate garden and fruit from her peach and pear trees, all out of the most frank and free benevolence; for she pitied the solitary creature, knowing in her own heart how forlorn loneliness is to any woman, though all the other good things of life be poured out abundantly into her hands. Miss Keziah had a heart, — somewhat torpid for want of exercise, perhaps, but still a heart, — and she felt Miss Yale's kindness, without finding words to express it to that lady; but she spoke of her so often to the professor that he learned to know her name, and thereby precipitated a certain impending catastrophe, set in motion by Jack Mason, the aforesaid student. On Valentine's day — a day of which Thomas Tucker was no more conscious and no better informed than Confucius or Aristotle — he received by mail a flowing ditty, of the most tender sort, written in a woman's hand, and signed "Eleanor." The professor stood aghast. Poetry had no charms for him; he had not the remotest idea of its figurative speech, its license, or its "tricks and manners;" to him it was merely curiously arranged prose, and this devoted and tender valentine seemed neither more nor less than an offer of marriage. His hair fairly stood on end, and his forehead was knit with perplexity. Who could have done this thing? Suddenly he remembered that Eleanor was the name of his sister's friend, and even on his learned and abstracted soul dawned a glimmer of the man's instinctive contempt for women, as he bethought himself how this woman had sought his sister's friendship and done her such kindnesses all for his sake. Still, being an exceptional man, he was moved rather to pity than scorn, on further reflection, thinking of all this wasted trouble and useless feeling on the lady's part. There was but one thing to be done. He did not want to marry any one; he had not planned or intended any such thing; his life and love were all centred in his studies, his books, his profession. And was not Keziah able and willing to do for him all those services which some men had no sisters to attend to, and therefore were obliged to marry?

But this poor woman, — she must not be deluded with so futile a hope. It was unpleasant to contemplate, but Thomas Tucker never shrank from duty; he must be honest or die. So he put on his hat and coat, and, presenting himself at Miss Yale's door, asked to see that lady. Miss Yale was astonished, but she received the professor a little more kindly because she was astonished, and afraid she should not put him entirely at his ease. But he was more formal, more awkward, more stiff than ever before. He sat down on the highest chair in the room, and, drawing the luckless missive from his breast-pocket, plunged at once into the middle of things.

"Madam!" he began, sternly, "I have received this epistle, bearing your name in superscription, which doubtless you recognize. I thank you for the regard herein expressed; but as an honest man, and one who is in bonds to the truth, I come to say to you that marriage has not entered into my plans at any time, nor is there any likelihood that it will."

Miss Yale looked at him with wide eyes. "What?" she cried, in amazement.

"I refer to this letter you have sent me, couched in the mode of verse," replied the professor, grim as a lion on a sign-post of old time, and full as wooden.

"Give me the letter, if you please," said Miss Yale, her color rising, and her eyes full of a dangerous glow. But the professor knew nothing of the sex and its ways, except theoretically; he handed her the document, without any fear of its explosive tendencies. Miss Yale read it through, and looked up at him. He was already lost in some problem, or evolving some theory; but her voice roused him.

"Do you think I sent you this?" she asked, in a very quiet voice, — altogether too quiet to be reassuring.

"Is not that your given name by which it is signed?" returned the professor.

"Yes. But I want to understand what you considered this letter to mean," she went on, with the same ominous quietness of manner, holding herself in leash, as it were, till the time for a spring.

"I think it has but one meaning, which he that runs may read: that you are desirous of entering the state of matrimony."

"With you?"

"With me," responded Thomas Tucker, with curt and ghastly honesty.

Miss Yale rose to her feet, and her clear eyes flashed. The professor felt danger; he shrank visibly into himself, yet fixed an undaunted gaze upon her. She looked at him a moment, and, with the vivid speed of thought, remembered herself, her position, his nature and his habits. Her anger died; she threw herself back on the sofa, and laughed till the tears rolled down her fair face.

The professor was entirely speechless; he knew not what to say, but at last, in honest indignation, opened his mouth, much like his Scriptural prototype, to the angel in the path: —

"It seems, madam, unsavory subject for mirth. I am in earnest."

"And so am I," said Miss Yale, drying her bedewed cheeks, and trying to be sober. "Professor Tucker, I did not write that letter. Some silly and impertinent boy sent it to you to deceive and disturb you. If I wished to marry you I should not take that method of obtaining my wish. I am a woman and a lady: good women and true ladies do not do such things."

She looked directly at him as she said this, and her eyes sparkled. Some manly shame stirred in the professor's bosom; he extracted a great red and yellow handkerchief, with much contortion, from his coat-tail pocket, and used it sonorously.

Miss Yale's lips quivered a little, and a sudden dimple flashed in her cheek; but she went on, certain, with her own perfect tact, that this man must be treated with absolute truth, like his own: "Moreover, in order to show you convincingly that I had no such intention, beside not having written that letter, I will tell you, in confidence, — a trust I feel will be safe in your hands, — that I have promised to marry President Winthrop some time next summer."

As Professor Tucker looked at the warm flush that covered the fine face of Eleanor Yale, and perceived the soft glow of her eyes, he thought that the widowed president was a happy man, but he did not say so. "Madam, I ask your pardon," he said, humbly. "And for that son of Belial, who hath made me his music, I trust due punishment is somewhere reserved," he gloomily added, and departed in a shambling fashion, that once more provoked Miss Yale's dimples and set her eyes dancing. And — alas for the feminine malice, of which a grain lurks in the best woman's heart! — that very night President Winthrop was entertained with a *résumé* of her afternoon's experience; and that genial gentleman roared and rolled with laughter, for he knew Thomas Tucker far better than Miss Yale did, and could more thoroughly enjoy the situation.

After this occurrence, which Hebrew points and crabbed Syriac idioms soon drove from the professor's mind, he went his way for a while quite undisturbed; but he was so unsuccessful as a teacher that, on some excellent pretext, it pleased the trustees of the college to remove him from his position. They recommended him to a church in the city, seeking for a clergyman to fill its pulpit, and then advised him to accept the call. It was at first an irksome employment for the professor, but he did not love teaching; it was far easier for him to produce two sermons a week, in the seclusion of his study, than to face daily a class of youths, more or less refractory, if they were students, and try to beat into them the beauties and intricacies of the dead languages.

The social duties of a settled clergyman might have pressed on him onerously; but, as if Providence saw that he was best fitted for a life of solitude, just as the Green Street church had listened to their learned and pious pastor for the first time after his installation in their pulpit, Keziah, his sister, was seized with a sudden and dangerous illness. The kind women of the church rallied around Thomas Tucker in this hour of his need, and nursed Keziah with unremitting kindness; but all in vain. She dropped out of life as silently and patiently as she had endured living, and it remained only to say that the place which knew her should now know her no more; for she left behind her no dear friend but her brother, and not an enemy. Even Thomas missed her rather as a convenience than a companion; profiting in a certain sense by her death, as it aroused keenly the sympathy of the church for his loss and loneliness, and attached them to him by those links of pity that are proverbially almost as strong as love. In any other circumstances the Green Street church would no doubt have discovered, early in their relation, that Mr. Tucker was as unfit for any pastoral position as he had been for that post in the college chapel; but much was forgiven him out of his people's abundant kindness; and their respect for his learning, his simplicity, and his sincere piety forbade their objecting at first to his great deficiencies in those things considered quite as needful to pulpit success as the power of preaching and the abundance of knowledge. It happened, soon after Keziah's death, that Mr. Tucker was called to officiate at the funeral of one of his wealthiest parishioners, a man who had just come back from Europe, and been killed in a railroad accident on the way to his home in Deerford. He was personally unknown to Thomas Tucker, but his character was notorious. He went to church, and bought an expensive pew there, merely as a business speculation; it gave him weight in the eyes of his fellows to be outwardly respectable as well as rich; but he was niggardly to his family, ostentatious, overreaching, and cruel as death to the poor and struggling who crossed his path or came into his employ.

The Reverend Mr. Tucker improved the occasion. He took for the text of that funeral address, "What shall it profit a man if he gain the whole world, and lose his own soul?" and after a pungent comparison between the goods of this world and the tortures of a future state he laid down his spectacles, and wound up with, "And now, beloved, I have laid before you the two conditions. Think ye that to-day he whose mortal part lieth before you would not utter a loud Amen to my statement? Yea, if there be truth in the word of God, he who hath left behind him the gain of life and greed is now crying aloud for a drop of water to cool his parched tongue, and longing for an hour of probation wherein to cast off the fetters of ill-gotten gold and sit with Lazarus gathering crumbs in the company of dogs. Wherefore, seeing that God hath spoken sharply to you all in the sudden requirement of this rich man's soul, let his admonition sink into your souls; seek ye first the kingdom of God, and cast in your lot with the poor of this world, rich in faith, and be ready to answer joyfully when the Master calls."

Of course the community was outraged; but for a

few kindly souls, who stood by the poor parson, and insisted that Keziah's death had unsettled his mind, and not a few who felt that he had manfully told the truth, without fear or favor, and could not help feeling a certain respect for him, he would have been asked, forcibly, to resign, that very week. As it was, the indignant widow went over to another denomination without delay. "I will never set foot in that church again!" she said. "How can one be safe where a man is allowed to say whatever he chooses in the pulpit? A ritual never can be personal or insulting. I shall abide by the Prayer-Book hereafter."

In due time this matter faded out of the popular mind, as all things do in course of time, and nothing came between pastor and people, except a gradual sense on their part that Solomon was right when he said, "Much study is a weariness to the flesh;" not only the student's flesh, but also theirs who have to hear reiterated all the dry outcome of such study.

But Parson Tucker's career was not to be monotonous. His next astonishing performance was at a wedding. A very pretty young girl, an orphan, living in the house of a relative, equally poor but grasping and ambitious, was about to marry a young man of great wealth and thoroughly bad character: a man whom all men knew to be a drunkard, a gambler, and a dissolute fellow, though the only son of a cultivated and very aristocratic family. Poor Emily Manning had suffered all those deprivations and mortifications which result from living in a dependent condition, aware that her presence was irksome and unwelcome, while her delicate organization was overtaxed with work whose limits were as indefinite as the food and clothing which were its only reward. She had entered into this engagement in a sort of desperation, goaded on by the widowed sister-in-law with whom she lived, and feeling that nothing could be much worse than her present position. Parson Tucker knew nothing of this, but he did know the character of Royal Van Wyck; and when he saw the pallid, delicate, shrinking girl beside this already worn-out, debased, bestial creature, ready to put herself into his hands for life, the " daimon" laid hold upon him, and spake again. He opened the service, as was customary in Hartland, with a short address; but surely never did such a bridal exhortation enter the ears of man and woman before.

"My friends," he began, "matrimony is not to be lightly undertaken, as the matter of a day; it is an awful compact for life and death that ye enter into here. Young man, if thou hast not within thyself the full purpose to treat this woman with pure respect, loyal service, and tender care; to guard her soul's innocence as well as her bodily welfare; to cleave to her only, and keep thyself from evil thoughts and base indulgences for her sake,—if thou art not fit, as well as willing, to be priest and king of a clean household, standing unto her in character and act in God's stead so far as man may, draw back even now from thine intent; for a lesser purpose is sacrilege here, and will be damnable infamy hereafter."

Royal Van Wyck opened his sallow green eyes with an insolent stare. He would have sworn roundly had not some poor instinct of propriety restrained him; as it was, he did not speak, but looked away. He could not bear the keen, deep-set eyes fixed upon him; and a certain gaunt majesty in the parson's outstretched arm and severe countenance daunted him for the moment. But Thomas Tucker saw that he had no intention of accepting this good advice, so he turned to Emily.

"Daughter," he said, " if thou art about to enter into this solemn relation, pause and consider. If thou hast not such confidence in this man that thy heart faileth not an iota at the prospect of a life-long companionship with him; if thou canst not trust him utterly, respect him as thy lord and head, yield him an obedience joyful and secure next to that thou givest to God; if he is not to thee the one desirable friend and lover; if thou hast a thought so free of him that it is possible for thee to imagine another man in his place without a shudder; if thou art not willing to give thyself to him in the bonds of a life-long, inevitable covenant of love and service; if it is not the best and sweetest thing earth can offer thee to be his wife and the mother of his children, — stop now; stop at the very horns of the altar, lest thou commit the worst sin of woman, sell thy birthright for a mess of pottage, and find no place for repentance, though thou seek it carefully and with tears."

Carried away with his zeal for truth and righteousness, speaking as with the sudden inspiration of a prophet, Parson Tucker did not see the terror and the paleness deepening, as he spoke, on the bride's fair countenance. As he extended his hand toward her she fell in a dead faint at his feet. All was confusion in an instant. The bridegroom swore and Mrs. Manning screamed, while the relations crowded about the insensible girl, and tried to revive her. She was taken at once upstairs to her room, and the wedding put off till the next day, as Mrs. Manning announced.

"And you won't officiate at it, old fellow! I'll swear to that!" roared the baffled bridegroom, with a volley of profane epithets, shaking his fist in the parson's calm face.

"Having taken the sword, I am content to perish thereby, even as Scripture saith," answered Thomas Tucker, stalking out of the door.

That night, as he sat in his study, the door opened softly, and Emily Manning came in and knelt at the side of the parson's chair. "I have no place to go to, sir," she whispered, with trembling lips. "You saved me to-day; will you help me now? I was going to sin, but I didn't know it till you told me."

"Then it was not sin, my child," said Parson Tucker, gently. "Sin is conscious transgression, and from that thou hast instantly departed."

"But what could I do?" she asked, her eyes full of tears. "I have no home. Marcia is tired of me, and I have no other friends. I wanted a home so much. Oh, I was wrong, for I did not love him. And now I have run away from Marcia, — she was so dreadful, — and what shall I do?"

"Poor child!" he said, tenderly. "Sit here. I will help. My old woman, in the kitchen below, shall fetch thee to a chamber. Keziah brought her with us; she is kind, and will care for thee, while I go to bring a friend." So saying, the parson rung his bell for old Jane, gave the girl over to her care, and set out himself for President Winthrop's house.

"I have brought you a good work," he said abruptly to Mrs. Winthrop. "Come with me; there is a soul in need at my house."

Mrs. Winthrop was used to this sort of summons

from the parson. They had been good friends ever since the eccentric interview brought about by Jack Mason's valentine, and when charity was needed Eleanor Winthrop's heart and hand were always ready for service. She put on hat and shawl, and went with the parson to his house, hearing on the way all the story.

"Mr. Tucker," she said, as he finished the recital, "aren't you going to make much trouble for yourself by your aggressive honesty?"

Thomas looked at her, bewildered.

"But the truth is to be spoken!" he replied, as if that were the end of the controversy. And she was silent, recognizing the fact that here conventions were useless, and self-preservation not the first law of grace, if it is of nature.

All Mrs. Winthrop's kindliness was aroused by the pitiful condition of Emily Manning. She consoled and counselled her like a mother, and soon after took her into her household as governess to the little girls whom Mr. Winthrop's first wife had left him; making for the grateful girl a happy home, which in after years she left to become the wife of a good man, toward whom she felt all that Parson Tucker had required of her on that painful day which she hated now to remember. And as the parson performed this ceremony he turned, after the benediction, to Eleanor Winthrop, and said, with a beam of noble triumph on his hollow visage, "Blessed be the Lord! I have saved a soul alive!"

But long before this happy sequel came about he had other opportunities to distinguish himself. There came a Sunday when the service of infant baptism was to be performed; and when the fair, sweet babes, who had behaved with unusual decorum, were returned to their mothers' arms, and the parson, according to order, said, "Let us pray," he certainly offered the most peculiar petition ever heard in the Green Street church. After expressing the usual desire that the baptized children might grow up in the nurture and admonition of the Lord, he went on: "But if it please thee, O Father, to recall these little ones to thyself in the innocence of their infancy, we will rejoice and give thanks, and sound thy praises upon the harp and timbrel. Yea! with the whole heart we will praise thee; for we know the tribulations and snares, the evil and folly and anguish, of this life below; and we know that not one child of Adam, coming to man's estate, is spared that bitter and woful cup that is pressed out from the fruit of the knowledge of good and evil, which our progenitors ate of in thy garden of Paradise, and thereby sinned and fell, and bequeathed to us their evil longings and habitual transgression. They are the blessed who are taken away in their infancy, and lie forever by green pastures and still waters in the fields of heaven. We ask of thee no greater or better gift for these lambs than early to be folded where none shall hurt or destroy in all thy holy mountain, and the love that is above all mother's love shall cradle them throughout eternity. Amen!"

Not a mother in that congregation failed to shiver and tremble at this prayer, and tears fell fast and thick on the babes who slumbered softly in the tender arms that had gathered them home, after consecrating them to that God whom yet they were so unwilling should literally accept their offering. Fifty pairs of eyes were turned on Parson Tucker with the look of a bear robbed of its cubs; but far more were drowned in tears of memory and regret, poignant still, but strangely soothed by this vivid presentation of the blessedness wherein their loved and lost were safely abiding.

Much comment was exchanged in the church porch, after service, on the parson's prayer.

"We ought to hold a special meeting to pray that the Lord will not answer such a petition!" cried one indignant mother, whose little flock were clinging about her skirts, and who had left twin babies, yet unbaptized, at home.

"It *is* rather hard on you, aunty!" said graceless Jack Mason, the speaker's nephew, now transformed into an unpromising young lawyer in Hartland. "You'd rather have your babies sin and suffer with you than have 'em safe in their little graves, hadn't you? I don't go with the parson myself. I didn't so much mind his funeral gymnastic over old Baker, and his disposition of that party's soul in Hades, because I never before supposed Roosevelt Baker had a soul, and it was quite reassuring to be certain he met with his dues somewhere; but he's worse than Herod about the babies!"

However, the parson did not hear or know what was said of him, and in an ignorance that was indeed bliss continued to preach and minister to his people in strict accordance with his own views of duty. His next essay was a pastoral visit to one of his flock, recently a widow, a woman weak in body and mind both; desirous above all things to be proper and like other people, to weep where she must, smile when she ought, wear clothes like the advance-guard of fashion, and do "the thing" to be done always, whether it was the right and true thing or not.

Her husband had spent all her fortune in speculation, taken to drink as a refuge from folly and reproach at home, and, under the influence of the consoling fluid, had turned his wife out-of-doors whenever he felt in the mood; kicked her, beaten her, and forced her, in fear of her life, over and over to steal from her own house, and take refuge with the neighbors, and ask from them the food she was not allowed at home. At last the end came. Parson Tucker was sent for to see the widow and arrange for funeral services. She had not been present at the Baker funeral, or indeed been in Deerford for some years after that occasion, so she adhered to the conventions; and when Parson Tucker reached the house he was shown into a darkened room, where the disconsolate woman sat posed already in deep mourning, a widow's cap perched upon her small head. A woman would have inferred at once that Mrs. Spring had anticipated the end of Joe's last attack of *mania à potu*, and prepared these funeral garments beforehand; but Thomas Tucker drew no such conclusions. He sat down silently and grimly, after shaking hands with Mrs. Spring, and said nothing. She began the conversation:—

"This is a dreadful affliction, Mr. Tucker. I don't know how I shall live through it."

"It is terrible, indeed," said the parson. "I do not wonder, madam, that you mourn to see your partner cut off in his sins, without time for repentance; but no doubt you feel with gratitude the goodness which hath delivered you from so sore a burden."

"What!" screamed the widow.

"I speak of God's mercy in removing from your house one who made your life a terror, and your days full of fear and suffering; you might have been as others, bereaved and desolate, and mourning to your life's end."

"I don't know what you mean, Parson Tucker," said Mrs. Spring, sharply, removing a dry handkerchief from unwet eyes. "Poor, dear Joseph is taken away from me, and I'm left a desolate widow, and you talk in this way! I'm sure he had the best of hearts that ever was; it was only, as you may say, accidental to him to be a little overcome at times, and I'm — I'm — O—h!"

Here she gave a little hysterical scream, and did some well-executed sobbing; but the parson did not mind it. He rose up before her, gaunt and gray. "Madam, did not this man beat, and abuse, and insult, and starve you, when he was living? Or have I been misinformed?"

"Well— Oh, dear, what dreadful questions!"

"Did he?" thundered the parson.

"He didn't mean to; he was excited, Mr. Tucker. He"—

"He was drunk. And is that excuse? Not so, madam. You know, and I know, that his death is a relief and a release to you. I cannot condole with you on that which is not a sorrow;" and he walked rigidly out of the door.

Is it necessary to say that Mr. Spring's funeral did not take place in Deerford? His widow suddenly remembered that he had been born in a small town among the hills of West Massachusetts, and she took his body thither, to be "laid beside his dear payrents," as she expressed it.

Things had now come to a bad pass for Parson Tucker. The church committee had held more than one conference over their duty toward him. It was obvious that they had no real reason for dismissing him but his ghastly honesty, and that hardly offers a decent excuse to depose a minister of the gospel. They hardly knew how to face the matter, and were in this state of perplexity when Mr. Tucker announced, one Sunday, after the sermon, that he would like to see the church committee at his study on Tuesday night; and accordingly they assembled there, and found President Winthrop with the parson.

"Brethren," said Thomas Tucker, after the preliminary welcome had passed, "I have sent for you to-night to say, that having now been settled over your church eight years, I have found the salary you pay me so much more than was needed for my bodily support that I have laid by each year as the surplus came to hand, that I might restore to you your goods. The sum is now something over eight thousand dollars, and is placed to the credit of your chairman, in the First Deerford Bank." The committee stared at each other as if each one were trying to arouse himself from sleep. The chairman at last spoke:—

"But, Mr. Tucker, this is unheard of! The salary is yours; we do not desire to take it back; we can't do it."

"That which I have not earned, Brother Street, is not mine. I am a solitary man; my expenses are light. It must be as I said. Moreover, I have to say that I hereby withdraw from your pulpit, of necessity. I have dealt with our best physicians concerning a certain anguish of the breast, which seizes me at times unawares, and they all concur that an evil disease lieth upon me. I have not much time to live, and I would fain withdraw from activities and duties that are external, and prepare for the day that is at hand."

The committee were pained as well as shocked. They felt guilty to think how they had plotted this very thing among themselves; and they felt, too, a certain awe and deep respect for this simple, unworldly nature, this supernatural integrity. Mr. Street spoke again; his voice was husky:—

"If this is so, Mr. Tucker, we must of course accept your resignation; but, my dear pastor, keep the money! You will need care and comforts, now this trouble has come on you. We can't take it back."

Parson Tucker looked at him with a grave, sweet smile. "I thank you, brother, but I have a private store. My sister left her worldly goods to me, and there is enough and to spare for my short sojourn," he answered.

"But it isn't according to the fitness of things that we should take your salary back, Parson Tucker," put in bustling Mr. Taylor. "What upon earth should we do with it?"

"Friend," said the parson, "the eternal fitness of things is but the outcome of their eternal verity. I have not, as I said, earned that wage, and I must restore it: it is for you to decide what end it shall serve in the church."

A few more words passed between them, and then each wrung the parson's hand and left him, not all with unmoved hearts or dry eyes.

"I don't wonder he's going to die!" exclaimed Mr.

Street, as the committee separated at a street corner. "He's altogether too honest to live!"

From that day Thomas Tucker sank quietly toward his grave. Friends swarmed about him, and if delicacies of food could have saved him the dainty stores poured in upon him would have renewed his youth; but all was in vain.

President Winthrop sat by him, one summer day, and, seeing a sad gleam in his sunken eye, asked gently, "You are ready and willing to go, Brother Tucker?" nothing doubting a glad assent.

But the parson was honest to the last. "No," he said, "I do not want to die; I am afraid. I do not like strange and new things. I do not want to leave my books and my study."

"But, dear brother," broke in the astonished president, "it is a going home, to your Father's house!"

"I know not what a home is, friend, in the sense of regret or longing for one. My early home was but as the egg to the bird, a prison wherein I was born, from which I fled; nor was my knowledge of a father one that commends itself as a type of good. I trust, indeed, that the Master will take me by the hand, even as he did Peter upon the water; but the utterance of my secret soul is even that of the apostle with the keys: 'Lord, save, or I perish!'"

"But you have been a power for good, and a close follower of Peter's Lord," said Mr. Winthrop, altogether at a loss for the proper thing to say to this peculiar man.

"One thing alone have I been enabled to do, Brother Winthrop, for which I can with heart and soul thank God, even at this hour. Yea, I thank him that I have been enabled to speak the truth even in the face of lies and deceptions, through his upholding." A smile of unearthly triumph filled every line of the wasted face, and lit his eyes with a flash of divine light as he said this. He grasped close the friendly hand he was holding, turned his cheek to the pillow, and closed his eyes, passing into that life of truth and love that awaited him, even as a child that lies down in the darkness, trembling, fearful, and weary, but awakes, in the dawn of a new day, in the heart of home.

"Still," said President Winthrop to his wife, as they walked home after the funeral, "I believe in the good old proverb, Eleanor, that 'the truth is not to be spoken at all times.'"

"And I never believed in it so little!" she cried, indignantly. "Think what a record he has left; what respect hangs about his memory! Do we know how many weak souls have relied on his example, and held to the truth when it was hard, because he did and could? It is something to be heroic in these days, even if it is unpopular!"

The president shrugged his shoulders.

THE FORGER'S BRIDE.

A very soft April day, now and then chilled by the wind off snow-drifts that spotted the hills even after a rainy morning, was about half over as Sally Tyler came up from the village street to the red house where she lived. She was extremely pretty: her features delicate and straight, her dark eyes sweet, her blue-black hair glossy; and now a little wild-rose bloom on her cheek, and a deeper crimson than usual on her lips, made her look like a flower with a white hood on.

She was evidently much engrossed by some new thought or plan, for she did not stoop to pat the old yellow dog who raised himself on his fore legs and slobbered a welcome as he lay in the sunshine; nor did she notice the threatening scream of a hen-hawk that circled high in air above her tiny brood of early chickens; or even look at the golden crocus that had sprung from the black mould of her posy-bed, a cup of sudden sunlight since last night; but took her way round to the back door, for nobody in New England country villages uses the front door, except for weddings or funerals. Many a house have I seen whose entire front half, with its darkened and musty parlors, and its " spare chambers," smelling of ill-dried feathers, fennel, and green mould, might have been sliced away and carried off, nowise to the detriment, and perhaps even without the knowledge, of the inhabitants behind.

So Sally followed the worn foot-track, past scraggy lilacs and sprawling cinnamon rose-bushes, round the house, and went in to the door of the back kitchen, where at the sink her mother stood chopping some cold potatoes. Sally was an only child, but her mother was so haunted by the one fear of spoiling her that she sometimes went too far the other way. The poor little girl was "tutored," as she said, till she was weary and aching, — aching for a little of the deep, real love that lay hidden away in her mother's heart, very much as the best parlor and bedroom were shut up: there, no doubt, but useless and unseen. To-day, as usual, the first words were reproof: —

"I told you there was too many pertaters biled yesterday, Sally, 'n now I've got to chop 'em for dinner, and chopped pertater aint real good 'long o' salt beef: you'd ought to be more considerin'. Supposin' you was to git married, and hev to see to the work yourself, I guess your husband'd come to woful want pretty surprisin' quick."

Sally sighed a little, but said nothing. She had learned how to hold her tongue at least, — perhaps a better preparation for marriage than the economizing of potatoes. Nor did she blush at her mother's illustration of her discourse, for in Wingfield there was nobody who could be called a beau for her: all the well-to-do farmers' sons had emigrated from its barren hill-sides, and the hired men were more often Irish than any other, or, if Yankees, of the very lowest class.

She waited a minute till the noise of the chopping-knife ceased and the potatoes were turned into the spider, and then said, shyly: —

"Mother, I went to the post-office after I'd carried the eggs, and I got a letter from Cousin Jerushy."

"Do tell!" said Mrs. Tyler, for a moment holding the big iron spoon suspended from her hand. "Why, we haint heerd from Jerushy quite a spell. How is all her folks?"

"They're all well, she says; only Grandmother Dyke has had a long spell of rheumatiz. They've got a bigger tenement now, and Jerushy wants me to come and stay with her for a while."

Mrs. Tyler stirred the potatoes so vigorously that Sally hardly dared to venture farther, but she did whisper, half audibly: —

"Can I go, mother?"

Mrs. Tyler was what the transcendentalists call "antagonistic," and her neighbors, "dreadful arbitrary." Her first impulse was to contradict every assertion and refuse every request. Of course, convenience and policy, and various other motives, better or worse, obliged her to come round to assertions and requests full half the time; but it was a weary and delayed victory that the opposite side gained, — one of those conquests almost as undesirable as a defeat. Her husband, with a shrewdness men do not often arrive at in dealing with this not uncommon type of women, always took care to say and ask nothing important if it could be helped, or otherwise to offer her the exact converse of his wishes. True, like all manœuvres, this sometimes worked its own defeat, from her habit of giving in at last; and then the squire shook his grizzled head and muttered to himself, winding up with a whistled psalm-tune, generally his best expression of doubt or consternation.

But to-day Mrs. Tyler was somewhat softened by Sally's shy look and tone, though of course she put out a sharp negative at first: —

"No, you can't. I don't see how you can think on't. Jest layin'-time, 'n all them hens to look after, 'n set, 'n feed; 'n two calves in the barn. Well, I s'pose I might see to them things myself" (she always would); "but *he* won't hear to 't, I know. I don't know but what I'd like to have ye go to see Jerushy; she's a smart woman, and a pretty woman as ever I see." (Mrs. Jerusha Phelps had about as much beauty as a chimpanzee, but "pretty" means only pleasant and well-mannered in our vernacular.) "I guess you might go ef you had two new gowns. You haint got really nothing fit to stay a spell, 'n I expect he won't want to give you no money. Well, it's nigh about dinner-time, 'n you might step out to the barn 'n call him — it'll save me a-blowin' the horn — and you can settle it, maybe, 'fore you come in. I don't want to have to jaw to the table: I like to eat 'n be done with it."

In her secret heart Mrs. Tyler knew that she didn't want to come into collision with the squire if he assented, or to give up her reluctant willingness to fight it out strenuously if he said no; but, as Sally replaced her hood and shawl and opened the outer door, her mother called after her: —

"Don't forget to tell him you've got to be fixed off to go, child. I expect he'll growl some, but the terbacker did real well last year, 'n he's a-packin' on't now."

There was a world of policy in this last remark, quite lost on simple Sally; so she trudged out to the big barn on the hill-side, and, stepping in at the little side door, threaded her way over milking-stools, pitchforks, wisps of hay, and all the nameless litter of an ill-kept barn, to the wide hay-floor, where her father and Peter, the hired Irishman, sat packing tobacco. Squire Tyler was a good specimen of an elderly Yankee farmer; his fine head was covered with iron-gray hair, curling all over it in spite of him; his face was wrinkled, but sagacious and kindly; while all the shrewdness ascribed to his race twinkled in the deep-set eyes, half lost under their big, shaggy brows. He was a quaint old creature, as far as his domestic life went, but nobody made more acute bargains than he, or understood better how to take the top wave of fluctuating prices and come off with flying colors just before his delaying neighbors lost all their ventures. He loved Sally better than anything else, and his Devon cows next; his wife came somewhere lower down in the scale, it is true, but that was her own fault; twenty years of persistent nagging and contradicting will somewhat stunt the growth even of a real affection, and whatever of love still lingered in this matrimonial tie had its balance altogether on the wife's side. Now, as he looked up and saw Sally leaning against the door, her white hood fallen off, and her face glowing with her walk and her errand, all his wrinkles and puckers vanished into a smile of welcome, and the sharp eyes softened at once.

"Hullo, Sally!" shouted he: "what be you after?"

"O father, please! I had a letter from Cousin

Jerushy"— Here she stopped a minute to take breath.

"Well, that aint no great thing to hev, is it? I thought mother was kind o' down on Jerushy, or you was, or somethin' or 'nother."

"Oh, not me! And, father, she wants me to come to Westboro' and see her a spell; and say, father, can't I go?"

Sally gave these last words in the true coaxing whine, and the squire looked up and laughed.

"You haint set your mind on't none, hev you, Sal?"

"I kinder have, father."

"What does mother say to't, eh?"

"Well, she said I couldn't, 'n then she said maybe I could if I had some new things; but I can't go unless I do."

The squire was purse-bearer evidently, and he began to tease Sally a bit. "Well, there's more'n four new things around here 't you can hev if you won't spile 'em; there's a new halter in that stall, 'n a new corn-basket; 'n I've got a fire-new axe to the house, 'f that'll help ye any"—

"Why, father! 'taint those kind of things I want; it's new gowns, and a hat, and"—

"What'n thunder do you want a hat for? Can't you wear a decent bunnet, 'n not put a tin pan with streamers a-top of your head, like them darned fools of Ruckers?"

"Why, I don't mean such a hat as that; I mean a big one to keep the sun out of my eyes. I've just got a new bunnet."

"Sun won't hurt your eyes none,— they aint everlastin' bright, anyway,— but I guess you can hev 'things,' as you call 'em, 'nough to go to Westboro'. An' seeing you can't get 'em without money, why, I expect I'll hev to give ye some. I'm a dreadful near old critter or'narily, ye know, but this here terbacker crop has kinder drawed out my heart, 'n I won't grudge you some on't."

With which speech the squire unlatched his pocket-book and fingered out from its capacious depths dirty bills to the amount of twenty dollars, which he handed to Sally, now drawn near enough to look over his shoulder; and was himself more astonished in his turn than she by the hearty hug she gave him.

"Good land! what's that for, you young critter? Haint been hugged so this forty year. Had to pay for't, though, didn't I? Well! well! go 'long, gal, when you git ready, and hev a first-rate time; but don't you go to fetchin' any o' them young fellers out of the iron-works home arter ye. I don't believe in luggin' a gal through teethin'," n measles, 'n all sorts o' knot-holes, 'n hevin' the first sassy chap 't comes along go 'n take her off, 'fore you've had a speck of comfort out on her."

Luckily the horn blew at this moment both loud and long, — irate signal of a domestic tempest brewing in the house, — and drove her father's caution quite out of Sally's head, — innocent little head! that had not even remembered before that there were iron-works or workers in Westboro', much less young men.

"Whew!" involuntarily sputtered the squire, as "the sound of that dread horn" fell upon his preternaturally sensitive ear.

Sally ran faster than his walk, but she stopped to wait for him behind the great water-butt, and smiled to herself as she heard him whistling "Dundee" with great earnestness. She was so happy she could afford to smile, even at the objurgations that met them both, little calculated as those sonorous remarks were to sweeten the dinner. However, the meal, like all New England penances of that sort, was soon over, and nothing was said between the parents of Sally's proposed journey; only that night, just as the squire was all but asleep, Mrs. Tyler suddenly came down upon him.

"So you went and let Sally go to Westboro', arter all, husband?" in a tone of mingled remonstrance and surprise.

"She aint gone yit," growled the squire, "'n I don't care a darn if she goes or stays. I kind o' like to hev her round sometimes, but if she's a mind to go, why, I don't care, only I aint a-goin' to have no young fellers a-follerin' on her home; 'n you kin jest drop a line to Jerushy and say so."

"I shan't do no such thing."

So the squire went to sleep, discreetly.

Sally was what some wise people would call foolishly happy for the next week. I don't know how much folly there was in her pleasure. I have seen rapture that was ingrain foolishness; I have seen despair quite as senseless; and I have my doubts, after all, if there is a much purer or simpler kind of happiness extant than danced in this sweet little girl's eyes and shone on her fair face in prospect of this first visit and her wonderful preparations for it; for she not only had a new gray *mousseline de laine* and delicate lilac calico, but her mother actually presented her with the dark green silk that had been her own wedding-dress, fortunately plain and thick, but altogether too strait for the goodly proportions of Mrs. Tyler now; requiring even every scrap of the long "cardinal" she had worn with it to eke out a dress for Sally. Then there were her white cambric dress and her old brown gingham. What more could she need or want? But the squire, going into Middletown to sell off some of his young stock, brought home a parcel and flung it into her lap.

"There!" said he, "that's Juno's calf. 'Taint half so good-lookin' as her shiny red skin; but I guess you'd ruther put it on your back, so I swapped."

Eager hands unrolled the parcel, and there lay a soft white shawl and a handful of ribbons, — delicate pink, tender green, and shades of aster color, with one trail of scarlet flashing through all. Sally was too happy to speak.

Why can't we make people happy oftener when they are young and simple enough to be made so? At forty, what are gowns, or shawls, or ribbons? But what are they not at sixteen?

At last the old cowskin trunk was packed, and Sally seated in the stage that was to take her over the hills to the railway station.

"Good-by, mother! Good-by, father!"

Mrs. Tyler only nodded.

"Good-by, little gal!" shouted the squire, muttering, as he turned away, "I shall kind o' hanker arter her, I swow! I guess I'll go 'n look arter that new heifer."

So Sally went safely off, and after a short drive and a long car-ride found herself at Westboro', and Cousin

Jerushy all ready to receive her at the station, as well as her husband, whom Sally had never seen, — a tall, serious-looking man, as quiet as his wife was gay. As soon as our little friend became known in Westboro' she also became, without knowing it, a social success: she was so pretty and delicate and fresh, and Cousin Jerushy always so popular, that a round of tea-parties and picnics and drives set in directly, till Sally thought she had never been in so delightful a place before.

Westboro' is a pretty village on a hill-side, beneath which runs a bright river, all its shores below the dam, on the village side, guarded by a huge rampart of workshops, where the trip-hammers clanged all day, and swarthy men with strong arms worked wonderful results out of the dull masses of iron before them.

These " shops," as they called them, were a dreadful institution to Sally: she was taken through them as the proper thing to do, but the furnaces and the hammers and the noise so confounded and frightened her that she was glad to get away to the cool green hill-side again and play with Jerushy's children. But many an admiring eye followed her progress among the forges; and that very evening no less than three spruce young men — all known to Mrs. Phelps, it is true, but not usually so attentive — called at her house. Sally did not recognize the Vulcans she saw in the morning in these washed and shaven and adorned youths; she only thought them very pleasant and kind. But after that it was surprising to see how popular Mrs. Phelps grew; how many calls she had of an evening, while her unconscious little cousin sat and smiled and talked, and behaved herself as a wild-rose might, transmigrated into a young woman.

A great many drives and walks Sally had, but after a while one gray horse seemed to her quite the best and gentlest she had ever known; and of all the wild-flowers given and sent her one basket of trailing arbutus surpassed all others. There were pinker clusters and larger flowers and bigger bunches, but the birch-bark basket, with its mossy covering, was so graceful, and the flowers so fresh and so deftly arranged; and then they were all gathered in her favorite walk,— a path in the woods by the river-side, so shaded and fresh, and sweet with such vernal odors as were never known to the bare hills of Wingfield.

It was rather odd that this was Joe Dyer's favorite walk also; that he owned that gray horse and made that birch basket. Perhaps it would have been odder still if Sally had not liked him even better than his gifts and belongings; for he was a good-tempered, handsome, gay young fellow, with overflowing spirits, a quick temper, and a kind heart; as lovable and honest as a child, yet with all a man's resolute will, strength, and fidelity. And Joe liked Sally; he had flirted with a dozen of the village girls and loved none of them. This shy, simple, sweet little country maiden was altogether different from the romping, boisterous creatures that are the growth of a manufacturing town; and, for a wonder, her voice, too, was sweet and low, — a thing rare enough among New England girls.

Under the circumstances it was hardly strange that Joe's liking and Sally's, with no intrusive elements about them, and the kindliest encouragement on Jerushy's part, should have ripened into a real honest love. Jerushy knew that Joe was a young fellow of thoroughly good character, earning high wages, and considered it a happy ordination of Providence that brought him and Sally together; and when it was time for Sally to go, and Joe appeared at the cars, Jerushy discreetly turned her head and appeared not to hear that perfectly audible whisper: " Dearest Sally, may I write you a letter?"

But I am afraid she heard, nevertheless, from the very significant speech that followed her good-by kiss of Sally's pensive, blushing face: —

"I expect you won't stay away a dreadful long while from Westboro', Sally; and you'll be just as welcome as summer-time when you *do* come back."

To which Sally only returned as an answer a deeper blush and a dimpling smile.

It would be impertinent to inquire what were Sally's meditations in the cars; they are open to conjecture; but when she arrived at the station where her father was to meet her, and, after a welcome, according to his own chestnut-burr fashion, of a growl and a kiss, was safely set beside him in the wagon, the squire looked round at her with a piercing stare, and expressed his opinion in the premises: —

"Well, seems as if you'd growed kind o' good-lookin', child. Had a good time?"

"O father, perfectly splendid!"

"I want to know! Any young fellers down to Westboro'?"

"Yes, sir," with a fresh blush, for her pure skin showed the heart-beats underneath with a lovely but annoying facility.

"Any on 'em ask ye to marry 'em?"

"No, sir."

O Sally! Sally! was that the letter or the spirit of

truth? Perhaps, after all, it *was* both, for she felt the sudden scarlet burn all her face, from the very folds of shining hair down to and through the white throat below.

Happily the squire's critical eye surveyed at that moment a piece of newly ploughed land, though he went on with his conversation: —

"Left your words behind, haint ye? Jerush' allers was a master-hand to talk, 'n I expect you've larnt how to keep still; 'n that's fust principles for women-folks. I never see furrows run like them on that hill-lot, — they're all cuterin'. Oughter be ashamed on't. Well, little cretur, be ye glad to get home?"

"Oh, yes, father!" with a very genuine love-look and smile.

"No desp'rit harm done, I guess."

"How's mother, father? — and the chickens?"

"Mother's real well, 'n spry as ever. She's follered up them old hens till they da'sn't call their souls their own another minnit, 'n went to settin' like sixty, jest to get rid on her. There's more'n six broods. Git up, old hoss! we must be a-joggin';" and in half an hour more they were at home.

"Well, here ye be, Sally! I'd kind o' gin ye up; thought you didn't mean to come at all, maybe."

"Why, mother! I'm sure you said I might stay till this week."

"Well, if I did, I didn't lot on your stayin' till Wednesday. Come, child, take off your things and stir round; it's 'most tea-time;" and with a cold kiss, that agreed well with her welcome, Mrs. Tyler returned to her rag-piecing as if life and breath depended on it, though her heart really glowed within her at the sight of her child's fair young face; but she had held the mother-love in fetters so long that it was too cramped to assert its strength even on an occasion of special demand like this.

Sally went upstairs with a wistful quiver on her lips. What a pleasant time she had had at Westboro'! How kind everybody was! how glad to see her! And then, there was that letter, — a bright spot of sunshine in the chilly dulness of home. Oh, when would it come? The weapons Mrs. Tyler had so long been forming against herself were to-day set in Sally's unconscious grasp, and she used them. It is the young soul's instinct to hunger after love, and bitterly are those to blame — more bitter is their punishment — who starve it at home and drive it out to wander after food.

If the postmaster at Wingfield had not been a deaf and gruff old man, who had no curiosity left in his wilted soul, he could not have failed to wonder at Sally's persistent haunting of the "store" where his pigeon-holes were fixed; and Sally's ingenuity was taxed for a week to find daily pretexts for her stroll toward the few clustered houses that were the nucleus of the village; but at last she was rewarded. If Joe had been delayed by a sudden journey on business at the express orders of his foreman, the letter was at least worth waiting for: it was short, strong, and earnest,—a true man's letter; and not the less precious to Sally that she felt a sort of pride in it. But if her joy had come, so came the trouble, hand in hand. As she walked along the green path homeward, the little white sun-bonnet shading her face, utterly absorbed in reading and re-reading the blessed epistle, not having the prudence or worldly wisdom to hide it in her pocket and read it at some other and more fit time, she felt a hand laid on her shoulder, and there was her father. Goodness! how she colored!

"What ye got there, so all-fired interestin', Sally? Jerushy ben a-writin' on ye some more?"

"No, father."

"What be ye a-colorin' up for so, jest like our old turkey? 'Taint none o' them Westboro' chaps ben a-sendin' ye love-letters, be it?"

The squire spoke in jest, but his word was true.

"O father!"

"The Lord above! Ef I haint hit the nail smack on the head this time! Come, Sally, let your old father see it. I don't allow no fellers to go a-writin' to my girl 'thout I know somethin' who they be, fust."

There was no place for Sally to escape; disobey she dare not. Her hand shook with apprehension as well as emotion when she put the fair sheet in the squire's hand, and her eyelids quivered with half-shed tears as she watched his inflexible visage.

"Darn it all! he's got brass enough for a meetin'-house bell! Wants to marry ye a'ready, 'n haint known ye but about three weeks: shows he's a fool on the face on't. Now I s'pose you think he's a real smart chap. Why, Sally! a-cryin', my little gal? Don't mean to tell me you like the critter so much? Well, well, well, I'll see about it. But I swan to man! there's your mother, 'n I don't know no more than Pharaoh which road she'll turn up. Whe—w!" and he took to whistling "China" five degrees worse than "Dundee." Poor Sally's heart sank.

"Stop a minnit!" said the squire, after the quavers of the last bar subsided. "Let's whittle it a bit. I guess you'd better show this here letter to her right away, 'n not say nothin' about me. She won't never surmise that I've come acrost ye; and then you'll know which way she's goin' to take, 'n let me know accordin'. Or I don't know's I will; I don't keer to be manooverin' round. It's sure as moonshine she'll set her face against it, jest as I'd oughter hev, 'n didn't."

Sally turned a face full of dew and bloom on her father for reply.

"Come, take your hankercher and wipe up them tears. I didn't eat ye, 'n maybe Mis' Tyler won't, but there's small chances but what she'll try to."

The squire turned down a lane with a grin at his daughter, thrown after her as a consolation. But, O dear reader, did you ever go to a dentist? Do you remember the sinking heart with which you forced yourself over the threshold while every fibre of your flesh recoiled? I think it requires less courage to face the flashing front of a battery, for there is a chance about bullets. Much like this felt Sally as she quickened her steps almost to a run to have this matter "over with."

Pale enough she was as she gasped, rather than spoke : —

"Mother, I've just got a letter from Westboro'."

Mrs. Tyler turned her cool gray eyes from the ironing-board and surveyed Sally, whose face certainly accorded with her tone.

"You hev?"

"Yes'm; here it is."

Her mother took the letter between her thumb and finger and deliberately read it.

"Of all things! Here's a pretty piece of business!

I told yer father 't I was clear against your goin' to Westboro', and now he'll see what comes on't. I guess he'll hark to me next time. Marry you, indeed! —'n talks as though he was pretty consider'ble sure you'd hev him!"

Harmless fell this acute arrow. Sally did love Joe, and knew he knew it.

"You kin jest answer that letter, Sally, 'n tell him we don't want nobody round after you: me'n your father can't spare ye. I aint a-goin' to hev no sech talk, not this ten year yet, 'n mebbe not then. Ef you know'd 's much 'bout the troubles o' matrimony 's I do, I guess ye'd ruther live single, a sight."

"But, mother, I — I — I don't want to write such a letter."

Sally burst into tears just as her father came in.

"Well, now, what is't, wife? What's broke loose now?"

"Nothin' great, only Sally's a fool; and another one o' the same sort, only a young feller, has ben a comin' round 'n askin' her to marry him."

"You don't say so!" ejaculated the squire, as naturally as possible. "That does beat all! I never did hear such brass! One o' them Westboro' chaps, I s'pose."

"Now there you go, right off the handle, slap! I *should* like to know who gev her things, 'n money 'n all to go to Westboro'? An' hevin' flung her at the poor young man's head, so to speak, lo you now! he turns around and jaws at him for pickin' on her up! That's real man-fashion, I do declare!"

"Goodness gracious! ef that aint jumpin' the fence! Anyhow, Sally, you've got to give him the mitten quick-step. I sha'n't hev it, 'n I won't, 'n I aint a-goin' to!"

"There you be ag'in, husband! How do you know but what he's a real clever young man? An' Sally seems to kind o' set her heart on't; 'n I s'pose she'll be a-gettin' married some time, anyhow."

"Thought you set your face ag'in matrimony, Miss Tyler?"

"Well, I can't fix the world over ef I want to, and folks will do so, whether or no. And ef he's got means, and is pretty respectable, 'n goes to meetin', why, in five or six years or so I might be brought to think on't."

"O mother!"

"Well, what?"

After that the battle raged, the squire opposing, Mrs. Tyler consenting, till at last, after myriads of words, Mrs. Tyler sat down to write Mrs. Phelps a letter of inquiry into Joe Dyer's morals, means, manners, etc.; and in due time got this hardly satisfactory letter from Cousin Jerushy: —

WESTBORO', June 3, 18—.

DEAR AUNT HULDAH: —

I got your letter two days ago, but Sophrony and Mary Jane are both down with measles, and I don't have much time. I don't know anything about Joe Dyer but what's good. He hasn't lived here a great while; he comes from Springfield, where he worked a good spell in the armory. He makes good wages here, and we think to our house he's a real pretty young man, and I guess a good one. Anyway, Uncle Tyler could write to the head man up to the armory and find out all he wants to know. I can't write much more, for the children have 'most got through their nap. Give my love to uncle and Sally.

Your affectionate niece,

JERUSHA PHELPS.

"Well!" groaned the squire, from the side of the room behind his wife, giving Sally a look as full of mischief as a boy's, "I wash my hands o' the hull business. You've took it up, Miss Tyler, ag'inst my feelin's, 'n you can kerry it out."

"Jest as ef I should go 'n write a letter to that man up to Springfield, husband! 'Taint my business; men-folks never want women a-writin' to them about sech things. I should make a mess on't; and reelly, ef you do care about Sally's feelin's, you'd oughter do it right off."

"Well, well!" groaned and grinned the squire, "it's no use talkin' no more. Fetch me the paper, Sally; I'll go 'n do it now, if I've got ter."

So the squire indited the following epistle, peculiar in more than its brevity:—

JUNE 4, 18—.

MR. ADKINS, ESQ.:—

SIR,—I have heerd that a young man called Joseph Dyer worked to your shops last year. What did he do and how did he do it? Leastways, what kind of a feller is he? I put in a stamp for answer, which will obleege

Yours to command,

'PAPHRO TYLER.

Nobody saw the letter before it went. In the meantime, Joe Dyer, getting no answer from Sally, but hearing through Jerushy that he had been inquired about by Mrs. Tyler, and drawing favorable augury from that fact, became desperately impatient, and travelled off one fine day to Wingfield to get a *vivâ-voce* answer to his proposal. It was the loveliest of June twilights when he walked over from the station;

the woods were full of that perfumed gloom that summer distils through the soft and tranquil air of evening; all the earth was quivering with vibrant whispers, as if its great heart palpitated with new life and murmured in sleep; myriads of blossoms drank the dew as at a fairy revel, and sent breathing odors skyward; the unutterable thrill and rapture of spring just blooming into summer pervaded even the worst places of Wingfield. Joe's heart was almost too accordant with the season, and it beat harder than was pleasant as he knocked at Squire Tyler's front door, standing open for once in its life, and letting into the usually musty parlor the whole breath of June and the delicate odor of two great white rose-bushes that guarded the portal on either hand, and trailed their wreaths of sunny blossoms, whose hearts glowed with the saffron tints of dawn, even across the quaint old lintel overhead.

Sometimes all powers are propitious to lovers, true though they be, and to-night the hour and the pair might have appeased the Eumenides themselves. Mrs. Tyler, dreaming of nothing less than Joe Dyer's vicinity, was in the farther barn coercing a refractory hen, that had a will of her own and declined to accept the situation; the squire was at the post-office waiting anxiously for the mail. So Sally herself appeared through the soft dusk like a glimmering blossom, and was stunned — perhaps not disagreeably — by finding herself in Joe's arms.

"O Sally!"

"O Joe!"

And then the parlor sank into a moment's quiet as they looked at each other and — said no more. If speech was given us to conceal our feelings they had very few to conceal, certainly; and I am inclined to think it was so.

But while they sat in this sweet silence, quite forgetful of adverse fate — possible to them as to all humanity — down the street came the squire, regret and consternation on his kind old face, holding a letter in one hand and wiping the sweat from his troubled forehead; not that it was warm, but he was agitated. He avoided the house, for he did not want to see Sally at first, and, hearing the angry squawks of the hen with which Mrs. Tyler was engaged in single combat, he traced his wife to the barn, and arrived there just as she emerged from the door, panting, but flushed with victory.

"Well! I've sot her at last! Got her into a nail-kag and put a milkin'-stool on top. I guess she'll stay put till to-morrer, and then I'll fetch the good eggs 'n put under her."

"Kind o' smother, won't she?" suggested the humane squire.

"Law, no! the hay aint up to the bung-hole. Got a letter, hev ye, there in your hand?"

"*Je*-rus'lem! I guess I hev; 'n I wish Sally'd stayed to hum, I tell ye. I'm dead beat, 'n I'd ruther be hung this minnit than tell her on't. Come along into the kitchen; she aint there, is she?"

"No; she's upstairs, I 'xpect. She seems to favor bein' alone considerable when the chores is done. I'm 'most allers sleepy, and you're up to the store, 'n there aint no company for her. Wait a minnit, 'n I'll light the lamp."

"Oh, dear!" said the squire, unfolding the letter. "It's a dreadful thing, wife — dreadful; but 'taint no use to jaw about it beforehand. Here! take 'n read it; I can't."

The superintendent had evidently thought Mr. Tyler's first questions were the important ones, and answered them in business fashion: —

Mr. 'Paphro Tyler: —

Sir, — Yours of the 4th came to hand this morning. I have recently come to this place, but find on inquiry that Joseph Dyer worked here a year ago. He was a forger, and a good workman; of his personal character I know nothing.

Yours, etc.,
T. Adkins.

"Goodness gracious!" exclaimed Mrs. Tyler, dropping the letter in her lap and looking aghast at her husband over her spectacles. "A forger! Why, it's a hangin' business, aint it?"

"I b'lieve 'taint now, but anyway it's State prison. Jest to think on't!"

"It's dreadful! dreadful! husband; 'n we've got to tell Sally! Well, she's had a great escape, 'n she'd oughter be thankful for't."

"I guess that'll be the least part on't," growled the squire, passing his hand across the shaggy eyebrows as if to brush away a mist. "Fetch the lamp, wife; the entry's mighty dark. I'll go 'n call her."

The squire opened the kitchen door, and Mrs. Tyler followed, but their steps were arrested by a strange sound in that house. From the parlor door flowed a stream of low talk, sweet as the kissing whispers that ripple behind a canoe silently paddled across silent water, and broken here and there with bubbles of laughter. The squire looked at his wife and advanced manfully, taking the light in his own hand. There, in the flood of light the rising moon poured in at the open windows, sat Sally and a young man, hand in hand, on the settee, — Sally blooming and dimpling and blushing in the most unscrupulous and delightful manner, and the "chap," as the squire mentally styled him, so handsome and so happy that Mr. Tyler involuntarily smiled.

"Father, this is Mr. Dyer. That is mother, Joe."

The squire fairly gasped with rage.

"How darst you come into this house, you raskil! — a-grinnin' and imposin' round jest as though you was as good as folks! I know ye, 'n I'll hev ye hauled up in State's prison pretty quick if there's law in the land, 'nless you clear right off."

"O father!" sobbed Sally; "don't! don't! What do you talk so for?" — Joe being, as he afterward expressed it, "dumbfoundered."

"Talk so! Facts is facts! I've found him out; he's ben and committed forgery, the everlastin' scamp!"

Joe found his tongue and blazed: —

"That's an infernal lie, whoever says it!"

"O Joe, don't!" interposed sobbing Sally; Mrs. Tyler being, for a wonder, quite silent, confessing at a later period of the evening that she "was so kind o' choked up she hadn't a word to throw to a dog."

"But it *is* a lie, Sally, and I can't be slandered so by any man, if he is your father."

"'Taint no slander!" thundered the squire; "'n if it was, 'taint me that slandered ye. I suppose you won't deny you worked to the Springfield armory a spell back?"

"Why, no; what should I deny it for?"

"Well, read that!" said the squire, charging down upon the angry and astonished young man with the letter.

Joe took the paper from the hand that brandished it, and the squire held the lamp nearer. As Sally's lover read the damnatory epistle a change passed over his features (isn't that the way they say it in novels?); but it wasn't livid, or pallid, or rigid, or purple, or anything but a growing broader and broader, till, as the last words were glanced at, Joe flung himself back on the old settee and burst into a roar of laughter that seemed utterly inextinguishable. He held his sides; he rolled and twisted; he laughed so that the tears made his ruddy cheeks shiny; he could not speak, but held out the letter to Sally. Was the girl bewitched? She, too, sat down in a chair and screamed with a laughter that would not be appeased, while the squire and Mrs. Tyler glared at them with wide-open mouths and blank eyes, as if they had suddenly gone mad.

"Oh, dear! O Lord! O goodness! I shall split — I certainly shall!" was all the explanation that could be got from Joe. He could not talk; but Sally, not quite so tickled with the joke, because she had been so scared to begin with, recovered her equilibrium first, and, wiping her streaming eyes, began, as well as she could for still-interrupting spasms of laughing, to expound: —

"Why, father! Goodness — oh, don't you know what Mr. Adkins means? Oh, dear! I can't stop! Why, he means Joe was a forger. Oh! there it is again! Well, he is now. He works at a forge, and *that's what they call 'em!*"

Joe exploded again, and the parlor rang with the squire's roars. Mrs. Tyler was the last to comprehend; but when she did she laughed too; and when at length the four, all red and shiny, had laughed themselves out and were fairly gasping for breath, the squire turned upon Joe: —

"Well, I haint hed sech a larf, not in twenty year. I can't do nothin' but shake hands with ye for the sake on't. Got any folks in Wingfield? No? Well, ye must stay here, — there's room enough, — and I shall hev a better chance to see how I like ye; 'n so'll Miss Tyler. I don't know but what Sally's made up *her* mind."

Sally had slipped away before Joe looked round. Is it necessary to detail Joe's triumphant progress into the hearts of the family? Perhaps the best proof of it is that on one October day, " expressly got up for the occasion," as Joe said, when the hills were gorgeous with color, the air transfused with sunshine, and the river blue as the fringed gentians on its bank, Sally descended once more from the cars at Westboro' station, — her first appearance in the new and highly-interesting character of "The Forger's Bride."

TOO LATE.

"'Tis true 'tis pity! pity 'tis 'tis true!"

In one of those scanty New England towns that fill a stranger with the acutest sense of desolation, more desolate than the desert itself, because there are human inhabitants to suffer from its solitude and listlessness, there stood, and still stands, a large red farm-house, with sloping roof, and great chimney in the middle, where David Blair lived. Perhaps Wingfield was not so forlorn to him as to another, for he had Scotch blood in his veins, and his shrewd thrift found full exercise in redeeming the earth from thorns and briers, and eating his bread under the full force of the primeval curse. He was a "dour" man, with a long, grim visage that would have become any Covenanter's conventicle in his native land; and his prayers were as long and grim as his face. Of life's graces and amenities he had no idea; they would have been scouted as profane vanities had they blossomed inside his threshold. Existence to him was a heavy and dreadful responsibility; a drear and doubtful working out of his own salvation; a perpetual fleeing from the wrath to come, that seemed to dog his heels and rear threatening heads at every turn. A cowardly man, with these ever-present terrors, would have taken refuge in some sweet and lulling sin or creed, some belief of a universal salvation, some epicurean "let us eat and drink, for tomorrow we die," or some idea in nothing beyond the grave.

But David Blair was full of courage. Like some knotty, twisted oak, that offers scant solace to the eye, he endured, oak-like, all storms, and bent not an atom to any fierce blast of nature or Providence; for he made a distinction between them. His wife was a neat, quiet, subdued woman, who held her house and her husband in as much reverence as a Feejee holds his idols. Like most women, she had an instinctive love for grace and beauty, but from long repression it was only a blind and groping instinct. Her house was kept in a state of spotless purity, but was bald as any vineless rock within. Flies never intruded there; spiders still less. The windows of the "best room" were veiled and double-veiled with green paper shades and snow-white cotton curtains, and the ghastly light that strayed in through these obstructions revealed a speckless, but hideous, homespun carpet, four straight-backed chairs, with horse-hair seats, an equally black and shining sofa, and a round mahogany table with a great Bible in the midst. No vases, no shells, no ornament of useless fashion stood on the white wooden mantel-piece over the open fireplace; no stencil border broke the monotonous whitewash of the walls. You could see your face in a state of distortion and jaundice anywhere in the andirons, so brilliant were their brassy columns; and the very bricks of the chimney were scraped and washed from the soot of the rare fire. You could hardly imagine that even the leaping, laughing wood-fire could impart any cheer to the funereal order of that chill and musty apartment. Bedroom, kitchen, shed, wood-house,

— all shared this scrupulous array. The processes that in other households are wont to give cheery tokens of life, and bounty, and natural appetites and passions, seemed here to be carried on under protest. No flour was spilled when Thankful Blair made bread; no milk ever slopped from an overfull pail; no shoe ever brought in mud or sand across the mats that lay inside and outside of every door. The very garret preserved an aspect of serenity, since all its bundles of herbs hung evenly side by side, and the stores of nuts had each their separate boundaries, lest some jarring door or intrusive mouse should scatter them.

In the midst of all this order there was yet a child, if little Hannah Blair ever was a child in more than name. From her babyhood she was the model of all Wingfield babies: a child that never fretted; that slept nights through all the pangs and perils of teething; that had every childish disease with perfect decency and patience; was a child to be held up to every mother's admiration. Poor little soul! the mother love that crushed those other babies with kisses; that romped and laughed with them, when she was left straight and solemn in her cradle; that petted, and slapped, and spoiled, and scolded all those common children, Thankful Blair kept under lock and key in her inmost heart.

"Beware of idols!" was the stern warning that had fallen on her first outburst of joy at the birth of one living child at last, and from that time the whole tenor of her husband's speech and prayer had been that they both might be saved from the awful sin of idolatry, and be enabled to bring up their child in the fear of the Lord, a hater of sin and a follower of the

Law: the gospel that a baby brought to light was not yet theirs! So Hannah grew to girlhood, a feminine reproduction of her father. Keen, practical insight is not the most softening trait for a woman to possess. It is iron and steel in the soul that does not burn with love mighty and outflowing enough to fuse all other elements in its own glow, and as Hannah grew older and read her mother's repressed nature through and through, the tender heart, the timid conscience, the longing after better and brighter things than life offered to her, only moved her child to an unavowed contempt for a soul so weak and so childish. In a certain way Hannah Blair loved her mother, but it was more as if she had been her child than her parent. Toward her father her feelings were far different. She respected him; he was her model. She alone knew, from a like experience, what reserved depth of feeling lay unawakened under his rigid exterior; she knew, for there were times when her own granite nature shuddered through and through with volcanic forces; when her only refuge against generous indignation or mighty anger was in solitary prayer and grievous wrestlings of the flesh against the spirit as well as the spirit against the flesh. So Hannah grew up to womanhood. Tall and slight as any woodland sapling, but without the native grace of a free growth, her erect and alert figure pleased only by its alacrity and spotless clothing. She was "dredful spry," as old Moll Thunder, the half-breed Indian woman used to say, — "dredful spry; most like squaw — so still, so straight; blue eyes, most like ice. Ho! Moll better walk a chalk 'fore Miss Hanner!"

And Moll spoke from bitter experience, for old Deacon Campbell himself never gave her severer lectures on her ungodly life and conversation than dropped with cutting distinctness from those prim, thin, red lips. Yet Hannah Blair was not without charms for the youth of Wingfield. Spare as she was, her face had the fresh bloom of youth upon its high, straight features ; her eyes were blue and bright ; her hair, smoothed about her small head, glittered like fresh flax, and made a heavy coil, that her slender white throat seemed over-small to sustain. She was cool, serene, rather unapproachable to lovers or love-makers ; but she was David Blair's only child, and his farm lay fair and wide on the high plains of Wingfield. She was well-to-do and pious, — charms which hold to this day potent sway over the youth of her native soil, — and after she was eighteen no Sunday night passed in solitude in the Blair keeping-room ; for young men of all sorts and sizes ranged themselves against the wall, sometimes four at once, tilted their chairs, twirled their thumbs, crossed one foot and then the other over their alternate knees, dropping sparse remarks about the corn, or the weather, or the sermon, sometimes even the village politics ; but one and all stared at Hannah, as she sat upright by the fireplace or the window, arrayed in a blue-stuff gown or a flowered chintz, as the season might be, and sitting as serene, as cool, as uninteresting as any cherub on a tombstone, till the old Dutch clock struck nine, the meeting-house bell tolled, and the young men, one and all, made their awkward farewells and went home, uttering, no doubt, a sigh of relief when the painful pleasure was over.

By and by the Wingfield store, long kept by Uncle Gid Mayhew, began to have a look of new life, for the old man's only son, Charley Mayhew, had come home from Boston, where he had been ten years in a dry-goods shop, to take the business off his father's hands. Just in time, too, for the store was scarce set to rights in symmetrical fashion when Uncle Gid was struck with paralysis and put to bed for the rest of his life, — a brief one at that. Wingfield gossips shook their heads and muttered that the new order of things was enough to kill him. After so many years of dust and confusion, to see the pepper-corns, candy, and beeswax sorted out into fresh, clean jars; the shoes and ribbons, cut nails and bar-soap, neatly disentangled and arranged; the ploughs, harrows, cheeses, hoes and bales of cotton and calico divorced and placed at different ends of the store; the grimy windows washed, and the dirty floor cleaned and swept, — was perhaps a shock to the old man, but not enough to kill him. His eighty years of vegetation sufficed for that; but he left behind him this son, so full of life, and spirit, and fun, so earnest at work, so abounding in energy, but withal so given over to frolic in its time, that it seemed as if even Wingfield stagnation never could give him a proper dulness or paralyze his handsome face and manly figure. Of course Charley Mayhew fell in love with Hannah Blair.

A mischievous desire at first to wake up those cold blue eyes and flush that clear, set face with blushes soon deepened into a very devoted affection. The ranks of Sunday-night lovers began to look at him with evil eyes, for not even the formality of the best parlor restrained his fun, or the impassive visage of David Blair awed him into silence. Even Hannah began to glow and vivify in his presence; a warmer

color flushed her cheeks, her thin lips relaxed in real
smiles; her eyes shone with deeper and keener gleams
than the firelight lent them, and, worst of all, the
sheepish suitors themselves could not help an occasional giggle, a broad grin, or even a decided horse-
laugh, at his sallies; and when at last David Blair
himself relaxed into an audible laugh, and declared to
Charley he was " a master hand at telling stories,"
the vexed ranks gave it up, allowed that the conquer-
ing hero had come, and left Charley Mayhew a free
field thereafter, which of course he improved. But
even after Hannah Blair had promised in good, set
terms to be his wife, and David had given his slow
consent, it was doubtful to Charley if this treasure
was his merely out of his own determined persistence
or with any genuine feeling of her own, any real response of heart; for the maiden was so inaccessible,
so chill, so proper, that his warm, impulsive nature
dashed against hers and recoiled as the wild sea from
a rocky coast. Yet after many days the rock does
show signs of yielding; there are traces on its surface,
though it needs years to soften and disentegrate its
nature. They were a handsome couple, these two,
and admiring eyes followed them in their walks.
Never had Hannah's face mantled with so rich a color,
or her eyes shone with so deep and soft a blue; the
stern, red lips relaxed into a serene content, and
here and there a tint of gayety about her dress — a
fresh ribbon, a flower at her throat, a new frill — told
of her shy blossom-time. She was one of those prim,
old-fashioned pinks, whose cold color, formal shape,
stiff growth, and dagger-shaped gray-green leaves,
stamp them the quaint old-maid sisterhood of flowers,

yet which hold in their hearts a breath of passionate spice, an odor of the glowing Orient or the sweet and ardent South, that seems fitter for the open-breasted roses, looking frankly and fervently up to the sun.

No, not even her lover knew the madness of Hannah Blair's hungry heart, now for the first time fed, — a madness that filled her with sweet delirium, that she regarded as nothing less than a direct Satanic impulse, against which she fought and prayed, all in vain; for God was greater than her heart, and he had filled it with that love which every wife and mother needs, strong enough to endure all things, to be forever faithful and forever fresh. But no vine-planted and grass-strewn volcano ever showed more placidly than Hannah Blair. Her daily duties were done with such exactness and patience, her lover's demands so coolly set aside till those duties were attended to, her face kept so calm even when the blood thrilled to her finger-tips at the sound of his voice, that, long as her mother had known her, she looked on with wonder, and admired afar off the self-control she never could have exhibited. For Hannah's wooing was carried on in no such style as her mother's had been. Thankful Parsons had accepted David Blair from a simple sense of duty, and he had asked her because she was meek and pious, had a good farm, and understood cows; no troublesome sentiment, no turbulent passion, disturbed their rather dull courtship. A very different wooer was this handsome, merry young fellow, with his dark curls and keen, pleasant eyes, who came into the house like a fresh, dancing breeze, and stirred its dusty stagnation into absolute sparkle. Mrs. Blair loved him dearly already; her repressed heart opened to him all its motherly instincts. She cooked for him whatever she observed he liked, with simple zeal and pleasure. She unconsciously smiled to hear his voice. Deeply she wondered at Hannah, who, day by day, stitched on her quilts, her sheets, her pillow-cases, and her napery, with as diligent sternness as ever she applied to more irksome tasks, and never once blushed or smiled over the buying or shaping of her personal bridal gear, only showing, if possible, a keener eye for business, a more infallible judgment of goods and prices, wear and tear, use and fitness, than ever before.

So the long winter wore away. Hannah's goods lay piled in the " spare chamber,"— heaps of immaculate linen, homespun flannel, patchwork of gayest hues, and towels woven and hemmed by her own hands; and in the clothes-press, whose deep drawers were filled with her own garments in neat array, hung the very wedding dress of dove-colored paduasoy, the great Leghorn bonnet, with white satin ribbons, and the black silk cardinal. Hannah had foregone all the amusements of the past months, at no time consonant to her taste, in order to construct these treasures for her new life. In vain had Charley coaxed her to share in the sleighing frolics, the huskings, the quilting-bees of the neighborhood. It did not once enter into his mind that Hannah had rather be alone with the fulness of her great joy than to have its sacred rapture intermeddled with by the kindly or unkindly jokes and jeers of other people. He never knew that her delight was full even to oppression, when she sat by herself and sewed like an automaton, setting with every stitch a hope or a thought of her love and life.

It was spring now. The long, cold winter had

passed at last; the woods began to bud, the pastures grew green even in Wingfield, and brave little blossoms sprung up in the very moisture of the just melted snow-drifts. May had brought the robins and the swallows back; here and there an oriole darted like a flake of fire from one drooping elm to another; the stiff larches put out little crimson cones; the gracious elm boughs grew dusk and dense with swelling buds, and the maple hung out its dancing yellow tassels high in air. The swamps were transfigured with vivid verdure and lit with rank yellow blossoms, where

"The wild marsh marigold shone like fire,"—

the quaint, sad-colored trillium made its protest in fence corners and by the low buttresses of granite on the hills far and near, and the rough-leaved arbutus nestled its baby faces of sweetest bloom deep in the gray grass and stiff moss beds. The day drew near for the wedding. It was to be the last Wednesday in May.

"Darned unlucky!" muttered Moll Thunder, drying her ragged shoes before Mrs. Blair's kitchen fire, having just brought a fagot of herbs and roots for the brewing of root-beer,— even then a favorite beverage in New England, as it is to-day. "Darned unlucky! Married in May, repent alway. Guess Hanner pretty good like ter set up 'ginst ole debbil heself. No good, no good; debbil pretty good strong. Moll knows! He! he! he!"

Mrs. Blair shivered. She was superstitious, like all women, and old Moll was a born witch, everybody knew. But then her daughter's pure, fair, and resolute face rose up before her, and the superstitious fear flickered and went out. She thought Hannah altogether beyond the power of "ole debbil." At last the last Wednesday came, — a day as serene and lovely as if new created; flying masses of white cloud chased each other through the azure sky, and cast quick shadows on the long, green range of hills that shut in Wingfield on the west. Shine and shadow added an exquisite grace of expression to the shades of tender green veiling those cruel granite rocks; a like flitting grace at last transfigured Hannah Blair's cold-featured face. The apple-trees blossomed everywhere with festive garlands of faint pink bloom, and filled the air with their bitter-sweet, subtle odor, clean and delicate, yet the parent of that luscious, vinous, oppressive perfume that autumn should bring from the heaps of gold and crimson fruit, as yet unformed below those waxen petals.

To-day at last Hannah had resolved to give her beating heart one day of freedom, — one long day of unrestrained joy, — if she could bear the freedom of that ardent rapture, so long, so conscientiously repressed. For once in her life she sung about her work; psalm-tunes, indeed, but one can put a deal of vitality into Mear and Bethesda; and Cambridge, with its glad, exultant repeat, has all the capacity of a love-song. Mrs. Blair heard it from the kitchen where she was watching the last pan of cake come to crisp perfection in the brick oven. The old words had a curious adaptation to the sweet, intense triumph of the air, and Hannah carried the three parts of the tune as they came in with a flexibility of voice new to her as to her sole hearer : —

> " 'Twas in the watches of the night
> I thought upon thy power;
> I kept thy lovely face in sight
> Amid the darkest hour!"

What a subdued ecstasy rose and fell in her voice as she swept and garnished the old house.

> "Amid the darkest hour!"

Oh, there could never be a dark hour for her again, she thought, — never a doubt, or fear, or trouble.

> "My beloved is mine and I am his,"

rose to her lips from the oldest of all love-songs. Half profane she seemed to herself; but to-day her deeper nature got the better of her deep prejudices; she was at heart, for once, a simple, love-smitten girl.

The quiet wedding was to be after tea. Nobody was asked, for the few relatives David Blair possessed were almost strangers to him, and lived far away. His wife had been an only child, and Hannah had made no girl friends in the village. The minister was to come at eight o'clock, and the orthodox cake and wine handed round after the ceremony. The young couple were to go to their own house, and settle down at once to the duties and cares of life. Charley had been ordered not to appear till tea-time, and after the dinner was eaten and everything put to rights Mrs. Blair went to her room to plait a cap-ruffle, and Hannah sat down in the spare room by herself, to rest, she said; really to dream, to hope, to bury her face in her trembling hand, and let a mighty wave of rapture overflow her whole entranced soul. The cap-ruffle troubled

Mrs. Blair much. Twice it had to be taken from the prim plaits and relaid, then to be sprinkled and ironed out. This involved making a fresh fire to heat the flat-iron, and it got to be well on in the afternoon, and Mrs. Blair was tired. There was nobody to reflect on her waste of time, so she lay down a moment on the bed. David had gone to plough a lot on the furthest part of the farm. He neglected work for no emergency. As a godless neighbor said once, "Dave Blair would sow rye on the edge of hell if he thought he could get the cattle there to plough it up!" A daughter's wedding-day was no excuse for idleness in him. So Mrs. Blair was safe in her nap.

Meantime, as Hannah sat a little withdrawn from the open window, where for once the afternoon sun streamed in unguardedly, and the passionate warble of the song-sparrows, and the indescribable odor of spring followed too, she was suddenly half aware of an outside shadow, and a letter skimmed through the window, and fell at her feet. Scarce roused from her dream, she looked at it fixedly a moment before she stooped to pick it up. Its coming was so sudden, so startling, it did not once occur to her to look out and see who brought it. She hesitated before she broke the broad, red seal, and swept her hand across her eyes as if to brush away the dreams that had filled and clouded them. But the first few words brought back to those eyes their native steely glint, and, as she read on, life, light, love, withdrew their tender glories from her face. It settled into stone, into flint. Her mouth set in lines of dreadful implacable portent, her cheek paled to the whiteness of a marble monument, and the red lips faded to pale, cold purple. What she read in that letter neither man nor woman save the writer and the reader ever knew, for when it was read Hannah Blair walked like an unrepentant conspirator to the stake, fearless, careless, hopeless, out into the small, silent kitchen, and laying that missive of evil on the smouldering coals, stood by stark and stiff till every ash was burned or floated up the chimney. Then she turned, and said in the voice of one who calls from his grave : —

"Mother!"

Mrs. Blair sprung from her doze at the sound. Her mother instinct was keen as the hen's who hears the hawk scream in the sky, and knows her brood in danger. She was on the threshold of the kitchen door almost as soon as Hannah spoke; and her heart sank to its furthest depth when she saw the face before her. Death would have left no such traces — given her no such shock. This was death in life, and it spoke, slowly, deliberately, with an awful distinctness.

"Mother, when Charles Mayhew comes here tonight, you must tell him I will not marry him."

"What?" half screamed the terrified woman, doubtful of her own hearing. Again the cold, relentless tones, in accents as clear and certain as the voice of fate itself : —

"When Charles Mayhew comes here to-night you must see him, and tell him I will not marry him."

"Hanner, I can't! I can't! What for? What do you mean? What is it?"

The words syllabled themselves again out of the thin, rigid lips : —

"I will not marry him."

"Oh, I can't tell him! he will die! I *cannot*, Hanner. You must tell him yourself — you must! you must!"

Still the same answer, only the words lessening each time : —

" I will not ! "

" But, Hanner, child, stop and think — do. All your things made; you're published; the minister's spoke to. Why do you act so? You can't, Hanner. Oh, I never can tell him! What shall I say? What will he do? Oh, dear! You must tell him yourself; I can't — I won't! I aint goin' to; you must ! "

A shade of mortal weariness stole across the gray, still face, most like the relaxation of the features after death; but that was all the shrill tirade produced, except the dull, cold repetition : —

" I will not ! "

And then Hannah Blair turned and crept up the narrow stairway to her bedroom; her mother, stunned with terror and amazement, still with a mother's alert ear, heard the key grate in the lock, the window shut quietly down, and heard no more. The house was silent even to breathlessness. In her desperation Mrs. Blair began to wish that David would come; and then the unconscious spur of life-long habit stung her into action. It was five o'clock, and she must get tea; for tea must be prepared though the crack of doom were impending. So she built the fire, filled the kettle, hung it on the crane, laid the table, all with the accuracy of habit, her ear strained to its utmost to hear some voice, some sigh, some movement from that bolted chamber above. All in vain. There might have been a corpse there for any sound of life, and

Mrs. Blair felt the awe of death creep over her as she listened. For once it was glad relief to hear David coming with the oxen; to see them driven to their shed; to watch his gaunt, erect figure come up the path to the back door; but how hard it was to tell him. He asked no question, he made no comment, but the cold, gray eye quickened into fire like the sudden glitter of lightning, and without a word he strode up the stair to Hannah's room.

"Hannah!"

There was no answer. David Blair was ill-used to disobedience. His voice was sterner than ever as he repeated the call: —

"Hannah, open your door!"

Slowly the key turned, slowly the door opened, and the two faced each other. The strong man recoiled. Was this his child, — this gray, rigid masque, this old woman? But he had a duty to do.

"Hannah, why is this?"

"I cannot tell you, father."

"But you must see Charles Mayhew."

"I will not!"

Still calm, but inexpressibly bitter and determined, like one repeating a dreadful lesson after some tyrant's torture. David Blair could not speak. He stood still on that threshold, without speech or motion, and softly as it had opened, the door closed in his face, the key turned, he was shut out, — not merely from the chamber, but forever from the deepest recess of Hannah's heart and life, if indeed he had ever, even in imagination, entered there. He stood a moment in silent amazement, and then went down into the kitchen utterly speechless. He swallowed his supper mechanically, reached down his hat, but on the door-step turned and said: —

"Thankful, you must tell Charles Mayhew: Hannah will not; I cannot. It is women's work — yea, it was a woman that first time in Paradise!"

And with this scriptural sneer he left his frightened wife to do the thing he dared not. Not the first man who has done so, nor the last. An hour later the joyful bridegroom came in, his dark eyes full of happy light, his handsome figure set off by a new suit of clothes, the like of which Wingfield never had seen, much less originated; his face fairly radiant; but it clouded quickly as a storm-reflecting lake when he saw the cold, wet face of Mrs. Blair, the reddened eyes, the quivering lips, and felt the close, yet trembling pressure of the kind old arms, for the first time clasped round his neck as he stooped toward her. How Thankful Blair contrived to tell him what she had to tell she never knew. It was forced from her lips in incoherent snatches; it was received at first with total incredulity, and she needed to repeat it again and again; to recall Hannah's words, to describe, as she best might, her ghastly aspect, her hollow, hoarse voice, her reply to her father. At last Charles Mayhew began to believe — to rave, to give way to such passionate, angry grief that Thankful Blair trembled, and longed for Parson Day to come, or for David to return. But neither thing happened, for David had warned the parson, and then hidden his own distress and dismay as far as he could get from the house in his own woodland, sitting on a log for hours, lest in coming back to the house he should face the man he could not but pity and fear both; for what reason or shadow of excuse could he offer to him for his daughter's cruel and mysterious conduct? So Mrs. Blair had to bear the scene alone. At last the maddened man insisted on going upstairs to Hannah's door; but that her mother withstood. He should not harass Hannah; she would keep her from one more anguish, if she stood in the door-way and resisted physically.

"But I will see her! I will speak to her! I will know myself what this means! I am not a fool or a dog, to be thrown aside for nothing!"

And with this he rushed out of the kitchen door, round the end of the house, to the grass-plat below Hannah's window. Well he knew that little window, with its white curtain, where he had so often watched the light go out from the hill-side, where he always lingered in his homeward walks. The curtain was down now, and no ray of light quivered from behind it.

"Hannah! Hannah! *my* Hannah!" he called, with anguish in every tone. "Hannah, look at me! only just look at me! tell me one word!" And then came the fondest pleadings, the most passionate remonstrances — all in vain. He might as well have agonized by her coffin side — by her grass-grown grave. Now a different mood inspired him, and he poured out threats and commands till the cool moonlight air seemed quivering with passion and rage. Still there was no voice nor answer, nor any that replied. The calmness of immortal repose lay upon this quiet dwelling, though the torment and tumult without stormed like a tempest. Was there, then, neither tumult nor torment within? At last, when hours — ages it seemed to the desperate man — had passed by, nature could endure no more. The apathy of exhaustion stole over him; he felt a despair, that was partly bodily weariness, take entire possession of him; he ceased to adjure, to remonstrate, to cry out.

"Good-by, Hannah; good-by!" he called at length. The weak, sad accents beat like storm-weary birds vainly against that blank, deaf window. Nothing spoke to him, not even the worn-out and helpless woman who sat on the kitchen door-step with her apron over her head, veiling her hopeless distress, nor lifting that homely screen to see a ruined man creep away from his own grave,— the grave of all his better nature, to be seen there no more; for from that hour no creature in Wingfield ever saw or heard of him again.

There was a mighty stir among the gossips of the village for once. Not often did so piquant and mysterious a bit of scandal regale them at sewing societies, at tea-fights, even at prayer-meetings, for it became a matter of certain religious interest, since all the parties therein were church-members. But in vain did all the gossips lay their heads together. Nothing was known beyond the bare facts that at the last minute Hannah Blair had "gi'n the mitten" to Charley Mayhew, and he had then and there disappeared. His store was sold to a new-comer from Grenville Centre, who was not communicative, — perhaps because he had nothing to tell, — and Charley dropped out of daily talk before long, as one who is dead and buried far away; as we all do, after how brief a time, how vanishing a grief. As for the Blairs, they endured in stoical silence, and made no sign. Sunday saw both the old people in their places early; nobody looked for Hannah, but before the bell ceased its melancholy toll, just before Parson Day ambled up the broad aisle, her slender figure, straight and still as ever, came up to her seat in the square pew. True her face was colorless; the shadow of death lingered there yet; and though her eyes shone with keener glitter than ever, and her lips burned like a scarlet streak, an acute observer would have seen upon her face traces of a dreadful conflict: lines around the mouth that years of suffering might have grown; a relaxation of the muscles about the eye and temple; a look as of one who sees only something afar off, who is absent from the body as far as consciousness goes. There she sat, — through short prayer and long prayer, hymn, psalm, and sermon, and the battery of looks, both direct and furtive, that assailed her, — all unmoved. And at home it was the same, — utterly listless, cold, silent, she took up her life again; day by day did her weary round of household duties with the same punctilious neatness and despatch; spun and knit, and turned cheeses; for her mother had been broken down visibly for a time by this strange and sad catastrophe, and was more incapable than ever in her life before of earnest work, so Hannah had her place to supply in part as well as her own. We hear of martyrs of the stake, the fagot, the arena, the hunger-maddened beasts, the rising tide, the rack, and our souls shudder, our flesh creeps; we wonder and adore. I think the gladdest look of her life would have illuminated Hannah Blair's face had it been possible now to exchange her endurance for any of these deaths; but it is women who must endure; for them are those secret agonies no enthusiasm gilds, no hope assuages, no sympathy consoles. God alone stoops to this anguish, and he not always; for there is a stubborn pride that will not lift its eyes to heaven lest it should be a tacit acknowledgment that they were fixed once upon poor earth. For these remains only the outlook daily lessening to all of us, — the outlook whose vista ends in a grave.

But the unrelenting days stole on; their dead march, with monotonous tramp, left traces on even Hannah's wretched, haughty soul. They trampled down the past in thick dust; it became ashes under their feet. Her life from torture subsided into pain; then into bitterness, stoicism, contempt, — at last into a certain treadmill of indifference; only not indifference from the strong, cruel grasp she still found it needful to keep upon thought and memory: once let that iron hand relax its pressure, and chaos threatened her again; she dared not. Lovers came no more to Hannah; a certain instinct of their sure fate kept them away; the store of linen and cotton she had gathered, her mother's careful hands had packed away directly in the great garret. The lavender silk, the cardinal, the big bonnet, had been worn to church, year after year, in the same spirit in which a Hindoo woman puts on her gorgeous garments and her golden ornaments for suttee. Mrs. Blair looked on in solemn wonder, but said not a word. Nor were these bridal robes worn threadbare ten years after, when another change came to Hannah's life; when Josiah Maxwell, a well-to-do bachelor from Newfield, the next village, was "recommended" to her, and came over to try his chance. Josiah was a personable, hale, florid man of forty; generous, warm-hearted, a little blustering perhaps, but thoroughly good, and a rich man for those days. He had a taunery, a foundry, and a flourishing farm. Newfield was a place of great water-privileges, sure to grow; it was pretty, bright, and successful; the sleepy, mullein-growing farms of Wingfield had in them no such cheer or life. Hannah was thirty years old; the matter was set before her purely as a matter of business. Josiah wanted a pious, capable wife. He had been too busy to fall in love all his life; now he was too sensible (he thought); so he looked about him calmly, after royal fashion, and, hearing good report of Hannah Blair, proceeded to make her acquaintance and visit her. She, too, was a rational woman; feeling she had long set aside as a weak indulgence of the flesh; all these long and lonely years had taught her a lesson — more than one. She had learned, that a nature as strong, as dominant, as full of power and pride as hers must have some outlet or burn itself out, and here was a prospect offered that appealed to her native instincts, save and except that one so long trodden under foot. She accepted Mr. Maxwell; listened to his desire for a short engagement favorably; took down the stores prepared for a past occasion from the chests in the garret, washed and bleached them with her own hands; and purchased once more her bridal attire, somewhat graver, much more costly than before, — a plum-colored satin dress, a white merino shawl, a hat of chip with rich white ribbons. Moll Thunder, who served as chorus to this homely tragedy, was at hand with her quaint, shrewd comment, as she brought Mrs. Blair her yearly tribute of hickory nuts the week before the wedding.

"He! he! She look pretty much fine; same as cedar tree out dere, all red vine all ober; nobody tink him ole cedar been lightnin'-struck las' year. He! he! Haint got no heart in him — pretty much holler."

One bright October day Hannah was married. Parson Day's successor performed the ceremony in the afternoon, and the " happy couple " went home to Newfield in a gig directly. Never was a calmer bride, a more matter-of-fact wedding. Sentiment was at a discount in the Blair family ; if David felt anything at parting with his only child, he repressed its expression ; and since that day her mother never could forget, Hannah had wrought in poor Mrs. Blair's mind a sort of terror toward her that actually made her absence a relief, and the company of the little " bound girl " she had taken to bring up a pleasant substitute for Hannah's stern, quiet activity. Everybody was suited ; it was almost a pleasure to Mrs. Maxwell to rule over her sunny farm-house and become a model to all backsliding house-keepers about her. Her butter always " came ; " her bread never soured ; her hens laid and set, her chickens hatched, in the most exemplary manner ; nobody had such a garden, such a loom and wheel, such spotless linen, such shiny mahogany ; there was never a hole in her husband's garments or a button off his shirt ; the one thing that troubled her was that her husband — good, honest, tender man — had during their first year of married life fallen thoroughly in love with her ; it was not in his genial nature to live in the house a year with even a cat and not love it. Hannah was a handsome woman, and his wife ; what could one expect? But she did not expect it ; she was bored and put out by his demonstrations ; almost felt a cold contempt for the love he lavished on her, icy and irresponsive as she was, though all the time ostensibly submissive. Josiah felt after a time that he had made a mistake; but he had the sense to adapt himself to it, and to be content, like many another idolater, with worship instead of response. Not even the little daughter born in the second year of their marriage thawed the heart so long frost-sealed in Hannah's breast; she had once worshipped a false god, and endured the penalty; henceforward she would be warned. Baby was baptized Dorothy, after her father's dead mother, and by every one but Hannah that quaint style was softened into Dolly. Never was a child better brought up, everybody said, — a rosy, sturdy, saucy little creature, doing credit to fresh air and plain food; a very romp in the barn and fields with her father, whom she loved with all her warm, wayward heart; but, alas! a child whose strong impulses, ardent feeling, violent temper, and stormy will were never to know the softening, tempering sweetness of real mother love. She knew none of those tender hours of caressing and confidence that even a very little child enjoys in the warmth of any mother-heart, if not its own mother's; no loving arms clasped her to a mother's bosom to soothe her baby-griefs, to rest her childish weariness. There were even times when Hannah Maxwell seemed to resent her existence; to repel her affection, though her duty kept her inexorably just to the child. Dolly was never punished for what she had not done, but always for nearly everything she did do, and services were exacted from her that made her childhood a painful memory to all her later life. Were there butter or eggs wanted from Wingfield on any emergency, at five years old Dolly would be mounted on the steady old horse that Josiah had owned fifteen years, and, with saddle-bags swinging on either side, sent over to her grandfather's at Wingfield to bring home the supplies, — a long and lonely road of five full-measured miles for the tiny creature to traverse; and one could scarce believe the story did it not come direct to these pages from her own lips. In vain was Josiah's remonstrance; for by this time Hannah was fully the head of the house, and the first principle of her rule was silent obedience. All her husband could do was to indulge and spoil Dolly in private, persistently and bravely. Alas for her, there was one day in the week when even father could not interfere to help his darling. Sunday was a sound of terror in her ears: first the grim and silent breakfast, where nobody dared smile, and where even a fixed routine of food, not in itself enticing, became at last tasteless by mere habit; codfish-cakes and tea, of these, "as of all carnal pleasure, cometh satiety at the last," according to the monk in "Hypatia;" then, fixed in a high, stiff-backed chair, the pretty little vagrant must be still, and read her Bible till it was time to ride to church; till she was taken down and arrayed in spotlessness and starch, and set bodkinwise into the gig beside her silent mother and subdued father.

Once at meeting, began the weariest routine of all. Through all the long services, her little fat legs swinging from the high seat, Dolly was expected to sit perfectly quiet; not a motion was allowed, not a whisper permitted; she dared not turn her head to watch a profane butterfly or a jolly bumblebee wandering about that great roof or tall window. Of course she did do it instinctively, recovering herself with a start of terror and a glance at her mother's cold blue eyes, always fixed on Parson Buck, but always aware of all going on beside her, as Dolly knew too well. At noon, after a hurried lunch of gingerbread and cheese, the child was taken to the nearest house, there to sit through the noon prayer-meeting, her weary legs swinging this time off the edge of the high bed, and her wearier ears dinned with long prayers. Then, as soon as the bell tolled, off to the meeting-house to undergo another long sermon, till, worn out mentally and physically, the last hour of the *séance* became a struggle with sleep, painful in the extreme, as well in present resistance as in certainty of results; for, soon as poor Dolly reached home, after another silent drive, she was invariably taken into the spare bedroom, and soundly whipped for being restless in meeting. And, adding insult to injury, after dinner, enjoyed with the eager appetite of a healthy child used to three meals on a week-day, she was required to repeat that theological torture, — the Assembly's Catechism, — from end to end. But in spite of all this, partly because Sunday came only once a week, partly because of her father's genial nature and devoted affection for his girl, which grew deeper and stronger constantly, Dolly did not miss of her life as many a morbid character might have in her place. She grew up a rosy, sunny, practical young woman, with a dominant temper toward everybody but her mother. Plump, healthy, and pretty, her cheeriness and usefulness would have made her popular had she been a poor man's daughter, — and by this time Josiah Maxwell was the richest man in the town; so Dolly had plenty of lovers, and in due time married a fine young fellow, and settled down at home with her parents, who were almost as much pleased with Mr. Henderson as was their daughter. But all this time Mrs. Maxwell preserved the calm austerity of her manner, even to her child. She did her duty by Dolly. She prepared for her marriage with liberal hand and unerring judgment; but no caress, no sympathetic word, no slightest expression of affection, soothed the girl's agitated heart or offered her support in this tender, yet exciting, crisis of her life.

Hannah Maxwell made her life a matter of business, — it had been nothing else to her for years; it was an old habit at sixty; and she was well over that age when one day Dolly, rocking her first baby to sleep, was startled to see her mother, who sat in her upright chair reading the county paper, fall quietly to the floor and lie there. Baby was left to fret while her mother ran to the old lady and lifted her spare, thin shape to the sofa; but she did not need to do more, for Mrs. Maxwell's eyes opened and her hand clasped tight on Dolly's.

"Do not call any one," she whispered faintly, and, leaning on her daughter's shoulder, her whole body shook with agonized sobs. At last that heart of granite had broken in her breast; lightning-struck so long ago, now it crumbled. With her head still on Dolly's kind arm, she told her then and there the whole story of her one love, her solitary passion, and its fatal ending. She still kept to herself the contents of that anonymous letter, only declaring that she knew, and the writer must have been aware she would know, from the handwriting as well as the circumstances detailed, who wrote it, and that the information it conveyed of certain lapses from virtue on the part of Charles Mayhew must be genuine.

"O Dolly!" groaned the smitten woman, "when he

stood under my window and called me I was wrung to my heart's core. The pains of hell gat hold upon me. I was upon the floor, with my arms wound about the bed-rail and my teeth shut like a vice, lest I should listen to the voice of nature, and, going to the window to answer him, behold his face. Had I seen him I must have gone down and done what I thought a sin; so I steeled myself to resist, although I thought flesh would fail in the end; but it did not. I conquered then and after. Oh, how long it has been! I meant to do right, Dolly; but to-day, when I saw in the paper that he died last week in a barn over Goshen way, a lonely, drunken pauper — Dolly, my heart came out of its grave and smote me. Had I been a meeker woman, having mercy instead of judgment, I might have helped him to right ways. I might have saved him — I loved him so."

The last words struck upon her hearer with the force of a blow, so burning, so eager, so intense was the emphasis: "I loved him *so!*"

Ah, who could ever know the depths out of which that regretful utterance sprang!

"Dear mother, dear mother," sobbed Dolly, altogether overcome by this sudden revelation of gulfs she had never dreamed of, — a heart which, long repressed, convulsively burst at last, and revealed its bleeding arteries.

"Dear, good mother, don't feel so — don't! You meant right. Try to forgive yourself. If you made a mistake then, try to forget it now. Try to believe it was all for the best — do, dear."

But all she got for answer was — "Dolly, it is too late!"

MY THANKSGIVING.

"I MUST go, Annie!" said Joe, speaking with a calm resolution that I felt to be final and fatal; all the more so that he put his arm round me as he spoke, and drew me to him in a clasp so close that it said more than words. Granny looked up from the chimney-corner where she sat, and said, in her feeble voice and deliberate accent:—

"Who died for us!"

These few words, so seemingly irrelevant, but merely seeming so because they drew a deeper significance than from the shallow present alone, smote on my ear like a knell. I looked up into Joe's face as it bent over me, brown and stern and sad, and as I looked, with all my life in the gaze, a cold shadow stole across that living countenance: it grew cold, rigid, ghastly; the mouth parted over its set teeth; the eyelids closed; it was a dead face. I involuntarily uttered a little shriek; and then for one second heard a word breathed through Joe's lips, and knew that he was not dead, but praying.

"What is it, Annie?" said he, gently.

"O Joe! I cannot, cannot bear it!"

"My child, you must. This is no time for a man to be at home, no time for a woman to be a coward. You must not make me weak, or send me away lonely;

for I should be doubly alone if I thought my — my wife, Annie, could not strike hand with me in this good cause."

The words breathed a steady glow of strength into me. I saw what I ought to do, what I must do for him; and from its broken deeps in my breaking heart the old Puritan blood that trickled from Winslow's veins down through mine answered to the appeal, and fired my brain and steadied my voice with its firm pulses. I pulled Joe's dark head down to mine and kissed his lips. I was not his wife yet, — perhaps now I never should be; but heart and soul we were indissolubly bound, and I had a right to kiss him without blushes or trembling. Hard, hard it was! Myriads of us all over this struggling, bleeding country know how hard; and know that even at this deadly crisis we could hold open arms to rebel women, and weep with them in the divine reconciliation of a mutual sorrow. Harder it was to me because, just now, I knew for the first time how utterly I loved Joe; and to tell why, I must go back a little into my past.

Granny Harding, who sat there in the fireplace corner, was Joe's great-grandmother as well as mine, though we were not even third cousins for all that. Joe's grandfather was her own son, my grandmother was her step-daughter; the relationship was scarce worth mentioning, nor would it have been recorded, unless in the big Bible, except that all the Harding race had always lived and died in Stoneboro. My grandmother was the parson's wife there; my father succeeded his father in the office, and was called "the minister" instead of "the parson." Father and mother both died when I was nine years old, and

Cousin Aristarchus Harding, Joe's father, was my guardian. So I went to his house — the old Harding homestead — to live, and found there Joe, three years older than I, and Cordelia, of my own age.

Probably the reason I had never fallen in love, as girls say, with Joe, was because I lived in the same house with him. He was always kind, and good, and considerate; but I was romantic, and in some respects a fool. I could not hang my ideal lover on the aspect of a young man I saw eating and drinking, and mowing, and splitting wood, and making fires, and driving oxen; a man in his shirt-sleeves and an old hat. It was impossible to find a sentimental and high-flown interest, such as Thaddeus of Warsaw would have excited, in an ordinary farmer, who only did his duty from day to day, and never talked about congeniality of soul or magnetic sympathies. Joe was not so hard to please; he began to love me very early; everything I did was right and pleasant in his eyes. I suited him exactly. My sauciness bewitched him; my prettiness, such as it was, pleased his taste. I always knew what he thought, and understood what he meant to say when he could not express it. I liked the things he liked, and I teased his monotonous farm-life into vitality. I was his romance; and it cruelly smote Joe when I fell in love with — somebody else!

Why, in the name of common-sense, when I had beside me this true, generous, gentle man, who was as much devoted to me as a man can be, I threw myself away on a hard, cool, selfish, imperious nature that only gave me the careless affection one bestows on a pretty child they have no time to love, Heaven only knows! It is a part of the mysteries we live in, that women have done, do, and will do so till time shall be no more; and there must be some good purpose of compensation or discipline in it; but it is a deadly experience, and where it is not mortal leaves frightful scars on heart and mind. I am inclined to think those whose ties of this kind culminate in marriage suffer more than those who escape before it; in either case it is bad enough. I was eighteen when I met this man, whose name I have no desire to recall; ten of my life's best years he wasted. In those ten years I loved him with the eager, faithful passion of youth and womanhood, grew slowly to know him, ruminated over this bitter herb of knowledge till my life was burnt with its acrid essence into pale ashes. For five years he made love to me, taught me to love, to doubt, to dread him; then, tired of his toy, he left me and Stoneboro, and for five years more I was broken in health and spirit down to the very dust. People in Stoneboro said I was "disappointed." So I was.

In the meantime Cordelia married and moved away. I did not miss her particularly. She was a good, placid, amiable creature, mildly pious and very commonplace. I should have loved her better if I had not been absorbed in my own affairs. The first thing that roused me from my self-absorbed misery was Cousin Martha Harding's falling into a severe illness. If I loved anybody then better than myself, which I doubt, it was Cousin Martha. She was the sweetest of sweet women; not with the super-saccharine manner of fashion and society, — no more like that suave and popular sweetness than maple-sugar is like Maillard's confectionery; but her nature was as fragrant and satisfying as wild honey. The homely flavor of a New England farm-life touched all she said with a certain quaintness, and her serene, but trenchant, common-sense and acute insight kept her unfailing good-nature from insipidity. She was quite deaf; a loss which added to her manner the exquisite gentleness rarely found except in the deaf, and very rarely among them; for it takes, as old Parson Winslow, my grandfather, used to say, " grace and gifts too " to bear such a deprivation with patience till it blossoms into a beauty. And this lovely, loving woman, who had been my mother in a certain imperfect sense, fell into a wasting consumption; and when I knew it I put aside my long repining, or rather it crept away before the face of so vital and inevitable a sorrow.

But all this long time Joe, though I did not see it, had watched me with the tenderest care, — his heart had been scarce less wrung with my trouble than my own, — but had given no sign to vex me. He had been my protector against rude tongues and the pangs that careless ones can inflict. He had tried with all his might to allay my physical suffering, and patiently striven to heal my mind; but in vain. I had adopted fully the girl's idea that constancy is a virtue instead of a fact; and long after I knew thoroughly how ill-placed my love had been, what sure and life-long misery I had lost in losing that love, I still clung to its ghost with dreary strenuousness, cherished its memory, dwelt on its frail souvenirs, recalled its raptures, and spent sleepless nights and long days in persuading myself that my heart was dead in my breast, that I had loved once for all, and lived my life out. All this Joe saw; but, with a fidelity that shamed my pretence to it, he really loved me still. He did not grieve, or fret, or give up his time and health, but, like the true man he was, only threw himself into harder work, and fed his self-denying love with such considerate care, such tender thought, such unflagging service for me, that he was almost happy in his pure self-devotion.

He grew gray, it is true, in those ten years; his dark curls were full of silver threads; the gay, bright face, scarce handsome, but full of intellect, and as gracious as summer in its smile, was thinner than it should have been, deep-lined about its grave lips, and serious even to sadness; but he went about his life's business so earnestly, with such energy and cheer,— was so helpful to everybody, so kind, so strong, — that nobody knew what he felt, or how he suffered, but Cousin Martha. To her he told every thought of his heart; and it was the very bitterness of death to Joe, when he at length was forced to see that mortal disease had fastened on that mother, dearer even than I.

Three long years life flashed and faded, and flashed again, in that racked frame, till it could bear no longer those terrible alternations. Consumption has in it a certain practical sarcasm that is hard to bear; it makes a mock of weakness with its sudden, but false, strength; it fires the eye, and paints the cheek, and sends vivid fever through the leaping pulse, till immortal youth and strength seem to defy death, and riot in their splendors; then comes the recoil of mortal weakness, a sunken cheek, a colorless lip, a dim and glazing eye, coughs that rend the panting breast, pains like the torture of rack and wheel in every wasted limb, the dreadful gush of scarlet blood, the utter prostration of arterial life, the passive sinking of nerve, and excitement of brain; and then again, reeling from the very abyss of death, the tormented prey of this vulture rises to life, blooms, brightens, exults, till another hour turns the descending scale. Three long years Joe and I watched and waited together. Cordelia was in Minnesota with a flock of little children, and we had Cousin Martha all to ourselves; for granny was now ninety-three, and could not help us, except that she was able, with very little aid, to take care of herself. And Cousin Aristarchus was no help; his great, slow-beating heart knew but one intense passion, and that was for his wife, and now he suffered accordingly. He would come into the room where she lay, stand and look at her with such an expression in his rough face, reddened with summer sun and winter frost through fifty-five years of a farmer's hardships, that I could not look at him. It was a dull, uncomprehending anguish at first, like the look of an animal in mortal pain; but deepening, as days went on, into the extremity of human suffering, heightened by wild conflict with the inevitable Will that could alone save, but offered here neither help nor hope. If she opened her large, languid eyes to look at him, or smiled, as she could sometimes smile, with a look that was almost supernatural in its triumph of love, pity, and patience over the extremity of pain, he turned at once and went away — where, nobody knew. I happened once to be in the barn, looking for a fresh egg, when he rushed by, without seeing me at all, and, flinging himself at length on the hay, groaned, and sobbed, and writhed, and cried out so bitterly, that it was terrible to see or hear. I crept away silently, awed and sick at heart. I had not supposed such feeling was possible in a man. I had judged them all with warped judgment, from the one

I knew best. I had no faith in them; but this was real. What could life offer to a woman better than such a mighty love as this? My unconscious egotism prompted one little question: would Joe ever love like his father?

So, as I said, Mr. Harding could not share our care;. he felt too much, and no discipline of life had ever taught him self-control. But we had no need of aid. Joe was one of those rare men who have a woman's perception as well as a man's strength, and with his aid Cousin Martha needed no other nurse than me.

At last she kept her bed; she could not sit up even for an hour; but still her cheerful voice, her unselfish regard for our strength and comfort, her patience in pain, her upholding religion, triumphed over these terrors and pangs of mortality. I could not understand her. To die; to be exiled forever from this body and this dear earth; to tempt an utterly untried existence, to lose that locality of place and time that the trembling soul lays hold of when it shudders at its own eternity and infinite capacities; to enter the cold newness of another world, austere from its very strangeness, with such simple courage, such certainty, such calm faith,—surprised me all the time; it seemed incredible. But Joe also partook of this vital belief. He talked calmly of that near and unseen world, and of his mother's passage thither. In the midst of his tenderest cares he had lips overflowing with the trumpet-blasts of the gospel; his face kindled with victory, his voice thrilled with assurance for her, even while the depth of settled sorrow in his eye showed no stir, no spark; it was for himself he had to grieve, and he forgot himself; for her he was triumphant. If I had stopped to look into my own heart I should have seen how effectually it was laying hold upon another love, as different from my first as the yellow wheat ear is from the springing blade.

But while day after day I drew nearer to Joe in feeling, and regarded him with such a quiet sense of safety and repose, I did not, could not, stop to dream of love. I was learning a new lesson, — learning to believe. The feeble emotional pretext I had called religion, and professed as such, that had crumbled away in the convulsive grasp of sorrow and left me unsupported, was being gradually replaced by a living faith. Blessed is the woman who loves a man better than she is! It is not often so; but it is the sure seal of that marriage that God ordained, and typified by his love for the Church, when King and Priest reign and minister in the sacred cloisters of home, and give themselves, even as he gave himself, for the love and teaching of the weaker. I did not know where I was, till one day, about a month before Cousin Martha died, I observed her look follow Joe wistfully out of the room, and then turn to me with a curious expression of regret and longing. Involuntarily I said: —

"What is it, dear?"

"Come here, Annie," said she. So I went and kneeled down by the bedside.

"I want to tell you something, my child: Joe loves you dearly."

"O cousin, you don't know! He doesn't; how could he?"

"But he does; and has for this fourteen years."

"Love me! I am not fit for Joe to love."

"Annie, I don't believe dying wishes are more to be

regarded than living ones; they are all liable to be short-sighted and selfish. You must promise not to feel bound by any desire of mine; but I must tell you how happy it would make me if you could love Joe enough to marry him."

I buried my head in my hands. "Cousin Martha, you *are* mistaken. Joe doesn't love me: think how old I am, — I was thirty last spring, — and how homely I am, and not good either; and — and, besides, I have loved somebody else."

A smile just glittered wanly in her eyes, and she laid her hand on my hair, as I looked up at her with a burning face. "Poor child!" said she. "I know how you have suffered, though I never said so to you. Those things are best kept silent. But Joe is a better man than that one; and he loves you better; believe it, for I know it. And now we will let the matter rest."

"God is good!" said granny. She had a strange way of coming out with apparently irrelevant bits of Scripture, or odd proverbs, or sayings of her own, at times when no one supposed she heard or saw what was going on, as she seemed sunk in her habitual revery.

"Yes, he is!" said Cousin Martha.

I think I said so, too, mentally, as I got up and went out of doors into the little bit of woods that sloped up the hill-side behind the barn, where I sat down under a great oak-tree through whose gnarled boughs, just roughened with buds, the March sunshine streamed strangely warm. I could not believe it! Was I in love again? Was this strong torrent of emotion a new freshet in the stream that had wrecked me before? Did I love Joe Harding? I'm afraid I did, even then.

I recognized with a certain pang the old rush of feeling, yet not now the vague, feverish emotion that had wrapped my whole nature in a light blaze before; but a deeper, steadier fire, that rose heavenward with solemn aspiration as from an altar, and promised to be life-giving instead of deadly. I ought, perhaps, to be sorry to confess that I did not stop to regret my beautiful theory of constancy; I never was a very introspective person. The thing was gone, and there was an end of it for me. The theory had disproved itself, and so was negatived; that was only another fact. I found time afterward to be heartily glad that I could love again, and so much more deeply. This unutterable rest, this serene rapture, one hour of which was worth a year of the excitement and restless wearying delight of my youth, was certainly a thing to be glad of, unless one had been more or less than a woman.

One thing struck me to the heart whenever I dared look that way: the possibility that Joe might not love me, after all; that Cousin Martha was mistaken. It seemed so impossible. My youth was gone, my beauty faded, my vivacity all fled; I had been made the sport of another man, and thrown away by him when he tired. Was there in humanity such redeeming love as could stoop to gather this weed of my life and wear it for a cognizance? I should as soon think of giving to a lover some wan and withered rose picked up from the pavement, without beauty or freshness, as the worthless gift I was. Cousin Martha must be mistaken. How could he love me? Before, and of that other, I had said so many times with hot and salt tears, "How could he help loving me?"

I went back to my room and looked into the glass; a

new bloom shone on the old face, but did not transfigure it. There were the pale, worn features; the sad eyes; the bands of hair still shining, but all threaded with snow; the lightly tinted lips that were so tremulous and grieving now, instead of smiling and firm. I was old: I turned away with a sigh from that vision. Men do not love beauty more than women, only they are more frank to own it; and to lose mine, which was always that of color and outline rather than feature, was hard.

Cousin Martha grew worse that night, and kept worse. No more respites for her; the hour came fast that should take her from us, and, except as a thought that I kept to rest myself with at intervals of watching and nursing, I heard and knew no more of Joe's love for me.

At length she died, not with any parting word or message, not with any scene; but fell asleep like a tired child, holding her husband's hand. There was no need of audible triumph in her testimony; her life was her witness, and they who had seen its quiet course knew from what source it sprung, to what glad sea it hastened. Joe and I also sat beside her, and when we saw that it was over he gently lifted her hand from his father's clasp and laid it back at her side. Mr. Harding looked up with dreadful questioning in his eyes, and then looked at her. He went out of the door and out of the house, and for hours we saw him no more. Joe would not let him be looked for, and at sunset he reappeared. He never said anything, but from that day was a broken man; his grizzled hair turned white, his keen eye was dimmed, his voice husky; even the rugged and set features learned to quiver with passing emotions; the firm temper became fitful; he asked help that he laughed at before; he clung to those about him in little ways hitherto unknown to him. I never loved him as much. Granny looked at Cousin Martha's pallid, but fair, aspect, and took the wasted hand in hers: she did not moan nor weep; all she said was, " Behold how He loved him! "

There was no other change than this inevitable change of loss. The fire seemed to have gone out of our lives, the light to be extinguished, it is true; but the household ways went on as usual, for I had taken charge of them long before, and now they were my sole occupation.

One day in May, when all the trees were full of opal tints, pink, or green, or dusky with young buds, and even the oaks put out tiny velvet leaves of tender pink from the heart of every new shoot, Joe asked me to go to the graveyard with him; and when we had planted by his mother's grave a rose-bush and some English violets, we strolled away into the woods and sat down on a log. Below us lay the Stoneboro valley, with its bright river sparkling in and out among the hills, and a soft south wind blew on us with odors of dead and new leaves, the fresh scent of grass, and breath of orchards in bloom. We sat a long time in silence, and then Joe said: —

" Annie, can you possibly love me enough? "

" I'll try," said I, with half a laugh, though I could hardly speak at all.

He put his arm round me and kissed me gravely, and that was all we said. I felt so safe, so rested, so consoled. I did not want words, and he seemed not to have them. I forgot how old and plain and undeserving I was: I ought to have refused him for his own good; but I couldn't. I was not very good, and I was so glad he loved me.

When we went home there was a little blaze kindled on the kitchen hearth; we sat there in winter and spring always, for it was never used as a kitchen, and granny's bedroom opened out of it. To-night she sat there in the flicker of the blaze, knitting placidly as usual. Her delicate, pale face; her soft hair, white as milk-weed down; her light gray dress and full-folded white cap, handkerchief, and linen apron gave her the look of a white moth, such as peers in through the window on some June night, with elfin visage and bright, dark eyes. She looked up as we came in, and gazed intently at us for a minute, then nodded with a satisfied air, and said, "Fulfilling of the law."

Joe smiled, and I believe I blushed; next morning Cousin Aristarchus, when I came down to breakfast, came and shook hands with me, and looked the other way all the time. It was all he could do, and a great effort for him; so I accepted it as a congratulation and welcome. It was about three weeks after this that Joe came in and told me he had enlisted and was going to the war, as I said in the beginning of my story. He had longed to go all the time, but could not think it right to leave his mother, especially as she begged him to stay with her while she lived. Now, when rebellion was higher-handed than ever, the army of the Peninsula in deadly straits, the West in terror, and two new calls proclaimed by the President, go he must. Now was the time for men, if ever.

I had to consent, of course. I am not a heroic woman. I was not glad to have him go, yet I should have been thoroughly ashamed had he stayed; doubly ashamed to have felt afterward that, even at the saving of his life, he had deserted his country at need. No. Unhappy enough are those women who lose their dearest in battle, though they fight and fall in the good cause; but wretched, far beyond any loss, are they whose unwomanly fears keep from the country's service men she needs — who must say to their children afterward, answering their child-questions, "Your father did not go to the war; I would not let him."

No such fate for me. Dear as Joe was to me, dearer every day, — far more dear than I thought any living creature could ever be, — I choked down my agonies of foreboding, and let him go. In this my sole comfort was preparing his outfit. Granny knit him more stockings than he could take, and every little contrivance that might add to his comfort I took pride in discovering and procuring. He enlisted as private in a company of the Sixteenth Connecticut Volunteers, which in August went into camp at Hartford. Once he came home to Stoneboro for a three-days' furlough, and we had one talk that I shall never forget.

"Annie," said he, "I want you to promise me something. I know how you will miss me, and how hard a time you will have; but promise you will not let your grief interfere with the usual routine of home. I don't mean simply on granny's account and father's, but on your own. Keep up all the old ways, for the sake of your own quiet. Don't let the farm go back because I'm not here; father will feel more interest in it if you are interested. Go to church, and to singing-meeting, and to sewing-society; wherever I am, dead or alive, don't omit to keep Thanksgiving; don't forget Christmas; and the poor — you know you have them always with you, He said."

"I will, Joe, if I can."

"You can, dear, if you begin straight. Habit is a great help, and in this quiet little village there is no excitement to divert your mind, which you must keep as firm and calm as you can; for, Annie, — you must look it in the face, — it is very probable I may not come back, and these old people will only have you left."

There was no answer to be made to this. The next day Joe bade us good-by and went off. We heard from him twice before they left Hartford: he was well and gravely cheerful.

As for me, there was but one course left, — I must work. No other quiet but that of constant action and effort could allay the dreadful fever of my thoughts. I was naturally both anxious and imaginative, — fatal combination for a woman whose place is to wait and endure! So by day I worked as I never had before. I let the girl whose place it was to take care of the milk, butter, and cheese, go home to her mother, as she had long intended to do at this time, without trying to supply her place. I could do her work, as far as skill went, better than she, and the constant excitement of anxiety made me strong. I had to rise early, and work hard; labor of real and stringent grasp held me all day; from dawn till blank night I was busy. There was the milk of twelve cows to strain, and set, and skim; the milk-room, and the cheese-room, and the ice-cellar to be kept spotless and of just temperature; there were rows of cheeses, pressing, ripening, drying, to be looked at twice a day; there was curd to set, and cut, and drain, and salt; moulds to be scoured, cloths to be scalded; daily the great churn, that a man had to turn, yielded me its crumbly mass of yellow butter, to be worked, salted, moulded, and packed for market, — butter that must be firm and sweet, hard as wax, and gold-yellow, lest our farm should lose its reputation for the best butter sent to Boston. Then came numberless pans, and cream-jars, and butter-pails to wash: these never passed out of my hands, lest the careless eyes of a servant might leave some grain of milk, some smear of cream, that should turn sour and spoil my work. Besides these things there was granny to care for; she needed some help to dress her in those quaint white folds and frills that she delighted to wear; help she needed, too, in order to lay them aside, and put herself into sleeping order, — for never by any chance was the delicately stiff cap permitted to rest by day against a chair-back, or the folds of cambric that covered her breast ruffled by one minute of repose out of position: if she slept by day, it was bolt upright, as she sat. The last thing at night was work too: the night's milk was to be strained and set; that of the night before must be skimmed, and the emptied pans scalded and dried; by nine o'clock I was so tired out that sleep caught me without my knowing it, and in dreamless exhaustion I knew nothing till the noisy fowls in the poultry-yard woke me to dawn and its necessary duties. Yet not all this work and weariness kept my eager, restless thoughts from Joe. They followed him, invisible, yet faithful, couriers, on every step of his journey, — into camp, at drill; farther I knew not, — till in so short a time after he left Hartford that it seemed to me scarce the lapse of three days, though I knew it was more, the news of Antietam struck us like a bolt from the clear sky.

I did not believe it when Cousin Aristarchus told me. I laughed.

"Why," said I, "it is impossible. The Sixteenth hadn't their arms, they were but just there; they could not have been sent into a battle."

"They were," said he, turning his keen gray eyes away from me, and dropping his white head slowly, as if it were heavy with some heavy grief. My heart fell.

"Is there any definite news? — any list of dead or wounded, cousin?" said I, the words faltering, as I spoke.

"No," said he. "The news came to Hartford yesterday morning, or Saturday night, — I don't know which. There was news of one officer killed; no particulars further."

He stopped, and looked aside out of the window; he had not finished. I waited breathless for the next words.

"No," he said, at length, drawing a long breath, and saying over, as if it were a lesson, the very words, I was sure, he had seen on the bulletin at the post-office: "Nothing definite as to names; the Sixteenth cut to pieces."

I sat down in the nearest chair, and he walked out of the kitchen. Grief never comes so; there is a shock, a paralysis, a shuddering novelty, but not grief. I sat there still as the dread grasp that stiffens every fibre holds the paralytic. I could not stir, because I forgot how. I was lost in one great spasm of resistance, of repulsion. I did not, would not, believe anything had come to Joe. Presently sense and strength returned to me. What a fool I was! I had heard nothing, knew nothing. Why should not Joe be saved as well as any other man? I tried to laugh, as one does sometimes in a dark room waking from fearful dreams, to reassure himself, but the old kitchen walls seemed to make a hollow echo of my forced mirth; or was it hollow of itself? Granny came out from her room, tottering on the cane that Joe had wrought and ornamented for her.

"Crackling thorns!" said she, lifting up her white head and looking vacantly before her. A cold shiver ran over me. I am superstitious, like all women; and granny's words, quaint and irrelevant as they seemed to others, I had a sort of reverence for that gave them prophetic significance in my eyes. Yes, my laughter was crackling thorns indeed! The fire was of briers that rankled in my grasp still; the flame but one flash, vivid and noisy, that quivered, flared, fell into ashes.

I helped her to her chair, and turned into the cheese-room for my work, sick at heart. There is a strange balsamic power in routine, when the very depths of life break up under your feet; the daily order of occupation is a light, but tenacious, crust above those volcanic surges; and though you feel their sickening undulations, and hear their threatening roar beneath, yet the gulf does not open and swallow you up, — the thunder is muffled, the fires smoulder. There is a place for human feet to tread, a point for the lever of divine faith to rest on. I think the cheeses I salted and put to press that day were as well done as ever. I knew what I had to do; yet it was not merely the grind of a machine. It demanded judgment, accuracy, attention; and it saved me from myself.

The next day I rode down to the post-office. Mr. Harding left me sitting in the wagon in a little pine-wood a few rods from the village shop where the office was kept, while he went for the news, however it might come. It was a hot, quiet autumn day. As yet no leaves were turned, but the indescribable foreboding of death and decay, that breathes in every air and sound of fall, hushed the whole land with funereal quiet; purple asters starred the edges of the road, golden-rods held their feathered masses upright in the paler sunshine, crowds of life everlasting crouched with their dead, yet deathless, blooms on every barren knoll, — a strange, dried sweetness filled the air everywhere. But here, under the pine-trees, the last fires of summer fused from the acute leaves and rough boughs their antique odor of fragrant resins, that has a breath beyond spice, and a perfume surpassing flowers. Both preservative and revivifying, it assailed other avenues of my nature than the sense it at once stimulated and satisfied; for the brain that it entered, through the subtlest of all entrances, expanded with insatiable longings, and fled away from the weary weight of space and sense into some upper air, where the ample ether was keen life and the light immortal knowledge; through all toned to finite capacities by the low whisper of awful, yet sweet, sorrow, that crept from the boughs with that exhaling odor, and breathed to the ear its ocean song of plaintive despair, the very pulse-tune of life and its immutable dead-march toward eternity. In that atmosphere that lulls my brain and exalts it beyond any other known influence I drew deep draughts of rest, and when I heard a man's tread coming, heavy and blundering, along the soft sand foot-path, though I knew by the very weight and stumble of that firm foot that he was blind with grief, I wore a calm face to meet Mr. Harding's blurred eyes, and held out a strong hand to help him find his way to the seat beside me. He thrust a telegram slip into my hands, seized the reins, struck the patient horse he never struck before a blow that sent it off at full speed, and I opened the crumpled slip. Its peculiar ominous mixture of print and writing ran thus : —

"A. Harding, Stoneboro. — Capt. A. H. Banks killed on the field. Private J. Harding missing. — A. J. BOLLES, 2d Lieutenant."

"Missing! only missing!" There must have been a great deal of latent hope in my nature to have seized on that frail straw as if it were a rock of refuge; but I did. Cousin Aristarchus looked around at me with eyes of such wonder and grief at my exclamation that I was half vexed.

"Why, cousin!" said I, — "*missing* is nothing. He is safe somewhere. We shall hear from him to-morrow."

"Shall we?" said he, vacantly.

"Why, of course we shall! Only think — not dead, like poor Banks; not wounded; only *missing!*"

He whipped the horse again with a fierce stroke, but said nothing. In ten minutes we were at home, and I had told granny. She looked at me with her bright, yet inexpressive, eyes, and said, slowly, "The letter killeth, but the spirit giveth life." What on earth had this to do with me or my news? I was used to her odd speeches, but this one seemed more irrelevant than usual. It haunted me all day in my thoughts of Joe, — merciful thoughts, sent, I believe truly, from above, that I might not be smitten at once, but rather led gently through the valley of the shadow. "The letter killeth!" At last it dawned on me: granny and his father had indeed taken the letter of the message, and their hope was dead. They were old and broken; but I was beginning life, and its vital spirit of love and action upheld me; but, then, why should they despair? I did not know then that granny's father, the hero of the race, who died in the Revolution, had been just so reported — "Missing," and found, after bitter weeks of winter, through which wife and babies waited and watched in vain, a stark and stiffened corpse near Ticonderoga, scalped, and pierced with English bullets through heart and limb. No wonder that they despaired.

Slowly the days went on. Cousin Aristarchus more than once resolved to go on and search for Joe; twice was all but ready, and then decided that it was worse than useless, for he could not follow him on the rebel track, and as yet there came no trace of him by report or message. He seemed all bowed and warped by sorrow in mind as well as body; his energy was gone, his life faded out. Oh, how I wished then to be a man! I longed and pined to go and look for Joe. I thought I could have tracked his flight, and rescued him whatever obstacles interposed. So the days crept on into weeks, and heavy gloom settled down upon us, broken only by rare gleams of hope as bits of detail, creeping out in the papers, recounted the death, or the illness, or the wounded condition of one after another at first, like ours, reported missing; gleams that only made the gloom heavier in its return, as the vivid track of lightning serves but to show, in a midnight storm, the awful height and blackness of overhanging clouds full of threat and terror.

By a month's end the blow came. As I said, Captain Banks, son of a near neighbor of ours, had been telegraphed as " killed on the field " by the same message that declared Joe " missing." Fortunately his mother, who was a widow, had left town for a day or two, and did not get the message till another followed close upon it to contradict the first. He had not been killed, but so fearfully wounded, that, seeing his lifeless face and streaming blood, in the panic of defeat he had been left by his men where he lay, with his rebel opponent dead beside him, and the cold corpse-face against his was his first sensation when he recovered from his swoon, somewhere in the dead of night. Happily for him he was found early in the morning alive, but too weak to speak. They took him to a hospital, where he was recognized, and did whatever they could for him; but fever set in, and when he was raving and apparently dying they sent for his mother. Under her care he began at length to recover, and six weeks after the battle, having regained his memory and strength enough to talk, he asked her to write and tell Uncle Harding that he saw Joe shot in the front rank, just before he himself fell. Not only that he saw him shot, but saw him reel to the ground just as a squadron of rebel cavalry charged and swept over him; so there could be no doubt of his fate.

Now, indeed, it was all over, — life and love and hope, — over forever! Like the mad whirl of chaos heaving before God clave it with his divine order, all my soul whirled and staggered. I could not bear it; I *could not!* Like a blind man fighting with a mortal enemy I fought with Fate, for I could not call it Providence then. I could not endure; duty was a blank negation to me. If I could have sunk on the floor and stayed there, unmoving and desperate till death released me, I would have done so; but instincts and habits tormented me forever back into life. Out of that desolate region to which I had fled, that arid desert on whose sands I fell, mad and blind, I was perpetually recalled by little daily needs, by the sting of hunger and the dry lips of thirst; by the demands upon my care and forbearance that others, perhaps suffering as much as I, though I would not believe it, daily made upon me. I have thought since what a mercy it was that He who made us, foreknowing the anguish and the lessons of life, put our souls into the conservating power of bodies. With no lesser wants, no failing of the flesh to distract the spirit from its awful pangs, how mortal would those pangs be! How beyond endurance, how lurid with the horrors of incredible, unimaginable essence and space! No; thank God that we *are* lower than the angels; for we sin and suffer as no angel could and live.

Mr. Harding was utterly broken down. He sat, with his head upon his hands, in the chimney-corner, hour after hour; nothing moved him. The farm-work he left entirely to his hired man, — a trustworthy person enough, but wanting in judgment and self-reliance. Another of the continual pin-pricks that daily roused me for a moment was his incessant demand for advice and direction. But at length Joe's last words to me recurred to my mind with strange force. What was I doing for him, for his? I saw suddenly what selfish sorrow mine had been; how everything I ought to do had gone undone, as, driven by the restless fury of my grief, I had spent those bright autumn days wandering over hill and field, through lonely woods and across wild ravines, where I startled the partridge and drove the rabbit from his lair; as I tore through bush and brier, regardless of all but the fierce impulse of motion, the necessity of some unreasoning activity; only coming home at the habitual hours of meals and rest, leaving those two other lonely souls to fight their trouble as they best might. I was ashamed now. I am ashamed still to reflect how little healing or constraining influence my religion — such as it was — had upon me. I had not yet been long enough under its influence to have acquired the habit of faith and submission; and under this deadly blow I knew nothing, felt nothing Christian or acquiescent, except the ever-present conviction that even in this whirling storm God was somewhere, — not with me, nor for me; but still living, and unchanged, and just, though all his world slipped away from under my feet like the sliding earth of a nightmare dream. I did not believe he was other than good, but I struck up against Heaven with my bleeding hands, and asked, with horrors of reproach and unbelief, "Why hast thou done this?" nor did Heaven reply!

Just as I have seen a mother with a wayward child, in its first passion of temper and grief, neither punish nor argue with it, but only divert its thoughts with some new story or external object, and then, when the sobs ceased, and the eyes were clear, and calmness had smoothed its fair little face into natural lines, quietly reprove, remonstrate, or even punish; so, as

I have since seen, did a diviner love than any mother's guide me, even by means of the very passionate human love that made me rebel, into a calmer sphere. Did he punish thereafter, or break my heart again with love instead of wrath?

I ceased after this to isolate myself, and resumed as best I could my neglected work; but something was necessary to rouse Mr. Harding: what could I do? As I was at work one day in the shed, Lemuel, the hired man, came in over the sill, and, leaning his back against the door, began one of his usual appeals: —

"I declare for't, Ann, I don't know what I be agoin' to do with the corn-stalks. Can't you jest step around and give me an idee?"

"I'll ask cousin," said I. Lem. stared, but kept his position, and began to tie a snapper which he produced from his pocket to the end of the long whip he held in his hand. I was glad he stayed behind. So I went into the great kitchen, where a fire of good hickory sticks sparkled and flamed on the hearth, for it was a chill November day. Granny sat in her own place, Mr. Harding on the other side, his head held in both his hands, the gray light from the window striking across its silver mass of tangled curls, and the red firelight flickering on the great, rough hands that concealed both face and forehead. I went up to him and stooped down beside his chair.

"Father," said I.

He started as if a shot pierced him; his hands dropped, and his dim, bloodshot eyes looked up with wild inquiry. I put one hand on his knee and laid my head on it; that was an old childish trick of Joe's I had often heard of, as being the only caress his father ever endured from either of his children. He was neither a gentle nor a demonstrative man.

"Father," said I again, "Lemuel wants to know where he shall put the corn-stalks."

Mr. Harding did not speak at once. He gave a low groan, like a sigh; then — "Lord, forgive me! I am worse'n a dumb ox. You come with me, my child."

He got up from his chair and shook himself, like a person bent on throwing off sleep, reached his old hat from the nail, and my shawl and hood, which hung beside it. As we went out of the door granny said audibly, "A Father to the fatherless, and the widow's God." He held my hand with a tighter grasp as the words met his ear, and held it still while we went the rounds of the barn, and he gave his directions to Lem. as clear and well-judged as ever, every now and then turning to me for an opinion. I knew afterward that Joe had said to his father nearly what he had said to me, and asked him, moreover, to care for and comfort me, if care and comfort should ever be needed as they were now. From this day he always called me "My child," and I always said "Father" to him.

So we settled down into the dull, gray calm of life again; very silent, very quiet, we all were. Granny now and then volunteered a proverb or a text, as strangely fit to the mood, rather than any occasion, as her utterances usually were. I remember once when Mr. Harding had gone to the village, and I sat by his empty chair sewing, I unconsciously drew a long, sobbing sigh. Granny took out her needle from the sheath, and laid her stocking down, saying, as she did so in a dreamy way, "Yet doth he devise means that his banished be not expelled from him." What did she mean? The words fell softly on my tired soul, yet there was neither special promise nor hope in them for my peculiar want; yet they sung in my thoughts long after, as if persisting on some tender errand, mysterious still to me.

Soon it was time to make Thanksgiving preparations. Last year how different had this all been! What dreadful changes had passed over us since! Cousin Martha and Joe both gone, — what had we to be thankful for? I had paused before going downstairs one morning, when these bitter thoughts had roused me long before light, to look out at the east from my window. A low range of hills barricaded the valley some two or three miles from our house; and now, lying level on their tops, were long bars of amber, flushing at the edges with red, that told of a sunrise far away, but sure in coming, while through the gray sky above that pallid blue streak on the horizon a dying aurora pulsated in flashes of faint light, that fled and throbbed out again, and fled once more, and quivered anew with mystic splendor that thrilled me to see. Strange and fair it was, that cold, bright meeting of dawn and the northern night-lightning; and strangely portentous, too, it seemed to me. Was that a "sign in the sky?"— were these fatal wars foreboding the world's great peace?— was it good or evil that danced and flickered in those ice-glittering flashes above?

Thanksgiving day came at last. My sole pleasure in its preparations had been in carrying out my resolve that no poor soul I knew of, within our township, should go without a good dinner to-day. Somebody should be thankful if I was not. So I had sent Lemuel round with a big basket of pies, and chickens, and tongues, and other necessities of Thanksgiving, the day before; and now, having laid out my dinner on the side-table in the summer parlor, as far as its cold viands were concerned, and leaving the girl to look after granny, who seemed feebler than usual of late, and giving her strong charges about the turkey, and the potatoes, and the turnips, that already were in their respective corners hissing, and bubbling, and sending savory odors up the chimney, I dressed myself in my best, and set off for church with "father."

Our old minister had gone away to keep Thanksgiving with his son in Boston, and to-day a stranger was to preach for us. Our village choir was a good one for the country, with several fine, though untrained, voices, and one remarkable soprano, that seemed in its purity and accuracy to defy the need of instruction; and as it rose alone in the anthem before service, and wandered along the exquisite music of those words, "Rest in the Lord; oh, rest in the Lord! Wait patiently for him, and he shall give thee thy heart's desire," more than one dull eye glittered with tears that did not fall. But on my heart tears lay like lead, nor sprung to cool my hot eyes. Ah! what patient waiting could ever bring to me my heart's desire? Not God himself, I said, could restore this ruined past!

I looked across the aisle and saw Mrs. Banks, the captain's mother; her handkerchief was at her face, but she wept for joy,—her son was home again, weak and helpless, but at home! It was Thanksgiving to her; but for me there was no restoration. Sitting there quiet in the corner of the pew, unable to exert myself to dispel the bitter thoughts crowding upon me, I became their prey. Hymn and prayer passed by unheeded. I neither heard the text nor the sermon till, when it was about half over, suddenly these words roused me: —

"But there is still heaven to be thankful for. Whatever sorrows bereave us here, whatever fatal mistakes darken our lives, whatever irredeemable losses befall us, we may yet rest in the Lord, and wait patiently for him in the little life that remains; for beyond this world's gain or loss, high in the serene air of heaven, when existence ceases to be a lesson and becomes vivid life, there and only there shall he give us our heart's desire in its immortal fulness. Here knowledge is defiled, love is imperfect, purity the result of fiery trial, wealth rusted with covetousness; but in heaven is the very native country of pure knowledge, perfect love, utter sinlessness, and riches that neither moth nor rust corrupt, that bless and curse not."

He went on to enumerate what we had to be thankful for, even under the reign of anarchy and war; but on these few sentences that I have written I dwelt till peace brooded over my tried heart. Yes! there was heaven to come; and an object still left to life, — to grow into fitness for that rest and its reuniting.

After church we went home without staying to speak to the neighbors, who seemed to understand and respect our silence. They all went home with groups of children and grandchildren about them; we were alone.

Soon as possible I had dinner on the table. I wanted to have it through; I wanted the day done. Anniversaries are like old wounds that reopen and bleed every year. I hurried to have the observances of this one over with. So we sat down to dinner — three, where last year had been five! Cousin Martha's fair, wan face, with its scarlet flush on cheek and lip, smiling beside granny; Joe's manly, sunburnt visage and handsome figure on the other.

We sat down in perfect silence. Mr. Harding carved, and we all went through at least the form of eating. Still in that dead silence, when just as I was about to lay down my knife and fork, a wagon came rapidly down the road and stopped at our door. "Lemuel come back from the post-office," said father.

But was that halting step in the entry Lemuel's?

The door flung open, and there stood Joe.

Sorrow is easy to describe, but what words can tell the incredible thrill of such joy as this? For the first time in my life I lost all consciousness for a blind blank moment. I did not faint, — for I never faint, — but I knew nothing from the moment I saw the door open on him till I found both his arms round me and my head lying against him as I still sat in my chair. It's no use trying to tell it. A few, blessed as I, have snatched this blossom out of blood-red battle-fields; they will know.

It seems Joe had fallen, as Captain Banks said, from two musket-bullets that pierced at once the upper part of his left arm; fortunately for him they were not Minié-bullets, but the old kind. Then the cavalry charge swept over him, and a horse stepping on his right leg broke it badly; he escaped marvellously with his life, and fortunately no artery was ruptured; but he lay on the field three days and three nights, was then picked up by a farmer, — a Virginian and a Union man, — who, passing by the field, heard him groan; he picked him up, took him home, drove off to the nearest doctor to be found, and had his leg set, and his wounds dressed; but Joe was too weak to talk or think, and before he had strength to do either fever set in, with delirium, and in consequence they neither knew who he was or where he came from. But the woman of the house nursed him like a mother. She had two sons fighting in the West with Rosecrans, and she said it was for thinking of them that she never let a soldier pass her door hungry or thirsty, and took such care of Joe. If gratitude and blessing and prayers can keep that woman's sons alive and well, they will come back to her scathless!

So for two months he lay there between life and death. Then he wrote, but the letter was lost, or delayed, or missent; and through his slow convalescence he expected to see his father or me daily, and so wrote no more till, as soon as he could sit up long enough, he got to Hagerstown, and from there home. True, his leg had been badly set, and he never would walk without limping, and his arm still lay in a sling; but it was Joe! No matter how battered or broken, no matter how wan and thin, he was back again!

The next week I laid aside my heavy crape and bombazine for a white dress, and we were married. Still bent and grave, but with a bright smile, father put both his arms round me, and kissed me for the first time in his life. "My *dear* child!" was all he said.

And the week after I put on those mourning garments again, for granny was gone. The only words she had spoken since Joe came home, except in answer to some question, were: "He that saveth his life shall lose it; but he that loseth his life shall find it." She sank into a sort of lethargy, and fell asleep like a contented child.

It is winter now. Heavy snow falls as I write, drifting from the north-east, and settling, shroud-like, over the earth; but in the house, at home, there is no climate but summer.

God has given me my heart's desire.

HOW SHE FOUND OUT.

"But I don't love you!" said Laura, in a lazy sort of way, as if it were a matter of no particular consequence.

"Yes, you do," answered Frank, lying at her feet in the short, sweet grass, and looking up in her face. A very pleasant face to look into, no doubt: piquant, sensible, humorous, with great capacities of sweetness not yet called out by life; for Laura's life had been as tranquil as that of the clover-blossoms he was punching with her parasol, and her dark eyes had never yet been dimmed or softened with sorrow. They were all sparkle. Yet what girl of twenty would sit quietly and hear a man tell her she loved him in that calm way, even if she had known him always, and was his step-cousin?

Not Laura Gay! A quick flush of angry color rose to the dark hair that lay in soft, fluffy clouds almost down to her eyes, and hid the low, wide forehead. She jumped up from the rock where she was sitting.

"You are impertinent. I shall go home!"

"O Laura! don't be cruel. Stay a moment — give me a chance. I do beg your pardon, ma'am;" and Frank Dyer put himself into such an absurd posture on his knees, with his hands dropped at the wrists, for all the world like Laura's own little spaniel which he had taught to beg, that she had to laugh, and after that there was no more to be said; so she sat down again and waited for the sunset which they had come to see.

Norfolk is a little village in western Connecticut: sleepy as Sleepy Hollow, except that it is partly on a hill, and that the north winds blow there straight from the Arctic regions, without let or hindrance. In winter Norfolk is a howling wilderness of snow or stones, where the people endure hardness, and keep alive by strenuous exertions. In summer it blooms with the reluctant foliage and flowering of New England. The barren hills put forth mullein and hardhack, with scant bloom of diluted yellow and unwilling pinkness. The ready ferns illustrate the wood-edges with their delicate grace and faint odor. The gnarled apple-trees writhe into rosy buds, and the knotted, straggling kalmia entertains angels unaware in its clouds of dawn-tinted or pallid flowers, that come and go almost too quickly to be discovered.

People go to Norfolk in summer to keep cool — and they do it. A few people live and die there. One of these few was Laura Gay's father. Mr. Gay was born in Norfolk, and, having made money enough to content him, elsewhere, returned to his birthplace and settled down in the old homestead. It can be inferred what sort of a man he was from the two facts, that he was content with fifty thousand dollars, and that he was willing to settle down in Norfolk after a long absence, money-making in New York. But he was very fond of his children, and city life had proved fatal to all of them but one; after that nothing would have persuaded him to leave the country. He took kindly to his life there,— pottered about his garden in summer, hoed his corn, brushed his peas, made wonderful scarecrows, and exterminated the worms from his currant-bushes. In winter he had full occupation in keeping his house warm. Seal-skin bags and blubber would have been a vast comfort to him, but civilization demands coal fires and roast beef.

Laura was never sent to school. A governess of some sense, and a good deal of sweetness, brought her up. Her mother was a fat, fair, incapable female, who liked her dinner and her novel, and who was abundantly careless of what other people said,— a happy gift in the country. It was Miss Greene, the governess, who was Laura's real mother; who directed her nature in its bright, simple, fearless fashion; who bought her clothes and saw that they were not *outré* enough to be remarkable; who bought, also, the books she read, and permitted novels of a certain class among them.

It was she who introduced Laura to the few mild dissipations of society she had ever enjoyed; for Mrs. Gay said she was too feeble to visit, being in fact too fat. Mr. Gay had never entertained as possible the idea that Laura would or could marry. She was his little girl still. She always would be. He felt a curious surprise when she began to go to the church sewing-society, and said, "Sh, sh, dear! children shouldn't talk about such things," when she piquantly retailed at breakfast all the gossip with which the unbleached cotton and cheap calico garments had been seasoned in their fashioning the night before. He even doubted in his secret heart if she could read well enough when she was asked to join a reading circle, which was to Norfolk what a ball is to New York. But he did not express the doubt, lest he should grieve her.

So she grew up as natural, as honest, as delightful as any wild blossom in the fields about her; and it was no wonder that Frank Dyer, whose father had married Mrs. Gay's sister, when his boy was some seven years old, should find out, after knowing Laura as long as he could remember, and much longer than she could, that she was the very sweetest girl in all the world, and the dearest to him.

But Frank manfully held his tongue till Laura was twenty. He did not want her to accept him before she knew her own heart fully. She had no lack of admirers, such as they were. The village post-office had a succession of clerks, who fell in love with her as fast as they came into position. At least three young farmers spent Sunday in worshipping a human idol with shining eyes and fluffy hair, and she counted among her scalps all those youths who administered dry goods to the Norfolk population, one after another, and forsook their counter because Laura had no smiles to measure off for them. One theological student, also, who came to try his new-fledged powers in the old white church, bowed and fell at her feet, and then went his way sorrowing. Frank might have despaired of such a Diana had he been a man given to despair; but he knew, without conceit, that he was a better man than these, and he saw with inward delight that Laura depended on him more and more every year.

So he spent his summers there with his step-mother, who preferred her sister's society and the cool *idlesse* of the deep country to Newport or Saratoga; and when his vacation was over and he plunged into business again, he kept Laura always reminded of him by occasional gay notes; sometimes a piece of music, a box of Maillard's delicate confections, books just published, birthday bouquets, and all the small munitions of war wherewith the *illuminati* besiege fortresses in these days. But in vain had he waited for Laura to spend a winter in New York, or even Hartford, or to be allowed a season at some gay watering-place, where she might see some other world than that of Norfolk. Her father would not hear of her going to a city; his early experience filled him with nervous horror of the idea. Was one child spared him out of five, — well, straight and strong, with bloom on her face, light in her eye, laughter on her lips, — and should he be insane enough to risk his treasure where all the others had been wrecked and lost? Never! No persuasion could induce him to trust her to Mrs. Dyer's care even for a month.

As to travelling, that, too, was not feasible. Mamma was altogether too supine. Railroads tortured her both by their punctuality and their speed; hotels were an astonishment and a hissing on account of their stairs and their chairs. She did not see why people wanted to travel when they could stay at home. So she stayed there! She could not be left alone, so they all stayed with her; and, therefore, it came to pass that Laura at twenty had seen no better man than Frank Dyer, and he took heart of grace that night they strolled off to see the sunset, and asked her to marry him, receiving the answer and making the response we have already revealed.

It is true they sat down quietly to wait for the sinking sun, but it was an outward quiet only. With all his audacity, Frank Dyer's heart was apprehensive enough, and Laura was disturbed deeply. Change of any sort had never come near her; life had never been a conscious thing; she had grown up in careless comfort, happy in her daily ways, as a child is happy unawares; and here came the first stone to vex the placid stream's career, that had hitherto known only a bright, shallow ripple in its grassy bed. But, like a child, she put the trouble aside for the moment and gazed before her. They sat on the precipitous edge of a little hill that holds on its summit the church, the green, and a few pleasant houses; the last step of a terrace rather, for beyond green and church the land rises again, and still again; but at their feet, and stretching out before them, lay the West Norfolk and Canaan valley, — a green ravine straight on to the sunset, its lofty sides clothed to their summits with tender foliage of birch, beech, and maple, shaded with masses of hemlock and dark spear-heads of pine. A brook babbled down through the verdant cleft in the hills; you could hear its distant fall over more than one dam, but its light and shining were hidden by thick leaves, and by the flood of golden, dusty, radiant mist that filled and overflowed all the valley from the fast-sinking sun. Now that day-star fell behind a dark blue slate cloud, and gilt its edge with a vivid fringe of fire. Silence brooded over all the woods, broken only now and then by the thrilling, vibrant, silver-smitten note of the wood-thrush, who sings at noon and night as if he disdained the song of other birds, and would have all ether to himself for the clear spirit of his fairy clarion to fill. Then the sun emerged; the livid cloud was flecked with cold crimson; pearl and golden scales of light dappled all the southern sky in streaming fans of splendor. The east was filled with warm rose tints flushing and fading, and deeper still the crimson grew, and softer the purple of the west. A parting cloud of fire and gloom revealed the high evening star; the sun was gone.

Laura drew a long breath. She had lost something, and tried to recover herself and remember. It came back to her, with a disagreeable thrill, that Frank had asked her to marry him. She pulled up her light shawl hastily, and stooped to pick a cluster of strawberry-blossoms to hide the hot blush that covered her face; but Frank Dyer saw it. He was wise, however, and said no more just then. They went home through the dew, the June grass brushing them with fragrant spires, and the cool evening air breathing promise of a storm to-morrow, as well as the heavy gathering clouds all about the horizon.

"It will rain to-morrow," said Laura, for want of some better thing to say; and here they were at the gate.

"Good-by," was all that Frank answered. He did not offer to come in. She did not ask him. For the first time in her life Laura was glad to be rid of her cousin. It did not strike her as significant that it was the first time. She was too young, too simple, to know why. She went into the house and sat down by the window. A tall white rose pushed its fragrant milky buds against the sash; the half unfolded roses showed their soft saffron depths, and stood pearled with dew, and breathing tranquil odors close to the sill. Laura loved roses, but she never looked at these. Her face was troubled and thoughtful, and nobody disturbed her; for her father was hunting cut-worms at the roots of his cabbage plants, her mother deep in a new novel, and Miss Greene had gone up the hill to prayer-meeting. Not that she would have told her thoughts or her trouble to either of the three; but the silence forced them upon her own attention, and she sat there a long time wondering if she really did care anything about Frank Dyer except as a cousin, and getting more and more indignant that he should have asserted it as a fact instead of asking it as a favor. For, as I said, Miss Greene had let Laura read novels. It was in fact making a virtue of necessity, for she knew what feminine nature is in the best of us; that from the days of Paradise down it has been forbidden fruit that tempted us all; and by permitting Laura to read novels she achieved for herself the power of selecting them.

But novels are not nature, save and except a noted few; and it was not in Laura's experience of gentlemanly love-making that the lady should be so curtly taken possession of as she had been, without so much as "by your leave." It is true her lovers — for a few of the enamored rustics had really committed themselves — had made their proposals with much stammering and dire confusion of face, but with proper humility. She had expected of a lover on her own plane the elegant diction, the well-turned phrases, the rapture and devotion, of a well-behaved man in a book; and Frank had first asked her in the simplest Saxon to marry him, and then, when she said she did not love him, assured her she did. Was this to be borne?

So she meditated long on the fact that she did not love

him; they were always quarrelling; not a week passed but their "little tempers" rose and flew to arms, for at least five minutes; then they were not in the least alike, — at least everybody said so. Frank was not afraid of anything; he was dreadfully rash; he had brown hair and blue-gray eyes; and so forth and so on, till she had catalogued the poor young fellow remorselessly, — the very police would have known him. Then femininity relented, of course, and the other side of the shield was interviewed; but good qualities are so tedious. Laura yawned, lifted her head from her hand, got up and lit her candle, and ignominiously went to bed, thinking all the way upstairs of the hero she always had meant to marry: tall, pale, with deep, glittering eyes and raven hair; a man dedicated to consumption and the ministry; a man to be adored, waited on, worshipped. Poor, dear little Laura! — she was so young! But she went to sleep very soon, and slept better than that audacious Frank, who was half scared at his first daring venture, and lay wondering how it would result — in what fashion he should follow it up. Night brought him no counsel; he made up his mind only to wait, having dim suspicion that these matters, out of novels, find their own way to a fit ending, much like the drop of water that works a patient way through sand, and stones, and tenacious clay, at last to the root which awaits it in thirsty longing. Even after a week's waiting, after walks, drives, hours of croquet, and two picnics, — opportunity-makers for the aid of all deliberating lovers, — all he contrived to say was one brief sentence, that escaped him almost before he knew it, as the two sat together one Sunday night on Mr. Gay's door-step, the rose-freighted air breathing softest balm about them, and the young moon, slender as a dream, floating down the twilight sky.

"Laura, have you found out yet whether you love me?"

"No!" snapped out this thorny young person, with a sudden red in her face that even the twilight could not hide.

She did not say "I do not," thought Frank to himself.

"Won't you try to find out?" he replied, with a certain strenuous meekness quite as masterful as a demand.

"I don't know," she answered; but the tone was far more subdued; the doubt was half assurance.

"*Chateau qui parle, femme qui écoute, tous deux vont se rendre,*" thought Frank, blessing the consolatory old proverb, as Laura abruptly rose and left him to welcome Miss Greene, just home from another prayer-meeting; for Miss Greene was a good woman,—conveniently good, thought Frank Dyer.

Matters went on very tranquilly after this. One little adventure occurred to Laura that was destined to be cut deep in her memory by after events. She went over to Winsted one day to the dress-maker, and Mrs. Dyer went with her. At the last moment Frank discovered important business would take him to the borough too; and, although both ladies assured him he would be dreadfully in the way, he was yet allowed to go on condition that he would not expect their society, but only meet them at the last train.

Now Mrs. Dyer, though not equal to Mrs. Gay in size, was a fairly stout woman, and of all things despised a hill; so, after Laura's dresses were talked over, fitted, tried on; her Sunday bonnet of last year a bit changed and sobered down for this year's daily wear, and a basket of peaches bought, Mrs. Dyer went to the hotel to take the carriage to the West-street station. But Laura at the last moment remembered she must have some candy, and really it was absurd to ride up a little hill like that; she could buy her sweets and run up the road very nearly as fast as Aunt Bell could be driven up. But she was long buying her candy; there was a delay about change, and when Laura at last crossed the Lake-street bridge she heard a whistle at the lower station, and, supposing the train to be coming, hurried up the steps to the track, intending to cross the railroad bridge, which there runs high above the road, and affords a quick way to reach the cars. Luckily for her the whistle she heard was that of the train just in from Hartford; but she did not know that, and hurried over the plank that is laid across the open floor of the bridge for pedestrians. Her aunt and Frank stood on the platform watching her, but neither felt anxious, for Laura was sure-footed, and prided herself on her safe passage of many a dangerous place in her walks. This time, however, between hurry and carelessness, one foot slipped just as she got to the last tie of the track, and went down into space as far as it could. She threw her bundles away instinctively, and grasped the rail with both hands; for an instant she recalled that coming whistle, and shivered; but the thought gave her desperate strength, and before Frank could reach her she had pulled herself forward on to the solid abutment, and was safe, though trembling with excitement and somewhat scraped and bruised.

Frank's face was white with terror, and he could not speak; he just gathered up her bundles, drew her hand into his arm, and hastened to the platform, where Aunt Bell stood wringing her hands, almost in hysterics.

After this good woman was quieted and Laura in the cars on her way home beside the still silent Frank, she remembered his white face, his look of pain, and wondered what made him care so much about her, and if she ever could or would care about him enough to marry him, half smiling, half sighing over the idea. So that summer passed, and the Dyers with it, though they only went to New York. Autumn again painted all the world about Laura with its wondrous pigments. Sober Norfolk became transfigured; respectable old Haystack flaunted in kingly robes of crimson and gold; the great green valley turned to a ravine of fire and blood, darkened with the constant evergreen sentinels that withstood all temptations of gay attire; the very ferns turned delicate bronze or faint yellow; and weeping blackberry-vines trailed garnet and saffron tracery over the scant grasses of the rocky hill-sides. Laura went nutting with more than one party; she gathered a bushel at least of gay leaves, and forgot to dry them; she took long, lonely walks and read volumes of nice, harmless poetry; her eyes grew dreamy, her manner abstracted; life out-doors seemed to have lost its flavor; she missed Frank everywhere; she began to hate the youths of Norfolk, who fluttered about her like uninteresting moths, only to burn their fingers. She wished it were summer, and, behold, here was winter; dreadful, more dreadful than ever, for it rioted among the deep figures below zero, — made the house dismal with cold o' mornings, and desperate with frozen water everywhere at night. There were days when the post-office was not accessible; when the railroad itself was over-drifted, and no New York paper even lifted the weight of their solitude with the assurance of a pleasanter world beyond, — a long and dreary winter, in which almost the only gleam of pleasure was the weekly pamphlet from Frank, or the frequent letter from either his mother or himself. But, after all, if one can endure, spring surely comes at last; and when May began to make the old hills green in patches, and dot the sward with shy, delicate blooms, Aunt Bell wrote that she had been so worn out with one influenza after another, a touch of pneumonia, and a long siege of rheumatism, that the doctor had ordered her to leave New York at once, and she had resolved to take board at a hotel in Winsted till July, when, of course, she should come to Norfolk. Mrs. Gay fussed a good deal in her harmless way about this new caprice of Mrs. Dyer's; but she knew long ago it was of no use trying to move her sister's fancy, however capricious it might be. Laura was very glad; if Aunt Bell was so near she could run down and see her any day. Nothing was said about Frank,— he never could leave New York so early; but by and by, when June began, and Aunt Bell had coaxed Laura into coming to stay a week with her, much to the (apparent) astonishment of both ladies, Frank appeared Thursday night, to stay till the next Monday.

How unfortunate! Laura had promised to go to Hartford with Miss Greene on Saturday. But then she was coming back at night; and, since she was to leave Miss Greene to spend Sunday with some friends, Frank promised to run down to Pine Meadow on the four-o'clock train and meet her there; he might be very useful, Aunt Bell said, to carry her bundles out of the car. Laura thought so herself. So at four o'clock the two simultaneously left Hartford and Winsted, flying toward each other on the wings of steam, though in a mighty prosaic fashion: Laura hot, tired, and cross; for Aunt Bell had made her wear a thick black silk dress and a black hat and feathers, — becoming enough, but fit for the cold Winsted morning, not for the hot Hartford noon; and then shopping is not always conducive to peace of mind: when you cannot possibly match your summer silk with trimming, or get the right shade of gloves, or suit yourself with a summer bonnet; when you are blinded with tints of blue, gray, and lavender; when your dresses demand white and black, with just a bit of rose-color in your bonnet, and you fall really in love with a wreath of dark and golden pansies; or you want that exquisite French cambric, with a border of daisies to its blue ground, and have spent all your money but two dollars, you have a right to be cross.

So Laura was cross, as, with half a dollar left in her porte-monnaie after buying her ticket and her inevitable candy, and six bundles in her arms and hands, she seated herself in the train and moved slowly out of the station.

In the meantime Frank bethought himself of the garnets that are to be found here and there in the rocks of Satan's Kingdom; and having a fitful fancy for geology, and remembering that he had an hour to wait for Laura, borrowed a hammer, and as the train crept at a snail's pace through this evil-named gorge dropped off the platform of the car, and proceeded to amuse himself. The day grew hotter toward night, as some days in the early season do. Geologizing is not done in the shade, and Frank got very warm indeed; Laura meanwhile getting cool, good-tempered, and rested, in the breezy cars, and thinking of Pine Meadow station more than she was aware. Suddenly the train stopped, and she was surprised to find the way so far passed over that they were waiting at the side track west of Stratton Brook for the four o'clock train from Winsted; fifteen minutes dragged on like an hour. By and by the steam-whistle shrieked from a distance, the train rattled on to the siding, and with a vexed yell the detained engine was off again. As they swept, half an hour after, through the Kingdom gorge, Laura, who sat looking out of the window, saw a man try to get on the platform of the car, and fail. She thought it might be the engineer of the construction train at first, and then, quick as light, it flashed on her brain that it was Frank, who expected the train to slow as usual, and could not reach it. She flew to the rear door of the car, — by this time just on the west end of the bridge, — and there he was, running across the open floor on the single plank over that black, swift river. Laura turned to the conductor with almost a cry: —

"Please, won't you stop the train? Mr. Dyer is left here, and it is Saturday night."

"I can't, Miss Gay." The conductor knew both Laura and Frank from their frequent transits over the road. "I wish I could; but we are fifteen minutes late."

She turned to look. Frank was gone. Laura felt her way back to her seat; she remembered her own fall on the bridge at Winsted; and there came back to her a horrid story, in the paper only yesterday, of an old lady whose daughter had come to bid her good-by at a train, and standing on the track to wave her handkerchief, the mother saw, as she rolled off in the car, another train run over her child, and kill her before her eyes. Laura shuddered; but, having a certain amount of sense for a girl, she sat down and considered what to do. At the Pine Meadow station there was no telegraph office. She could not stop there; she could not go home in this horrible anxiety; she must know the worst — if anything is worse than doubt. She went to the conductor again and asked him to tell the station-master at the Meadow that if Mr. Dyer came there he might tell him that a wagon would be sent down for him from Winsted at once. Now, Laura did this partly not to let the conductor know she was frightened, — for she already, with the logic and justice of most young ladies, regarded this poor man as a callous and cruel brute not to have stopped for Frank; and partly to give Frank himself information that would set him at rest, if by any possible chance he had escaped the ghastly river, with its rocks and pools; for Laura had enough poise left to remember that such a thing might be. But little did this young person know the ways of men if she expected the conductor to give such a message, or the station-master to deliver it. They knew very well that any average man could take care of himself without a girl's intervention. Laura hates them both to this day; but I do not know that it troubles either of them.

Then she resolved to leave the train at New Hartford, for she knew certain Winsted people whom she knew well would get into the cars there, and she could send after a carriage to come down for her from the hotel and take her home. So, gathering all her bundles, she hurried to the door, and, as soon as they stopped, seized upon the first gentleman she saw entering and charged him to tell the driver of the Blank House carriage to send a man down to New Hartford for her as soon as possible,—" For my cousin, who was to meet me here, has been left at Pine Meadow, and I must wait."

Diplomatic little Laura! She did not see the furtive smile that curled the corners of Mr. Blinn's mouth as she so carefully avoided personal pronouns. She did not know that he came down on the train with Frank, and knew perfectly well who *he* was waiting for; much less did she know the conclusions he drew at once from her white, anxious face and wistful eyes. But he promised to give her message. Then where to leave her bundles? The station-master assured her he should immediately shut up for the night, as there was no later train, but kindly advised her to go to the tavern. She would have asked where she could find a wagon and driver; but, alas! there was only half a dollar in that depleted pocket-book. So she found her way to the tavern, interviewed the landlord, and left her parcels in his keeping, telling him she expected to be sent for, and if the man from the Blank House, Winsted, came there before she got back, he must wait for her. Laura's parcels were valuable,—among them her pretty French Cashmere shawl, rolled up in its case, and the results of her day's shopping. But do you think she cared, when Frank was perhaps lying dead in that black river, what became of things? So she gathered up the long train of her heavy dress, which had been torn from its loopings before she left Hartford, and prepared to walk down to Pine Meadow.

How hot and dusty the road was! How long as a bad dream its dull track! One wagon after another passed her, but Laura had no courage to ask for a ride. Two ladies in a pony-carriage drove down, and one turned and looked at her. Laura felt uneasily how peculiar her appearance must be then and there, but she kept on till the Canal railroad station was in sight. Then she paused to consider. If Frank had not been drowned, of course he would walk up to the village; if he got her message he would stop at the station; if not, he would probably take the track as shortest; at any rate the road ran parallel to the railroad, and the Connecticut Western track went for a mile side by side with that of the Canal. She would walk down the rails, and look across at the highway; then she should be sure not to miss him; so holding up her gown, that kept increasing still in weight, she stumbled on across the ties, her head turned toward the highway, till the two paths diverged so far that in the deepening twilight she could scarce discern figures, and in despair she took a little cart-path back to the road, and found herself close to the Pine Meadow station. It was shut tight; nobody to be found. She looked along the lonely track toward the Kingdom bridge, but no figure appeared; she heard the rushing river and the whispering trees sighing in the soft, damp air of the valley; her heart sank very low. She could not walk to the bridge, and then back to New Hartford; her strength was all but gone now. Sadly she turned back and hunted up the station-master, only to find that he had shut up as soon as the train passed, because he "allers did." "Hadn't nobody ben there!" Then there lay all that walk to be retraced; and by this time hope had almost left her; the tears came hot and fast to her eyes, and dropped unheeded. She went over, with the fertile imagination of a woman, not only all the probabilities, but all the possibilities, of the case. How should she tell Aunt Bell; how glad she was that she had not confided her terrors to Mr. Blinn, for Aunt Bell might have had a real fit and died, to hear such a rumor, and not be able to search it out, and Uncle Dyer not there either! Poor Frank, — poor Laura rather, she thought, — what should she do without him? If she asked herself any further questions they are unknown to this deponent.

But the hot night grew hotter to her all the time; her feet ached as well as her heart; it is well that we have bodies to deaden the aches of our souls sometimes. Just then the pony phaeton passed her again, this time with but one lady. She drove very slowly, and Laura, with her heart in her mouth, took courage, and said timidly, though clearly: —

"Are you going to New Hartford, madam?"

The lady stopped and assented.

"Can I ride up with you, please? I am so tired."

"Certainly."

And in another moment Laura was safe beside this friend in need, inexpressibly relieved as to her weariness, and very glad to have her companion ask, "Are you not Miss Gay, of Norfolk?" And then Laura told her story, too glad to be known and befriended to remember or care for any possible inferences.

Blessed are the sympathizers! — they give the most precious gifts of earth. Man does not live by bread alone, even in this mortal life; we exist on other food that that which is physical. Had Mrs. Parker been sarcastic, and sniffed at Laura as a foolish girl, scared at nothing, and assured her a man was always able to look out for himself, or teased her for her sentimentality and devotion, Laura might have added a third to her list of hates; but Mrs. Parker was a lady, and knew better. Life had not made her bitter any more than nature. She soothed poor Laura with the kindliest words; assured her she should feel just so in the same circumstances, and proposed at once that they should drive right back to the tavern, and see if Mr. Dyer had by any chance been there; but he had not. The landlord had seen somebody who looked like a stranger ride by; but he was with another man, and went up to the depot. So to the depot they went, to find that all closely shut; then Mrs. Parker suggested that he might have come up to the telegraph office and sent a message for her to Winsted, thinking she would be alarmed; but when they got there the operator had gone to tea. She must be looked for, and when they found her there was no record of any message for the last hour. Mrs. Parker, with unweary kindness, then insisted Laura should go home with her, bundles and all, to wait for the "team" from Winsted, which the landlord of the tavern promised to send to Mrs. Parker's when it came; and the homesick, heartsick girl was only too glad to go.

The cool, quiet house, the friendliness, the rest, seemed to Laura's undisciplined soul only aggravations; she wanted to do something; she could not swallow the nice supper set before her, — she could not even drink the tea. She paced up and down the piazza in restless misery, till at last the idea occurred to her to telegraph to a friend of Frank's, who was boarding at the hotel in Winsted with his wife, and find out if her cousin had been heard from there. So she wrote a hasty message : —

Has Frank come home? I am left in New Hartford.
LAURA GAY.

Further particulars she spared, thinking of that half dollar; and when Mrs. Parker's little boy had gone down to the office she began to count the minutes for his return. It was seven o'clock now; by eight at most she ought to see the wagon from Winsted, and before that she should hear from Mr. White. An hour! The next fifteen minutes were like a day to her; and at every roll of wheels over the bridge below her heart jumped. But nobody came! By and by the boy returned; but there was no answer to her message. At eight — oh, how long first! — Mr. Parker came home, and, proving to be an old acquaintance of Laura's, was as kind as his wife. He went at once down to the livery-stable, which they had not thought of, to see if any one had been there to hire a horse, as it was the only place where one could be had, and surely Mr. Dyer would not think of walking to Winsted. Laura was by this time nearly frantic. Nobody came for her; no answer arrived to her telegram; nothing could be heard of Frank. The mystery and silence of death seemed to close about her like an awful nightmare. She beat against these bars of circumstance like a newly-prisoned bird; she begged Mr. Parker to order a carriage for her at ten o'clock, for if nothing happened by that time she must and would go back to Winsted; she must reach her aunt; she must know something!

They all pitied her; they were all good to her. Perhaps her fervent gratitude to them stands balanced in her record against her hatred of the conductor and station-master. I think the gratitude outweighs the hate if that be so, it is so much the rarer emotion. But even the kindness and pity could but pacify the external expression of Laura's wild and impatient distress. The minutes passed in slow torture; her nerves were racked with doubt and dread; her incisive and impatient nature could know no more unendurable pangs than those of suspense. Mr. Parker did not come home; he had then no good news to bring. Night darkened over the hills about her; mists curled up from the long pond above the dam; the river murmured below; the tranquil stars came out softly into the misty heaven. Laura looked at this still world with dumb rage and reproach. Frank dead in that whispering river, and all the world so silent, calm, and sweet! It was horrible. Where should she go? What should she do? Her head throbbed with pain and excitement. She walked up and down in the night-air till she was shivering with the chill, though her head and her eyes were still aflame. Kind Mrs. Parker, with pity in every tone, tried to make her sit down and rest; she did not try to comfort her any more. Laura noticed that. Nine o'clock; must she give up all hope? Just then hoofs rattled on the bridge, clattered up the hill. Mr. Parker's cheery voice cried out that there was news, and in a moment more Laura tore open a telegram from Winsted:—

I am coming for you. Wait where you are.
FRANK DYER.

Laura gave one dry sob and sat down in a chair somebody gave her. Her strength was all gone. There are human words enough for pain: how few there are for joy! — nowhere near enough to describe the blessed relief and rapture that made our little girl so weak, so content. Now she could remember her politeness, and try to express her vivid gratitude to these kindest of all people who had helped her in time of need. But it seemed to her as if words failed even there; she had to cease herself, and hear how Mr. Parker had heard nothing at the stable, and, being then a little alarmed himself, had kept the telegraph office open as long as he could, hoping to hear from Winsted.

Let us take the time while Laura is waiting in hope — far different dispensation from the waiting in fear — to explain how this missing young gentleman had spent his time for the three hours during which his fate had been so doubtful to his dismayed "cousin." When Frank found himself, at five o'clock, in the gorge, tired and heated with climbing, his pockets full of specimens, and his hands bruised against the rocks, he resolved to wait there for the train, which ordinarily slows quite enough for any one to reach the car-steps easily, rather than to walk in a hurry up to Pine Meadow. When the cars passed him so fast he still thought they would stop for him on the other side of the bridge, as the conductor had seen him, he supposed, from the baggage car; so he ran over the single plank, never thinking it to be dangerous, and coming to no harm, except, indeed, that he perceived the train did not slacken speed, and that further effort was useless; so he turned at once into the highway, and prepared to walk to New Hartford. Just then it must have been that Laura turned to look again after speaking to the conductor; for the road turns at right angles with the bridge, while the train curves but little there; and, standing back in the car, she could not see the road, but only the bridge and the track, and Frank not on either!

He walked but a few rods before meeting an old farmer, whom he persuaded to put one of his horses into a wagon and carry him to Winsted; and so it happened that while Laura, hot and anxious, was trudging down the Canal railroad track, Frank was quietly driving up the highway, and she had failed to recognize him so far off, having moreover made up her mind that he would walk. They had driven up to the depot at New Hartford, for the farmer had some errand there, and would have been seen again, and probably recognized in passing the hotel, had they not, to save time, taken a little by-road that cut off a corner and put them sooner on the turnpike. Frank thought of sending a telegram, but supposed the conductor had seen him, and would tell Laura he was left, as she would ask probably, on his not appearing at the Meadow station, if he had come down in the four-o'clock train. When he got home and did not find Laura, his mother having gone to bed with a sick headache, he could get no information from her. Mr. and Mrs. White had gone to ride, and the telegram from Laura lay safely on the floor of their room, shoved in through the crack of the door! The landlord asserted that Laura did not come home in the carriage, and now both driver and carriage were gone to the Naugatuck train. Frank naturally supposed she was left in

Hartford, and very tranquilly sat down and ate his supper, and then went up street to hunt up Mr. Blinn and see if he had seen her on the train, as it was just possible she might have heard from Miss Greene news to take her back to Norfolk, though he felt a certain chagrin that she had not in either case thought of her aunt's natural anxiety and telegraphed to her. Mr. Blinn was not in his office, so Frank went on to send a telegram to Hartford, and there learned of Laura's message to Mr. White, sent his own down to her, and waited till her answer came. Then he took a conveyance from the nearest stable, and drove back to the hotel for wraps and to interview the driver who had received Mr. Blinn's order at the cars, and find out why it was not executed. But that worthy was in a muddled frame of mind, not unusual to him, and "didn't remember nothin' 'beout it anyhow." So, with a mildly derogatory remark, Frank went his way to New Hartford, quite unconscious of Laura's anxiety, and wondering not a little how she came to be so silly as to get off the last train at New Hartford, and on Saturday night too. Her reply to his message had been, "Will wait at Mr. E. B. Parker's"; so, after an inquiry or two, he drove directly to the house.

It was dark by this time, or Laura, who was at the door to meet him, might have been a little confused at his look of surprise when she threw herself into his arms and began to sob.

Here was an event, to be sure! Laura, who never had kissed him even as a child, hanging on his neck in tears, and before utter strangers. Mrs. Parker came to the rescue.

"Mr. Dyer, I presume. Miss Gay has been dreadfully frightened."

"Frightened?" echoed the bewildered man.

"O Frank! — for three hours I have not known if you were dead or alive. I thought you were drowned."

"Come," said he, in a curt, masculine way, being in fact mightily tickled with the obvious state of affairs; "put your things on, Laura; we ought to go directly, — it is late;" and while Laura, meek as any nun, folded herself in the wraps he brought and hunted up her bundles, Mr. Dyer made his warm acknowledgments to Mr. and Mrs. Parker, and obtained some idea of the complications he had unwittingly caused.

It was after ten o'clock when they drove out of the little village; the moon glittered just above the crest of an eastern hill, red and hot through the purple haze; the soft and fragrant June night brooded like a tender dream over the woods and drew out all their delicate odors into the cool and wooing air; no light shone from any window; no voice of man intruded on the peace; the dropping brooks tinkled from stone to stone or rippled whisperingly under long grasses in the meadows; a whip-poor-will's lonely cry accented the silence and made it felt. With broken speech, and tears that could not be restrained, Laura told her pitiful little tale, and Frank supplied its vacancies with his own. Laura ended with a long, sighing breath and an unfinished sentence: —

"Oh, I am so glad" —

Frank did not speak — he could not. He grasped Laura's little hand in his own very closely, but she did not reclaim it. They were both silent for a while, thrilled with the same emotion; doubtful if, after all, this darkness, stillness, this silent passion, this sweet agony of relief and rest, were not a dream; if it could be true; if it were vanishing, — at least this was Laura.

Frank, perhaps, was more assured, more exultant, more courageous; for it was he who broke the silence.

"Laura, have you found out?" and for answer the lovely head dropped on his shoulder, and she nestled into his arms. Probably she had.

Laura always said that Frank took a mean advantage of her, and extorted his answer when she was so tired she really didn't know whether she meant it; but as she never said this to any one but him, and they were married the next October, I don't know that it was of any consequence.

ANN POTTER'S LESSON.

My sister Mary Jane is older than I, — as much as four years. Father died when we were both small, and didn't leave us much means beside the farm. Mother was rather a weakly woman; she didn't feel as though she could farm it for a livin'. It's hard work enough for a man to get clothes and victuals off a farm in West Connecticut; it's up-hill work always; and then a man can turn to, himself, to ploughin' and mowin'; but a woman aint of no use, except to tell folks what to do; and everybody knows it's no way to have a thing done, — to send.

Mother talked it all over with Deacon Peters, and he counselled her to sell off all the farm but the home-lot, which was sot out for an orchard with young apple-trees, and had a garden-spot to one end of it, close by the house. Mother calculated to raise potatoes and beans and onions enough to last us the year round, and to take in sewin', so's to get what few groceries we was goin' to want. We kept Old Red, the best cow: there was pasture enough for her in the orchard, for the trees wa'n't growed to be bearin' as yet, and we lotted a good deal on milk to our house; besides, it saved butcher's meat.

Mother was a real pious woman, and she was a high-couraged woman too. Old Miss Perrit, an old widder-

woman that lived down by the bridge, come up to see
her the week after father died. I remember all about
it, though I wa'n't but ten years old; for when I see
Miss Perrit comin' up the road, with her slimpsy old
veil hanging off from her bumbazine bunnet, and her
doleful look (what Nancy Perrit used to call " mother's
company-face"), I kinder thought she was comin' to
our house; and she was allers so musical to me, I went
into the back-door, and took up a towel I was hemmin',
and set down in the corner, all ready to let her in. It
don't seem as if I could 'a' been real distressed about
father's dyin' when I could do so; but children is just
like spring weather,—rainin' one hour and shinin' the
next,—and it's the Lord's great mercy they be; if they
begun to be feelin' so early there wouldn't be nothin'
left to grow up. So pretty quick Miss Perrit knocked,
and I let her in. We hadn't got no spare room in that
house; there was the kitchen in front, and mother's
bedroom, and the buttery, and the little back-space
opened out on't behind. Mother was in the bedroom;
so, while I called her, Miss Perrit set down in the splint
rockin'-chair, that creaked awfully, and went to rockin'
back and forth, and sighin', till mother come in.

"Good-day, Miss Langdon!" says she, with a kind
of a snuffle, "how *dew* you dew? I thought I'd come
and see how you kep' up under this here affliction. I
rec'lect very well how I felt when husband died. It's
a dreadful thing to be left a widder in a hard world, —
don't you find it out by this?"

I guess mother felt quite as bad as ever Miss Perrit
did, for everybody knew old Perrit treated his wife
like a dumb brute while he was alive, and died drunk;
but she didn't say nothin'. I see her give a kind

of a swaller, and then she spoke up bright and strong: —

"I don't think it is a hard world, Miss Perrit. I find folks kind and helpful, beyond what I'd any right to look for. I try not to think about my husband any more than I can help, because I couldn't work if I did, and I've got to work. It's most helpful to think the Lord made special promises to widows, and when I remember him I aint afeard."

Miss Perrit stopped rockin' a minute, and then she began to creak the chair and blow her nose again, and she said: —

"Well, I'm sure it's a great mercy to see anybody rise above their trouble the way you do; but, law me! Miss Langdon, you aint got through the fust pair o' bars on't yet. Folks is allers kinder neighborly at the fust; they feel to help you right off, every way they can; but it don't stay put, — they get tired on't; they blaze right up like a white-birch stick, an' then they go out all of a heap; there's other folks die, an' they don't remember you, an' you're just as bad off as though you wa'n't a widder."

Mother kind of smiled, — she couldn't help it; but she spoke up again just as steady: —

"I don't expect to depend on people, Miss Perrit, so long as I have my health. I aint above takin' friendly help when I need to, but I mean mostly to help myself. I can get work to take in, and when the girls have got their schoolin' they will be big enough to help me. I am not afraid but what I shall live and prosper, if I only keep my health."

"Hem, well!" whined out Miss Perrit. "I allers thought you was a pretty mighty woman, Miss Langdon, and I'm glad to see you're so high-minded; but you aint sure of your health, never. I used to be real smart to what I am now, when Perrit was alive; but I took on so when he was brought home friz to death that it sp'iled my nerves; and then I had to do so many chores out in the shed I got cold an' had the dreadfulest rheumatiz; an' when I'd got past the worst spell of that, and was quite folksy again, I slipped down on our door-step an' kinder wrenched my ankle, an' ef't hadn't 'a' been for the neighbors I don't know but what Nancy and I should 'a' starved."

Mother did laugh this time. Miss Perrit had overshot the mark.

"So the neighbors were helpful, after all!" said she. "And if ever I get sick I shall be willin' to have help, Miss Perrit. I'm sure I would take what I would give. I think givin' works two ways. I don't feel afraid yet."

Miss Perrit groaned a little, and wiped her eyes, and got up to go away. She hadn't never offered to help mother; and she went off to the sewin'-circle, and told that Miss Langdon hadn't got no feelings at all, and she b'lieved she'd just as soon beg for a livin' as not. Polly Mariner, the tailoress, come and told mother all she said next day; but mother only smiled, and set Polly to talkin' about the best way to make over her old cloak. When she was gone I begun to talk about Miss Perrit, and I was real mad; but mother hushed me right up.

"It aint any matter, Ann," said she. "Her sayin' so don't make it so. Miss Perrit's got a miserable disposition, and I'm sorry for her. A mint of money wouldn't make her happy. She's a doleful Christian;

she don't take any comfort in anything, and I really do pity her."

And that was just the way mother took everything.

At first we couldn't sell the farm. It was down at the foot of Torringford Hill, two good miles from meetin', and a mile from the school-house; most of it was woodsy, and there wa'n't no great market for wood about there. So for the first year Squire Potter took it on shares, and, as he principally seeded it down to rye, why, we sold the rye and got a little money, but 'twa'n't a great deal, — no more than we wanted for clothes the next winter. Aunt Langdon sent us down a lot of maple-sugar from Lee, and when we wanted molasses we made it out of that. We didn't have to buy no great of groceries, for we could spin and knit by firelight, and, part of the land bein' piny woods, we had a good lot of knots that were as bright as lamps for all we wanted. Then we had a dozen chickens, and by pains and care they laid pretty well, and the eggs were as good as gold. So we lived through the first year after father died pretty well.

Anybody that couldn't get along with mother and Major (I always called Mary Jane "Major" when I was real little, and the name kind of stayed by) couldn't get along with anybody. I was as happy as a cricket whilst they were by; though, to speak truth, I wasn't naturally so chirpy as they were. I took after father more, who was a kind of a despondin' man, down-hearted, never thinkin' things could turn out right, or that he was goin' to have any luck. That was my natur', and mother see it, and fought ag'inst it like a real Bunker-Hiller; but natur' is hard to root up, and there was always times when I wanted to sulk away into a corner and think nobody wanted me, and that I was poor and humbly, and had to work for my living.

I remember one time I'd gone up into my room before tea to have one of them dismal fits. Miss Perrit had been in to see mother, and she'd been tellin' over what luck Nancy'd had down to Hartford: how't she had gone into a shop, and a young man had been struck with her good looks, an he'd turned out to be a master-shoemaker, and Nancy was a-goin' to be married, and so on, — a rigmarole as long as the moral law, — windin' up with askin' mother why she didn't send us girls off to try our luck, for Major was as old as Nance Perrit. I'd waited to hear mother say, in her old, bright way, that she couldn't afford it, and she couldn't spare us if she had the means, and then I flung up into our room, — that was a lean-to in the garret, with a winder in the gable end, — and there I set down by the winder with my chin on the sill, and begun to wonder why we couldn't have as good luck as the Perrits. After I'd got real miserable I heerd a soft step comin' upstairs, and Major come in and looked at me and then out of the winder.

"What's the matter of you, Anny?" said she.

"Nothing," says I, as sulky as you please.

"Nothing always means something," says Major, as pleasant as pie; and then she scooched down on the floor and pulled my two hands away, and looked me in the face as bright and honest as ever you see a dandelion look out of the grass. "What is it, Anny? Spit it out, as Reub Potter says; you'll feel better to free your mind."

"Well," says I, "Major, I'm tired of bad luck."

"Why, Anny! I didn't know as we'd had any. I'm sure, it's three years since father died, and we have had enough to live on all that time, and I've got my schooling, and we are all well; and just look at the apple-trees, — all as pink as your frock with blossoms; that's good for new cloaks next winter, Anny."

"'Taint that, Major. I was thinkin' about Nancy Perrit. If we'd had the luck to go to Hartford may be you'd have been as well off as she; and then I'd have got work, too. And I wish I was as pretty as she is, Major; it does seem too bad to be poor and humbly too."

I wonder she didn't laugh at me, but she was feelin' for folks, always. She put her head on the window-sill along of mine, and kinder nestled up to me in her lovin' way, and said, softly: —

"I wouldn't quarrel with the Lord, Anny."

"Why, Major! you scare me! I haven't said nothin' against the Lord. What do you mean?" said I; for I was touchy, real touchy.

"Well, dear, you see we've done all we can to help ourselves; and what's over and above, that we can't help, — that is what the Lord orders, aint it? And he made you, didn't he? You can't change your face; and I'm glad of it, for it is Anny's face, and I wouldn't have it changed a mite. There'll always be two people to think it's sightly enough, and may be more by and by; so I wouldn't quarrel with it, if I were you."

Major's happy eyes always helped me. I looked at her and felt better. She wasn't any better-lookin' than I; but she was always so chirk, and smart, and neat, and pretty-behaved, that folks thought she was handsome after they knowed her.

Well, after a spell there was a railroad laid out up the valley, and all the land thereabouts riz in price right away; and Squire Potter he bought our farm on speculation, and give a good price for it; so't we had two thousand dollars in the bank, and the house and lot, and the barn, and the cow. By this time Major was twenty-two and I was eighteen; and Squire Potter he'd left his house up on the hill, and he'd bought out Miss Perrit's house, and added on to't, and moved down not far from us, so's to be near the railroad-depot, for the sake of bein' handy to the woods, for cuttin' and haulin' of them down to the track. 'Twasn't very pleasant at first to see our dear old woods goin' off to be burned that way; but Squire Potter's folks were such good neighbors we gained as much as we lost, and a sight more, for folks are greatly better'n trees, — at least, clever folks.

There was a whole raft of the Potters, — eight children of 'em all, — some too young to be mates for Major and me, but Mary Potter, and Reuben, and Russell, they were along about as old as we were. Russell come between Major and me; the other two was older.

We kinder kept to home always, Major and me, because we hadn't any brothers to go out with us; so we were pretty shy of new friends at first. But you couldn't help bein' friendly with the Potters, they was such outspoken, kindly creturs, from the Squire down to little Hen. And it was very handy for us, because now we could go to singin'-schools and quiltin's, and such-like places, of an evenin'; and we had rather moped at home for want of such things, — at least I had; and I should have been more moped only for

Major's sweet ways. She was always as contented as a honey-bee on a clover-head, for the same reason, I guess.

Well, there was a good many good things come to us from the Potters' movin' down; but by and by it seemed as though I was goin' to get the bitter of it. I'd kept company pretty steady with Russell. I hadn't give much thought to it, neither. I liked his ways, and he seemed to give in to mine very natural, so't we got along together first-rate. It didn't seem as though we'd ever been strangers, and I wasn't one to make believe at stiffness when I didn't feel it. I told Russell pretty much all I had to tell, and he was allers doin' for me and runnin' after me jest as though he'd been my brother. I didn't know how much I did think of him, till, after a while, he seemed to take a sight of notice of Major. I can't say he ever stopped bein' clever to me, for he didn't; but he seemed to have a kind of a hankerin' after Major all the time. He'd take her off to walk with him; he'd dig up roots in the woods for her posy-bed; he'd hold her skeins of yarn as patient as a little dog; he'd get her books to read. Well, he'd done all this for me; but when I see him doin' it for her, it was quite different; and all to once I know'd what was the matter. I'd thought too much of Russell Potter.

Oh, dear! those was dark times! I couldn't blame him; I knew well enough Major was miles and miles better and sweeter and cleverer than I was. I didn't wonder he liked her; but I couldn't feel as if he'd done right by me. So I schooled myself considerable, talkin' to myself for being jealous of Major. But 'twasn't all that, — the hardest of it all was that I had to mistrust

Russell. To be sure, he hadn't said nothin' to me in round words, — I couldn't ha' sued him; but he'd looked and acted enough; and now, — dear me! I felt all wrung out and flung away!

By and by Major begun to see somethin' was goin' wrong, and so did Russell. She was as good as she could be to me, and had patience with all my little, pettish ways, and tried to make me friendly with Russell; but I wouldn't. I took to hard work, and, what with cryin' nights, and hard work all day, I got pretty well overdone. But it all went on for about three months, till one day Russell come up behind me, as I was layin' out some yarn to bleach down at the end of the orchard, and asked me if I'd go down to Meriden with him next day, to a picnic frolic, in the woods.

"No!" says I, as short as I could.

Russell looked as though I had slapped him. "Anny," says he, "what have I done?"

I turned round to go away, and I catched my foot in a hank of yarn, and down I come flat on to the ground, havin' sprained my ankle so bad that Russell had to pick me up and carry me into the house like a baby.

There was an end of Meriden for me; and he wouldn't go, either, but come over and sat by me, and read to me, and somehow or other, I don't remember just the words, he gave me to understand that — well — that he wished I'd marry him.

It's about as tirin' to be real pleased with anything as it is to be troubled, at first. I couldn't say anything to Russell; I just cried. Major wasn't there; mother was dryin' apples out in the shed; so Russell he didn't know what to do; he kind of hushed me up, and begged of me not to cry, and said he'd come for his answer next day. So he come, and I didn't say "No" again. I don't believe I stopped to think whether Major liked him. She would have thought of me, first thing; I believe she wouldn't have had him if she'd thought I wanted him. But I aint like Major; it come more natural to me to think about myself; and, besides, she was pious, and I wasn't. Russell was.

However, it turned out all right, for Major was 'most as pleased as I was; and she told me, finally, that she'd known a long spell that Russell liked me, and the reason he'd been hangin' round her so long was, he'd been tellin' her his plans, and they'd worked out considerable in their heads before she could feel as though he had a good-enough lookout to ask me to marry him.

That wasn't so pleasant to me, when I come to think of it; I thought I'd ought to have been counselled with. But it was just like Major; everybody come to her for a word of help or comfort, whether they took her idee or not, — she had such feelin' for other folks's trouble.

I got over that little nub after a while; and then I was so pleased everything went smooth ag'in. I was goin' to be married in the spring; and we were goin' straight out to Indiana, onto some wild land Squire Potter owned out there, to clear it and settle it; and what Russell cleared, he was to have. So mother took some money out of the bank to fit me out, and Major and I went down to Hartford to buy my things.

I said before, we wasn't either of us any great things to look at; but it come about that one day I heerd somebody tell how we did look, and I thought considerable about it then and afterwards. We was buyin' some cotton to a store in the city, and I was lookin' about at all the pretty things, and wonderin' why I was picked out to be poor when so many folks was rich and had all they wanted, when presently I heerd a lady in a silk gown say to another one, so low she thought I didn't hear her, "There are two nice-looking girls, Mrs. Carr."

"Hem — yes," said the other one; "they look healthy and strong; the oldest one has a lovely expression, both steady and sweet; the other don't look happy."

. I declare, that was a fact. I was sorry, too, for I'd got everythin' in creation to make anybody happy, and now I was frettin' to be rich. I thought I'd try to be like Major; but I expect it was mostly because of the looks of it, for I forgot to try before long.

Well, in the spring we was married; and when I come to go away Major put a little red Bible into my trunk for a weddin' present; but I was cryin' too hard to thank her. She swallowed down whatever choked her, and begged of me not to cry so, lest Russell should take it hard that I mourned to go with him. But just then I was thinkin' more of Major and mother than I was of Russell; they'd kept me bright and cheery always, and kept up my heart with their own good ways when I hadn't no strength to do it for myself; and now I was goin' off alone with Russell, and he wasn't very cheerful-dispositioned, and somehow my courage give way all to once.

But I had to go; railroads don't wait for nobody; and what with the long journey, and the new ways and things and people, I hadn't no time to get real down once before we got to Indiana. After we left the boat there was a spell of railroad, and then a long stage-ride to Cumberton; and then we had to hire a big wagon and team, so's to get us out to our claim, thirty miles west'ard of Cumberton. I hadn't no time to feel real lonesome now, for all our things hed got to be onpacked, and packed over ag'in in the wagon; some on 'em had to be stored up, so's to come another time. We was two days gettin' to the claim, the roads was so bad, — mostly what they call corduroy, but a good stretch clear mud-holes. By the time we got to the end on't I was tired out, just fit to cry; and such a house as was waitin' for us! — a real log shanty! I see Russell looked real beat when he see my face, and I tried to brighten up; but I wished to my heart I was back with mother forty times that night, if I did once. Then come the worst of all, clutterin' everything right into that shanty; for our frame-house wouldn't be done for two months, and there wa'n't scarce room for what we'd brought, so't we couldn't think of sendin' for what was stored to Cumberton. I didn't sleep none for two nights, because of the whip-poor-wills that set on a tree close by, and called till mornin' light; but after that I was too tired to lie awake.

Well, it was real lonesome; but it was all new at first, and Russell was to work near by, so't I could see him, and oftentimes hear him whistle; and I had the garden to make, round to the new house, for I knew more about the plantin' of it than he did, 'specially my posy-bed, and I had a good time gettin' new flowers out of the woods. And the woods was real splendid, — great, tall tulip-trees, as high as a steeple and round as a quill, without any sort o' branches ever so fur up, and the whole top full of the yeller tulips and the queer, snipped-lookin', shiny leaves, till they looked like great bow-pots on sticks; then there's lots of other great trees, only they're all mostly spindled up in them woods. But the flowers that grow round on the ma'sh edges and in the clearin's do beat all.

So time passed along pretty glib till the frame-house was done, and then we had to move in, and to get the things from Cumberton, and begin to feel as though we were settled for good and all; and after the newness had gone off, and the clearin' got so fur that I couldn't see Russell no more, and nobody to look at, if I was never so lonesome, then come a pretty hard spell. Everything about the house was real handy, so't I'd get my work cleared away, and set down to sew early; and them long summer days, that was still and hot, I'd set, and set, never hearin' nothin' but the clock go "tick, tick, tick" (never "tack," for a change), and every now'n'then a great crash and roar in the woods where he was choppin', that I knew was a tree; and I worked myself up dreadfully when there was a longer spell 'n common come betwixt the crashes, lest that Russell might 'a' been ketched under the one that fell. And settin' so, and worryin' a good deal, day in and day out, kinder broodin' over my troubles, and never thinkin' about anybody but myself, I got to be of the idee that I was the worst-off cretur goin'. If I'd have stopped to think about Russell, may be I should have had some sort of pity for him, for he was jest as lonesome as I, and I wasn't no kind of comfort to come home to, — 'most always cryin', or jest a-goin' to.

So the summer went along till 'twas nigh on to winter, and I wa'n't in no better sperrits. And now I wa'n't real well, and I pined for mother, and I pined for Major, and I'd have given all the honey and buckwheat in Indiana for a loaf of mother's dry rye-bread and a drink of spring-water. And finally I got so miserable I wished I wa'n't never married,—and I'd have wished I was dead, if 'twa'n't for bein' doubtful where I'd go to if I was. And, worst of all, one day I got so worked up I told Russell all that. I declare he turned as white as a turnip. I see I'd hurt him, and I'd have got over it in a minute and told him so, only he up with his axe and walked out of the door, and never come home till night, and then I was too stubborn to speak to him.

Well, things got worse, an' one day I was sewin' some things and cryin' over 'em, when I heerd a team come along by, and before I could get to the door Russell come in, all red for joy, and says:—

"Who do you want to see most, Anny?"

Somehow the question kind of upset me,—I got choked, and then I bu'st out a-cryin'.

"Oh, mother and Major!" says I; and I hadn't more'n spoke the word before mother had both her good, strong arms round me, and Major's real cheery face was a-lookin' up at me from the little pine cricket, where she'd sot down as nateral as life. Well, I *was* glad, and so was Russell, and the house seemed as shiny as a hang-bird's nest, and by and by the baby came;—but I had mother.

'Twas 'long about in March when I was sick, and by the end of April I was well, and so's to be stirrin' round again. And mother and Major begun to talk about goin' home; and I declare my heart was up in my mouth every time they spoke on't, and I begun to be miserable ag'in. One day I was settin' beside of mother, — Major was out in the garden, fixin' up things, and settin' out a lot of blows she'd got in the woods, and singin' away, — and says I to mother: —

"What be I going to do, mother, without you and Major? I 'most died of clear lonesomeness before you come!"

Mother laid down her knittin', and looked straight at me.

"I wish you'd got a little of Major's good cheer, Anny," says she. "You haven't any call to be lonely here; it's a real good country, and you've got a nice house, and the best of husbands, and a dear little baby, and you'd oughter try to give up frettin'. I wish you was pious, Anny; you wouldn't fault the Lord's goodness the way you do."

"Well, Major don't have nothin' to trouble her, mother," says I. "She's all safe and pleasant to home; she aint homesick."

Mother spoke up pretty resolute: —

"There aint nobody in the world, Anny, but what has troubles. I didn't calc'late to tell you about Major's; but sence you lay her lively ways to luck, may be you'd better know 'em. She's been engaged this six months to Reuben Potter, and he's goin' off in a slow consumption; he won't never live to marry her, and she knows it."

"And she come away to see me, mother?"

"Yes, she did. I can't say I thought she need to; but Russell wrote you was pinin' for both of us, and I didn't think you could get along without me; but I told her to stay with Reuben, and I'd come on alone. And says she, 'No, mother, you aint young and spry enough to go alone so fur, and the Lord made you my mother and Anny my sister before I picked out Reuben for myself. I can't never have any kin but you, and I might have had somebody beside Reuben, though it don't seem likely now ; but he's got four sisters to take care of him, and he thinks and I think it's what I ought to do ; so I'm goin' with you.' So she come, Anny ; and you see how lively she keeps, just because she don't want to dishearten you none. I don't know as you can blame her for kinder hankerin' to get home."

I hadn't nothin' to say ; I was beat. So mother she went on : —

"Fact is, Anny, Major's always a-thinkin' about other folks ; it comes kind of nateral to her, and then bein' pious helps it. I guess, dear, when you get to thinkin' more about Russell an' the baby you'll forget some of your troubles. I hope the Lord won't have to give you no harder lesson than lovin', to teach you Major's ways."

So, after that, I couldn't say no more to mother about stayin' ; but when they went away I like to have cried myself sick, — only baby had to be looked after, and I couldn't dodge her.

Bym-by we had letters from home. They got there all safe, and Reuben wa'n't no worse, Major said, — ef't had been me wrote the letter I should have said he wa'n't no better, — and I fell back into the old lonesome days, for baby slept mostly, and the summer come on extreme hot ; and in July, Russell, bein' forced to go to Cumberton on some land business, left me to home with baby and the hired man, calc'latin' to be gone three days and two nights.

The first day he was away was dreadful sultry ; the

sun went down away over the woods in a kind of red-hot fog, and it seemed as though the stars were dull and coppery at night; even the whip-poor-wills was too hot to sing; nothin' but a doleful screech-owl quavered away, a half a mile off, a good hour, steady. When it got to be mornin' it didn't seem no cooler; there wa'n't a breath of wind, and the locusts in the woods chittered as though they was fryin'. Our hired man was an old Scotchman, by name Simon Grant; and when he'd got his breakfast he said he'd go down the clearin' and bring up a load of brush for me to burn. So he drove off with the team, and havin' cleared up the dishes I put baby to sleep, and took my pail to the barn to milk the cow, — for we kept her in a kind of a home-lot like, a part that had been cleared afore we come, lest she should stray in the woods, if we turned her loose. She was put in the barn, too, nights, for fear some stray wild-cat or bear might come along and do her a harm. So I let her into the yard, and was jest a-goin' to milk her when she began to snort and shake, and finally giv' the pail a kick, and set off, full swing, for the fence to the lot. I looked round to see what was a-comin', and there, about a quarter of a mile off, I see the most curus thing I ever see before or since, — a cloud as black as ink in the sky, and hangin' down from it a long spout like, — something like an elephant's trunk, and the whole world under it looked to be all beat to dust. Before I could get my eyes off on't, or stir to run, I see it was comin' as fast as a locomotive. I heerd a great roar and rush, — first a hot wind, and then a cold one, and then a crash, — an' 'twas all as dark as death all round, and the roar appeared to be a-passin' off.

I didn't know for quite a spell where I was. I was flat on my face, and when I come to a little I felt the grass against my cheek, and I smelt the earth; but I couldn't move no way. I couldn't turn over, nor raise my head more'n two inches, nor draw myself up one. I was comfortable so long as I laid still; but if I went to move I couldn't. It wasn't no use to wriggle; and when I'd settled that I just went to work to figger out where I was and how I got there, and the best I could make out was that the barn-roof had blowed off and lighted right over me, jest so as not to hurt me, but so't I couldn't move.

Well, there I lay. I knew baby was asleep in the trundle-bed, and there wa'n't no fire in the house; but how did I know the house wa'n't blowed down? I thought that as quick as a flash of lightnin'; it kinder struck me; I couldn't even see, so as to be certain. I wasn't naterally fond of children, but somehow one's own is different, and baby was just gettin' big enough to be pretty; and there I lay, feelin' about as bad as I could, but hangin' on to one hope, — that old Simon, seein' the tornado, would come pretty soon to see where we was.

I lay still quite a spell, listenin'. Presently I heerd a low, whimperin', pantin' noise, comin' nearer and nearer, and I knew it was old Lu, a yeller hound of Simon's, that he'd set great store by, because he brought him from the old country. I heered the dog come pretty near to where I was, and then stop, and give a long howl. I tried to call him, but I was all choked up with dust, and for a while I couldn't make no sound. Finally I called, "Lu! Lu! Here, sir!" and if ever you heerd a dumb creature laugh, he barked a real laugh, and come springin' along over toward me. I called ag'in, and he begun to scratch and tear and pull, — at boards, I guessed, for it sounded like that; but it wa'n't no use, he couldn't get at me, and he give up at length and set down right over my head and give another howl, so long and so dismal I thought I'd as lieves hear the bell a-tollin' my age.

Pretty soon I heerd another sound, — the baby cryin'; and with that Lu jumped off whatever 'twas that buried me up, and run. "At any rate," thinks I, "baby's alive." And then I bethought myself if 'twa'n't a painter, after all; they scream jest like a baby, and there's a lot of them, or there was then, right round in our woods, and Lu was dreadful fond to hunt 'em, and he never took no notice of baby; — and I couldn't stir to see!

Oh, dear! the sweat stood all over me. And there I lay, and Simon didn't come, nor I didn't hear a mouse stir; the air was as still as death, and I got nigh distracted. Seemed as if all my life riz right up there in the dark and looked at me. Here I was, all helpless, may be never to get out alive; for Simon didn't come, and Russell was gone away. I'd had a good home, and a kind husband, and all I could ask; but I hadn't had a contented mind. I'd quarrelled with Providence, 'cause I hadn't got everything — and now I hadn't got nothing. I see just as clear as daylight how I'd nussed up every little trouble till it growed to a big one; how I'd sp'ilt Russell's life, and made him wretched; how I'd been cross to him a great many times when I had ought to have been a comfort; and now it was like enough I shouldn't never see him again — nor baby,

nor mother, nor Major. And how could I look the
Lord in the face if I did die? That took all my
strength out. I lay shakin' and chokin' with the idee,
I don't know how long; it kind of got hold of me and
ground me down; it was worse than all. I wished to
gracious I didn't believe in hell; but then it come to
mind, What should I do in heaven ef I was there? I
didn't love nothin' that folks in heaven love, except the
baby. I hadn't been suited with the Lord's will on
earth, and 'twa'n't likely I was goin' to like it any
better in heaven; and I should be ashamed to show my
face where I didn't belong, neither by right nor by want.
So I lay. Presently I heerd in my mind this verse,
that I'd learned years back in Sabbath school, —

"Wherefore He is able also to save them to the uttermost."

There it stopped, but it was a plenty for me. I see at
once there wa'n't no help anywhere else, and for once
in my life I did pray, real earnest, and — queer enough
— not to get out, but to be made good. I kind of
forgot where I was, I see so complete what I was; but
after a while I did pray to live in the flesh. I wanted
to make some amends to Russell for pesterin' on him
so.

It seemed to me as though I'd laid there two days.
A rain finally come on, with a good, even down-pour,
that washed in a little, and cooled my hot head; and
after it passed by I heerd one whip-poor-will singin',
so't I knew it was night. And pretty soon I heerd
the tramp of a horse's feet; it come up; it stopped.
I heerd Russell say out loud, "O Lord!" and give a
groan, and then I called to him. I declare, he
jumped.

So I got him to go look for baby first, because I could wait; and, lo! she was all safe in the trundle-bed, with Lu beside of her, both on 'em stretched out together, one of her little hands on his nose; and when Russell looked in to the door she stirred a bit, and Lu licked her hand to keep her quiet. It tells in the Bible about children's angels always seein' the face of God, so's to know quick what to do for 'em, I suppose; and I'm sure her'n got to her afore the tornado; for though the house-roof had blowed off, and the chimbley tumbled down, there wa'n't a splinter nor a brick on her bed, only close by the head on't a great hunk of stone had fell down, and steadied up the clothes-press from tumblin' right on top of her.

So then Russell rode over, six miles, to a neighbor's, and got two men, and betwixt 'em all they pried up the beams of the barn, that had blowed on to the roof and pinned it down over me, and then lifted up the boards and got me out; and I wa'n't hurt, except a few bruises, but after that day I begun to get gray hairs.

Well, Russell was pretty thankful, I b'lieve, — more so'n he need to be for such a wife. We fixed up some kind of a shelter, but Lu howled so all night we couldn't sleep. It seems Russell had seen the tornado to Cumberton, and, judgin' from its course 'twould come past the clearin', he didn't wait a minute, but saddled up and come off; but it had crossed the road once or twice, so it was nigh about eleven o'clock afore he got home; but it was broad moonlight. So I hadn't been under the roof only about fifteen hours; but it seemed more.

In the mornin' Russell set out to find Simon, and I

was so trembly I couldn't bear to stay alone, and I went with him, he carryin' baby, and Lu goin' before, as tickled as he could be. We went a long spell through the woods, keepin' on the edge of the tornado's road; for't had made a clean track about a quarter of a mile wide, and felled the trees flat, — great tulips cut off as sharp as pipe-stems, oaks twisted like dandelion-stems, and hickories curled right up in a heap. Presently Lu gave a bark, and then such a howl! — and there was Simon, dead enough! A big oak had blowed down, with the trunk right acrost his legs above the knees, and smashed them almost off. 'Twas plain it hadn't killed him to once, for the ground all about his head was tore up as though he'd fought with it; and Russell said his teeth and hands was full of grass and grit where he'd bit and tore, a-dyin' so hard. I declare, I shan't never forget that sight! Seems as if my body was full of little ice-spickles every time I think on't.

Well, Russell couldn't do nothin'; we had no chance to lift the tree, so we went back to the house, and he rode away after neighbors; and while he was gone I had a long spell of thinkin'. Mother said she hoped I wouldn't have no hard lesson to teach me Major's ways; but I had got it, and I know I needed it, 'cause it did come so hard. I b'lieve I was a better woman after that. I got to think more of other folks's comfort than I did afore, and whenever I got goin' to be dismal ag'in I used to try 'n' find somebody to help; it was a sure cure.

When the neighbors come, Russell and they blasted and chopped the tree off of Simon, and buried him under a big pine that we calc'lated not to fell. Lu pined, and howled, and moaned for his master, till I got him to look after baby now and then, when I was hangin' out clothes or makin' garden, and he got to like her in the end on't near as well as Simon.

After a while there come more settlers out our way, and we got a church to go to; and the minister, Mr. Jones, he come to know if I was a member, and when I said I wa'n't, he put in to know if I wa'n't a pious woman.

"Well," says I, "I don't know, sir." So I up and told him all about it, and how I had had a hard lesson; and he smiled once or twice, and says he: —

"Your husband thinks you are a Christian, Sister Potter, don't he?"

"Yes, I do," says Russell, a-comin' in behind me to the door, — for he'd just stepped out to get the minister a basket of plums, — "I haint a doubt on't, Mr. Jones."

The minister looked at him, and I see he was kinder pleased.

"Well," says he, "I don't think there's much doubt of a woman's bein' pious when she's pious to home; and I don't want no better testimony'n yours, Mr. Potter. I shall admit you to full fellowship, sister, when we have a church meetin' next; for it's my belief you experienced religion under that blowed-down barn."

And I guess I did.

ACELDAMA SPARKS; OR, OLD AND NEW.

"I TELL yew what 'tis, Miss Sparks," said the deacon, "that are boy's got ter hev a Scriptur' name. I wa'n't born an' bred in Hanover, an' hed a father and gran'ther deacons afore me to be a-goin' an' givin' the boy sech a jography name as Wallis; now don't ye set to no more."

Mrs. Sparks laughed; she always laughed; it was currently reported that she laughed once in church, but that was scandal. Eleven years had she been married, and now for the first time the ponderous old cradle was lugged from the garret to hold a baby. No wonder Mrs. Sparks laughed now. And such a baby!

Only imagine Deacon Ebenezer Sparks dressed in a long white frock and a red-edged blanket, seen through a reversed spy-glass, and you behold his baby. Just such yellow hair, sedulously brushed on end; just such a mottled red complexion, a nose just so indefinite, a mouth that lacked only certain ominous yellow stains to repeat the paternal feature, and eyes of that blank and amazing blue that awed naughty boys, peeping over a stupendous shirt-collar in the deacon-seat every Sunday. But outside the resemblance stopped; for that baby, like its mother, always laughed; from a broad grin to a sputtering chuckle it progressed, slowly and surely, till it was time for it to be baptized. "Six months old!" exclaimed Mrs. Little, at sewing-society, "and not yet presented for baptism!" That was one of Deacon Sparks's crotchets; he was a good man, and somewhere, a great way down behind his ribs, he had a kind heart; but it was overlaid with so much work, and caution, and prejudice, and starch, that it beat very feebly, almost invisibly, even to the angel that is supposed to look after such institutions in every man, specially deacons.

If Deacon Sparks had one horror above another, it was of babies, particularly in church, most particularly when they cried and made a disturbance at their baptism, — a thing he believed to be effected by a special interposition of Satan; and from the hour his baby was born he had looked forward with dreadful doubts to this crisis, resolving that his child at least should be old enough to obey before it was risked in an ecclesiastical public; doubly resolved that it should have a Bible name, in spite of Mrs. Sparks's desire that the boy should be called by her family name; but, positive as the deacon was, Mrs. Sparks only laughed.

"I don't care no gret what you dew call him, Betsey, so's'ts out o' Scriptur'," relented the deacon. "I guess it's jest as good not ter call him Cain, 'cause likely he'd feel as though he didn't want ter hev jest that callin'; but you ken call him anything else you're willin'."

"Well, I do'no', husband," responded Aunty Sparks. "I haint no great admiration for Timothy, nor Reuel, nor Nahum; them was all our folks's names, too. Let's open the Bible kinder easy, and call him the first name we see."

So the trial by lot was agreed on, and the fatal proper name was Aceldama.

Mrs. Sparks and her husband were rather pleased than dismayed at this. The name was, so to speak, an unclaimed grant, and they the first settlers on it; besides, it afforded such unprecedented advantages for nicknames, so many syllables, such natural diminutives, and then it began with the first letter of the alphabet.

So the day of baptism came, — a bright, mild Thanksgiving morning, — and Master Sparks was arrayed in gorgeous attire for the occasion; a long dress, embroidered surprisingly with little holes and big holes, small dots and large dots, impossible leaves with a great development of veins, and tendrils that spiralled the wrong way and executed bow-knots on this occasion only, — all fenced in with insane scallops, that branched, and sidled, and crooked perseveringly, but did their duty, after all.

Over this reposed a long and full yellow cloak, bound with pink ribbon, refreshingly suggestive of dandelion-blossoms, while above the stiff lace frill that inclosed the beaming red visage of this "tender youth" towered a blue silk construction of the pagoda style, popularly supposed to be a puerile cap.

Who shall describe the trig, prim, and withal sheepish, expression of Ebenezer Sparks as he squeaked up the aisle in advance of this wonderfully got-up baby? No amount of stationery would suffice. It was like unto no mortal creature but himself, and was produced by an unlimited quantity of collar, flour-starch, sole-leather, paternal pride, and intense conservatism; for it was the ruling passion of Deacon Sparks to preserve things as they had been.

Even now, in this crowning ceremony, his soul was troubled with the novelty of having a baby to baptize, and his hair stood on end more pertinaciously than ever, over a yet redder face, and the dead blueness of his eyes caused Timothy Little, the pastor's graceless son, a nine-year sinner, to quake and quiver in his pew corner, self-conscious of sundry apples hooked from Deacon Sparks's tree of russet-sweets but a few weeks ago

Poor Timothy! the deacon personified his conscience, for that officer of the church was thinking of nothing else but his baby. Clothed in garments of blue broadcloth set off by brass buttons, followed by Mrs. Sparks in a dress we dare not venture to describe, the deacon and his baby presented themselves before Mr. Little, a meek, sentimental, florid man, with a big head and a weak voice, and of the straitest sect, an Old-School man. Dear reader, unlearned as yet in the variations of style and title, ask not rashly what an Old-School man means. Plunge not headlong into the sea of metaphysics and terminology that these hard-headed Yankees call theology. Leave the scientific Greek and Latin names of these unknown trees and shrubs to those who gave and use them; look and see what fruit hangs on the gracious boughs; which spreads widest shelter for the lame, and the weak, and the evil-smitten race of men; to which the birds of heaven fly with gladdest instinct and purest song; where flowers are sweetest and fruit most abundant and nutritive: that tree is one out of Paradise, whatever name labels or libels it; and it is good to thank God for it, and fashion one's own growth after its pattern. But Deacon Sparks is holding his baby all this time.

The ceremony began. The deacon held Aceldama with a tight grip; but, as ill-luck would have it, the trembling cap on top of the child's head toppled forward and extinguished those staring eyes, into one of which, in his awkward attempts to replace the structure, Deacon Sparks thrust his huge, horny finger.

Poor, dear Aceldama! What a roar and yell was that which pierced his father's ears, and made the old meeting-house ring again! No efforts could quiet the war-cry of the half-gouged baby, and the ceremony proceeded in a din likest to nothing ecclesiastical but the exorcising of a bad spirit.

Deacon Sparks was furious. He held the shrieking infant with fingers that left their sign-manual upon flesh and skin; and when Mr. Little, with a preternatural exalting of the voice that made him more than ever florid, at length struggled through the baptism and bestowed the strange name Aceldama upon a decent Yankee child, Deacon Sparks, without waiting for the prayer, shouldered his baby, marched out of the meeting-house in double-quick time, followed by his wife at a rapid, scuttling trot, and having arrived at the porch deliberately sat down, and, lowering the infant, administered to it a severe personal castigation; while Mrs. Sparks, recovering breath behind him, only laughed, well knowing what layers upon layers of linen, flannel, cambric, and merino rendered her precious boy's person impervious to slaps.

It seemed, from that hour forward, as if some unruly spirit had entered into Aceldama with his name. Instead of lying still in the old cradle, like an orthodox baby, he was always scrambling up on end therein, and peeking over the side. He behaved like some tricksy elf, uttering his most pertinacious screeches in time of family prayer, and distorting his visage at poor Mr. Little into such curiously ugly shapes, as daunted the feeble divine from any caressing approaches whatever.

When the child began to creep, dire conflicts ensued in the peaceful kitchen of Mrs. Sparks. He seemed to have a natural proclivity for tubs of scalding suds, hot flat-irons, ley-kettles, and old cats. Once he sat down in a kettle of hasty-pudding, just off the boil, and nothing but an instantaneous grip of the maternal red right hand and triple folds of domestic flannel saved him from an untimely end. Twice he entered into single combat with the old tabby on account of her kittens (which he liked to carry by the tail), and came off both times with honorable scars in the face. Once he pulled the wooden churn over, and deluged himself and the spotless floor with thick cream, besides bumping his nose till it bled. Once he narrowly escaped death from eating potash; and three times his red flannel frock was patched over holes he burned in it by cultivating an intimacy with the fore-log, for the sake of its sweet and smoky drip of sap.

Nor were matters composed at all when Master Sparks, having survived his first infancy by dint of a certain elder-witch element in his nature that always brought him off "right side up" from any danger, emerged into a full suit of butternut cloth, trousers and all, thickly buttoned with brass.

The wildest colt in the deacon's pasture he coaxed into a near approach with tempting handfuls of oats and apples, and then, bestriding the creature, with his dumpy legs almost horizontal across its back, and clinging on to its mane like a monkey, Aceldama careered full tilt about the meadow till he was speedily thrown over the colt's head, luckily for him, into a soft and swampy spot full of flag and coarse grass, from which he crept out slightly subdued and very wet.

Nothing daunted by this, the next morning he resumed his equestrian feats by striding the old black cow, very unexpectedly to that respectable animal, causing her to behave in a manner set aside since her calfish days, — a sudden plunge and fling of the tail, a wonderfully energetic prance, — and away she went down the high road, Aceldama hanging on to the brass knobs of her horns, beating her ears with his heels till, out of breath, his grip relaxed, and just as the cow reëntered the barn-yard he dropped off into the deepest pool therein, adding the last drop to Deacon Sparks's righteous indignation, he having viewed the whole affair from the upper door of the barn.

That night 'Celdy got his deserts after true Solomonic prescription, and went to bed very rueful indeed, but not quite penitent; for two days after, capturing the biggest rooster in the yard, he dressed it up in a white cravat, tied after the strictest clerical fashion, and turned it loose upon astonished Mr. Little, just emerging from the door after a pastoral visit.

In fact, though Aceldama was drilled morning, noon, and night in the Assembly's Catechism, till a profound disgust for that ancient institution was thoroughly implanted in his mind; though he was kept in a straight-backed chair, and forbidden to laugh or look out of the window all day Sundays; though his father treated him with the severest justice and his mother with the mildest mercy (popularly called indulgence), Aceldama offered every prospect of becoming the wildest boy in

Hanover, and the soul of Deacon Sparks groaned within him.

At school nobody did or dared half the pranks that he amused himself with. At the academy no other boy could compete with him in tormenting the master, kissing the prettiest little girls, tying up the bell-rope out of reach, plugging the logs destined for the fire with tiny charges of powder, and filling the key-holes with divers sticky mixtures that cost an hour's delay of school in the effort to extract them.

It is true 'Celdy learned his lessons irreproachably. In class he never vexed his master by being stupid or perverse. He was no fool, nor yet a knave, though the latter trait predominated, for he was mischievous and acute. His faults were the faults of vivid animal spirits and pure courage. No little boy, no coward, no sweet-tempered and forgiving comrade, owed Aceldama a grudge, or received from him a blow. The big boys, who bullied all the rest, the savage and brutal natures that will crop out in every crowd of boys as well as men, — all these he fought, and cowed, and ruled, with the generous bravery of a thoroughly fine temper and noble disposition.

But all this availed him nothing with his father. Night and day Deacon Sparks lamented over the boy, not merely as a torment and tease at home, but as a branch and offspring of Satan, — a child evidently formed for and bent on eternal misery; in short, a reprobate.

The stern Calvinism of the deacon's creed would have allowed him no hope of 'Celdy's salvation had he died in his first innocent babyhood. He would have resigned himself to the justice, as he called it, of God.

His mercy was mythical to the deacon. Judge, then, what a state of mind this really sincere father was in when, to the certainty of original sin and total depravity, 'Celdy had added such a muster-roll of actual transgressions!

Truth to tell, Deacon Sparks's faith and practice were not of a kind to attract the fresh and sensitive heart of youth; not that outgrowth of the loving soul that draws itself into the souls of its brethren on the plea of a common father and a yearning fraternal tenderness for all its kind; not that self-forgetting, tender, gentle charity that lives in the wants and woes of others, and bears their burdens as the Master did, glorifying the daily routine of life with love, and praise, and cheerfulness. Exceedingly set in his way, for no better reason than that it was the old way of his fathers, he believed in the Law, and only tolerated the Gospel. His strictness was so purely honest and earnest as to demand respect from any candid mind; but it was, nevertheless, a strictness of the letter from which the spirit fled away deprecatingly, and which bound upon him and his a grievous yoke that Aceldama found impossible to be borne.

As the boy grew older the deacon's rule grew more stringent, and he fretted and galled beneath it, and but for his mother might have ended his days, as many a wild boy with a strict father has done before, in the noisome hold of a whaler or the barrack hospital of an army; but Aunty Sparks was certainly especially ordained to be the deacon's better half.

No heroine of novel or story was this honest, good-tempered, cheerful, steady, healthy woman. A dozen Matilda-Marias might have been made physically out of her goodly proportions, and forty from her mind and heart. Not a particle of sentimentality tinged her nature. She neither screamed nor shrunk at a hop-toad, or fainted when Aceldama chopped his foot half off or was thrown over the pony's neck and taken up for dead. She never cried all night over her own troubles or anybody's else, but took her natural rest like a common-sense woman, and got up in the morning ready to do her duty, with bright eyes and a hearty laugh.

The sick people in Hanover thought "Miss Sparks beat the doctor;" the poor believed her bread-tray and pie-shelf never could be emptied; the deacon consulted her on all emergencies, grimly scorned her advice when given, and always took it. Aceldama loved her as a dandelion loves sunshine or a bobolink singing.

Heaven bless Aunty Sparks! If there were a hundred like her where there is one slightly resembling that type of woman, the world would be saved from half its evils and all its Women's Rights Conventions.

And under these conflicting influences 'Celdy grew up to be fourteen. At that time another person began to bend him. Mr. Samuel Fletcher came to Hanover to keep the Academy, and Master Sparks found his master.

There was nothing very subduing, either, in the aspect of Mr. Fletcher: spare, tall, shabby, with a face that might be the index of extreme youth or maturity, so supra-temporal — to coin a phrase — was the inner fire that used that wan, hectic visage, that keen outline, and wonderful azure eye for its mask and servant.

Aceldama came home the first morning and told his mother, in confidence, that the new master "wasn't much;" at night he came back and said he was mistaken; and before the first quarter was out Master 'Celdy would have walked up to a cannon's mouth and put his head therein at Mr. Fletcher's request.

No man attains that personal ascendency over boys without good reason in himself. Girls adore anybody they happen to fancy, as nine-tenths of their marriages and ten-tenths of their friendships show; but the *besoin d'aimer* is not so potent with the stronger sex; they must know the reason why, and feel it, before they submit to it. Mr. Fletcher was one of those rare natures whose special gift is a vast power over others, — a character difficult to analyze, only to be explained by classing it under the all-sufficing head, genius.

He was an extraordinary teacher, of course. Under his direction his scholars' minds expanded and absorbed knowledge, as vegetation is said to thrive in certain gases. No dull boys were to be found in Hanover Academy under his sway. His acute and vivid intellect seemed to transpierce whatever it would, and transfuse it with its own light and power for the time being. School became a pleasure and an excitement; and Aceldama, being the smartest boy there by gift of nature, proportionately grew and flourished in the new dispensation, and added to his increased knowledge a most absorbing and devoted attachment for Mr. Fletcher.

But after some weeks rumors of a startling nature came to Deacon Sparks's ears; somebody told somebody else that some third body had said the new master was a New-School man in theology, and, on investigating the matter, the deacon became more and more convinced of the fact.

Now Mr. Fletcher was as earnest in religion as he

was in teaching. The boys and girls of Hanover Academy could not listen to his morning prayers and readings without profound convictions that, whatever they might think about it, the Bible, and God, and Goodness, and Sin, were deep and living realities to their eloquent master; and gradually, at first by mere sympathy, then as the safer result of thought and study, a religious interest sprung up and made steady progress throughout the school.

Deacon Sparks groaned. He could not have his only son a New-School man; that would be the final drop in the cup!

He sat thinking the matter over one night by the kitchen fire, Aceldama having retreated to his own room overhead, where, — truth to tell, — instead of studying, he, too, was meditating, with his head on his hands, as boys will meditate for whom the great problems of Life and Nature just begin to show their colossal outlines and stir their mighty forces.

"Miss Sparks," uttered the deacon, after sundry stifled grunts and uneasy creaks of his old chair, "I'm a-goin' to take Aceldamy out of the 'Cademy."

"Why, husband, you do beat all! What for, eh?"

"Well, I aint satisfied with that Fletcher; he aint right; he ai—nt right!" musingly retorted Deacon Sparks.

"What on 'arth's the matter of him?" said aunty, dropping a stitch in her blue yarn knitting from pure astonishment, for Mr. Fletcher had got at her heart through 'Celdy's.

"Well, I've heerd, and I expect it's true, that he's a New-School man, — ralely and ondeniably a New-School man."

"Sakes alive!" exclaimed aunty, with one of her own laughs; "is that all, husband? I thought he'd turned out a forger, or a burglar, or somethin' or other orful bad!"

"I don't know what you call bad, Miss Sparks, if 'taint hetererdoxy!"

The deacon delivered this dictum with indescribable weight; it was evidently intended to settle the thing at once.

"He! he! he!" furtively choked out from behind aunty's checked apron, held up to stifle the naughty laugh in its bud. "It's a bad word, I'm sure; but what harm is it, husband?"

"Harm! Why, they don't believe in the catechism, Miss Sparks! And they don't believe in total depravity, nor in reprobation, nor in infant damnation, nor in — well, a good many things."

"Well, husband, the Scriptur' don't say them is needful to salvation, does it? I shouldn't think Mr. Fletcher could be very bad, judgin' from his prayers that he makes to conference meetin's, and the gentle way he gets the mastery over them boys by. And, you know, the Lord didn't make us all jest alike; some on us thinks some way, and some another."

"Miss Sparks, I tell you New-School folks is all wrong; and ef I thought 't I was goin' to live to see Aceldamy grow up a New-School man, I'd ruther he'd never seen the inside of a school'us; and ef I don't stir up the school committee and get that Fletcher sent packin', my name aint Ebenezer Sparks!"

Aunty recommenced her knitting, knowing that words would be but fuel to light the deacon's rage withal; but 'Celdy, overhead, had heard the whole discourse, and was swelling with rage and grief; and that hour laid the first stone of a barrier between him and his father that long years could not break down.

Deacon Sparks was true to his intent; by dint of perseverance and orthodoxy he got the school committee to dismiss Mr. Fletcher; and that New-School man, after listening to a farewell address, got up by the boys and spoken by 'Celdy, — who made it most expressive by totally breaking down in the middle, — bid good-by to his charge, in a chorus of tears and sobs from the girls, and choking adieus and sturdy hand-shakings from the boys, and betook himself to his boarding-house to pack his trunk; during which operation a timid knock called him to the door, there to find Aceldama Sparks.

"Come in, 'Celdy!" kindly said Mr. Fletcher; "come, sit down in that chair, where you won't get tangled in my things."

He had too much tact to seem surprised at the boy's appearance, or his utter failure to speak what was choking in his throat. So 'Celdy sat down; and, after turning his cap round and round a dozen times in his hands, at length sputtered out, "If you please, sir, can I go with you?"

Mr. Fletcher laughed; not a derisive or altogether an amused laugh, but as if he were pleased, and surprised, and doubtful, — all three. "Go where, my dear boy?" said he.

"Oh, anywhere, sir. I want to get away; I want to get out of Hanover."

"What's the matter?" said Mr. Fletcher, flinging himself into an arm-chair, and looking 'Celdy in the face with those keen eyes that seemed to read one's soul.

"Sir, I can't stand it! I can't live with my father! I cannot!" 'Celdy's face glowed with scarlet indignation.

"Ah!" said Mr. Fletcher, coolly, both hands in his pockets, and his eyes fixed now on the wary manœuvres of a spider overhead; "how has he tried to kill you? — poison, or bludgeons, or the old musket?"

'Celdy moved uneasily on his seat, blushed deeper yet, and at length stammered out, "Why, Mr. Fletcher, he hasn't tried to kill me, of course."

A line, fine as the spider's thread, quivered about Mr. Fletcher's mouth and was still again.

"But I thought you said you couldn't live with him?" gravely interrogated he.

"Well, sir, I can't; I'm miserable. He talks so, he makes me so angry; he says such things about"—

"Stop there, my boy! You have no right to tell me what your father says about anybody. And as for you — look here!" Mr. Fletcher pulled from the top of his trunk a little book, thin, and cheaply bound; and, with his peculiar, expressive voice, read aloud one passage from the wisest and best of all books, — *the* book among men's works, — Thomas à Kempis's "Imitation of Christ":—

It is no great matter to associate with the good and gentle; for this is naturally pleasing to all, and every one willingly enjoyeth peace, and loveth those best that agree with him. But to be able to live peaceably with hard and perverse persons, or with the disorderly, or such as go contrary to us, is a great grace, and a most commendable and manly thing.

'Celdy's head drooped.

"Nothing gives you any right to leave your father,

my boy, even if he treated you far worse than he does; neither God's law nor man's permits it. You have hoped lately that you began a new life; and here is your place to test it. If you are in earnest the trial of your sincerity is here, and will strengthen it; if you are half-way, lingering, undecided, you will fail and fall. God knew your need, and he arranged your life. Dare you run away from it? Don't be a coward."

'Celdy's face flushed, and his head rose.

"That's right! you have a right to be indignant at the idea; only be indignant, too, at the thing; for it is as cowardly to run away from duty as to run away from a battle; and it never helped any living soul out of trouble, but rather into it, to run away from one's post. Besides, your father is a good man, and one whom I respect truly. He has his own ideas, and he has strong prejudices, — strong natures often have. Isn't it enough of an object for your life to try and live down those prejudices, — try and show him that religion is a life of duty rather than of doctrines? Can't you do a noble service for your Master just here, and one that the world needs as much as this one man? 'Do the duty that lies nearest thee; all the rest will follow.'"

'Celdy's eye kindled. "I'll try, sir."

"I believe you will," said Mr. Fletcher. "And one thing more: if you want to be free of the world's bonds don't be troubled by what anybody says of anybody else or of you; if what they say is true, they have a right to say it; if it is a lie, it is a lie then, and neither mars nor shames any but the teller. The worst slavery in life is slavery to what 'they say.' If you want to be bound and tortured you can try the experiment, but you will repent it."

'Celdy got up from his chair with a glowing face, full of new resolution. Mr. Fletcher smiled, half sadly, to see that look. He knew what lay before the boy, — what days of futile endeavor, of lapses and recoveries, of sinking heart and struggling hope; for he, too, had lived under bondage, and cherished a Christian life in the clefts of the rock, as it were, till the strong tree had wound its roots firmly into every crevice, and now stood stately and fair.

"Only never be discouraged," said he, laying his hand on the boy's shoulder. "Remember that not one fall, nor forty, discourages the child learning to walk — why should it the Christian? Distrust yourself, but not God; for what does St. Augustine say? — 'He is patient, because he is eternal.' And here, my boy, is a Bible for you, with these same passages I read you written on its blank leaf. I was going to carry it to you myself. I shall come and say good-by to your father in the morning. Shall I see you?"

"Yes, sir," said 'Celdy, choking as he spoke, and hurrying out of the door without one word of thanks. But his master was already thanked.

Mr. Fletcher did call in the morning to see Deacon Sparks. 'Celdy sat demurely in the kitchen corner, with his eyes shining and his lips apart, to drink in every word. Mr. Fletcher was as kindly and as genial to the hard old man as to his best boys in school. Nothing was said about the deacon's agency in dismissing him, even in the way of distant allusion; and those blank blue eyes seemed to stare wider than ever at the unmistakable kindliness of the young man's manner. Now if Mr. Fletcher had gone away, as the vernacular of Hanover hath it, "in a huff," and never come near Deacon Sparks, or if he had " improved the occasion" of his farewell call to rebuke the deacon for his interference, and then magnanimously forgiven him, the carnal man, who still sneaked about the premises of the deacon's heart, would have become at once a pugnacious animal, and called itself righteous indignation, or a martyr to duty; but now, overawed by a phenomenon rarely visible in more extended parishes than that of Hanover, — the thorough Christian courtesy of a Christian gentleman, — the said carnal slunk into obscurity, and the deacon's conscience spoke a good word for the school-master, like an honest conscience as it was, though generally rather stinted and starved.

"I hope you've found another school, sir?" said Deacon Sparks, with an accent of real interest.

"Why, no, sir," answered Mr. Fletcher, the least bit of fun glinting in his eye. "I have never intended to teach anywhere after this time. I am about to enter the —— Theological Seminary, as I wished to last year, but found my funds did not quite hold out."

Deacon Sparks's countenance fell in spite of himself. He had had his labor for his pains, literally. 'Celdy's face sparkled; his secret soul exulted. I regret to say the boy triumphed in his father's discomfiture. Strange, hard, unnatural position! Where there should have been confidence and sympathy, only this perpetual antagonism, this utter want of tenderness, this repulsion between old and new; as if the new were not always an outgrowth of the old,— no fresh creation of God, but the spring sprouting of the old stock, the result of air and light and warmth upon a long-delayed and chilled embryo. But no such light dawned on Deacon Sparks; no such breadth of perception as yet illuminated 'Celdy. The deacon's hair bristled with horror at the idea of novelty. The Gospel was an old and fixed fact to him, divisible into so many doctrines; cribbed up to fifty-two days in the year. Works were a legality for six days in the week, and a strict, stony necessity on the seventh. Six days he ground the faces of the poor, snarled and snapped at his wife, looked like a Yankee Gorgon at every child that he passed, overworked his horses, and underfed his hired man. The seventh day he held his tongue and read the Old Testament in the house, or went to church and sung psalms with much fervor and no tune. Yet for all this the deacon had his good traits, both gracious and natural. He was honest in letter and spirit; earnest as a child in what he believed; working righteousness and fearing God. Shall man say that the loving Christ, who bears through all these ages the burden of earth's sin and anguish, had not a tender care for this old man, who had not so learned him? Did not those eyes, that looked into the heart of publican and sinner with never-failing pity, pierce also the crust of this groping life, and behold, with compassionate affection, its truth and its earnestness? "Judge not, that ye be not judged."

Now when Mr. Fletcher made this little disclosure, that discomfited the deacon and delighted 'Celdy, Aunty Sparks laughed. If anybody else had laughed there would have been some warm words forthcoming from the conscious deacon. But nobody minded aunty. She always laughed; not specially because things were amusing, or because she was particularly pleased, but out of her overflowing good-will, and the good time she always had, living and loving. Just as a bobolink, filled with June scents and glory, can't possibly wait a minute, but lights on the first thing at hand, and bubbles over with singing and fun; not because it is a cavatina or a bravura from any opera, and he knows exactly how it ought to be sung, with La Grange's trills and Gazzaniga's expression; nor because it is an exquisite day, and deserves a musical interpretation of its splendor and verdure and perfume; but simply because he-can't-help-it-and-he-don't-want-to-and-he-don't-know-why-and-he-don't-care-and-nobody-knows-and-he-must-sing-sing-sing-and-bubble-over-whether-or-no!

Just so aunty laughed, and said, in the interludes: —

"Why, dew tell, Mr. Fletcher, if you're a-goin' into the ministry!"

"Yes, ma'am, I am," returned that gentleman, with a mixture of reverence and joy that was delicately defined to a quick ear, and one quick ear received it.

"Well, I'm glad on't," replied aunty, no way daunted by the ominous rigidity that Old School drew over her husband's face. "There's so many poor sticks in the ministry I always feel as though 'twas a partic'lar providence when a smart man takes to preachin'. Folks always think anybody's good enough to make a minister of, or a missionary, an' 'taint so. I think they'd come a sight nearer facts ef they'd think nobody's good enough; for I'm sure skerce anybody is."

"That is true," said Mr. Fletcher; and he was about to add that we might take a lesson therein from the

Romish Church, that culls her ministers from men of physical perfection and mental power, and thereby carries half her wide-spread influence; but Mr. Fletcher remembered Deacon Sparks's prejudices, and with fraternal charity spared them, for he went on: "I think we should oftener remember the answer of David to Araunah: 'Shall I offer to the Lord God that which cost me nothing?'"

Deacon Sparks's visage relaxed. He liked the Old Testament. The Jews and their observances interested a certain natural formalism in his character; while for want of living the Gospel he had not yet come to loving it, nor did he suspect the delicate apprehension of, and regard for, this very trait that had prompted Mr. Fletcher's quotation. Strange it is that we so often hear a man accused, as of a fault, of "being all things to all men," when the most fervent of all apostles, the one least fitted by birth or training to conciliate or concede, uses it as a triumphant assertion of his pure zeal and ardent endeavor that he *is* "made all things to all men, that I might by all means save some."

And Mr. Fletcher knew when to go. He knew that a further discussion of his future work would only lead to some stumbling-block of doctrine or theological nettle-bed for the deacon. So he shook hands all round, but 'Celdy went with him to the yard-gate.

"I sha'n't write to you, 'Celdy," said he, answering a dumb inquiry in the boy's look; "but I shall often be in Hanover, I hope. The Seminary is not far away, and there are long vacations. I never forget anybody," added he, with a smile, the blank look of 'Celdy's face prompting him, so full as it was of doubt and regret. And so Mr. Fletcher left Hanover; nor did 'Celdy know till years afterward that he had refused to write him simply lest he should thereby widen the breach between the boy and his father.

Three years in the Seminary fast rolled by to Mr. Fletcher, but they dragged a slow length to Aceldama Sparks. It is true that he went to the Academy, and did his best to learn in spite of teachers and text-books; all the time longing in his soul for the clear and vivid mind that had interpenetrated his own, and made knowledge and study more keenly sweet than any freedom to be idle. Yet, after all, this discipline was best for the boy; it threw him on himself for strength and support; and a boy who learns to stand alone, even in school, is half a man; and in the better knowledge of himself that self-reliance gave, he learned a broader charity for his fellows, and learned how blind were his own eyes when he would teach others to see. At home one change lightened 'Celdy's time, though it separated him yet farther from his father. Mrs. Sparks's mother was a widow when her daughter Eunice married Ebenezer Sparks, but soon after that event she herself married a man by the name of Case, a widower, whose only daughter had married and gone to Illinois. Daniel Case was a farmer, — kind-hearted, well-meaning, and honest, but emphatically what we Yankees call shiftless. His house-roof leaked, and the crevice was stopped up with rags, because he was "goin' to get a hundred o' shingles to-morrer." But Mr. Case's to-morrow never came. His barn-floor rotted and fell in, and was mended with old plank laid across the floor, so that when harvest-time came he had to sell his rye as it stood, for he had no place to thresh it. Then the fences began to give way, and were propped with white-birch poles, or stopped with bushes, because he was " goin' to cut them chestnut-trees next week, and have a lot o' new rails." But, somehow or other, the trees were never cut in his day, and house and farm slipped out of his easy, listless hands, till at length it all went, and Daniel Case; his wife, who was " a sickly cretur;" and his little grand-daughter, a legacy from his dead daughter in Illinois, — all came on to the town some twenty-six years after Mrs. Sparks's marriage.

This was the great trouble of Aunty Sparks's life, — something that stopped her laughter whenever she faced its reality; for not one cent of help for her poor old mother or her kindly, inefficient husband could be wrung from the deacon's pocket. He would not have her in the house, or feed her from the kitchen. He said, as mightier men have said in better phrase and more polished accent: " No, you needn't pester me, Miss Sparks; she made her bed, and she's got to lie on't now; I aint going to work my legs off to feed Daniel Case's laziness; they can hang on to the town if they want to, but they aint goin' to hang on to me!"

So, in process of time, Mr. and Mrs. Case were put up to auction, — as we do put up poor people in New England and did black people at the South, — to be sold off to the lowest bidder; and an old woman, whose bedridden husband had a pension that helped them both to starve at their own expense instead of the town's, bidding off the old couple at a lower rate than anybody else, they were forthwith carted down to her dwelling, furnished with a lean-to in the garret, fed on salt pork and potatoes, but neither abused nor despised, for a sum so small that I will not record it; for the same reason that Mungo Park held his tongue about the wonders he saw in Africa,— lest the rest of my history should thereby have its credibility endangered.

And then Hannah Jones, the little girl, was to be bound out. Here Aunty Sparks could interfere, though at no small expense of goodness and labor. She persuaded the deacon, ever accessible on his economic side, that she didn't need a grown girl to help her in the kitchen, and receive wages as well as board; that it would be far better to have a little girl, who would eat less, cost no money but for shoes, and be clothed from her own old garments. Powerful arguments all these were to the deacon, whose secret soul was eaten into, wide and deep, by that money-rust that curses the blessings of nine-tenths of our northern population, and makes the very foundations of their lives rotten and tremulous. Oh! had I but one hour more of life to hold a pen; one hour of reason to guide my thoughts to its tip and send them flying over the land, — I should think that hour well spent if I consumed it in preaching on the one text that no man dare expound in its awful power and significance to a "respectable" congregation: "And he cast down the thirty pieces of silver in the temple, and departed, and went and hanged himself!"

So there was another fresh young soul set to endure the discipline of Deacon Sparks's household, but with far better chance to escape its contracting influences than 'Celdy, whose very soul boiled over in a torrent of righteous indignation, when he found his grandmother, a sweet-natured, patient, helpless, and gentle old woman, whom 'Celdy loved almost as well as his mother, was farmed out as town poor to the tender mercies of old Peggy Myers. Much ado had Mrs. Sparks to keep 'Celdy's wrath out of the deacon's way; for the boy of sixteen felt himself to be a man, and looked at his father from a conscious level, for, as a father, in the divinest sense of the word, never could he regard Deacon Sparks; and long years of dutiful, outward respect were yet needful to make him reverence the relation where he could not reverence the man.

Aunty Sparks soothed and reasoned and persuaded in vain, till at length she cried, and 'Celdy, who never saw his mother cry before, gave a reluctant promise not to say anything to his father; but Aunty Sparks had well-nigh undone her own work the next minute, by saying, as a sort of amends to the unwilling youth: —

"And if you made him wrathy, 'Celdy, you'd just kick over your own dish, for he wouldn't give you an apple nor an egg for grandmother; so you'd better keep cool."

"O mother!" burst out 'Celdy, "that's enough to make me speak! Do you think I'd keep quiet for such a reason? Do you think I'd let him help grandmother now? No, indeed, I wouldn't! I'll hold my tongue because I promised, and it troubles you; but I'd work my fingers off before granny should touch anything of his."

"Miss Sparks!" interrupted a low voice, and 'Celdy turned round just in time to see Hannah, in her check apron, holding the door apart, her great black eyes full of tears and anger, her rosy cheeks red as an apple, and the words, that her pretty red lips tried to make into "Mr. Little's in the keepin'-room," choked back with something between grief and rage: from that day 'Celdy and Hannah were sworn friends.

In the meantime Aceldama had many letters from Mr. Fletcher, full of good and kind advice; for which the boy's life thanked him even better than his words. Hard had been the struggle with himself before 'Celdy could persuade that stubborn self that it was right to set the seal of Christian profession upon his new life within by joining Mr. Little's church. "How can I," he wrote to his old teacher, "join the same church that holds such men as you know belong to Mr. Little's, — and who live down, in their niggardly, selfish, unlovely natures, all that the Gospel publishes, and I believe? How can I profess their faith, when I do not, and dare not, follow their practice? How can I hold them as brethren whom I must despise and dislike, from their utter want of goodness and honesty?"

Mr. Fletcher pondered sorrowfully over this letter, for it had to him more significance than merely the expression of Aceldama's candid perplexity and pain. It was the outcry of a whole world lying in sin against a passive and neglectful Church. Nay, more — it was the solemn voice of that Church's Head, like the heavy pulses of a knell, tolling down through ages of denial and scorn his own words, uttered where the fruitful Judean valleys illustrated the sentence, "By their fruits shall ye know them. Do men gather grapes of thorns, or figs of thistles?" Yet, ponder as he might, there was but one thing to do, for truth is never unsafe or unjust; and, though it be sometimes the cautery, and sometimes the salve, it is the need of the patient to which it fits itself; and it was not in Mr. Fletcher's nature to tamper with or mitigate any truth, however bitter, so he answered 'Celdy on this wise: —

"I cannot deny that what you say of those church-members is true. But you have to consider two views of the question before you judge them: one is, the influence of education on their minds,—such education in both theology and practical religion as you may fairly infer men in their station and their age received. It is one thing to adhere to wrong because you have been brought up in it till it has become a habit, and another to build it up about yourself as a wall against good influences and full light. And the other view is, consideration of what you do not know about them; the good that you do not see; the real earnestness to do right when one is habit-blind; the inward struggles with sin; the depression of physical disease or domestic trouble: these are known to God only, and, if you could discern with his sight, would not your judgment be modified? And then there is the harder truth that some of these men are not Christians; that the tenderest charity and the most gentle judgment cannot set aside the bitter fact of their living in sin, though professing righteousness: with such men you cannot fraternize, nor are you bound to attempt it. So much for other people; too much, indeed; for this is a matter which concerns yourself, and you only. Mr. Little's church is the only one in your village, the only place where you can confess Christ before men, and that you own to be a duty of direct importance. Go, then, and fulfil this duty. It is not made contingent on any circumstance. If there was not one Christian besides yourself in the list of members, that would not affect what you ought to do. Nay, it ought rather to stimulate you, since it opens a field of action wider and more hopeful than makes the station of many a missionary, and the Lord has said, 'To every

man his work.' Let me caution you against one thing,
— contempt. Despise no one; there is no human
heart that is all evil, and the solitary fact that Christ
came to die for every man should place all far above
your contempt. Dare you despise where he pitied?"

If this advice seemed hard to 'Celdy, at least he took
it, and was admitted to Mr. Little's church in due time,
not a little to his father's satisfaction, though he could
not repress a lurking doubt of 'Celdy's orthodoxy on
several points, luckily for both, not included in the
Confession of Faith common to most New England
churches.

But there were all the time troubles and doubts wedging apart Deacon Sparks and his son, first of one kind
and then of another. If the deacon began a theological
discussion after supper 'Celdy was sure to hear a noise
in the barn that needed direct attention, or some barrels in the cellar called for his care, or Hannah wanted
help to set up her tubs and take her cheeses out of
press, — hardly legitimate work for evening; but her
quick instinct provided excuses for 'Celdy when his
own failed. So, after a time, the deacon let doctrines
drop; for when 'Celdy was eighteen his school-time
ended, and he came home to "farm it." Here was
fertile subject for trouble; the untiring kindness of
Mr. Fletcher furnished him with a good agricultural
paper, and his own acute sense seized at once on the
practical advantages of a better style of farming than
that which prevailed in Hanover. But he might better
have harangued the mulleins and golden-rods that
adorned his sheep-pasture on the benefits of being
pulled up than attempt to convert the deacon to draining, lime-manuring, or rotation of crops. Rye had been

grown on a certain slope year after year till the spindling stalks could be counted, and then the lot was given over to lie at ease till nature should cover it with poor grass again, and sheep should be turned in to starve. Potatoes and corn had their allotted places as much as the horses and wagons in the barn; and, when corn dwindled and potatoes rotted, the deacon's luck was miscalled, and the weather helped bear the blame. Twenty acres of "muck" swamp, in various patches, that would have made the eyes of a modern farmer open with delight, and his crops laugh on the hill-sides, that now were dry and sunny enough to raise the best blackberries, lay altogether idle, except for the frogs that basked in its black and shallow pools, or the mud-turtles that sunned themselves on every stump, and scuttled away at the rare approach of step or voice.

But draining was not to be heard of; lime, and guano, and compost heaps took rank with fairy stories in the deacon's mind. His father and his grandfather had been farmers before him, and squeezed a living from the soil; and what his father and grandfather did was good enough for him, especially as any change of method involved an outlay of money; and though the deacon was willing to lay out his own labor and Aceldama's at lavish expense of comfort and health,—perhaps life,—money was out of the question; he would rather have opened a vein to enrich his corn-lot than spent the dollars that a course of drain-tile or a barrel of lime implied.

So Aceldama fretted over his work; mowed and hoed, and raked and ploughed with grudging effort, and strayed into the swamp, whenever he got a leisure moment, to turn up the rich black soil and speculate on its value, as a miser might count his useless gold, and sigh over its stationary existence. Nothing could be done with the deacon; no argument could convince him that Aceldama knew more than the three generations before him, as he was pleased to put the case; and now he retaliated 'Celdy's neglect of his theology by sniffing at the young man's new-fangled ideas on farming, and treating his opinions with an open contempt that kept them, eventually, silent. Only for his mother and Hannah, 'Celdy would have packed up his Sunday suit and gone to seek his fortune elsewhere; but his mother more and more depended on him for help and society as she gradually grew older, and Hannah, who was as merry as a cricket, even under the deacon's hard eye, set herself to work, woman-fashion, to make 'Celdy comfortable and contented as far as she could.

And unsentimental as it may seem to Sacharissa, who alleviates the sorrows of Strephon with smiles and Cologne-water, it was no small comfort to 'Celdy, who was only flesh and blood, to have his dough-nuts made and fried just right, his stockings mended smoothly, his shirts never lacking a button, his room kept in faultless order, his own special lamp—with which he read in his own room those offending agricultural papers and various other works that would have equally enraged the deacon—always filled and trimmed, and spotlessly clean. And it was more than all these to have that bright, pretty face and trim figure, animated by a character of sparkling common-sense and gay good-temper, always at hand,—always somebody to feel for and with him; to admire and arrange the wild flowers he brought home from that obnoxious swamp and its edges; to trudge over the three-mile hill of a moonlight night with some trifle for "grandmother;" to escort to singing-school; to go berrying with; to make "posy-beds" for,— in short, to love; for it came to that, without either 'Celdy or Hannah's knowing it; and a very good plan it was.

For in those yet primitive regions servants were made of the same clay with their masters; were men and women of like passions, whose feelings and tastes were really allowed to have room, and whose personality was acknowledged as much as anybody's else; and it was thought no more for a man to marry "their hired girl," who ate and drank at the kitchen-table with the rest of the family, sat in their pew Sundays, and belonged to the same sewing-society with her mistress, than it is in these parts for Mr. Van Tromp, who had a great-grandfather of some sort, to marry Miss Spratte, whose grandfather founded the family in a new hair-dye.

So between bitter and sweet, strife and peace, 'Celdy grew to twenty and Hannah neared eighteen. By this time old Mrs. Case had grown stone-blind in her attic at Peggy Myers's house, and her husband was bent double with rheumatism, and, at the annual auction of the poor, Peggy had been underbid by an old half-breed Indian known as Peter Piper, whose shackling house of two rooms and a garret stood on the top of a bare hill, exposed to every wind that blew, and leaky enough to drown out at least all hope of comfort even for Peter and his dirty, drinking wife. It was nothing to the public, who paid their board, that so many years had made Peggy Myers's house home to these old and feeble people; that Mrs. Case had learned to grope her way about the rooms and even through the garden; still less did it matter that Peter's house was wet, cold, and shackling enough to be dangerous in a high wind: it was all in all that he had offered to take them for ten dollars less than Peggy could afford, and no town could be so foolishly benevolent as to throw away ten dollars a year on non-producers like these. Besides, if they did die, why, then, the whole sum was saved. But the selectman, unluckily for him, had a heart, — a thing selectmen ought never to be troubled with, and sometimes are not; but Mr. Steel, being so afflicted, was troubled enough at the prospect before these kindly and suffering old folks. Had it been in his power he would gladly have kept them with Mrs. Myers; but he was only the agent of the town, and the town's nose was ringed with a silver ring, — it answered only to the appeal of dollars; nor could Mr. Steel pay the extra sum himself, for he was poor enough to look twice at even a cent before he dared spend it. In this dilemma Deacon Sparks occurred to him. He was able to put the matter at rest directly; *he* was well-to-do; in possession of a good farm, with only one son, he could hardly help giving so much aid as this to his wife's mother. So Mr. Steel put on his Sunday coat, tackled up, and set out for Hanover Corners, where the deacon lived, some four miles west of the Centre, and was soon welcomed to a seat by the kitchen fire that a March wind without made doubly welcome. Your true Yankee never comes to the point at once; there is a pleasing satisfaction to him in veering to every point of the compass before he indicates his stopping-place, and Mr. Steel drew largely upon everything in general before he came to his proposition, which was succinct and clear enough when he did reach it. Aunty Sparks dropped her knitting as he began to state the case, Hannah intermitted her sewing, and 'Celdy's cheeks gathered a hot flush as Mr. Steel went on; but the deacon sat still till he finished, and then spoke.

"I don't know but what you're correct, Mr. Steel, about this business, but reelly I can't say as I feel called to pamper Dan Case and his wife beyond payin' my reg'lar tax to the town." 'Celdy moved as if to speak, but his mother looked at him, and her eyes were bright with tears; so 'Celdy held his tongue, and the deacon went on: —

"It's allers been my principle to let folks reap as they've sowed, and I can't see no justice in my grubbin' and sweatin' the year round to set up a feller, that was allers as shiftless as a cow-buntin', in luxury and ease. I aint a wealthy man myself; I pay my debts and calc'late to subscribe to some objects, but I haint got money to throw away. Besides, I don't see no gre't call for't; when folks gets old in shiftless ways I expect they aint partic'lar about where they do put up. I guess Miss Case an' Dan 'll be about as well off with Peter Piper as they was with Miss Myers."

'Celdy got up and flung out of the room. Mr. Steel twiddled his restless fingers in and out in confusion, and finally ventured: —

"Well, I thought I'd call an' say how it was, and maybe you'd feel to help 'em; they're pretty poor off anyhow"— Here he stopped, for he saw a big bright drop fall into Aunty Sparks's lap, and he knew her nature well enough to know how hard tears came; all the harder for the thought that this change would take her mother a mile and a half farther, where the homely dainties, and necessities too, that she had, till now, contrived to smuggle down to her once or twice a week, could scarcely reach her by any available messenger. Hannah had stolen out of the room to comfort 'Celdy, — luckily for the deacon, as it reduced his audience to two before he answered Mr. Steel.

"Well, Brother Steel, I don't feel no call to help 'em. I don't mind Miss Sparks's sendin' of 'em bits an' ends now an' then; but payin' out money's a different thing; and I can't see my way clear to be sinkin' ten dollars a year, jest so's to pamper them old folks. If Dan Case had had a grain of common-sense he could ha' had a house over his head to-day, and got his livin'; but now he'd oughter be thankful to be kep' from starvation, and he'll profit by 'xperience, I guess."

Mr. Steel said "Good-by," the deacon went to bed, and Aunty Sparks, throwing her apron over her head, sat a long time rocking back and forth by the fire, sometimes crying softly over her poor old mother, dear to her as a mother should be; sometimes trying to devise any plan by which that ten dollars could be raised in time to pay Peggy Myers, who would gladly have kept the desolate couple if she could, though she did not make two dollars a year out of her "boarders."

'Celdy and Hannah came in softly from the shed as soon as Deacon Sparks's snores testified his absence from the kitchen; and Hannah, giving Mrs. Sparks a hearty hug and kiss, went off to her own little room with a heart full of pity and indignation, not a little consoled, however, by the quiet, determined way in which 'Celdy had said to her, out in the shed: —

"I'll make it straight, Hannah."

How this was to be done Hannah never stopped to

question. She believed in him with all the innocence and strength of her fresh and loving nature. Happy child! It was enough for her that he undertook anything. Though it wore impossibility on its face to all the world beside, it would have seemed practicable to her since 'Celdy did it; and she rested on this faith to reverse all the evil and wrong in both their lives. So she fell asleep, child-fashion, without a care for the morrow.

'Celdy sat down by his mother, who had dropped her apron and resumed her knitting as soon as he came in, and for a while neither of them spoke. At length he said:—

"Don't be troubled, mother; I'll see that granny never goes to Indian Peter's. Don't you lose heart over it."

Mrs. Sparks laughed just a little, partly by way of reassuring 'Celdy about herself, and partly because of his confident and grown-up manner, that both pleased and amused her even then.

"You can't help it, 'Celdy," said she, "and I can't either; and if 'twasn't best, why, the Lord wouldn't permit it when he knows it can't be helped. I feel bad to think how you'll lay it up against your father. I know you feel hard toward him; but you must call to mind his natur' and his bringin' up. His father was a close man, and I've heerd his mother was inclined that way. She come of a family that was always called very near; so't your father was brought up that way, and you can't blame him, nor I can't neither, so much as if he'd ha' been differently inclined in his youth. I do feel bad about mother, and about Father Case, for I don't feel as if Indian Peter was a faithful man, and his house is dreadful leaky and shacklin'; but then we must make the best on't, and I oughter be thankful your father lets me take 'em vittles, — that's a great deal."

"You always do make the best of everything, mother," said 'Celdy, in a tone of mixed admiration and affection; "but there's scarce any best to this. I shall be twenty-one next week, and you'll see how I shall help the matter if I live."

So the affair rested for that night, and for several days after nothing was heard of it, till the week before 'Celdy's birthday, when he was busy in the barn with his father. He thought best to enlighten the deacon.

"Father," said he, "Sam Myers, who used to work for you when I went to the 'Cademy, is here, down to the Centre. Don't you want to hire him?"

"Why, no," said the deacon, facing 'Celdy with a grim look of surprise; "I don't cale'late to keep a hired man. I guess you an' I can do all the work on this farm if you don't go to runnin' arter your new idees, an' I guess you won't have no chance arter the worst on 'em, for I sold the hull o' that are swamp to Squire Willet yesterday."

'Celdy set his face into its most dogged look.

"But you won't have me, sir. I'm twenty-one next week, and I've taken Squire Willet's farm on shares, from the fifteenth of April."

The deacon dropped the broom he was sweeping up hay-seed with.

"Well," said he, "I s'pose that's your New-School idee of honorin' parents, aint it? I've ben an' brought you up, an' paid your schoolin', and now you go off."

"I don't know, sir, as you've done anything more'n

what everybody does for their sons," remarked 'Celdy between his teeth.

"Where be you a-goin' to live?" said the deacon.

"I'm going to live in the farm-house on Long Pond that he built for Mrs. Willet's brother before he went West. The squire's going to Congress for four years, and I've got the farm on trial."

"Two fools together!" growled the deacon.

'Celdy set down his peck measure, and set his back against the manger.

"Father," said he, "I don't think you can say anything to me about honoring parents when you'll let Grandmother Case go to Peter Piper's because you won't pay ten dollars to help it. I can't stand that. You may give your money to the heathen; I shall take care of my own household first. I'm a man now, and I shouldn't dare show my face before God or man while grandmother was starved and miserable in that old Indian hut. I don't know anything about what you call Old and New School; but I know what my duty is, and I've got to do it; and as long as grandmother and Dan Case live I'll take care of them, if I work my hands off."

The deacon stood stock-still. 'Celdy walked out of the barn into the woods. He was afraid to trust his temper farther; he was afraid of having indulged it even in what he had said. He lay down at the foot of a huge pine-tree that towered up above him, a spire of verdure and fragrance and sad music. The chords of its whispering anthem soothed his excited brain; the blue sky above shone through those waving boughs like a glimpse of God's eternity through the flickering of time. Young as he was, the troubles and doubts of every earnest mind already had wearied him with their assaults, so that a prospect of heavenly rest was sweet even when all life's hope lay tempting before him. The mournful character of New England scenery, the sober nature of a life that must needs be one long labor, the repressive system of his home, — all tended to make his buoyant nature pensive, if not sad; and as he lay there under the tree, no hermit in his rocky cell, on desolate mountains, or sandy deserts, could have looked at the world with more pitying contempt than did 'Celdy, when all at once one of those poems God has scattered in the wilderness, that birds and brooks alone set to music, met his eye. Under the next tree, right at its foot, basking in a gleam of sunshine, stood a tiny cluster of blue squirrel-cups, — "liverworts," as the country people call them; at the foot of that massive tree, from the shrivelled heap of last year's leaves, that bunch of crowded azure blossoms and gray, downy buds looked up to the rare sun, as bright, as fearless, as serene as — Hannah!

'Celdy sprung up from the turf, and stooped over the pretty creatures, with a shy longing to kiss them, which, being a Yankee boy, he did not indulge; then he felt for his knife to dig them up and carry them away bodily; but, as he opened the broad blade, a better impulse filled him. He would not move them; they belonged there. Amidst the thousand odors of spring in the woods, glinting against the golden-brown of the dead leaves about them, neighbored by the chattering squirrels, and praised by the first song of the year, there they bloomed and there they should die, rather than in a cracked teapot on Hannah's window.

But 'Celdy went home comforted, though he didn't

know how, and though he avoided his father and spent the mild, smoky evening chiefly on the step of the back shed in the moonlight, Hannah was there too, with a shawl over her head, and 'Celdy's arm round her, — to keep her warm, I suppose; and whether he learned his lesson of the squirrel-cups, or not, I cannot tell, but Hannah left him at bedtime with the remark that he "beat all for persuadin' folks out of their own mind."

Deacon Sparks preserved a grim silence. Pride forbade that he should relent toward 'Celdy, even so far as to speak with him a word that was not absolutely necessary. He hired a man, but not the one his son had recommended. He went his way to work, and when on Sunday, the second day of April, Deacon Sparks heard the Rev. Mr. Little read from his pulpit the intention of marriage between Aceldama Sparks and Hannah Jones, he so far held the outer man in tight subjection that his eyelash never quivered, nor his mouth stirred from its grim lines.

So Hannah and 'Celdy were married at the minister's house the next Sunday, and, taking the old couple off the town's hands, were all settled in the new house at Long Pond by the fifteenth of the month. Scarce anybody but Hannah and 'Celdy would have begun life on such small foundations; but 'Celdy never forgot a sentence in Mr. Fletcher's letter answering one of his that asked advice on this matter: "Don't be ashamed of anything but sin; if you have enough to eat and keep warm with, and a clear conscience, no man is better off than you." Just these requisites Aceldama had. Squire Willet, a good man, and a progressive one, knew enough of his circumstances and education to give him a helping hand with true pleasure. Hannah found a barrel of pork and two of potatoes in the cellar, which Mrs. Willet sent over because she was going to Washington, and from there to spend the summer at the sea-side, and stores wouldn't keep. What should have been the parlor was given up to the old folks for a bedroom, and they had bedding of their own, and a rickety bedstead, with one chair, an old rocker, and a hair trunk, — that made all the furnishing their room could boast. Mrs. Sparks had made over to Hannah the bed that belonged to her in right of her term as "bound girl" having elapsed, and added to it some linen and blankets that she had brought with her when the deacon married her. A few coarse towels, a kettle, a spider, and a little tin, with a plain set of absolutely necessary crockery for the table, completed Hannah's equipage, taken in lieu of the heifer-calf, — that is, besides the bed, — a bound girl's general portion on her release. She and Aceldama had two boxes for their clothes, and they spread their bed on the floor in an upper room.

Yet, if ever a philosopher wanted an illustration to vindicate his contempt for circumstances, we should have recommended him to 'Celdy's home. No young wife of a boyish millionnaire, in her morning robe of silk, with laced and embroidered garments peeping from under its soft and heavy folds, and every delight or glory that money can bring gathered about her, ever shone more cheerfully lovely than Hannah, in her dark print dress and clean white collar, doing up "chores," with old Dan Case poking about in vain attempts to help her, and granny in her chair by the sunny south window, knitting at her blue stocking, her face as quiet as a child's, and her eyes closed as if will, not power, were wanting to see with. 'Celdy had read enough fiction in his life to have a due value for surroundings, and would have liked as well as any man to see his wife in a romantic cottage, overhung with roses, gracefully doing nothing; but we doubt if he would have loved her half as much under those pleasing aspects as he did now, when every day showed him more and more how neat, how cheerful, how contented she could be in the midst of absolute poverty with him.

It was the most subtle flattery he could receive, because the most unconscious in its giver; and to him perhaps the thought came, as it does to us, why might not thousands of other men, who dare not marry because they are poor, attempt and find the same happiness by the same faith in the woman they love?

Heaven knows that women are the weaker sex; that they are full of faults and full of follies; but where one woman in ten would make a man's life wretched by pining after show and luxury, the other nine would ask nothing but love and trust enough to make them happy in four bare walls. It is not here that women's sins lie. The whole life of thousands, as poor as utter destitution can make them, tells another story. Love a woman enough to trust her, and if she loves you, doubting and sneering man! she will upset all your woman-hating theories in a year; but treat her like a doll and a fool, and she will be both. Is it an unnatural result?

Mrs. Sparks stole down as often as she found the deacon's work took him to a distant field to see her boy and his wife, as well as to comfort her old mother; but the deacon never came, nor did 'Celdy's Christian charity get the better of him yet, enough for him to go home at all. He could not forget that when he left his father, and stifling all his worse feelings in the real affection that only slept within him, he said, "Good-by, father," holding out his hand, the deacon had held his own still before him, and, turning red with rage, answered: —

"You'll come back here begging yet!"

"Never, if I die on the town!" said 'Celdy, equally red. And so father and son had parted.

Squire Willet had left his farm on 'Celdy's hands, with full power to work it as he pleased, swamp and all, and 'Celdy was faithful to his trust. He hired but two men to help him, and made the eyes of all the farmers round about open wide by the barrels of lime and courses of drain-tile that he laid in for the campaign; but he knew what he was about. Up early, and out late, never idle a moment, never looking on, but always at work with his men, he showed the most incredulous how much more a head is worth than hands alone; and when Squire Willet came back to Hanover for a visit in the autumn, to inspect his farm and settle accounts with Aceldama, the twenty-acre swamp waved with such a crop of corn as no field in the township ever saw before, and there was more hay and rye harvested than even his big barns could hold. 'Celdy made enough out of his farming that year to buy a bedstead and a new cloak for Hannah, and lay up a small sum besides for future emergencies; since he had discovered that he was as happy as he need be — with Hannah, and without furniture!

In the winter the trimming and thinning of the wood-lot, and the clearing of a hill-side swarming with white birches, gave them wood enough to defy even a New

England winter; and, unable to be idle, 'Celdy set up two coal-pits, and brought new profit out of the hitherto waste lands on the place.

Toward the end of their first year's life there, old Dan Case died. He was not sick long, and his feeble mind lost nothing during that brief illness. He paid Hannah richly for all her care by his grateful words on those few days; she was good enough to be rewarded for any trouble, by feeling that she had made the last year of her grandfather's life on earth both comfortable and happy, and she never could be glad enough that his last words were: —

"Hanner! you've got a good husband; the Lord'll bless him an' his'n, because he haint forgot the Lord's poor. I can't rightly remember things now; I'm kinder riled in my head; but there is a text somewheres that means him; it's about doin' it to 'the least of these.' Oh, yes! I remember!" He raised his head and looked full at 'Celdy coming in at the door. "The Lord says, 'Ye have done it unto me!'"

"He's been a great burden to you," said Mr. Little to Aceldama, on the day of the funeral, which was held in church on Sunday.

"Oh, no, sir!" was the almost indignant reply; "he has been a great blessing!"

Deacon Sparks heard it.

The second year of 'Celdy's farming kept the promise of the first good, and was brightened all through by a visit from Mr. Fletcher, who slept on the floor, and lived on pork, potatoes, and rye-bread, with as much apparent enjoyment as if they had been the luxuries of a palace. It was a great refreshment to 'Celdy, mentally, to have his company at his daily work; not that Mr. Fletcher worked much, for he had come there to rest, and he therefore conscientiously rested; but his quick, practical insight, that he always exerted for others, though never for himself, and his poetic faculty of seeing the beauty in every common thing, seemed to illustrate even labor, and make it vivid with power and loveliness. Then he appreciated Hannah; and there is no man who does not like to have his wife praised by another, especially by one whom he admires and respects. A woman loves for love's sake; it makes no difference to her what the world says: it is enough that she loves her lover; praise intrudes, and blame is simply outside barbarism. But a man loves for his own sake; pride and self-gratulation mingle with his passion and affection; he is commercial enough in his very nature to feel better satisfied with a bill the more good indorsers it has. "Pity 'tis, 'tis true."

So this visit left 'Celdy in good heart for the summer's labors — all the more that "granny" elevated "that are Mr. Fletcher" into a household oracle, and quoted him on all possible occasions; and Hannah kept alive in her husband's mind a hope too sweet not to be cherished, small as it was, that Hanover people would some day call Mr. Fletcher to be colleague with Mr. Little, now stricken in years and extremely feeble.

"No, they won't, Hannah!" 'Celdy would say, with great emphasis. "They don't know him, and he aint orthodox enough." But, for all that, a vague hope existed in his mind, till it was finally quashed by Mr. Fletcher's receiving and accepting a call to Hanover Centre, four miles from the Corners, and inaccessible to anybody but 'Celdy, because they kept no horse.

Six months he trudged that distance every Sunday to hear his old friend preach; for Hannah had now a little occupation at home that made "meeting" impracticable; till one Sunday in the second spring after their marriage she did contrive to walk to church, and Mr. Little being too ill to preach, Mr. Fletcher supplied his place and baptized Aceldama Sparks' baby and his own namesake.

This was rather too much for Deacon Sparks. If 'Celdy had shown one sign of relenting toward his father — if he had even called his baby Samuel Ebenezer — the deacon might have "come round;" but to go and name his first grandchild after the man, of all others, who had been, in the deacon's eyes, the primary cause of their separation, was not to be forgiven.

It is true Mrs. Sparks and Hannah both begged this mitigation of the name, but 'Celdy was not to be persuaded; the dogged old Adam, who gets credit for all his children's sins, lurked deep in 'Celdy's heart, and made him uncomfortable through every duty of his life, religious or secular. He knew he did not feel as he should toward his father; but he laid the blame on his father's shoulders, and refused to own that both could be wrong as well as one.

That year the farm-work needed a horse; so 'Celdy bought one, and built a barn, and removed his membership and Hannah's to the Centre church. This was the climax of Deacon Sparks's affliction. He couldn't any way understand the works of Providence; he could not see why a New-School man, and one who set light by his father, and called him to naught by his actions, as he phrased it, should be blessed in all his temporal undertakings, — have the best wife, and the finest child, and the biggest crops in the township. He had eaten sour grapes, and it was against Scripture that 'Celdy's teeth were not set on edge.

So matters progressed for three years, during which the deacon's farming plodded slowly backward, and Squire Willet's farm got the premium at the county fair. Hanover people began to wake up to the merits of modern farming; and 'Celdy worked his way into the respect of everybody who knew him, not merely by his agricultural success, but by the never-failing care and kindness with which he treated his old blind grandmother. Still Aceldama was not happy, and Mr. Fletcher saw it, and treated him accordingly.

"What is the matter with you?" said he to Aceldama, one Sunday night, after tea was over, and they sat on the door-step, looking at the sunset, while Hannah "cleared off" within.

"I don't know, sir," said Aceldama.

"Then I shall have to tell you," said Mr. Fletcher; "you have everything at home here, in your family and in your success, to make you happy; but you don't feel right to your father."

"Well, what can I do?" answered 'Celdy, with a sudden burst of angry grief: "he don't treat me as if I was his son; he is not so civil to me as to the commonest beggar. What can I do?"

"I don't see that what he is or does has anything to do with your duty; if he neglects his, that is his affair. Have you tried all you can to be friends with him?"

Aceldama was honest; he hung his head and said, "No."

"Then go and do it at once. Go to-night. I cannot offer you any hope of peace unless you are willing to do a known duty as soon as you see it. If you have spoken disrespectfully to him, say so, and ask his pardon ; tell him you want to be at peace with him ; that you have suffered from your estrangement. Do this, and, whatever answer he gives you, I can promise you a light heart and a pure conscience then ; but not till then."

"I will," said Aceldama, and, quite forgetful of Mr. Fletcher, afraid only of delaying so disagreeable a duty, he took his hat and went; leaving his pastor in the door, no longer interested in the sunset, but thinking in himself, with increasing respect and affection for 'Celdy, how few men in all the world kept in their life of business the directness and honesty that had sent the young man on such an errand, with so slight an impulse. He did not know himself how much he had to do with it; how far his own stainless life, and practice of what he preached, had given him the great power he possessed over all who knew him.

It is almost always true that Providence smooths before us the path to any duty from the moment we enter it. A thicket of doubts and fears may present itself before us, but the boughs bend and the briers part as we face them, and we find a straight way ready for our feet. So Aceldama found it, for his mother met him on the step with tears in her eyes. His father had been taken sick the night before, with a heavy cold apparently ; it had increased now to fever, and he lay on his bed seemingly stupid, but flushed with heat, and restless, though unconscious. The doctor had just been there, and pronounced him in danger; and Mrs. Sparks, full of apprehension, thought he had sent Aceldama up on his way back to his house; and so he would have, but that 'Celdy came across the lots, and Dr. Brooks went by the road. Aceldama was glad always that he came of his own will.

For many long days and nights Deacon Sparks groaned and tossed in the anguish of a raging fever. 'Celdy only went home to direct his men about the work; he was always at hand at night, and watched and wore himself to a shadow, — too glad to show how earnest his resolutions had been, by some visible act of witness. Deacon Sparks neither knew wife nor son for ten days. His first consciousness ensued on a heavy sleep, from which he woke early one April day, free from fever, but weak as a child; and, gathering his fluttered senses so far as to know where he was, heard 'Celdy say, in the next room, in a voice which only the extreme sensitiveness of weakness could have rendered audible to his father: —

"No, mother; I can't leave him now; tell Jay to let the wheat-lot go. I don't care if there isn't a blade of grain on that lot this year: I shall not leave father."

Deacon Sparks could not believe his ears; his mind was too weak and dreamy to linger long on anything; but the sentence lived in his memory, and was there turned over and over again during his long convalescence, and resulted in his slow conviction that, after all, 'Celdy must have a strange affection for his old father, since he risked a crop worth at least a hundred dollars, net profit, to stay with him over the crisis of his illness.

For dollars were the deacon's standard, and when a man has one habitual gauge of value he reduces strange things to that measure; however, it is significant to himself, though it be even ludicrous to another.

He was a long time getting well. Week after week rolled by, and still 'Celdy was needed often to lift his father from one bed to another; to watch by him at night, when his mother was altogether worn out; to oversee the deacon's neglected affairs, over which he fretted and worried enough to have made a well man sick; and all this time he said nothing of reconciliation or affection to his son, — not one word.

By no means because he did not feel it, and show it, too, in his own way; but a genuine Yankee is lost for words to express emotion, however deep it may be. Perhaps he is used rather to consider language as so potent an ally in cheating and chaffering, that he hesitates to profane truth and feeling by utterance; or perhaps he is conscious that the nasal twang of dear old New England is scarce fitted to adorn or intensify the tenderer and sweeter sentiments of life. Be that as it may, the fact remains true; nay, we recall now one man of profound mind and intense sympathies, whose professional attempts at consolation or advice almost always give pain and excite anger, from the simple inability existing in him to speak what he feels with the same depth and delicacy that he feels it. When will somebody annex to the "school of the prophets" most in vogue, a "school of expression," and get a woman to teach it? But Aceldama knew that his father had restored him to his old place quite as well as if he had orientally fallen on his neck and wept, and was rather pleased to have the reconciliation tacit himself. As Deacon Sparks grew better, and came out again into life to do for himself, every one who saw him perceived that he was softened toward things in general, as well as toward 'Celdy. He gave more to the poor-box, and quite as much to the heathen; he went all over Squire Willet's farm, and did not sniff once at the new-fangled machines and operations for its management. He volunteered a call on Hannah, in return for the many she had made him, and shook hands with old Mrs. Case, who was as earnestly glad to welcome him as if he had been the best son-in-law living, and coaxed Master Sammy into the beginnings of a friendship so fervent that thereafter neither grandfather nor grandson were ever so happy as when together; and Sam led the old deacon into all sorts of places, at all times and seasons, simply by pulling at his knotty forefinger, till Hannah had to interfere for her father-in-law's sake, much to the little master's disgust, who had no idea but that grandfathers were made to be useful.

Before another year expired, bringing to an end 'Celdy's lease of the Willet farm, old Mrs. Case had gone home to heaven in her peaceful sleep, and was mourned as a sweet and quiet example of Christian loveliness must be mourned always; though it is for the world and ourselves we grieve, not for those whom death restores to their native atmosphere. Deacon Sparks came to the funeral early, and, standing by the coffin to take a last look at the placid, withered face within it, was heard to say by Hannah, who was in the next room, and was attracted to the door by his musing soliloquy: —

"Well! the Lord has his own ways of levellin' stubborn folks. I wouldn't keep her out o' want, and now she'll be in the upper story up there. She'll be a saint, and I don't know as I shall even keep the door."

Deacon Sparks gave up his farm to 'Celdy, to have and to hold and to work his own way, while he himself "lived on his interest," in Hanover phrase. We only hope our readers may have been able to live on the same fund up to this point. 'Celdy's profits on the Willet place enabled him to build a little frame house, for neither his wishes nor his judgment permitted him to accept his father's proposal that they should all live together. And a few years of real sunshine gilded what remained of Deacon Sparks's life; but he never quite rebounded from that fever. And when a slow consumption at length set in, and gradually beguiled him to his grave, he had many long talks with Mr. Fletcher, whom he had learned both to admire and love; and in one of the last he said : —

"I'm a real changed man about a good many things, Parson Fletcher, an' 'Celdy's done it. I can't think hard of folks's religion when I see how it's worked him, out of the kiting-est boy ye ever see into a real, downright good man. He's better'n I am, a sight! He don't take sech an amazin' grip o' this world as I did. There's suthin better'n dollars to him. An' seein' him, he's kinder upset all my old hard feelin's about New-School folks. I tell ye what, Parson Fletcher, there aint no preachin' like livin'; an' if you want to convert the world, jest you preach to folks in your church to live as though they b'lieved the Bible, and liked to b'lieve it. Your pretty Sunday talk about natur', and ph'losophy, and doctrines, and one thing and 'nother, isn't goin' to bring the millennium round very spry. It aint no good to deny the Lord six days in your works, and be entertained spec'latin' about him the seventh. The children o' this world are too knowin' to be caught with sech chaff. They've got the Bible as well as professors, and they know 't when the Lord says religion is doin' justly, and lovin' mercy, and walkin' humbly with God, that a man who don't do nary one of them things aint religious, if he is deacon in three churches, and shells out to all the societies a-goin'.

"I've ben a stumblin'-block myself long enough to know jest how't's done; and the fust thing't brought me to was seein' one live Christian, an' that's 'Celdy; an' you done it, next to the Lord, ef you *are* a New-School man. Besides," added the old man, after a paroxysm of coughing that interrupted his speech had passed away, "I'm too near to Jordan now to b'lieve there's any schools on t'other side. It's jest like gettin' right into the sunshine's track when it's settin', an' seems near, close to; you can't see nothin' partic'lar because of the light an' glory on't; all you know how to say is, it's all light, and brightness, and warm all over; there aint no spots; it's all together, and it's all good."

"Amen!" said Mr. Fletcher, bending his head, and closing the rude simplicity of the old man's speech with the only words fit to finish and seal it: —

"'Where there is neither Greek nor Jew, circumcision nor uncircumcision, Barbarian, Scythian, bond nor free: but Christ is all, and in all.'"

SALLATHIEL BUMP'S STOCKING.

> "Sallathiel Bump,
> He sat on a stump.
> I hit him a thump
> That made him to jump,
> And" —

"OH! ow! ow! Stop a-hittin' of me, C'lesty! I aint doin' nothin'; haint a feller got a right to sing, I'd like to know?"

"Depends considerable on what he sings," said Celestia, glowing like an indignant rose, "angry and brave," as she stood there in the October sunshine, with a milk-pail in one hand, and the palm of the other pink and tingling with the blows she had just bestowed on Jehiel Burr's ears.

"Well, what in thunder's a feller got such an outlandish name for, if he don't want it poked fun at?" muttered the aggrieved youngster, rubbing his scarlet ear with his hand, and casting black glances at Celestia.

"If you was half as good-lookin' or as good as he is, you'd be glad enough to take his name, you limb! I do'no' as Jehiel Burr is much better, neither."

"Stan' up for him, don't ye?" sniffed Jehiel, commonly called Hi. "Well, do! I see ye last Sat'day night under that apple-tree a "— here he skipped madly out of reach, for Celestia's firm hand descended, only just escaping his ears again; and, feeling that discretion was better than valor, he fled to the barn and sung his doggerel there in safety; but poor Celestia carried her milk-pail round to the sunny stoop of the kitchen, and, having tilted it at just the right angle to catch the sun, she sat down on the steps, flung her gingham apron over her head and began to cry noiselessly. In this moist state her mother found her as she stepped out to hang up a dishcloth in the air.

"Why, C'lesty!" she asked; "what under the canopy ails ye? What are ye takin' on about?"

"Oh, nothing," said the girl, as women always say.

"Well, nothing's easy mended," answered the mother, having good reasons of her own for not asking Celestia's confidence; indeed, she knew enough of the trouble in her girl's heart to be pretty sure these tears were but its outlet and relief; and she knew, too, from long experience, that sympathy is not always the best thing for trouble that is inevitable, and the meek, weak, patient woman had been Jehiel Burr the elder's wife so many years that she regarded his will quite as powerful and sure as the will of that higher power whom she called Providence.

The fact was that old Jehiel had made up his mind that Celestia should marry the school-master at Pompton Academy, and Celestia had made up her mind to marry Sallathiel Bump.

There is very little in a name when one falls in love with a tall, handsome young fellow, kind-hearted, well made, with the handsomest steel-blue eyes you can think of; a dimple in his chin, and teeth white as rows of corn kernels under the green husk of the fresh cob. All these good gifts belonged to Celestia's lover; but her father did not pay such respect to them as they deserved. In his eyes Sallathiel — I should like to leave out one l in the name, but he never did — Sallathiel, I say, had two glaring faults; he was poor, and he was born and bred an Episcopalian. If Jehiel Burr had started the old war-cry against popery and prelacy he would have added poverty to complete the triad; he hated all three. He was a rigid sectarian of his own sort, and despised every other form of religion; and to be poor was to be "shiftless," — the New England unpardonable sin.

Moreover, Celestia had a little money of her own, just enough to add another charm in the eyes of some people to those with which nature had endowed her; and every poor man who looked at her was considered by her father to be rather captivated with her money than herself. But Celestia felt in her heart that Sallathiel loved her, and not her dollars; possibly she judged him by herself, as we all judge others, but this time her opinion was right: this lover would have laid his heart at her feet with just as much alacrity and passion if her Grandmother Green had left her five thousand cents, instead of five thousand dollars.

Not content with thwarting this true love, however, Jehiel Burr was also determined that his daughter should marry as he pleased, and had already determined that Mr. Algernon Sydney Howard Middleton, principal of Pompton Academy, should be his son-in-law. Here was a man after his own heart: orthodox as Calvin, learned enough to be writing a wonderful work on higher mathematics, powerful in prayer-meeting, setting his face, not exactly as a flint, but rather as a flour-pudding, against amusements, and rattling off the Shorter Catechism from his tongue's end on all occasions as fluently as a Tartar praying-machine. Of course Celestia hated him; and not without other reason than his pretensions to her favor. He was very fat, — fat as to his colorless, puffy cheeks, as well as his person, which possessed the even symmetry of a large chestnut worm; and his little, beady, black eyes gleamed from under the gold-rimmed glasses perched on his thick, flat, upturned nose, with a glare by no means heavenly; while his protuberant lips wore an expression of conceit and impertinence almost insufferable to beholders. His gait was a pompous swagger, and the stove-pipe hat tilted on his bullet head added another expression of character to his figure. He was vain as a peacock, and could not believe that any girl could resist his charms; indeed he felt that he stooped from a proud eminence to address Celestia Burr, and he made her feel it. But for that five thousand dollars of hers he knew, and she knew, that he never would have condescended so far. Hi, a real little pickle, hated the school-master with all his heart, and liked Sallathiel, but he loved to tease Celestia; it tickled his very soul to see the angry crimson rise in her smooth, dark cheek, her beautiful soft eyes flash from their midnight depths with fire, and her rich red lips quiver with distress. He was a boy, and, if all men are born free and equal, as our glorious Constitution plausibly declares, all boys are born savages. Really Hi loved his sister as well as anybody, but he tyrannized over her and his mother because his father was a tyrant to him, and instinctively he imitated the parent he feared; it was a curious sort of relief to pass the terror along.

But when Jehiel Burr resolved that Celestia should marry Master Middleton he did not remember that she was his daughter. Heredity is a troublesome thing sometimes. Men forget that their children generally share their own traits, and Celestia had quite as strong a will as her father. In her firm chin, on her low, straight brow, in the darkness of her great, steady eyes, lay dormant a strength he did not dream of, waiting only for an emergency to call it out.

Now Grandmother Green had the forethought to ordain in her will that Celestia should not have her money at all if she married before she was twenty-one, but at that age she should come into full possession of it with her other legal rights; and this October afternoon she was still twenty. Her birthday was coming on Christmas day, though she knew about that festival only from the pleasant stories Sallathiel Bump had poured into her ears concerning his own childhood.

His father and mother had both been of English descent, and their form of religion was an inheritance. Poor as they were no Christmas had ever passed without some observance in their family, some decoration about the tall clock, some festoon of evergreen about the old rusty halberd that lay across two spikes above the fireplace, and had a tradition invisibly tied to it, longer by far and more sempiternal than the ground-pine streamers floating from its sharp pike-end. Sallathiel always hung up his stocking over-night, and always found something, if only a home-made top and home-knit mittens, distending its blue ribbed leg, and if there was but one mince-pie falling to their lot in the whole year it was served for their Christmas dinner.

It was a sort of romance to Celestia, this cheerful observance, this happy religion. Her clean, bare, silent home knew no feast-days but the annual Thanksgiving, which meant to them a tedious political sermon from Parson Pitcher, an inordinate dinner, at which Master Middleton, for the last two years, had gorged himself to repletion, leering at Celestia like an enamored boa-constrictor between vast mouthfuls of turkey, onions, and pie; and after which "cold bits" from the overloaded table were their daily food for at least a week.

During these last six months, urged by parental encouragement and the fact that Celestia was nearly twenty-one, Master Middleton had " courted " her with unfaltering assiduity. Every Sunday night found him seated on the big rocker by the sitting-room hearth when fires began to burn there, or by the window when summer reigned, his fat pomposity seeming to fill and overflow the small apartment, and his thick-skinned conceit keeping him complacent under all Celestia's coolness or angry rebuffs.

But Sallathiel had no entrance to the house. When he met her it was by stealth, under the fragrant, flowery apple-trees of the orchard, or Sunday noons in the pine grove back of the graveyard, when her father was grinding out the conjectural history of Melchisedec, the problems of election, infant damnation, free-will and responsibility, or the war record of the Maccabees, to his yawning Bible-class, and thought C'lesty had gone home to get her lunch, or to a noon prayer-meeting. Hi kept them both in terror, for he was ubiquitous; and, if he did not know when and where they met every time, he said he did, which was quite as unpleasant to the lovers.

To-day Celestia had reason for her tears of vexation when the little rascal intimated he had been a witness of their last interview, for it had been an important one. She had stolen away to the orchard, while her father dozed by the kitchen fire, in obedience to a word from Sallathiel, as he passed her on the road two days before on her way to a quilting.

"C'lesty," said the handsome fellow, after the shy greetings had passed between them, "that feller Middleton's a-boastin' and tellin' round how that you're a-goin' to marry him sure, come New Year, and I can't stan' it no more."

"I don't know as his sayin' of it makes it sure," said Celestia, with a bewitching little laugh.

"No, I do'no' as it does, but it's everlastin' hard, C'lesty, to look on and see him courtin' of you when I can't put in a look except on the sly. Now, why won't you say the word, and we'll get Jim Perkins's fast horse and click it over the line, and be married without any to-do about it?"

"I like that!" said the girl, meaning she did not like it at all. "No, sir! when I git married 'twon't be over no State line, as though I was ashamed on't. Besides, Sallathiel, I should lose all Granny Green's money."

"I don't care an individooal darn if you do!" said Sallathiel, flushing hotly in the moonlight. "I don't want your money, nor I never did. I want you; and I am afeared your pa'll set to and pester you so, and make it so hot for you to hum, that — well"—

Here he choked. The prospect was too hard. Celestia blazed up at once.

"Do you think I'm a fust-class fool, Sallathiel Bump? Do you think I'm sech a rag-baby that any man 't ever was born could make me marry that feller?

If you do, you're entire mistook. I'd give him lamb-kill before I'd marry him."

"No, you wouldn't," said Sallathiel, rather startled by the flashing eyes of his sweetheart. "You wouldn't hurt a fly, C'lesty. I know ye."

"I'd kill a snake, though!" she retorted, but it was an aside.

Sallathiel went on : —

"I can work, and I will work for my wife. I've got two stout good arms, and I've got the old homestead and four acres to't. We couldn't starve noway, C'lesty. Don't, *don't* wait for that confounded money!"

Celestia laughed.

"Never you mind, dear. I shall wait for the money. I want it; but that Middleton feller shan't have it, not a red cent. Besides, I don't want to go out of the State to be married; it aint seemly, and if I'm twenty-one I don't need to. Can't you have patience?"

"It's everlastin' hard to," sighed Sallathiel, looking at the lovely upturned face in front of him. "But there's one thing, C'lesty. I've got as good a right to come to your folks's house Sunday evenin's as he has, and I'm a-comin'."

"W-e-e-ll," she answered, doubtfully, not without a thrill of consciousness that her master would some time grow out of her lover, "you know father'll make it real unpleasant for you, S'lathil, and that other feller'll be worse."

"I aint afraid of 'em," said he, calmly, closing his big, shapely hands into ominous fists as he spoke, with masculine instinct. "I can't come to-morrow night, for I'm goin' to set up with old Perkins. He's had a stroke, and I told Jim I'd come and spell 'em. But look out for me next Sunday evenin' for sure as shootin' I shall come." And with that they parted.

It was Saturday again when Celestia caught Hi singing his ditty about Sallathiel Bump's unfortunate name, and this was the one straw that quite broke down her vaunted courage. She had worried all the week about that coming Sunday evening. It was right, quite right, that Sallathiel should assert himself. Her father had never forbidden him to come to the house further than grim looks and bitter words went; and it was owing to her own entreaties that he had consented to meet her elsewhere, for, like most women, Celestia dreaded a domestic storm. Alas, how many meannesses, subterfuges, lies, have been forced upon trembling wives, sisters, and daughters, in order to avert these uncivil wars in the household! How rare is the woman who dares adhere to facts in the face of masculine fury! Celestia was not of that exceptional sort. She looked forward to this coming encounter with dread, and when Hi added his small jeer to the weight already oppressing her, what could she do but cry? But, tears or no, the unlucky Sunday came; and when meeting, Bible-class, and the late dinner were over, old Burr turned to Celestia, as she passed through the kitchen with the sitting-room lamp, and growled: —

"Look-a-here, C'lesty, I want ye to understand that you aint a-goin' to keep Master Middleton on tenter-hooks no longer. You've hed him a-danglin' long enough, and he's a-comin' for his answer to-night; you let him hev it, do ye hear?"

Celestia's courage returned. She looked her father square in the face.

"Yes; he'll get it!" she said, curtly and sharply.

Jehiel stared at her with dull surprise in his cold, angry eyes.

"Look out, gal! he nor me won't stan' no nonsense."

"Nor me, neither!" she said, looking back at him as she went through the door.

The old man glared after her, a little doubtful, but still confident of his own coercive powers, and waited for the master's arrival. Celestia, too, waited. Never had she looked lovelier than to-night. Her dark red woollen dress, with its delicate white frills, became her well, her cheek glowed with excitement, and in the coiled masses of her night-black hair she had fastened, with instinctive taste, a graceful spray of golden-rod, and clasped another in the tiny breastpin at her throat.

Her eyes were brighter than soft, something defiant looked out from them; but when Master Algernon Sydney Howard Middleton waddled into the front parlor, and put his shiny hat down on a chair near by the door, he only perceived her beauty, and simpered to think how soon she would be his own. Celestia was cool and haughty. She seated Master Middleton on the old sofa, whose feeble springs creaked as he deposited his weight on the slippery horsehair surface; but he did not mind that: he had no consciousness of small things, he was going to make the final plunge, and emerge triumphant. But, just as the early commonplaces of weather and season were over, a confident knock was heard at the outer door. Country-fashion, Celestia answered it, just in time to prevent her father's thorough rousing from his doze by the kitchen fire. A repetition would have brought him out; as it was he thought a rat had disturbed him and nodded again. But it was something worse than rats,— it was handsome, happy, assured Sallathiel Bump, who walked into the parlor beside Celestia, blushing divinely, though her heart beat almost to suffocation. Algernon Sydney Howard Middleton stared with beady eyes at the intruder, but said "Good-evening," in the hope that this was but a call, and determined to outstay him; a determination all in vain. There were awful pauses in the conversation; there were essays at talk on the school-master's part that fell dead to the ground, and sallies from Sallathiel that were supported by Celestia with giggling response or interested question. Master Middleton grew furious, yet had sense enough left to appreciate the situation. When the clock struck ten he took up his shiny hat and said good-night.

"Going my way, Mister Bump?" he remarked blandly to Sallathiel.

"Not jest yet," was the exasperating answer, and the master left the lovers together. Father Burr long since had gone to his bed, secure that his plans were all going on as he desired, and Celestia and Sallathiel sat up in that stiff, chill parlor till midnight, happy as they ought to have been; happier, no doubt, because they knew their bliss was precarious, and Master Middleton not always to be so balked.

Not he! Scarce a day had passed before he complained to Jehiel Burr of his disappointment.

"I'll fix it," said the furious parent, and forthwith he hunted up Sallathiel, and forbid him to enter his house or speak to his daughter.

"If you wa'n't her pa, and an old feller to boot, I'd thrash ye to strings!" said the outraged lover.

"Do! oh, do, now," sneered Jehiel. "I'd jest like to tackle ye, young feller! Maybe I be old, but I'm gritty as sin; jest you try."

"I'd despise to tech ye, Mister Burr; but I will say one thing, an' thet is, as sure as I live I'll marry C'lesty in spite of you."

And with this defiance Sallathiel went, leaving Father Burr choking and sputtering with rage, which he drove home to pour out on Celestia.

The girl shut her teeth and said nothing. It was but a few weeks now to her birthday; her mind was made up. Master Middleton came again, and this time without interruption; but, to his disgust and surprise, when he laid his heart and hand at Celestia's feet she resolutely refused him. His face grew tallow white, his little black eyes glowed red with rage, his upturned nose quivered; he looked like a fat fiend, and Celestia's deep contempt inspired her expressive countenance.

"But your father said you should," he gasped and stammered.

"And I say I shall not," was her calm, cool answer.

"I believe it's a law of Christianity that children shall obey their parents," he retorted, taking high moral ground.

"I shan't never obey nobody to do wrong," replied Celestia, trumping his trick.

"Well, I s'pose you're whifflety, like other girls, Celestia; but I've got your pa's consent, and I'll give you time to change your mind. I'm a patient man; I can wait, for I'm sure you'll come round."

"Never!" said the angry girl. "I wouldn't marry you, Master Middleton, if there wa'n't another man in the created universe!"

She said these indignant words as she lighted him to the door, looking so handsome in her excitement that the master's feelings got the better of him. He turned on the sill, threw his arms about her and tried to snatch a kiss. Celestia screamed and dashed the lamp at his face; a rough hand seized him by the collar, hustled him down on to the gravel path, and the foot that corresponded to that hand dismissed him ignominiously from the premises, too confounded and out of breath to do more than skip along with an alacrity uncomfortable enough to a man of his avoirdupois, and only able to gasp: —

"Ow! oh! ow!"

While an elfish giggle from the gate-post preluded another stave of Hi's impromptu ditty: —

> "Sallathiel Bump
> Hit the master a thump,
> And how he did jump
> All up in a hump!
> Oh my!"

"Hi Burr! hold your tongue!" whispered Celestia, who had stayed to pick up the pieces of her lamp-chimney on the steps.

"Taint me!" shrieked Hi, as he disappeared round the corner.

Perhaps Sallathiel did not further his cause by this outburst. The master could not bring suit against him for assault, for there were no witnesses, nor did he even see the face of his assailant; but he uttered vast threats of vengeance, at which Sallathiel laughed; and he still proceeded to persecute Celestia with weekly visits on the Sunday evenings sacred in New England to courtships. Besides this, her father assumed that the marriage was a fixed affair; and her mother, while she weakly cried and sniffed about the house, dared not offer one word of comfort or help to Celestia. As the year drew near its close the girl became conscious that things were closing up about her. Her father gave up his Bible-class at noon, and brought the family home to lunch. He would not let her go to quiltings or to evening meetings any more, and every night he locked the front door, put the key in his pocket, and sat in the kitchen till midnight, so that no one should go out or come in without his knowledge.

Celestia's heart sank; for weeks she had not seen Sallathiel, and she began to feel that despair which the native impatience of woman accelerates before it is inevitable.

But Sallathiel was not idle meantime. With a lover's instinct he cultivated a friendship with Hi; he let him gather the chestnuts off the big tree behind his little red house, a tree noted in Pompton for its large and abundant nuts; he took him hunting Saturdays; helped him with advice as to his water-wheel; and had many a laugh with him over Master Middleton's alert departure from Jehiel Burr's door on that Sunday evening.

Hi grew very fond of Sallathiel, and correspondingly pitiful of Celestia's hard case. Hi kept his eyes and ears open, and reported the condition of things to the lover with great zeal; it was so pleasant to feel of importance!

Christmas came very near. It was only two days

before its arrival that Hi followed Celestia into the pantry, on a pretext of seeing that she put some ginger-snaps as well as pie into his dinner-pail, and whispered to her: —

"Say, C'lesty! I heered pa a-sayin' to ma last night when you went down suller for th' apples an' cider, thet come your birthday he was a-goin' to tell ye to clear out o' here for good or marry Master Middleton. I was up-stairs a-harkin' an' a-peekin' through the pipe-hole, for I 'xpected something or 'nother was up. Ma said, kinder cryin', thet you wouldn't never marry him, she was afeared; and then pa fetched his fist down and sed he'd hev the minister here that mornin' 't you was comin' to your money and marry ye right up. I do'no's he could, an' do'no' *as* he could; but I thought you'd oughter know. Land, there's pa! Put in them things quick, C'lesty. Don't keep a feller waitin' all day." And with an aggrieved air he took up his pail and hurried off.

Celestia, trembling and pale, went upstairs to her chamber. Could it be, after all, that her father had such power over her? Had she mistaken her own rights under the law? There was nobody to advise or reassure her. She fell into an unreasoning terror.

What if, after all, it *was* in her father's power to make her marry Master Middleton? She shuddered at the thought. If only she could get to Sallathiel! At last it occurred to her that Hi could perhaps carry him a letter. But if her father should find it on the boy? She sat down and fell to thinking, for she knew no one but her lover could help her in this strait; yet how could she send and word the letter, so that if it fell into other hands it need not betray her? Woman's wit at last came to the rescue. She remembered Sallathiel's stories of his Christmas gifts in the old time. She knew he was now at work at a saw-mill just beyond the village, and that it was but a little farther for Hi to go to school by the lane past his red house; so she wrote him a note, instructing Hi to push it under the crack of Sallathiel's door the next morning, and went about her work with a lighter heart.

Sallathiel himself was pleased enough with the brief epistle which he found in his kitchen as he entered the door, though all it said was: —

> To-morrow night is Christmas Eve, that you used to tell about. Hang your biggest stocking outside of your door, instead of up chimney, and see what you'll get. C.

It seemed to link a happy memory to a blessed future that Celestia should think of sending him a Christmas gift, and remember about the stocking, for years had gone by since the childish custom had been observed for him; and it was with a saddened gladness that he obeyed her wish, going late out of the door to nail up on the casing a long blue yarn stocking he had hunted up in his mother's chest; the very stocking — one of his father's best pair — that had always been used in his childhood for this purpose.

It was early dawn when he awoke, after a night of dreams, in which his mother and his sweetheart seemed both to visit him, with smiling faces. He thought he heard steps on the crisp snow outside, and with the old boyish eagerness sprung up, hastily dressed himself in the pale, cold light that stole into his little window, and lifted the latch to explore his stocking for the expected love-token.

Did he dream still? There stood Celestia herself, one arm deep down in the blue stocking, the other hand holding her shawl close about the blushing, tearful, dimpling face.

"My Christmas present!" said Sallathiel, in a sort of rapture, drawing her into the tiny kitchen, and putting her into his mother's chair.

Truly it was Celestia whom he found in his stocking! Desperate at the prospect before her she had stolen into Hi's room before light, not daring to open even the closet door to find a bonnet; but, as the bedroom doors were always left ajar in winter, she reached the boy's window silently, managed to lift it without waking him, since he had long ago taken out the spring in order to make his own exits, and, as it opened on a shed roof slanting to a few feet from the ground, she had dropped off into a snow-drift, and made her way by the gray light to Sallathiel's door.

Luckily there was an early service in the small Episcopal chapel at Pompton, for the rector lived ten miles away, and did duty in this mission chapel as well as in his own church, and when Sallathiel had lit the fire in his stove, and brewed Celestia a cup of tea with awkward devotion, he locked the door on her lest some one might track her thither, and, hurrying to Jim Perkins's house, borrowed his buggy, his fast horse, and his mother's Sunday bonnet, to Jim's speechless astonishment.

So before three people had gathered to this early service, just as the tinkling bell begun its summons, Celestia was made Sallathiel's wife; and to this hour, though, like us all, they have endured life's evils as well as its joys, Sallathiel still blesses the Christmasday when he hung up his stocking.

SALLY PARSONS'S DUTY.

The sun that shines on eastern Massachusetts, specially on buttercups and dandelions, and providentially on potatoes, looks down on no greener fields in these days than it saw in the spring of 1775, fenced in and fenced off by the zigzag snake-fences of 'Zekiel Parsons's farm.

"About this time," as almanacs say, young orchards were misty with buds, red maples on the highway shone in the clear light, and a row of bright tin pans at the shed door of the farm-house testified to a sturdy arm and skilful hand within, — arm and hand both belonging to no less a person than Miss Sally, 'Zekiel Parsons's only daughter, and the prettiest girl in Westbury: a short, sturdy, rosy little maid, with hair like a ripe chestnut shell, bright blue eyes full of mischief, and such a sunny, healthy, common-sense character one is almost afraid to tell of it, it is so out of date now.

But of what use is it to describe her? How can I impress upon moderns how enlivening and refreshing was her aspect, as she spun, or scoured pans, in a linsey-woolsey petticoat and white short-gown, wearing her pretty curls in a crop? George Tucker knew it all without telling; and so did half a dozen of the Westbury boys, who haunted the picket fence round 'Zekiel's garden every moonlight night in summer, or scraped their feet by the half-hour together on his door-step in winter evenings. Sally was a belle; she knew it and liked it, as every honest girl does,—and she would have been a belle without the aid of her father's wide farm and pine-tree shillings; for she was fresh and lovely, with a spice of coquetry, but a true woman's heart beneath it all.

It was very hard to discover whom Sally Parsons favored among her numerous beaux. Her father seriously inclined to George Tucker; not because he was rich,—for 'Zekiel had not arrived at fashionable principles,—but because he was honest, kind-hearted, and reliable; but as yet Sally showed no decided preference; time and the hour were near, but not in sight.

One Sunday night, early in April, after the nine-o'clock bell had scattered Sally's admirers far and wide, and old 'Zekiel sat by the chimney-corner, watching his sister, Aunt Poll, rake up the rest of the hickory log in the ashes, while he rubbed away sturdily at his feet, holding in one hand the blue yarn stockings, "wrought by no hand, as you may guess," but that of Sally; the talk, that had momentarily died away, began again, and with a glance at Long Snapps,—a lank, shrewd-faced old sailor, who, to use his own speech, had "cast anchor 'longside of an old ship-met fur a spell, bein' bound fur his own cabin up in Lenox,"— 'Zekiel spoke after this wise:—

"I expect, Long, you sailors hev a drefful hard, onsartin time navigatin', don't ye?"

"Well, skipper! that are depen's on folks. I don't calc'late to hev no sort of a hard time, ef I don't get riled with it; but these times I doo rile easy."

"What onsettles ye, Snapps?"

"Well, there's a squall to wind'ard, skipper; 'taint no cat's-paw neither; good no-no-east, ef it's a flaw. And you landlubbers are a-goin' to leeward, some on ye."

"You don't say! What be you a-hintin' at?"

"Well, there's a reel blow down to Bostin, Zekle; there's no more gettin' out o' harbor with our old sloop; she's ben an' gone, an' got some 'tarnal lawyer's job spliced to her bows, an' she's laid up to dry; but that's a pesky small part o' judgment. Bostin's full o' them Britishers, sech as scomfishkated the 'Susan Jane,' cos our skipper done suthin' he hedn't oughter, or didn't do suthin' he hed oughter; and I tell *yew* the end o' things is nigh about comin' on here!"

Sally, in the chimney-corner, heard Long Snapps with open eyes, and, hitching her wooden chair nearer, inquired solemnly: —

"What do you mean, Mister Snapps? Is the end of the world comin' here?"

"Bless your pooty little figger-head, Sally! I don't know as 'tis, but suthin' nigh about as bad is a-comin'. Them Britishers is sot out for to hev us under hatches, or else walk the plank; and they're darned mistook, ef they think men is a-goin' to be steered blind, and can't blow up the cap'in no rate. There aint no man in Ameriky but what's got suthin' to fight for, afore he'll gin in to sech tyrints; and it'll come to fightin' yet, afore long!"

"Oh, my! oh, goody! the land's sakes! yew don't mean ter say that, Long?" wofully screeched Aunt Poll, whose ideas of war were derived in great measure from the tattered copy of Josephus extant in the Parsons family, and who was at present calculating the probable effect of a battering-ram on their back buttery, and thinking how horrible it would be to eat up Uncle 'Zekiel in case of famine, — even after long courses of rats and dogs.

"Well, I dew, Aunt Poll. There'll be some poppin' an' stickin' done in these parts afore long!"

"The Lord deliver us! an' the rest on't!" devoutly ejaculated Poll, whose piety exceeded her memory; whereat 'Zekiel, pulling on the other blue stocking that had hung suspended in his fingers while the sailor discoursed, exhorted a little himself: —

"Well, the Lord don't deliver nobody without they wriggle for themselves pretty consider'ble well fust. This aint the newest news to me; I've been expectin' on't a long spell, an' I've talked consider'ble with Westbury folks about it; and there aint nobody much, round about here, but what'll stand out agin the Britishers, exceptin' Tucker's folks; they're desp'rit for Church an' King; they tell as ef the Lord gin the king a special license to set up in a big chair an' rewl creation; an' they think it's pertic'lar sin to speak as though he could go 'skew anyhow. Now I believe the Lord lets folks find out what he does, out o' Scriptur'; and I haint found nothin' yet to tell about kings bein' better than their neighbors, and it don't look as ef this king was so clever as common. I s'pose you haint heerd what our Colony Congress is a-doin', hev ye, Snapps?"

"Well, no, I haint. They was a-layin' to, last I heerd, so's to settle their course; I 'xpect they've heaved up an' let go by this, but I haint seen no signals."

"Dear me!" interrupted Sally; "a real war coming, and I aint anything but a woman!"

Her cheeks and eyes glowed with fervent feeling, as she said this; and the old sailor, turning around, surveyed her with a grin of honest admiration.

"Well said, gal! but you're out o' your reckonin' ef you think women aint nothin' in war-time. I tell *yew*, them is the craft that sails afore the wind, and does the signallin' to all the fleet. When gals is full-rigged an' tonguey, they're reg'lar press-gangs to twist young fellers round, an' make 'em sail under the right colors. Stick to the ship, Miss Sally; give a heave at the windlass now 'n' then, an' don't let nary one o'them fellers that comes a-buzzin' round you the hull time turn his back on Yankee Doodle; an' you won't never hanker to be a man, ef 'tis war-time!"

Sally's eyes burned bluer than before. "Thank you kindly, Mister Snapps. I'm obleeged to you for putting the good thought into my head. (If I don't pester George Tucker — the plaguy Tory!)"

This parenthesis was mental, and Sally went off to bed with a busy brain; but the sleep of youth and health quieted it; and if she dreamed of George Tucker in regimentals I am afraid they were of flagrant militia scarlet, — the buff and blue were not distinctive yet. However, for the next week Sally heard enough revolutionary doctrine to revive her Sunday-night enthusiasm; the flame of "successful rebellion" had spread; the country began to stir and hum ominously; people assembled in groups, on corners, by church-steps, around tavern-doors, with faces full of portent and expectance; ploughs stood idly in the fields; and the rawboned horses, that should of right have dragged the reluctant share through heavy clay and abounding stones, now, bestridden by breathless couriers, scoured the country hither and yon, with news, messages, and orders from those who had taken the right to order out of the hands of sleek and positive officials.

Nor were Westbury people the last to wake up in the general *réveille*. Everybody in the pretty, tranquil village, tranquil now no more, declared themselves openly on one side or the other, — Peter Tucker and his son George for the king, of course; and this open avowal caused a sufficiently pungent scene in Miss Sally Parsons's keeping-room the very next Sunday night, when the aforesaid George, in company with several of his peers, visited the farm-house for the laudable purpose of " sparkin' " Miss Sally.

There were three other youths there besides George; all stout for the Continental side of the question, and full of eager but restrained zeal; ready to take up arms at a moment's notice; equally ready to wait for the ripened time. Of such men were those armies made up that endured with a woman's patience and fought with a man's fury, righting a great wrong as much by moral as by physical strength, and going to death for the right, when death, pitiless and inevitable, stared them in the face.

Long Snapps had been, in his own phrase, " weather-bound" at Westbury, and was there still, safe in the chimney-corner, his shrewd face puckered with thought and care, his steady old heart full of resolute bravery, and longing for the time to come; flint and steel ready to strike fire on the slightest collision. On the other side of the hearth from Snapps sat 'Zekiel, in his butternut-colored Sunday suit; the four young man ranged in a grim row of high-backed wooden chairs; Sally, blooming as the roses on her chintz gown, occupying one end of the settee, while Aunt Poll filled the rest of that institution with her ample quilted petticoat and paduasoy cloak, trying hard to keep her hands still, in their unaccustomed idleness, — nay, if it must be told, surreptitiously keeping up a knitting with the fingers, in lieu of the accustomed needles and yarn.

An awful silence reigned after the preliminary bows and scrapes had been achieved, — first broken by George Tucker, who drew from under his chair a small basket of red-cheeked apples and handed them to Aunt Poll.

"Well, now, George Tucker!" exclaimed the benign spinster, "you dew beat all for sass out o' season! Kep' 'em down sullar, I expect?"

"Yes'm, our suller's very dry."

"Well, it hed oughter. What kind be they?"

"English pippins, ma'am."

"Dew tell! Be you a-goin' to hev one, Sally?"

"No, Aunt Poll! I don't want anythin' English 'round!"

The three young men grinned and chuckled. George Tucker turned red.

"Hooray for you, Sally!" sung out old Snapps. "You're a three-decker, if ever there was un!"

Again George reddened, fidgeted on his chair, and at last said, in a disturbed, but quite distinct voice: —

"I think the apples are good, Miss Sally, if the name don't suit you."

"The name's too bad to be good, sir!" retorted Sally, with a decided sniff and toss of the head. Old 'Zekiel gave a low laugh and interfered.

"You see, George Tucker, these here times is curus. It wakes up the wimmen folks to hev no tea, nor no prospects of peace and quiet, so's to make butter an' set hens."

"O father!" burst out Sally, "do you think that's all that ails women? I wouldn't care if I eat samp forever, and had nothing but saxifrax tea; but I can't stand by cool, and see men driven like dumb beasts by another man, if he has got a crown, and never be let speak for themselves."

Sally's logic was rather confused, but George got at the idea as fast as was necessary.

"If 'twas a common man, Miss Sally; but a king's set up on high by the Lord, and we ought to obey what he sets over us."

"I don't see where in Scriptur' you get that idee, George," retorted 'Zekiel.

"Well, it says in one place that you're to obey them that has the rule over you, sir."

"So it do; but ef the king haint got no rewl over us (an' it looks mighty like it jes' now), why, I don't see's we're bound to mind him!"

This astute little sophism confounded poor George for a minute, during which Sally began to giggle violently, and flirt in her rustic fashion with the three rebels in a row. At length George, recovering his poise and clear-sightedness, resumed : —

"But he did rule over us, Mister Parsons, and I can't see how it's right to rebel."

"There don't everythin' come jest square about seein' things," interposed Long Snapps; "folks hed better steer by facts sometimes, than by yarns. It's jest like v'yagin'; yew do'no' sumtimes what's to pay with a compass; it'll go all p'ints to once; mebbe somebody's got a hatchet near by, or some lubber's throwed a chain down by the binnacle, or some darned thing's got inside on't, or it's shipped a sea an' got rusted; but there's allers the Dipper an' the North Star; they're aller's true to their bearin's, and you can't go to Davy Jones's locker for want of a light'us so long's they're ahead. I calc'late its jes' so about this king-talk; orders is very well when they aint agin common-sense an' the rights o' natur'; but you see, George Tucker, folks will go 'cordin' to natur' an' reason, ef there's forty parliments an' kings in tow. Natur's jest like a no'west squall; you can't do nothin' but tack ag'inst it; and no men is goin' to stan' still and see the wind taken out o' their sails, an' their liberty flung to sharks, without one mutiny to know why!"

"No!" burst out Sally, who had stopped flirting, and been listening with soul and body to Long; "and no man, that *is* a man, will go against the right and the truth just because the wrong is strongest!"

This little feminine insult was too much for George Tucker, particularly as he had not the least idea how its utterance burned Sally's lips, and made her heart ache. He got up from his chair with a very bitter look on his handsome face.

"I see," said he, quite coldly, "I am likely to be scarce welcome here. I believe the king is my master, made so by the Lord, and I think it is my honest duty to obey him. It hurts me to part otherwise than kind with friends; but I wish you a good night, and better judgment."

There was something so manly in George's speech, that, but for its final fling and personality, every man in the room would have crowded round him to shake hands; but what man ever coolly heard his judgment impeached?

Sally swallowed a great round sob; but being, like all women, an actress in her way, bowed as calmly to Mr. George as if he only said adieu after an ordinary call.

Aunt Poll snuffled, and followed George to the door; Uncle 'Zekiel drew himself up straight, and looked after him, his clear blue eyes sparkling with two rays,— one of honest, patriotic wrath, one of affection and regret for George; while Long, from the corner, eyed all with a serpent's wisdom in his gaze, oracularly uttering, as the door shut: —

"Well, that are feller is good grit!"

"All the worse for us!" growled Eliashib Sparks, the biggest of the three, surprising Sally into a little hysterical laugh, and surprised himself still more at this unexpected sequence to his remark.

"Pooty bad! George is a clever fellow!" ejaculated 'Zekiel. "He haint got the rights on't, but I think he'll come round by'n'by."

"I do'no'," said Long, meditatively; "he's pooty stiff, that are fellow. He's sot on dooty, I see; an' that means suthin' when a man that oughter be called a man sez it. Wimmin-folks, now, don't sail on that tack. When a gal sets to talkin' about her dooty it's allers suthin' she wants ter do and haint got no grand excuse for't. Ye never see a woman't didn't get married for dooty yet; there aint nary one on 'em darst to say they wanted ter."

"O Mister Long!" exclaimed Sally.

"Well, Sally, it's nigh about so; you haint lived a

hunderd year. Some o' these days you'll get to know yer dooty."

Sally turned red, and the three young men sniggered. Forgive the word, gentle and fair readers!—it means what I mean, and no other word expresses it; let us be graphic and die!

Just then the meeting-house bell rang for nine o'clock; and every man got up from his seat, like a son of Anak, bowed, scraped, cleared his throat to say "Good-night," did say something like it, and left.

"Well, Sally, I swear you're good at signallin'," broke out Long, as soon as the youths were fairly out of sight and sound; "you hev done it for George Tucker!"

Sally gave no answer, but a brand from the back-log fell, blazed up in a shaft of rosy flame, and showed a suspicious glitter on the girl's round, wholesome cheek.

Aunt Poll had gone to bed; 'Zekiel was going the nightly rounds of his barns, to see to the stock; Long Snapps was aware of opportunity,—the secret of success.

"Sally," said he, "is that feller sparkin' you?"

Sally laughed a little, and something, perhaps the blaze, reddened her face.

"I don't know," said the pretty hypocrite, demurely.

"H'm! well, I do," answered Long; "and you aint never goin' to take up with a tory?—don't think it's yer dooty, hey?"

"No, indeed!" flashed Sally. "Do you think I'd marry a Britisher? I'd run away and live with the Indians first."

"Pooty good! pooty good! you're calc'lating to make George into a rebel, I 'xpect!"

Long was looking into the fire when he said this; he did not see Sally's look of rage and amazement at his unpleasant penetration.

"I'm sure I don't care what George Tucker thinks," said she, with a toss of her curly head.

"H'm!" uttered Long, meditatively, "lucky! I 'xpect he carries too many guns to be steered by a woman; 'tis a kinder pity you aint a man, Sally; mebbe you'd argufy him round then; it's plain as the gulf you can't crook his v'yage; he's too stiff for wimmin folks, that's a fact!"

O Long Snapps! Long Snapps! how many wives, in how many ports, went to the knowledge of feminine nature that dictated that speech? Sally set her lips. From that hour George Tucker was a doomed man; but she said nothing more audible than "Good-night." Long looked at her, as she lit the tallow dip by the fire, and chuckled when he heard her shut the milk-room door in the safe distance. He was satisfied.

The next afternoon Sally was weeding onions in the garden, — heroines did, in those days, — the currant-bushes had just leafed out; so George Tucker, going by, saw her; and she, who had seen him coming before she began to weed, accidentally of course, looked up and gave him a very bright smile. That was the first spider-thread, and the fly stepped into it with such a thrill!

Of course he stopped, and said : —

"What a pleasant day!" — the saving phrase of life. Then Sally said something he couldn't hear, and he leaped the low fence without being asked, rather than request her to raise her voice; he was so considerate. Next he remembered, just as he turned to go away, that there were some white violets down in the meadow, that Sally always liked. Couldn't she spend time to walk down there across lots and get some? Sally thought the onions could not be left. Truth to tell, her heart was in her mouth. She had been playing with edge-tools; but just then she smelt a whiff of smoke from Long Snapp's pipe, and the resolve of last night came back: her face relented, and George, seeing it, used his utmost persuasiveness; so the result was, that Sally washed her hands at the well, and away they went, in the most serene silence, over fences, grass-lots, and ditches, through bits of woodland and by fields of winter-rye, till they reached the edge of the great meadow, and sat down on a log to rest. It was rather a good place for that purpose. An old pine had fallen at the feet of a majestic cluster of its brethren, so close that the broad column of one made a natural back to part of the seat. The ground was warm, dry sand, strewn with the fine dead leaves of past seasons, brown and aromatic. A light south wind woke the voices of every bough above, and the melancholy susurrus rose and fell in delicate cadences; while beyond the green meadow, Westbury river, a good-sized brook, babbled and danced as if there were no pine-tree laments in the world.

I believe the air, and the odor, and the crying wind drove the violets quite out of both the two heads that drooped silently over that pine log. If Sally had been nervous or poetical she would have been glad to recollect them; but no such morbidness invaded her healthy soul. She sat quite still till George said, in a suppressed and rather broken tone: —

"I was sorry to vex you last night, Sally; I could not be sorry for anything else."

"You did grieve me very much, Mister George," said Sally, affecting a little distance in her address, but sufficiently tender in manner.

"Well, I suppose you don't see it the way I do," returned George; "and I am very sorry, for I had rather please you than anybody else."

This was especially tender, and he possessed himself of Sally's little red hand, unaware or careless that it smelt of onions; but it was withdrawn very decidedly.

"I think you take a strange way of showing your liking!" sniffed the damsel.

George sat astounded. Another tiny spider-thread stopped the fly; a subtle ray of blue sped sideways out of Sally's eye, that meant "I don't object to be liked."

"I wish with all my heart I knew any good way to please you," he fervently ejaculated.

"*I* should think any way to please people was a good way," retorted Sally, saying more with her eyes than with her voice, — so much more, that in fact this fly was fast. A little puff of wind blew off Sally's bonnet; she looked shy, flushed, lovely. George stood up on his feet, and took his hat off.

"Sally," said he, in the deepest notes of his full, manly voice, "I love you very much indeed! Will you be my wife?"

Sally was confounded. I rejoice to say she was quite confounded; but she was made of revolutionary stuff, and what just now interfered with her plans and schemes was the sudden discovery how very much indeed she loved George Tucker, — a fact she had not left enough margin for in her plot.

But, as I said, she was made of good metal, and she answered very low:—

"I do like you, George; but I never will marry a Britisher and a tory."

A spasm of real anguish distorted the handsome face, bent forward to listen.

"Do you mean that, Sally? Can't you love me because we don't think alike?"

Sally choked a little; her tones fell to a whisper. George had to sit down close to her to hear.

"I didn't say I didn't love you, George." A blissful pause of a second; then, in a clear, cold voice, "But my mind's set. I can't marry a Britisher and a tory, if I died sayin' so."

George gasped.

"And I cannot turn traitor and rebel, Sally. I cannot. I love you better than anything in the world; but I can't do a wicked thing; no, not even for you."

He was pale as death. Sally's secret heart felt proud of him, and never had she been so near repenting of her work in the good cause before; but she was resolute.

"Very well," replied she, coolly; "if you prefer the king to me it's not my fault. When your side beats you can take your revenge!"

The thorough injustice of this speech roused her lover's generous indignation.

"If you can think that way of me, Sally, it is better for us both to have me go! Good night!" And away strode the loyal fellow, never looking back to see his sweetheart have a good cry on the pine log, and then an equally comfortable fit of laughter; for she knew very well how restless Mister George would be, all alone by himself, and how much it meant that they both loved each other, and both knew it.

Sally's heart was stout. A sort of Yankee Evangeline, she would not have gone after Gabriel; she would have stayed at home and waited for him to the end of time; doing chores and mending meanwhile, but unmarried, in the fixed intention of being her lover's sixth wife possibly, but his wife at last.

So she went home and got supper, strained and skimmed milk, set a sponge for bread, and slept all night like a dormouse. George Tucker never went to bed.

"Hooraw!" roared Long Snapps, trundling in to dinner, the next day; "they're wakin' up down to Bostin! Good many on 'em's quit the town. Them are Britishers is a-gettin' up sech a breeze; an' they doo say the reg'lars is comin' out full sail, to cair' off all the amminition in these parts, fear 'o mutiny 'mongst the milishy!"

"Come along!" shouted 'Zekiel, "let 'em come! like to see 'em takin' our powder an' shot 'thout askin'! Guess they'll hear thunder, ef they stick their heads inter a hornet's nest."

"Dredful suz!" exclaimed Aunt Poll, pulling turnips out of the pot with reckless haste, and so scalding her brown fingers emphatically; "be they a-comin' here? Will they fetch along the batterin'-rams?"

"Thunder *an'* dry trees," ejaculated 'Zekiel, "what does the woman";—but at that instant Long made for the door, and flung it open, thereby preventing explanations.

"Goin' to Concord, George?" shouted he to George Tucker, who, in a one-horse wagon and his Sunday-best clothes, was driving slowly past.

"No; goin' to Lexington, after corn. Can I do anything for you?"

"Well, no, I 'xpect not. When be you a-comin' back?"

"I don't know."

"Well, go 'long; good-luck to ye! Keep to wind'ard o' squalls, George."

Long nodded, and George drove on. That day the whole village of Westbury was in an uproar. News had come from Boston that the British were about to send out forces to possess themselves of all the military stores in the country, and forestall rebellion by rendering it helpless. From every corner of every farm and village young men and old mustered; from every barn horses of all sizes and descriptions were driven out and saddled; rusty muskets, balls of all shapes and of any available metal that would melt and run, disabled broad-swords, horse-pistols, blunderbusses, whatever wore any resemblance to a weapon, or could be rendered serviceable to that end, — all were hunted out, cleaned, mended, and laid ready; an array that might have made a properly drilled and equipped army smile in contempt, but whose deficiencies were more than supplied by iron sinews, true blood, resolve, and desperate courage.

Sally and Aunt Poll partook the gale of patriotism. They scoured the "ole queen's arm" to brilliancy; they ran bullets by the hour; baked bread and brewed spring beer, with no more definite purpose than a general conviction that men must and would eat, as the men of their house certainly did, in the intervals of repairing harness, filling powder-horns and shot-belts, trotting over to the tavern after news, and coming back to retail it, till Aunt Poll began to imagine she heard the distant strokes of a battering-ram, and, rushing out in terror to assure herself, discovered it to be only Sam Pequot, an old Indian, who, with the apathy of his race, was threshing in the barn.

Aunt Poll took down Josephus to refresh her memory, and actually drew a laugh from Sally's grave lips by confiding to her this extreme horror of the case; a laugh she forgave, since Sally reassured her by recommending to her notice the fact that Jerusalem had stone walls that were more difficult to climb than stone fences. As for Sally, she thought of George all day, — of George, all night; and while the next day deepened toward noon was still thinking of him, when in rushed Long Snapps, tarpaulin in hand, full of news and horror.

"I swan! we've got it now!" said he. "Them darned Britishers sot out fur Concord last night, to board our decks an' plunder the magazine; the boys heerd on't, and they was ready over to Lexin'ton, waitin' round the meetin'us; they stood to't, an' that old powder-monkey Pitcairn sung out to throw down their arms, darned rebels; an' 'cause they didn't muster to his whistle he let fly at 'em like split; an' there's some killed an' more wounded; pretty much all on 'em our folks, though they did giv the reg'lars one round o' ball afore they run."

"Hooray!" shouted 'Zekiel; "that's the talk; guess they'll sing smaller next time!"

"They'll do more'n that, Zekle," responded Long; "this aint but the beginnin' o' sorrers, as Parson Marsh sez, sez he; there'll be a hull gulf stream o' blood afore them darned reg'lars knows the color on't well enough to lay their course."

Sally glided past Long, and plucked him by the sleeve, unseen by the rest. He followed her into the shed. She was ghastly pale. "Long," said she, hurriedly, "did you hear who? Was anybody shot?"

"Bless ye, gal! a hull school on 'em was shot; there wasn't many went to the bottom, though; haint heerd no names."

"But George?" gasped Sally, — "he went to Lexington yesterday."

"Well, I am took aback!" growled Long. "I swear I never thought on't. I'll go see."

"Come back and tell me," whispered Sally.

"Lord-a-massy, yes, child! — jest as soon's I know myself trewly; but I shan't know nothin' more till sundown, I 'xpect. Desire Trowbridge is a-ridin' post; he'll come through 'bout that time with news."

Long did not come back for several hours, some time after sundown, when he found Sally in the shed, waiting for him. She saw the news in his face. "Dead!" said she, clutching at the old sailor's hand.

"No! no! he aint slipt his moorin's yet, but he is badly stove about the figger-head; he's got a ball through his head somewhere, an' another in his leg; and he aint within hail; don't hear no speakin'-trumpets; fact is, Sally, he's in for the dock-yard a good spell, ef he aint broke up, hull and all."

"Who shot him?" whispered Sally.

"That's the best on't, gal; he's took an' tacked beautiful; he went into port at Lexin'ton yesterday, and hecrin' there all sides o' the story, an' thet them critters sot up for to thieve away our stores, he got kinder riled at the hull crew like a common-sense feller, an' when Pitcairn come along George finally struck his colors, run up a new un to the masthead, borrered a musket, an' jined the milishy, an' got shot by them cussed reg'lars fur his pains; an ef he doos die I'll hev a figger cut on a stun myself, to tell folks he was a rebel and an honest man, arter all."

"Where is he?" asked Sally, in another whisper.

"He's.to the tavern there in Lexin'ton. There aint nobody along with him, 'cause his father's gone to Bostin to see 'bout not gettin' scomfishkated, or arter a protection, or sumthin'."

"And his mother is dead," said Sally, slowly. "Long! I must go to Lexington to-night, on the pillion, and you must go with me. Father's got too much rheumatiz to ask it of him."

"Well!" said Long, after a protracted stare at Sally,—"wimmin is the oddest craft that ever sailed. I swan, when I sight 'em I don't know a main-top-sail from a flyin' jib! Goin' to take care o' George, be ye?"

"Yes," said Sally, meekly.

Long rolled the inseparable quid in his cheek, and slyly drawled out, "W–ell, if ye must, ye must! I aint a-goin' ter stand in the way of yer dooty!"

Sally was too far away to hear, or she might have smiled.

Uncle Zeke and Aunt Poll were to be told and coaxed into assent,—no very hard task; for George Tucker was a favorite of 'Zekiel's, and now he had turned rebel, the only grudge he had ever owed him was removed; he was only too glad to help him in any way. Aunt Poll's sole trouble was lest Sally should take cold. The proprieties, those gods of modern social worship, as well as their progenitors, the improprieties, were unknown to these simple souls; they did things because they were right and wrong. They were not nice, according to Swift's definition, nor proper in the mode of the best society, but they were good and pure; are the disciples and lecturers of the "proper" equally so?

Sally's simple preparations were quickly made. By nine o'clock she was safe on the pillion behind Long Snapps, folded in Aunt Poll's red joseph, and provided with saddle-bags full of comforts and necessaries. The night was dark, but Sally did not feel any fear; not Tam O'Shanter's experience could have shaken the honest little creature's courage, when George filled the perspective before her. The way was lonely; the hard road echoed under the old cart-horse's hoofs; many a black and desolate tract of forest lay across their twenty miles' ride; more than once the tremulous shriek of a screech-owl smote ominous on Sally's wakeful sense, and quavered away like a dying groan; more than once a mournful whip-poor-will cried out in pain and expostulation, and in the young leaves a shivering wind foreboded evil; but they rode on. Presently Sally's drooping head rose erect; she listened; she laid her hand on the bridle. "Stop, Long!" said she. "I hear horses' feet, and shouts."

"Look here!" said Long, after a moment's listening, "there's breakers ahead, Sally; let's heave to in these 'ere piny bushes side o' the track; it's pitch-dark, mebbe they'll go by."

He reined the horse from the road, and forced him into a group of young hemlocks, which hid them entirely from passers-by. Just as he was well ensconced, a company of British cavalry rode up, broken and disorderly enough, cursing and swearing at the Yankees, and telling to unseen ears a bloody story of Concord and its men. Sally trembled, but it was with indignation, not fear, and as soon as the last hoof-beat died away she urged Long forward; they regained the road, and made their way at once to George in Lexington.

Is it well to paint, even in failing words, such emotions as Sally fought with and conquered in that hour? Whoever has stood by the bed of a speechless, hopeless, unconscious human being, in whom their own soul lived and suffered, will know these pangs without my interpretation. Whoever knows them not need not so anticipate. If Sally had been less a woman I might have had more to say; but she was only a woman, and loved George, so she went on in undisturbed self-control and untiring exertion to nurse him.

The doctor said he could not live; Long said he was booked for Davy Jones; the minister prayed for " our dying brother; " — but Sally said he should live, and he did. After weeks of patient care he knew her; after more weeks he spoke, — words few, but precious; and when accumulating months brought to the battle-fields of America redder stains than even patriotic blood had splashed upon their leaves; when one nation began to hope, and another to fear, both hope and fear had shaken hands with Sally and said good-by. She was married to George Tucker, and with the prospect of a crippled husband for life was perfectly happy; too happy not to laugh, when, the day after their wedding, sitting on the door-sill of the old Westbury homestead, with George and Long Snapps,

George said, "Would you ever have come to take care of me, Sally, if I'd 'a' been shot on the side of the reg'lars?"

Sally looked at him, and then looked away.

"I 'xpect she'd 'a' done her dooty," said Long Snapps dryly; and Sally laughed.

A HARD LESSON.

"Is he worse, doctor?"

"No, madam, no. I cannot say he is worse."

"But he is no better?"

"Madam Fontaine, the secrets of the profession — h'm — I'm an old fellow as you know, but damme! I might as well be honest for once, — I must own I am at my wit's end about the judge."

"Dr. Lèvis!"

A shocked exclamation, that did not seem to pain the doctor, — a fat, flabby, elderly man, yellow as an orange with malaria, whiskey, and tobacco: a trio that had taken full possession of him for many a year, yet had not altogether quenched the keen ray of his deep-set eye, and could not change the contour of his head and face, or do more than degrade and darken the evident intellect they expressed.

Mrs. Fontaine was a slight, delicate woman, with soft, dark eye, languid lips, abundant black hair, small feet and hands, a typical Southern woman, a tender mother and a devoted wife, full of the inborn conviction that the black race were made for slavery, and the white for masters. Judge Fontaine, her husband, was judge by courtesy; he had studied law and been admitted to the bar of Louisiana; but he put a definite end to his legal usefulness by marrying Marie Le

Baron, an orphan girl, and an heiress. Soon after this marriage his father died, and left him master of another great plantation beside Le Rivage, — the inheritance of his wife.

But they did not live at Le Rivage, — it was not a wholesome place for white people; all the Le Barons had died young, saturated with malaria from the swamps that lay all about the great fields of cotton and cane from which they coined their dollars. Marie had been educated from her childhood in a New Orleans convent, and on her first entrance into society had met Louis Fontaine, and married him from her aunt's house there; for Le Rivage was uninhabited except by the overseer. Marie's father, mother, brothers and sisters lay on the tiny enclosure on the only bit of rising ground in the plantation, and she expected to live out her life in the city, when Colonel Fontaine died, and Louis took possession of Rosières, — his inheritance. Rosières was a vast and productive estate, and lonely as only a home can be set miles away from any other human habitation. It was higher than the Le Barons' estate, and its crops were of upland cotton; the heavy woods that hemmed in those rolling acres did not hide altogether the distant river that half circled Le Rivage, and took away the sense of solitude by its ever-varied, never-ending procession of smoke-wreathing steamers. Rosières was far away from the nearest village, — miles lay between its centre and the homes on other plantations; hospitalities passed between them at rare intervals, and the men found in their hunting and fishing the sole amusement of their lives, and their only labor in the ordering of their estates, the buying and selling of slaves, the shipping of cotton, and the semi-annual visits to New Orleans for purposes of traffic and pleasure; while the women had the children to rear, their irresponsible house-slaves to scold, and the ignoble army of the quarters to clothe, feed, and aid as far as they might when sickness and death entered the lowly hut as inevitably as the lordly mansion. Schools there were none; every house had its governess or tutor; and Dr. Lèvis, the only physician within reach, had a plantation of his own, and practised his profession rather as an occupation than a necessity. His patients were his friends; for the slaves preferred their own healers to this rough, contemptuous master, who treated them as he would not treat his superb horses or his thorough-bred dogs.

To-day Dr. Lèvis was puzzled. He had an acute brain, some perception, much common-sense, and such knowledge added to his course of study in a celebrated northern college as thirty odd years of experience gave him. He was a fair, old-fashioned physician, but none of the remedies and experiments of modern times were at his command. He took no medical journals, for he considered that he knew by heart all the range of diseases that prevailed in the neighborhood; he had even had yellow-fever himself, and believed it perfectly manageable; while the various forms of malaria were to him an old story. He knew just where a *tisane* of bitter sour-orange was of use, and where a small dose of quinine was good for nothing; but for a case not in his books or his experience he had nothing to do but to confront his ignorance and own it.

He had to do this now. Judge Fontaine had been in a languid, irritable, feeble condition for weeks; quinine did not seem to bring him up except for the hour; food was disgusting to him; he could not swallow stimulants, and a heavy depression, impossible to throw off, settled down upon him like a pall. He was drowsy or fretful most of the time, and nothing Dr. Lèvis did seemed to be of any use.

He turned and looked sharply at Mrs. Fontaine as she said, " Dr. Lèvis!" in that pained, frightened voice.

"Yes, madam! Doctor as I am, I don't know what to do for Fontaine any more than you do!"

"Did Louis show you his left arm this morning?"

"His arm! No. He was so glad to get rid of me, or, I should say, so infernally snappish at seeing me, that I made a short visit, I can tell you. What's to do about his arm?"

"Why, there's a black spot on it as big as my nail; and there's one on his forehead, too, since yesterday."

"H'm!" Dr. Lèvis knitted his gray brows, and set his loose, thick lips hard together. "How long since the spot came on his arm?"

"Stephen found it last night when he bathed him."

"I'll go back and inspect," said the doctor; and Mrs. Fontaine followed him into the sick man's chamber.

A cool, airy room it was; scrupulously neat, with all the air that stirred that warm spring day blowing across it from the half-turned Venetian blinds on either side. Judge Fontaine was stretched on a light framework of bamboo and cane near the northern window, with only a sheet thrown over his stalwart figure. He was a handsome man in health, with black hair, tolerably fair complexion, and dark, long eyes; now he was pale, thin, and a sort of feverish brightness lit his usually calm countenance; he was impatient of his illness, and turned his head, as the door gently opened, with a vexed look.

"Here again, Fontaine! Bad penny, you know. But I want to inspect you once more, for I've got to go down to the city to-morrow, and maybe I can counsel there with my brothers, if I take a thorough account of your symptoms along."

"You might go or stay, Lèvis, for my care. I don't get better with all your doses, and I never shall."

"Fudge!" growled the doctor. "I believe you're a d—d humbug, Louis. Let me look at you with my spectacles. Steve, open the blind!"

Stephen, Judge Fontaine's body-servant, stepped forward, unfastened the catch, and gently swung the blind backward. He was a tall, well-made mulatto, like enough in every feature to have passed for his master's brother, except for the deep olive of his skin. And why not?— for he *was* Judge Fontaine's brother; only Louis was the son of the free woman and Stephen of the slave!

As the warm light streamed in on the sick man's face he shut his eyes, unused to even the tempered glare of day, and Dr. Lèvis saw on his temple a dark spot like a mole, that certainly was not there two days before. It was not a mole, though, for not even the slightest roughness, or rising, indicated any such thing; it was merely a dark spot, as if the juice of some fruit, or the stain of a drug, had touched it.

Dr. Lèvis turned back the shirt-sleeve on the sick man's left arm a little way, as if the better to feel his pulse, and there on the wrist, or rather just above the articulation of the wrist, on the inside of the arm, another dark spot showed against the unsunned skin more blackly than on the temple.

For a moment Dr. Lèvis was startled. Could it be the black flag of mortification? But the steady pulse forbade such a diagnosis; there was no other symptom to further the idea. Some chronic derangement of the liver Judge Fontaine had long suffered from at intervals; now there were symptoms also of digestive trouble, but nothing that could or would induce gangrene, — nothing that, to the doctor's eye, meant vital mischief. He fell back on the last resort of all physicians, — change of place and air.

"Look here, old fellow," he said, putting on a hilarious air, as Stephen closed the blinds again, — "what you want is a course of Saratoga water. Take Steve and the madam, and start off Monday for Congress Hall."

"I can't do it, Lèvis! You know I can't."

"Fudge! Don't tell me. By George! you shall go, if I have to carry you to the boat. Half that ails you is hypo. Get up your will, man! The moment you're out of this slew you'll begin to pick up."

Judge Fontaine laughed feebly. To him the "slew" of this dreadful depression and irritation seemed the very valley of death, and it tickled his sense of humor that hearty, jolly old Lèvis, standing hale and heartsome in the sunshine, should tell him to take up his bed and walk, with divine prerogative.

"Since when did you go into miracle-working?" he asked, looking up at the doctor with an odd twist of his pale lips.

"Get up, I say; don't talk blasted nonsense! You can, if you've a mind to. If I stuck a lighted fagot under the veranda you'd run like a lapwing in five minutes; you want excitement, push, — not a cool lounge and unlimited lemonade or orange-juice."

Judge Fontaine's eye kindled; much as he liked Dr. Lèvis he did not like to be bullied in this fashion. He rose on one elbow, and a certain warmth that was not color lit his sallow cheek.

"I wish I could fight you, Lèvis! One would think I was your red setter, to hear you order me about."

"Good!" laughed the doctor. "Got your blood up a little. Gad, man! I'd fight you with a good will if you could stand up long enough; 'twould stir you up roundly, better than Saratoga. But, seriously, Louis, I am at the end of my track with you. I can't put my finger on the mischief. I'm old, and not up to modern sciences. You *must* go North, and see an abler man than old Hubert Lèvis. If you stay here you'll just sink; the heats are coming on; May will be here in a fortnight, and I want you to get to New York by the first of the month. Set off to-morrow; don't wait to think."

Judge Fontaine sunk back wearily on to his pillows.

"I don't care a picayune, Lèvis, whether I get well or not."

"D—it!" roared the doctor, in a most unseemly passion. "Haven't you got a wife and children to think of?"

Mrs. Fontaine burst into a flood of tears; she was not well, and she was worn out with anxiety.

"O Marie! don't cry, child!" sighed her husband. "Don't·mind my petulance, dear! I was just weary enough to feel like dying that minute, Lèvis has badgered me so; but you know I don't want to leave you and the babies."

Mrs. Fontaine choked her sobs, and kissed her husband's cold forehead, while the doctor paced up and down, growling under his breath all the anger he felt. He had small patience with what he called "fudge,"— his favorite term for anything that seemed to him pretence or feebleness of will.

Judge Fontaine looked tenderly at his wife's pale face and tear-filled eyes; he was not more selfish than other men are by nature, and Marie was a part of himself; he would try to live for her sake, and for the sturdy boy of five, and the twin girls of two, who were laughing and prattling under the great catalpa tree, that dropped its spotted bells on the pavement of the court-yard, and sent its odorous breath into his chamber.

"I'll try, doctor," he said, with an evident effort.

"Good! Man can't do more. Mammy is safe to take care of the youngsters; or I'll carry them off to Lone Palm, if you like, while madam is away."

"Doctor, I can't go; you forget," said Mrs. Fontaine, in a half whisper, a wave of faint color rising to the edges of her shining hair.

"So you can't! I'm an old fool. Well, Fontaine will have the less care, and Steve will watch over him like a brother!"

A flash in Stephen's eye, as he stooped to pick up his master's handkerchief, might have warned Dr. Lèvis that he had forgotten again, had he seen it; but he saw nothing except a change in the judge's face, a look he liked to see there, for the far-off expression of the eye was gone; it seemed to have recalled sight to the things at hand, to have taken a new outlook on life, to be once more a vital spark, not a fading glimmer.

So the next day Judge Fontaine and Stephen, in the easiest of carriages, with every appliance to be procured in that lonely region, began their journey to the nearest landing-place on the river, leaving a pale, but tearless, woman on the veranda looking after them with sorrowful longing, and three wondering children, who could not understand why papa should go away and mamma cry. It was a tedious journey to Judge Fontaine, and when he reached New York he was quite exhausted; but the physicians there seemed to be as much at fault as Dr. Lèvis. None of them noticed the dark spots on his forehead and arm, and Stephen did not know that the old doctor had ever observed them. One man, whose specialty was disease of the liver, immediately pronounced him "Bilious, nothing more." Another, who had studied affections of the heart, laid his condition at the door of that long-suffering organ; and each one he consulted fixed his malady on some part of his organization that the last diagnosis had omitted; but in one thing all agreed: change of air and cheerful society must be tried at once. It was a late season and too cold for Saratoga, so Judge Fontaine went to Newport for a month, and, in pleasant lodgings in that quaint old town, fancied that the pure sea-breeze revived him.

So it did, a little; but as he grew somewhat better Stephen noticed that the black spots spread; another showed on one cheek just under the eye, and on one leg a patch appeared as large as a child's palm.

"It is nothing mortal," said the little Quaker physician whom he had called in, — a quaint, considerate, old man, with almost a life's experience of diseases and their treatment. "Thee can call them moth-patches if thee likes, friend Fontaine; it is a disorder of the true skin, or rather of the pigment therein; we regard it as a rather obscure ailment, probably connected with the liver. A thorough course of Congress water, fresh from the spring, will probably prove beneficial to thee."

So early in June the judge established himself in a private boarding-house in Saratoga. He grew more languid and depressed here; the sick people who filled the house were not altogether a cheerful crowd. To sit down at table thrice a day with exemplifications of paralysis, brain-softening, spinal distortion, jaundice, and other evils too numerous to mention, is not calculated to raise the spirits of a well man; and the increasing size of the dark spot on the judge's face began to annoy him: he thought that all eyes were fixed upon it; that he was a marked man, in a most obnoxious sense. He had always been conscious, to say the least, of his handsome face and figure; but now he shunned a mirror as if it were a poisonous reptile, and only Stephen knew that the spot on his leg was fast covering it, and that the other ankle was blackening too, while the blotch on the temple spread daily.

Saratoga is a very stupid place to people who do not care for fashion, show, or horse-racing. There is but one pleasant drive near it, and walking is dreary and difficult in the sand-barrens or yellow-pine groves on its outskirts. June was not well over before Judge Fontaine was as weary of it all as Mariana of the Moated Grange; and he and Stephen set off for the mountains of Vermont, finding a resting-place on a lonely, but lovely, mountain side, where some enterprising Yankee had built a tavern and now took summer boarders. There the judge grew stronger; but the plague-spot spread more and more rapidly. To be brief, by the time September set in, the blackness on his temple had invaded his face, his arms, his hands, his legs and feet, and a part of his body. Louis Fontaine was a negro to every eye but his own; and, at last, an overheard conversation between two of the hotel servants opened his eyes to his condition.

Words are very weak sometimes; never weaker than in the attempt to express the darkest and most evil experiences of man; the inward hurricane and tempest of rage, despair, and agony, that sometimes ravage and lay waste the soul which is helpless to avoid or avert an overwhelming calamity. There was but one thing left to Louis Fontaine, that which is left to the mortally smitten wild beast, and is the instinctive action of man; he must go home and hide himself. But to Stephen, a slave, a man with more than half white blood, running its subtle currents under his dark skin, here was an opportunity.

The Fontaines had been fairly kind to their slaves, not sparing of castigation, to be sure, — a little more than ordinary parental discipline demands. Stephen's mother was the daughter of Louis Fontaine's uncle, and General Fontaine's favorite slave.

Favorite! What depths of degradation that same word means from a master to a slave! Her daughter, an exquisitely beautiful quadroon, had held the same relation to Louis Fontaine's father, and, being found in the house by Colonel Fontaine's bride, — a French creole heiress from New Orleans, — had been, by several instalments, to save appearances, whipped to death by Anastasie Fontaine's orders, and her baby given to an old woman in the slave-quarters to "raise."

Stephen, the grandson of Louis Fontaine's uncle, and his father's son, had double portions of the fiery Fontaine blood in his veins, and yet he had not escaped the lash or forgotten the story of his mother's death. For years he had been madly athirst for freedom; but the Caucasian subtlety he inherited taught him to conceal his wishes and intent till the time should come. It had come now.

Judge Fontaine had regained his physical health almost entirely, and when he set out for home he had money enough to take him and his servant to Rosières, and some to spare for emergencies. Stephen possessed himself of half the gold in his master's trunk, and half the judge's wardrobe.

What did he know about the rights of property? He had never even owned himself!

At the station where he should have taken the train southward two trains met, — one for New York, one for Canada. Stephen dutifully checked his master's baggage, bought his ticket, and as the northern train slipped on to a siding for the other to pass, the son of the bondwoman, valise in hand, with his master's stiff hat on his fine head, and his master's coat on his back, stepped into the Canada train, — a well-behaved, good-looking, rather dark-complexioned gentleman, who sat down in that first-class car a slave, and emerged from it, five hours later, a free man on Canadian soil.

For, dear reader, this was *ante-bellum*.

Judge Fontaine, quite forgetful of his own aspect for the moment, and supposing Stephen, as usual, was in another car, entered that at whose door his valet had left him, and proceeded to a seat.

"You can't sit here!" bawled the conductor, a little way from the door; but Mr. Fontaine did not at all understand that the remark was intended for him. The conductor came forward just as the judge seated himself by the window. "Say! You can't sit here, I tell ye. Come along to the back car," the peremptory official said.

"What do you mean, sir?" retorted the angry planter.

"Mean! I mean niggers aint allowed on this car."

"Good God, sir!" roared the judge, "do you mean to insult me? Me!—Judge Fontaine, of Louisiana."

A general laugh echoed the statement.

"Put him out, conductor!" said the nearest man, and "Put him out!" was reëchoed all about.

"Come along," said the sturdy conductor, "or I'll hev to fetch ye."

And promptly the irate judge knocked him down.

This was too much. Ready hands caught the aggressor's arms, set the conductor on his feet, and Judge Fontaine, of Louisiana, was ignominiously hustled into a baggage-car, locked in, and left to digest his wrath.

He roared and swore, and planned vengeance on his captors, but wondered where was Stephen. At the end of the route he must find him, and prove to the officials his status as a gentleman.

Before that came, however, the conductor of the train left at a station, and when the cars were again moving another one unlocked the door and came in.

"Look here!" he said quietly to Mr. Fontaine; "the conductor of t'other half told me to look after you.

What's the matter't you blew out so, my man? Haven't you never travelled before? Don't you know colored folks aint allowed in first-class cars?"

"Good God, man! do you take me for a black boy?" burst out the unfortunate judge.

"I don't know what else you be, to look at you," said the cool Yankee.

"I tell you I'm Judge Fontaine, of Louisiana; I'm a white man. This dreadful color of my skin is a disease."

"Oh, come now," said the conductor, "that's rather too steep; don't tell yarns that are too big to swaller, friend. Sam was goin' to have you up for knockin' him over, but he thought better on't; he couldn't afford to be off for lawin' of it, and I'm tryin' to deal reasonable with you. Don't try to stuff me."

"But my servant is on board somewhere; he'll swear to my identity. Find him, for God's sake! — he's a light mulatto, with curly brown hair and an aquiline nose. He's in the rear car."

"No, he isn't. No such feller round. You're addin' too many circumstances."

"But, look here!" said the baffled judge. "Here's my check; find the trunk and see if my name isn't on it, if that will convince you."

The conductor poked about among the baggage and came back.

"It's there; but I smell a rat, young feller! It looks to me as though you was goin' off with your master's trunk and things without his pussonal knowledge an' consent, as you may say; but you'd ought to have headed for Canady, if that is so; your ticket was bought pretty near the border."

Judge Fontaine started; a new idea struck him. But, no, it was nonsense. Stephen never would have left so good a master, so pleasant a home; he must have been confused, and taken the wrong train.

The conductor stood glaring at him with stern suspicion.

"Prove it, then, if you can," said the judge, his legal training coming to his aid.

"Well, I shan't try; if you're a poor devil tryin' to run away from them nigger-owners down South, as I mistrust you be, why, joy go with ye; I wouldn't lift a finger to hender." And the kindly conductor went his way, little guessing that the rushing wheels alone prevented his hearing the epithet Judge Fontaine hurled after him: "Damned abolitionist!"

But silence and solicitude brought counsel; in a few hours the train would reach the ferry and New York. He could go at once to the hotel where he had stayed before, and from there telegraph back to Split Rock House, — the mountain hotel he had just that morning left, — and have Stephen come after him. The conductor had left the door unlocked, and the judge had no trouble in finding his way out of the station. It was night by this time, and tying a handkerchief about the lower part of his face, and slouching his soft hat far on his forehead, he managed to secure a carriage and have his trunk brought to it. He gave the order to drive to Blank Hotel, and drew a relieved breath, sure of a place where he should be known, and could wait till his body-servant returned. Poor man! he had not yet discovered that people with black bodies could have no servants, nor yet serve themselves alone. He paid the hackman, and, following his trunk into the hotel, walked up to the desk in the office, and addressed the clerk: —

"Peters, how are you? Give me a good room, will you? The one I had before, if you can."

The dapper clerk, famous for never forgetting a countenance, turned to look at the new-comer, and his face blazed with anger.

"You can't have a room here, my man. Don't you know better than to ask for it?"

"Peters, don't you know me? Don't you remember Judge Fontaine? Why, I was here a month in May."

"Come, now, that *is* cheeky. Judge Fontaine ought to be here. You'd get your quietus and a flogging beside. Go off, fellow, or I'll call the police!"

"I tell you I *am* Judge Fontaine," angrily answered the poor planter, wrath and distress raging in his breast. "This skin is the result of a dreadful disease. I am a white man!"

"I like that!" sneered the clerk. "About as white as coal, you are. But the disease dodge is a new one. By George!" seizing the judge by the collar, and drawing him to a near gas-jet, which he turned on to its full blaze, "I've got you now. I thought I knew your features. You're Stephen, the judge's body-servant, or else his twin-brother!"

Just then his eye fell on the trunk, a foreign article of luggage, which he had noticed when Mr. Fontaine was there before.

"And there's his trunk, by Jove! Rascal, what have you done with your master?"

A pang, keener than any blade of Damascus, went through the judge's soul. Some long-past time, when he had been to church with his old grandmother in the city, himself only a youth at school, he had heard in the lesson for the day certain quaint morals about the sins of the fathers being visited on the children; and now, by some divinely-ordered palimpsest, the fearful sentence returned on him. Stephen was his brother, if he was his slave His father's sin, hitherto scarce a peccadillo in the son's judgment, stared him close in the face, and threatened vengeance. The likeness that was Stephen's right was to be his own condemnation

In a moment the clerk had a porter at his side, and between them the angry planter was shut into a small bedroom, the door locked, and the proprietor of the house summoned to a consultation. To arrest the man on suspicion of murdering his master was the clerk's first idea; but the cooler head of the landlord demurred.

They had no proof except the trunk, which he probably had stolen. It was not like a murderer to attempt to pass himself off as a white man. The story he told the clerk looked more like the figment of a disordered brain than the subterfuge of a criminal, and at last, after much conversation pro and con, the landlord resolved to see and question the man himself.

But the man was not there! Shut up by main force to await the judgment of his fellows — no, the judgment of white men on a black — Louis Fontaine perceived how hopeless was his case.

He remembered, almost against his will, by a reluctant recollection, how little reliance *he* had ever placed on the word of a slave; how protestations, prayers, cries, had vainly interceded with him for mercy when his superior intellect had once decided on guilt — even on mere disobedience. Had not Stephen himself— his brother according to the flesh—been beaten with stripes, mangled, and scarred, because he refused to take to himself a wife picked out for him by the overseer, and add other items to the sum of slavery's wrong and woe?

He began to see that "If lions could paint," works of art would depict men as sometimes victims rather than always conquerors, and that a slave might tell a different and sadder story than the master, could he only have the gift of tongue and pen.

But the practical result of these meditations as related to his own case was the immediate resolve to escape rather than await justice — white justice.

Luckily for him a painter had been at work on the outside of the house, and left his ladder hanging on an awning fixture outside the little window-balcony of Mr. Fontaine's temporary prison; this he perceived as he cautiously lifted the sash and peered about him for means of flight. His hands were strong, the street was a side street, the room he was in on the corner of a gangway shut in by an iron grating and door from the sidewalk; in a few moments he had made his way to the ground, climbed the iron fence where it was in shadow, and on the platform of a horse-car, that came by at an opportune moment, he rode as far as the belt-line went, and found himself at a pier on the North river. That night Louis Fontaine, with abundance of money about him, a man used to all luxury and elegance, to sleep soft and eat daintily, curled himself up in an empty hogshead and tried to forget his fate till day should dawn.

He did not occupy his thoughts, however, with great

questions of wrong and right; it was not in him to accept the awful lesson set him, with eager desire to learn; he was far more disturbed about the immediate future of Judge Fontaine than the whole slave population of creation, and he at last resolved to push homeward at once, leaving the dangerous trunk behind him.

He ventured out at early dawn from his tub, feeling much less philosophic than Diogenes, and at a coffee-stall kept by a fat old negress made a rude, but palatable, breakfast, and set out for his home. It would take a volume to relate what a week of torture he passed before he could reach the great river: scorned, flouted, sworn at for a " damned nigger," treated to even viler and severer pellets of profanity, relegated to dirty emigrant cars, forced to sleep in the unclean attics of hotels, where he had to eat with the black servants, if there were any, or have food served to him in wash-house or shed, as a dog might be served, if none of the obnoxious color were at hand to befriend him; ordered here and there by " high-toned " gentlemen, of the sort whose boon-companion he once had been, the poor wretch suffered agonies of humiliation and rage.

At last he reached St. Louis, and took a deck passage — all he could take — on one of the splendid steamers where he had been used to the airest stateroom and the best seat at table. Now he carried his food in a great basket, for he must provide for the rest of his journey; and his cheap valise served for pillow by night and seat by day, holding as it did only a few changes of linen purchased at a shop in New York. Here, coiled up in a corner, he watched men and women whom he knew at least by sight, some of them personally, promenading on the upper deck, laughing and talking together as once he had laughed and talked with his compeers.

Now his sole notice was a rough jest from the hands of the boat, or a curse from some official thrown at the "sulky nigger," who never offered a helping hand in any strait, but kept himself in his nook, neither eating nor drinking with any of his color, nor exchanging cheery word or wholesome laughter with his kind. Gangs of slaves were driven on and driven off, but he never looked at them! What were their deprivations to his? They were born into an estate of sin and misery in a sense the divines of Westminster never knew; he had been hurled out of Paradise, his birthright, into a howling wilderness full of thorns and briers. But there was one gleam of light that led him on: he was going home, home to his wife, his children; there, in the solitude of Rosières, healing and rest awaited him. Marie, the most devoted wife and mother, a woman of women, given soul and body to him and their children, living utterly for and in them, on her he could rely to console him for these agonies of flesh and spirit; for, with all outside tortures, there came also the horrors of prophetic imagination, pictures rising before him of all the future could, must, bring; even his dreams were lurid with horrid or fantastic situations, all turning on the pivot of his discolored visage.

Weak and weary with all this, at length the boat reached that lovely landing where he and Stephen had embarked on their northern journey.

No luxurious carriage waited for him here; he had not sent for it when he wrote that he was coming; he did not want to face his slaves, to assert and vindicate to them his identity; his one thought was to reach home and Marie, to find counsel as well as comfort. He could hire neither horse nor wheeled vehicle here; there was nothing at the landing but a negro hut and a wood-yard. With a sinking heart Judge Fontaine set out for the plantation on foot. He dared not be out at night without a pass, still less dared he sleep in the malarious open air; his pride fell to its lowest depth, it seemed to him, when he was forced to ask shelter at the quarters of some plantation, and sleep beside the slaves of a friend or acquaintance. The fourth day of his pilgrimage, which was neither a penance nor an enthusiasm, but a heart-broken journey, he arrived just before sunset at Rosières. He did not enter at the front door, but stole through a young orange-grove planted close to the veranda, on which his room opened, as well as his wife's morning-room, and, sheltered by the glossy boughs, went softly up to the open window. There sat Marie, in a light dress that set off her delicate loveliness, a single pomegranate blossom flaming in her shining hair, and with one cry of relief and joy he stepped in beside her.

She rose to her feet swiftly, and looked at him with colorless lips; but her courage was high.

"What do you want here?" she asked, haughtily.

"Marie!"

The name burst from his lips like the cry of a murdered man. She moved toward the bell, but he was nearest it and stepped before her.

"Marie! Don't you know me? I am Louis."

A look of disgust and terror passed over her pale face; before he could prevent it she drew a little dog-whistle from her belt, and, at its shrill call, a great mastiff hustled itself through the door and flew at the intruder.

Fontaine lifted his hand and said, "Down, Bear!"

The great brute knew his master! He crouched, fawned, slavered on the black hand, leaped to the stalwart shoulder, and licked the black face, taught by the instinct, that had shown the wife nothing, to recognize the man he loved, and loved still, spite of color.

Judge Fontaine looked at Marie with bitter sadness. "The dog knows me, but you" —

She trembled from head to foot; every inborn prejudice of race and usage revolted at the assertion that this black was her husband; but Bear's glad recognition, the well-known voice, the peculiar growth and color of the hair, — what could she think of these? — how account for them? With burning anguish at his heart, Louis Fontaine controlled himself sternly, for he must explain before there was any interruption.

"Sit down, Marie!" he said. "Let me tell my story; I dared not write it." And, with the eloquence of a hunted slave added to the power of thought and language owed to his education, he laid before her in every wretched detail the life he had led since the unpardonable color had invaded for once the skin of a master. Her lips quivered, her eyes poured floods of tears; she overflowed with pity, but her heart fainted at his aspect.

He could only see the tears, and they fell like balm on the wounds he had bared before her; he came toward her with eager steps and opened wide his arms to embrace her. Alas! she shuddered and recoiled. She could no more help it than she could help breathing. A black her husband!

It was loathsome, unnatural, impossible. And the revolt of her whole nature was evident in face and form.

Louis Fontaine stood paralyzed; this was an abyss he had never imagined. What could be done? Where was the end? With a dreadful effort he recalled himself to sense and composure.

"Marie!" he said, coldly and curtly, "you must face the situation. I will go to my room and to bed. Tell the servants I have come home ill; let none of them come to me, but send a boy over to Lone Palm for Lèvis. Has Stephen come back?"

"Stephen! Is he not with you?" she asked, feebly.

Then he knew what had happened. Stephen had taken to himself the liberty his father and his brother denied him; and now Judge Fontaine understood why his money had seemed to melt away, for, with the lavish carelessness of his kind, he had never counted the gold he had carried always hidden about him when he travelled, and its deficiency had not troubled him since he had enough to reach home; but he wondered vaguely that so little was left. Stephen had spared him ample means to reach home, but he did not ask himself if, in a reversed situation, he would have been so considerate of Stephen. The lesson was far from learned as yet.

It was midnight before the rapid hoofs of Dr. Lèvis's horse rattled up the approach, and when Marie, pallid, sad, agitated, told him the story, and brought him into the same chamber where he last saw the judge, and confronted him with this blackened white man, curses deeper and more savage than had ever passed his rough lips before were his welcome to his friend. That useful creation of Sterne, the well-known recording angel who forgave Uncle Toby's oath, must have had a hard time with Hubert Lèvis! And yet there was not a particle of intended profanity in his words; they were the outcome of strong, indignant sympathy and emotion, and surely for this once were unrecorded against him.

A sadder conclave could scarce have been held than these three formed that night in the judge's chamber. Already mental torture, and what to him were physical privations, had hollowed Louis Fontaine's cheek and sharpened his temples. Marie's eyes were red with weeping, and her face drawn and sallow with the fearful shock, while Dr. Lèvis wore the aspect of a grimmer sphinx than ever glared over the sands of an Egyptian desert.

Yet, after all, there was but one decision to arrive at. Judge Fontaine must be kept in hiding till time and skill should be brought to bear on this calamity, and to that end a suite of rooms were set apart for him, and no one but his wife and Lèvis, through all that weary winter, allowed to see his face. He heard his children's prattle and laughter outside. He gazed at them through the half-turned blinds as a soul in purgatory might regard the cherubs of heaven; but he could not feel their soft kisses, their clinging arms, their exuberant caresses. From them — ah, worst fate! — from his wife, he was parted by an abyss neither hand nor foot might cross.

Dr. Lèvis wrote to all the physicians at home or abroad whom he knew by name or reputation, and paid fees untold for their advice; but none of their experiments availed anything. Some inscrutable change in the pigment of the true skin had taken place, and no human power could blanch it. Louis Fontaine had been relegated to the place of his slaves in a deeper fashion than he was ready to understand. But could he understand it?

His father, his grandfather, his ancestors for generations, had held and accepted slavery as the natural and needful adjunct of their lives. They were born to it, steeped in it, made by it what they were. It was not to them an accident, or a *fiat voluntas*, but a thing as matter-of-course as the air they breathed, or the earth they trod on. Not even this personal convulsion of nature opened Louis Fontaine's heart to perceive the woes and wrongs of bondage and bondsmen; he could only feel his own.

But another, mightier revolution was at hand; for, while he lay secluded in the lonely luxury of his chambers, Lincoln was elected, and war inaugurated. It was long before the news reached Rosières, but it fired Judge Fontaine's heart and soul with indignant fury. Lie there he could not and would not, nor did Marie seek to detain him. She had no longer a husband, and yet he was there. Love and loathing set her in a condition as unnatural as painful. In her heart she was glad to evade it for a time, for she knew the South must triumph!

So, as Dr. Lèvis's body-servant, Louis Fontaine joined a Louisiana regiment.

By one of those incidents we call " dramatic," as if the drama were not an inadequate expression of life, instead of its imaginative exaggeration, at the first great battle of his experience, rushing, in defiance of discipline or his position, to the front, Louis Fontaine was shot through the lungs, and the bullet that sped him came from Stephen "Fontaine's" rifle. For Stephen, too, had risen at the call of his brethren, and Cain met Cain on the red field of war!

Yet it was Stephen who picked up Louis from the ground where he fell, and carried him to the surgeon's tent.

The doctor shook his head as he lifted it from the examination. "No hope; but he deserved it for fighting against his race," he said.

"He is a white man, doctor," answered Stephen, sadly; "born white, blackened by what you doctors call disease, and I call God. He was put into our place to see what was the curse of the slave; but, after all, you see that he did not learn it."

"My brother," said the grave, strong voice of the chaplain, who stood beside the dying man, "do not be too harsh in your judgment. 'Who did sin, this man or his parents, that he should be born blind?'"

'LIAB'S FIRST CHRISTMAS.

"There's yer punkin!"

—And he set down on the kitchen table a small, irregular-shaped pumpkin; not a big, smooth, golden sphere, such as lay heaped on the barn-floor in hundreds.

"O father!" said his wife, very gently, being a little, wan, meek-faced creature, with scarce the pungency of a mouse, or the spirit of a weakly lamb.

"Well! what now?" snapped Eliab Hoskins, turning on the door-sill to look at her under his shaggy eyebrows.

"Why, haint ye got no better than that? It's real slim-lookin'; seems as though we'd ought to kinder put the bes' foot foremost, seein' Abner's comin' to Thanksgivin', and Netty's comin' to stay."

"It's good 'nough, Sary Ann. I got a first-rate offer for the rest on 'em to Hickory farm, and they won't take no runts there, now I tell ye. It's good 'nough. I do'no' why folks has got to guzzle and stuff jest because it's a Thanksgivin' day. It's bad enough to have ye set to that the bronze turkey had to be slartered for't. I never see his ekel for a faowl, and I begrutch him to be used to hum, when he's worth five dollars good money to the city, 'most anywhere."

Sary Ann held her peace, and the tyrant of the

family took himself off. In his remarks about that bronze turkey he said nothing of the fact that his wife had given her black silk apron to a neighbor's wife in exchange for six eggs of this mighty breed, three of which hatched out into two cocks and a hen; a pair were kept for breeding, and this one, foreordained to be the chief figure at Thanksgiving, Mrs. Hoskins had petted, pampered, waited on, watched over, and run after with an anxious care its real parent never could have equalled. She had put pepper-corns on its unwilling tongue for the good of its digestion; she had rubbed sulphur and lard, kerosene oil, wormwood tea, and nobody knows what else, into its infant feathers; and chopped onion-tops and scalded meal and "pussley" for it till the kitchen was odorous; and now it was plump and glossy as a ripe chestnut, and all ready to be killed for the feast. Yet 'Liab grudged it. There are "more than four" people like Eliab Hoskins in the world. He had been born into a state of sin and misery, as the catechism says; ground into the dust by penurious and narrow parents, and the awful poverty that is the lot of some New England farmers, who drag out a life on its lonely hill-sides more frugal in its fare than a hermit's, and far more dreadful to endure, since its privations and distress are not to be endured alone.

'Liab had inherited, however, the fruit of all this laborious poverty in the shape of a farm more extensive than profitable; but free from mortgage or debt of any kind. Principally woodland, it had been unproductive enough, and when he married Sarah Ann Parks he inducted the gentle, shy, young girl into a life of hard work and of self-repression which had almost worn her out; but for her children she would have been very glad to take the place ready for her in the lonely little graveyard at the foot of Saltash mountain, where her father and mother had slept this long time; but she had that motherly heart that is faithful to the very end, and she resolved not only to live, but to be as cheerful as her life would allow, for the sake of Abner and Netty, her boy and girl.

Abner had long since left home and the stern rule of his father, and worked his way up from the youngest clerk in a country store to be cashier in Haverford bank, and now he was married, and had a little girl of three years old; but he had not seen his home for ten years. He was coming home to this Thanksgiving for the second time only since he left the farm, twenty years ago, a boy of fifteen. Perhaps if he had stayed with his father, and spent his life in that hand-to-hand battle with the elemental forces of nature that farming means on the highlands of New England, Abner would have repeated him in character; but what was greed in the elder man developed only into care, economy, and thrift in the younger; and to his work he carried the same energy, persistence, and shrewdness that distinguished Eliab. Living among other people he learned his own powers and failings soon enough to balance and correct them, and marrying a woman of generous temper, high spirit, intelligence, and warm heart, all that was best within him grew and prospered. Netty was much younger than Abner; and when she was fourteen years old her father suddenly discovered that his acres of wild woodland had become valuable; a railroad was laid out through the valley just below the Hoskins farm, and wood for ties and sleepers were in demand. Every cent Eliab Hoskins received he laid out in buying more wild land, till he owned forests far up on the Canadian border, sold for nominal prices by owners who did not see, as he did, that the railroad meant an outlet and a sale for the lumber hitherto valueless for want of transportation.

If Mrs. Hoskins had asked her husband, when she by chance discovered he was selling timber to the Northern Railway Company, for new dresses, or furniture, or household conveniences, she would have received but one answer, brief and hard enough, and she knew it; but when she took her life in her hand, as it were, and asked him to let Netty go to Haverford to school he did not refuse to consider the matter. It is the glory and the strength of New England that education is to its people an inborn necessity; the Gospel is a matter of choice as to its support and furtherance: highly respectable, and not to be set aside if it can be supported cheaply enough; but even a New England infidel — if there be such an anomaly on its lonely hills (an infidel in open opinion, I mean; practical infidelity is another matter) — would be unwilling enough to let his son or daughter grow up without a certain amount of "book-learning." So it was at last decided that Netty should go to Haverford, as Abner would give her her board; and there she stayed for three years, brief to her gay girlhood, suddenly emancipated from home solitude and thrift; but, oh! how lonely to the weary mother, who toiled on in solitude without her.

They were all coming home now, and Netty's schooling was over; if she had learned other lessons than Haverford Academy included in its scholastic year she did not report them; nor dared she confess certain strayings from the church of her fathers, induced as much by the grave young rector as by the beautiful liturgy of his church. She was half glad and half sad to come back to the mountain farm; but her tender heart leaped when she saw how her mother's wan face glowed to see her again, and at first, when Abner and Lizzy and tiny Ruth were all there, she did not feel regret sharply; but when mother had toiled through the festival, made hard work by her devices to spread a generous feast, for out of home products, only grudged at that, she wrought the dinner of the day; when Abner and his family had just endured the solitude and bare cleanliness of the farm-house for three days and gone away, then life shut down on Netty like a blank cloud. There was nothing to do but strain milk, peel potatoes, churn, mend, bake, sweep and dust, except the early week's change of work in washing and ironing. Netty had to question of what use was her education; to what end her narrow life? Suddenly she bethought herself of another holiday approaching, one she had kept in Haverford so joyfully, and yet her memory never recalled the least observance of the day at home.

"Mammy," she said abruptly, one afternoon, ten days after Thanksgiving, as they sat together at the week's mending, "what shall we do for Christmas this year?"

"What?" said the astonished woman; "what be you talkin' about, Netty?"

"Why, Christmas, dear! We used to keep it at Abner's,—have a real time hanging up stockings and giving things, you know, and greens all over the house. Don't you ever do it here?"

A smile sadder than tears stole over Mrs. Hoskins's tried face.

"Why, Netty! — we don't keep Thanksgivin' most years. Father aint one of them that b'lieves in play-spells, ye know. Come to think, I've read about it somewheres; mebbe 'twas in the paper Amarinthy Snow sent over one time for me to see about that medicine that's good for rheumatiz. I guess I did; some folks think the Saviour was born that day, I b'lieve. I do'no' how they know."

"Well, but, mammy, supposing they don't know just the very time, isn't it good to take a day to be glad in, for all that? And I don't feel sure they don't know; folks that know more than I do have thought He was, for years untold; and it seems as if we ought to do something to tell what day it is thought to be, anyway."

Mrs. Hoskins's face fell.

"I don't b'lieve I'd try, dear. Father aint one to give in to new-fangled ways a mite. I don't b'lieve he'd like it."

Netty laughed; so far she had not come into opposition with her father, and she had most abundant faith in her powers of pleasing.

"We'll see," she said, confidently. "I could trim up the house beautifully; there's lots of young hemlocks up the hill, and it's such mild weather the ground hasn't frozen yet, and I remember that old lot full of sumachs, where there are three kinds of ground pine; and I'll coax father to give me some money, and we'll have your first Christmas-day kept in good fashion, mammy."

Mrs. Hoskins turned her head away, and pretended

to see something out of the window. She hated to nip Netty's hopes in the bud; she knew the girl might as well hope to move that dismal old gray barn she was staring at, with its littered yard and rickety fences telling the story of neglect and penuriousness, as to move her father; and yet — poor mother! — it was perhaps possible that those clear, sweet, gray eyes, that rippled wealth of hair, those firm, red lips and warm, flushing cheeks she found so irresistibly lovely, might touch 'Liab's heart as she herself had never touched it. Yet so small was her faith that when after supper was over and the dishes washed, and Netty drew up her own low chair to 'Liab's side, as he sat in the chimney-corner warming his feet, Mrs. Hoskins went away up-stairs on some poor pretext, and shivered in Netty's cold bedroom rather than see her darling hurt.

But of all this Netty was unaware; she had never yet since she came home from Haverford asked her father to do anything for her, and her courage was like all untried courage, — very strong.

"Father," she began, "didn't you ever keep Christmas when you were a boy?"

"What?" growled 'Liab.

"Didn't you hang up your stocking and give people things, Christmas?"

"I don't know what you're talkin' about, girl. I put my stockins' on my feet since I was big enough to do't. I wa'n't fetched up to no nonsense."

"Well!" said Netty, a little less cheerily, "I suppose, come to think of it, there weren't any Episcopalians round here then any more than there are now; but we always kept it at Abner's, and everybody gave presents all around, and we went to church, and I thought if you'd give me some money, dear, — ten or fifteen dollars, — why, I would make Christmas here, and have it so nice for mother and " —

"Stop sech talk right off. I won't hear to't! Ten dollars! Why, be ye out of your head, girl? 'Piscopals, indeed! meetin'-house is good enough for me, an' I've been a purfessor this forty odd year. I guess not! It's darned nonsense, the hull on't. I haint got no money to throw away on sech stuff, nor Sary Ann don't want no sech notions put into her head, now I tell ye; nor don't ye go to doin' on't. Ten dollars! I wonder ye don't want a hundred! I aint no man to throw away dollars. I've spent a heap too much on yer edication a'ready, partickler if this notion comes on't; hevin' food an' raiment you had ought therewith to be content, as Scriptur' says. Moreover an' where-withal I don't mean to hev ye a-idlin' round all yer days; there's a school deestrict over to 'Sable Four Corners, where they're a-goin' to want a teacher next spring. I'm school committee, and I'll give ye your time so't you can take that school come April, and 'arn your livin'. Come to that, I guess you won't hanker after no Christmas nonsense. Well — it's bed-time pootty near. I'll go 'n' shake down a little fodder for them caows, and you'd better go 'long up charm-ber."

Netty did not answer; she sat quite still in her chair, like one after a blow which has stunned. 'Liab got up, lit his lantern, and tramped off by the shed-door; but she never moved. She had been away from home three years, and the halo of separation had softened her remembrance of her father much. She herself had changed, too, and whatever was painful in that memory she had learned to think might have been caused by her own childish waywardness. In the few days Abner and his wife and child had been with her at home her father, who had a certain respect for Abner's success in life, had been as agreeable as he knew how; and since then he had been so busy that Netty had scarcely seen him except at meals, and never before had she had occasion to ask of him a favor. Now all her delusions were gone: she saw him as he was, a hard, cold man, penurious and insensitive even to the only child left him; and a man so intrenched in his profession of religion that he could not see himself to be in the wrong. That he was honest, thrifty, and a constant attendant at meeting, though it was a five-mile ride to the church in the valley, went for nothing in Netty's mind; for her heart was hurt, and she was a woman. She bent her head on her hands and cried bitterly and silently, lest mother should hear; it was not the mere disappointment of the day,— that she could have borne; but it was the blank, chill outlook on a denied and repressed life lying before her; a life of exacted labor and loveless thrift. Netty had a generous soul, ready to lavish itself and all its possessions on those she loved as freely as the odorous ointment was poured out by Mary on the feet of Him whom she adored; but she had also sense and courage. If it had been her lot to marry the aforesaid young rector in Haverford she would have spared and pinched and twisted and turned his small salary till every cent was put to good purpose, burnt her fingers ironing his bands and cooking his savory dinners, spoiled her eyes making his shirts, and broken down her health taking care of him and, that clerical blessing that never fails, his children; but she would have dispensed wealth, had it fallen to her share, with the liberality of a born queen. Now she was not thinking of the ten dollars or the Christmas gifts, but of her father's hard heart and niggard nature.

She sat there when 'Liab came back; he had left his boots at the shed-door and came in to hang up his lantern and cap, so softly Netty never moved. Something in her dejected attitude stirred a throb deep down in his rugged nature; there is sap even in the gnarled boughs of an apple-tree that, bent and broken by the stormy wind of year on year, looks dead to the core; and even in 'Liab Hoskins there was nature, though he had overridden and starved it.

But he did not speak, and as he crept back into the shed and clattered about with his boots, dropping one of them in the dark, Netty jumped up from her chair and fled. When he came back she was gone; and he went into his own room, where Sary Ann lay, having retreated there from Netty's chamber, when she heard the girl come upstairs, by a back way, and slipped into her place speedily while 'Liab raked up the fire. Mrs. Hoskins was naturally a frank woman, if a coward ever can be frank; but she was so afraid of her husband that she had learned all those domestic deceits which are the shield of weak women; nobody could be more deaf than she when she preferred not to hear, or more forgetful when she did not care to remember. She made cream-cookies for Netty when 'Liab went to mill, and told her that her father never ate such things, they did not agree with him; which was true — in a sense. She was asleep now; so fast asleep that she heard every breath her husband drew and every movement he made; so fast asleep that she did not close her eyes till near dawn, her tender motherly heart aching for Netty, and shrinking from hearing 'Liab's hard, sneering story of the girl's presumption.

When they all met at the early breakfast neither of the three looked at each other. 'Liab ate like a bear at its meal of throttled game; it is true he had a knife, and a symbolic fork, which helped him to hold fast the thick sliced pork and spear the potato floating in hot fat that he bolted ravenously; but he none the less ate and drank like a beast of the forest, and neither knew nor cared that Netty nibbled only a crust of bread and sipped the decoction they called coffee with a pallid face and heavy eyes, and his wife did not eat or drink at all.

At last he pushed his chair away, and, wiping his mouth with the back of his rough hand, made for the door, turning back to say, "Sary Ann, fetch them old saddle-bags down from up charmber, will ye, and put in a change of things? I'm a-goin' up to them lots on the Canady line this afternoon. It's nothin' more'n a trail after ye get to the Forks, so't I might as well go a hossback all the way, and I expect it'll take me full a week; and like enough I shall get soaked afore I get through, and want them red flannels the wust way. Darn rheumatiz!"

Netty's heart gave a leap of joy, and then sunk again to think how undutiful she was. "Honor thy father and thy mother,"—what does it mean in a case like this? Netty's conscientious New England soul began to torment itself, but her natural heart *did* feel enlivened and glad for all that; and by and by, opening her Bible for the daily reading, another text flashed upon her with that aptness texts of Scripture have,— "Fathers, provoke not your children to anger," — and seemed to restore her balance; people who occupy themselves with ethics sometimes forget that duty is individual, not natural.

But her mother had no scruples of this kind; her conscience toward her husband had long been dulled. She had enough to do to evade his exactions and cruelties when and how she could. Love for him she had never known, marrying him because he asked her to, and she was afraid to refuse him, and exchanging one bondage for another. She was heartily glad 'Liab was going away, and packed his saddle-bags with the flannel he grudged carrying, with a light in her eyes not at all flattering to a husband; but 'Liab did not care. Neither had he loved her; it was needful to have a woman on the place when his mother died, and old Parks's daughter was a good worker, and not a talker or gad-about. So he mounted the old sorrel horse, adjusted his saddle-bags, and rode off with only a nod. He did look through the open door as if he missed something, to be sure; but Sary Ann did not notice it, nor did she or Netty, who was in no mood to be tender now, know how the thought of his child's bent head and dropping tears would recur to 'Liab now and again on his cold ride, till he angrily fought the unpleasing vision away, and began to cipher out in his head the probable feet of lumber his saw-mill on that mountain-brook in the forest would run out this year; or the prospect of snows heavy enough for his loggers to draw their squared logs down to the nearest slide from which it would pay to haul them to the railway station. It was two days before Eliab reached the end of his tiresome journey;

two nights he slept in log-cabins, or shanties, by the wayside, and the third day found him at the mill, energetic and harsh. The men who worked for him dreaded his coming, and bestirred themselves while he stayed with an activity put on for the occasion. He went from one camp to another, found fault, rated them in terms more forcible than kindly, planned for transportation, estimated time and costs, and pared down expenses with a shrewd thrift that made him unpopular enough with the loggers, who swore at him behind his back with alacrity and energy. The fifth day he set out for the farthest camp. He had already outstayed the time he allowed himself, and was impatient to have his business over, for he had been more than once wet through with cold rain, and the rheumatism he so dreaded twinged ominously in his bones; but he was not a man to mind an endurable ache, so he set out on his long ride over a mountain trail, not on the old sorrel, which had given out entirely, but on a little, rough, Canadian pony. He had not gone ten miles when the long-delayed snow set in; fine, small flakes filled the darkening air, beat in his face, gathered thickly on his shaggy brows, and chilled him to the heart. He went on, however, trusting to his pony's sagacity some ten miles farther, when it seemed to him, from the thick bushes and crowded trees through which the little beast scrambled, that it had lost the trail. He dismounted to brush away the snow and see if any track could be discovered, stepped on a slippery stone, and, trying to recover his footing, slipped again,—for the rocks were covered with ice,—fell headlong, and lost his consciousness entirely. When it returned, he was lying alone in the dark forest, the snow still whirling and whispering in air all about him with the ominous hiss and rustle of a heavy storm, his pony gone, and night coming on. 'Liab Hoskins was a man of courage; his heart did not fail. He was strong in constitution, and used to the shifts of a woodsman's life enough to feel no dread of being lost; but when he tried to rise to his feet he could not: his right leg was broken.

Then despair set in; never before had he been helpless; and here he was, in a lonely forest, with a broken leg, neither food, fire, nor shelter to be had, and no prospect of help at hand; while his nerves, of which he had never before been conscious, at last rebelled. It seemed to him that through the dark pine vistas, for all the whirling storm, he saw his home-fire, the clean, bare kitchen, the low flicker of the dying blaze, and before it, — not Sary Ann, as she was at that moment, busy in cooking a savory supper of cream toast and dried beef with gravy; but Netty, her bright face hidden in her hands, and tears dropping down and glittering against the flashes of the fire.

Persistently the vision haunted him; much as he longed to be in his own bedroom, to be fed and tended by his wife's patient hands; hungry as he was, cold, weary, and almost desperate, — he could not get that sorrowful little figure from his thought; and the wind, sighing bitterly in the pine-boughs, the hissing hush of that relentless snow, the stealing and increasing gloom about him, only intensified his anguish, which began to be pain of mind as well as body. He must die there in the storm; there was no doubt of that. Would anybody ever find him? They would not even know where he died, there at home. There would be no funeral; pleasing and solemn prospect as a funeral always is to the genuine New Englander, he must forego it. With the curious perversity of that intangible and wayward comrade we call the soul, he figured to himself how it all should have been: the decent coffin, and this old body, instead of lying a shrivelled wreck for the wild creatures to prey on, and the stormy wind to rob of all its proper covering, dressed in his Sunday suit, — a shocking waste of good clothes, to be sure; but then Abner wouldn't wear them, and the women couldn't, — neighbors flocking in from far-off homesteads, tip-toeing into the cold parlor and eying the corpse with that ghoulish delight characteristic of country funeral-goers. He knew how Granny Griggs would peer at him and say to Mis' Mather: "Looks very nateral, don't he?" and how Priest Dyer would make a long prayer including the heathen and the isles of the sea; then how they would sing China, — that was what the wind was wailing now, — rising and falling in funereal shrieks and sobs, frozen into a despairing calm by harmony of parts and rhythm of verse; then "friends will view the remains;" and then — He started, for the dream had been too real! He was alone in the forest, and the storm singing his funeral hymn, while still he could hear it. And Netty? — she would lift up her head when he didn't come home and stop crying! What had he ever done to make her cry for him? Educated her? Well, that was what he must do, and he had looked to making it pay. He meant to have her take herself out of his care, and he had even looked forward to repayment of her school expenses. And Sary Ann? What on earth *could* she cry for? She never had her own way, or what she wanted; now she would have it all! He meant to make a will, and leave something handsome to Foreign Missions and Blank College; it would sound well; but he hadn't done it. Sary Ann and the children woud have it all, and *The New York Deserver* never would print an obituary notice of him, saying how much he had left to deserving institutions, and what a good man he was; and how he was now reaping the reward of — He started again; going to die; and where after that? It was the very blackness of darkness, that outlook! Nobody to mourn him here, was there anybody to welcome him there? What could he do where there was no farm, no lumbering tract, no bank to keep his gold in, no gold to keep? Another of those plaguing texts that he had heard in the meeting-house as if he heard them not, and laid up in the dark chambers of his brain all unknowing, rung now in his ear: —

"Lay up to yourselves treasures in heaven, where moth and rust do not corrupt."

He had not; no, he had not even shared his money with good works on earth, nor even by will; how should he show his face in that glorious country where loving and giving are the breath of life? Perhaps this was not his conscious thought; it was rather an instinct of unfitness that made him shrink from the transference to a nobler sphere; but another word pierced his soul again, and made him cower in spirit as if under a lash: —

"Friend! how camest thou in hither not having a wedding-garment?"

What grave, calm voice, having in it an awful authority, spoke thus to him? At that moment a soft rush came through the snow, something cold and wet touched his cheek, and a hound threw up his head and bayed loud and long. What a thrill ran through 'Liab Hoskins at the sound! His old hard, practical nature slipped back to him like a coat of armor. He did not think about Netty, or dying, or heaven any more; not he! Here was a chance for life, dear life! sweet life! so bitter and tasteless and weary to live as we all find it, yet so hard to lose and leave!

He lifted himself a little on his elbow and spoke to the dog; it bayed again, and presently he saw a gleam of light, and heard a voice call, "Brave! Brave!" and the dog bounded to meet his master and another man. They were two French Canadians, burning charcoal on the next tract to Hoskins's lumbering lots. The pony had, it seemed, once belonged to Jacques Dupont, and had taken the track to its old home on the coaling instead of that to the lumber camp. It had gone on after losing its rider, and when Jacques came home from the pits at night he found it at his shed, and gathered from its saddle and the bags that something had happened on the track. Fortunately he had a helper boarding with him, and the two set out with their dog to help or rescue, as the case might be.

It was with much difficulty that they managed to get 'Liab to Dupont's shanty, though the distance was not great. Once there Dupont's wife made up a clean bed on the floor and laid the weary man on it, cut off parts of his clothes, and laid warm cloths on the broken leg, which was beginning to swell and be painful; then they fed him with tea and crackers, their best and carefully hoarded luxuries, and the two men sat down to supper, leaving the wayfarer to meditate and plan the next step. That, no doubt, was to get a doctor; he would not trust his leg to the rude surgery of a charcoal-burner. Dupont, being promised a reward for his services, left early the next day for a Canadian village, where he said lived a surgeon of repute in the wild country, where he had enough of such practice to keep his skill from rusting. The slow days went by wearily. Mrs. Dupont was kind, neat, and voluble; she did her utmost for her guest, and now and then her broken speech brought a grim smile to 'Liab's face; but the food she had for him was not to his liking, and the fever and rheumatism that set in to enhance the pangs of his broken leg made him loathe the dark bread, the slapjacks drowned in molasses, the constant pot of beans, the potato soup, and herb tea that were the daily fare of the coal-burners. When the doctor came at last he had to stay three days to reduce the swelling of the leg so that the bone could be set, and the only promise he could hold out to the patient was that in six weeks he might be able to be set on a pony and led down to the village on the lake below, thence go by sled to the nearest town where there was a railway station, and so home.

Eliab groaned; this was a prospect of bondage! Six weeks to lie here and think, — he did not enjoy thinking, he had tried that in the forest.

The doctor read his face.

"It is a long time, I know," he said, kindly. "But you are no more young, my friend; it is the young bones that knit themselves quickly; you must wait; yes, it is necessary."

"O-h!" groaned Eliab; he knew it was truth, but what a prospect lay before him! He had asked the surgeon to write to his wife: she could not come up there, nor could Netty; women could not endure the peril and fatigue of such a journey, nor was there a place for them. Jacques and the doctor together had contrived a sort of cot for him, which was at least better than the floor, and Jeanne did all a tender heart and womanly instincts could do with her poor means and appliances; but he heard his sentence with disgust and revolt. Six weeks of helplessness at home would have been wretched; here it was unendurable! Yet he had to endure it. The five rosy children who danced and clamored about the shanty were a great nuisance, too, though they were banished out of doors whenever the weather allowed, and set to such helpful tasks as they could fulfil when storms prevented them from playing outside. But after a time, for want of any other interest, 'Liab grew to watch them from his cot as a diversion to the cruel and weary thoughts which harassed him. How they loved their mother! Naughty, mischievous, provoking as they were, she had a divine patience with them that almost exasperated this spectator. Her mild, sweet, dark eyes never flashed with anger; her hand never lit in wrath on round cheek or curly head. She was grieved and hurt sometimes at their waywardness, but never impatient or angry. And they loved their father as well; though they feared him more, for Jacques had the despotic element in him, and ruled with stern justice his small kingdom; but the children always ran to meet him, hung round him, waited for him with eager expectation. 'Liab was forced to reflect that neither of his own children had ever greeted him so; but rather shrunk from his presence and kept out of his way.

Then there came one night he long remembered. Jacques had been down to the village below for supplies, which was a two days' journey; the children had brought in from the shed long wreaths of ground-pine and boughs of fir, with which they adorned the rude shanty till it was like a bower. Jeanne strung threads with scarlet cranberries, and festooned them here and there among the evergreens, and in one corner of the room, behind a screen of old quilts, gave every one of her brood such a thorough scrubbing that when they emerged in their Sunday clothes they shone and glowed like new dolls. A certain joyful decorum pervaded their manners, astonishing to behold; but when Jacques entered, loaded with bundles, the decorum vanished; they threw themselves on him like a pack of busy wolves, as he laughingly called them.

"Will you cease then?" called the mother, in laughing tones.

"Leave the father for one time; he is tire, terrible children! He have hunger, I say."

"Get down, rascals!" thundered Jacques. Then, exchanging a few voluble French sentences with his wife, he hurried up into the loft with the basket he carried, and Jeanne put his other bundles into the old red chest.

"Come now!" he called to the children, who were skylarking about the fire, not at all abashed by their dispersion. "Come now! it is to sing the hymn of Noel; here is the father again."

The little crowd ranged themselves in line, folded their hands, and, looking up like adoring cherubs, began to sing in sweet, childish voices that hymn of the ages, in its stately Latin syllables: —

"Adeste fideles! læti triumphantes."

Not a word of its meaning did 'Liab understand, or the rapt look of Jeanne's face and the glistening eyes of Jacques as they listened; but the tones were sweet, the harmony pure, and his heart softened unconsciously under its influence. Had he heard it pealing through the high arched ceiling of some vast cathedral, with all the splendor and color of religion's most gorgeous ritual to illustrate it; or from the lips of cloistered virgins, in a dim convent chapel, it could not have impressed him as it did in this bedecked shanty, from these red childish lips. It was only when the children gathered about the table for their supper, to-night made a feast for them by certain sugar-cakes Jeanne had baked, and raisins in their porridge, that 'Liab got a chance to speak.

"'Taint Sunday, is't?" he asked Jacques.

"No; it is the — what you call? — night of before Noel."

"Well, I thought I'd lost my reck'nin' ef 'twas Sunday; but what the dickens is Nowell?"

"I forget to say it to you right; it is the French I tell you; it is in your talk the Chrees-mas!"

"Hm!" growled 'Liab, moving uneasily on his cot.

Jacques shot a keen glance at him, whispered under his breath, "Heretique!" and moved away to the table for his own share of cakes and porridge.

Strangely enough Netty's bent head and dropping tears rose up before him; it was Christmas to-morrow, then, and she had wanted to celebrate it, — if he would have let her.

Presently the children were despatched to their bed in the loft, and Jeanne began to tie small stockings, of graded sizes, to the fir-boughs here and there, till five dangled limply along the wall; then Jacques fetched down the basket he had brought, and with happy faces and sparkling eyes the simple couple began to fill the stockings with their gifts. What poor little treasures they were! A stick of candy to each, a red pin-ball in one, a rough wooden top in another, a pair of gay mittens, a long blue comforter, a rattle-box made from an old sleigh-bell with a knit cover, — all these home-made by Jeanne's tired fingers, as she sat by the fire at night after the children's bedtime. There was a knife for Paul, the oldest; a ribbon, cheap but scarlet, for each of the twin girls; a pair of good, stout shoes for four-year-old Jean, and a wooden doll for the baby, — these Jacques had fetched from the village; then a red apple atop in every woollen leg, and the father and mother rubbed their hands and congratulated each other in rapid French. 'Liab watched it all; he had a question to ask, but not yet; he, however, asked another of Jacques : —

"Say! why don't ye allus talk French, if 'tis that you're a-talkin' now. Seems to come a sight easier to ye than Yankee."

"It is that; the French is my born tongue, friend; but for the children it is. Some time we shall move down, when the forest burns away, when I do stop the coal job; it is then the children must speke Ingleesh for to school. You see?"

'Liab nodded. He was a man keen enough to perceive issues and draw conclusions in his business; he was not dull now, but stared with a certain pained wonder at these poor, ignorant people with their tender parental feeling. He did not understand it. Pretty soon Jeanne sat down by the fire and surveyed her work; Jacques went out to feed his goat and tie it for the night. 'Liab seized the opportunity.

"Say, Mis' Dupont, what do ye make all this fuss for about Chris'mas?"

Jeanne started.

"Eh?" said she. "For why? and does not sir also keep holiday at the house?"

"I? No, marm! I wa'n't fetched up to no sech goin's-on. What's it for, anyway?"

"Ah! do you not know, poor friend? Why, it is that the good God did come to-night, — oh, many, very many, long years ago. He was to the poor born, a leetel poor one; it is in hay of the manger where beasts eat that they laid him. Oh, the good, good God! — to die on that cross he came for men. He gave, — yes, himself he did give; and it is to-day he was leetel child, so we give to the childs. You see?"

"But you hev to work real hard to get them things, and Jack has to foot it a long stretch to fetch 'em; ef 'twas to give to missionaries now, why, 'twould look reasonable."

"I know not those; I have my children. Ah! I should to them give heart's blood, so not to forget their little Jesus, the good God's child. Him in the manger, so poor as we, so troubled, and die on the cross, that Son of God, so as Paul is my son. Ah! it is not much, but it is dear."

And Jeanne's honest face glowed with such tender devotion, such earnest love, that 'Liab fell back on his pillow awed. He slept little that night; the message of Bethlehem had found him literally a sheep lost in the wilderness; yes, the Shepherd had left the rest, and gone out upon the mountains seeking him.

There, in the dull glow of the dying fire, he recalled his heartless fatherhood, his loveless home, his sins of omission, that mocked the outward cold uprightness of his life; before him, in this nook of the forest, were piety and affection, the like of which never blossomed out of his money and lands; here were children who loved their parents; here a father and mother ready to give up all things and do all things for the happiness of their children; what had he ever done for his? Abner had gone out from him as soon as he possibly could, and made his own home. Netty had stayed, and he had made her wretched. Poor Netty! her first innocent request cruelly denied and scorned! It was not a merry Christmas Eve for 'Liab; not even the joyful shouts of the five children next morning, as they rifled their stockings, caused more than a transient smile on his rugged face; but he had set that face in a new direction at last, even toward Bethlehem, and the New Song was creeping, note by note, faintly, yet surely, into his heart; even as the herald angels sang it above that lowly manger cradling their King: —

"Glory to God in the highest; and on earth peace, good-will toward men."

Yes, Eliab Hoskins was an old scholar, but he learned his lesson at last; not in days, or weeks, or months; nay, not in all his life did he learn it fully, or without struggle; but when at length he rose up from that cot-bed, and left the shanty to go home, he wondered at himself that it was so easy, even so pleasant, for him to overpay Jacques Dupont for his care and shelter; and still more he wondered to find how his lips quivered when he tried to say good-by to Jeanne and the children. Netty was unfeignedly glad to see him, and Sary, placid as usual, did not refuse a slow smile as he came to his own door. It is true she confided to Netty, months after: —

"I thought pa was struck with death cert'in, when he come home; he was real flabby and meechin' for a spell; and to my mind he haint never been himself sence."

He never had. The old things had passed away from 'Liab; but he said nothing; like all his tribe he had no speech for the best and deepest feelings of his soul. He changed in all his ways, however, slowly and securely. Netty was never permitted to teach the school at 'Sable Four Corners, and she and her mother were both well supplied with food and raiment, even in their own opinion, thereafter. The bare, niggardly aspect of the house also softened by degrees, and at Netty's instigation, Abner, too, was asked to let his wife and child come home to spend the summer; and sometimes when he drove over to see them that grave young rector came too,— not altogether to 'Liab's satisfaction, who did not like the prospect; but, to his credit be it said, spoke no word of objection, and did his best to be gracious.

And when Christmas drew near again Netty had so relearned her father that, without fear or hesitation, she said once more: —

"Can't we keep Christmas this year, father?" and 'Liab answered: —

"Cert'in! cert'in, child! — only I want ye to fix up a box of things for them folks up on the coalin' who took sech care of me last winter. There's five children,

— they'll like most anything, and I'll fetch a gown from Haverford for Mis' Dupont, and I guess I'll get him an overcoat. The rest ye must fix to suit ye, Netty. I'll pay the bills."

Never in his life had 'Liab received such a hearty hug and kiss; he turned away without a word and stared out of the window; the old barn stood there still, but he was moved!

"I do wonder what made father change his mind so!" said Netty to her mother, after joyfully reporting her success; but neither of them ever knew; nor that God had changed his heart, too, in that coal-burner's hut in the forest, by the power of His life, love, and death, who came to us at the sacred Christmas-tide.

www.ingramcontent.com/pod-product-compliance
Lightning Source LLC
Chambersburg PA
CBHW051848300426
44117CB00006B/303